Managing Cognitive Load in Adaptive Multimedia Learning

Slava Kalyuga
University of New South Wales, Australia

Information Science REFERENCE

INFORMATION SCIENCE REFERENCE

Hershey • New York

Director of Editorial Content: Kristin Klinger
Managing Development Editor: Kristin M. Roth
Assistant Development Editor: Deborah Yahnke
Editorial Assistant: Rebecca Beistline
Director of Production: Jennifer Neidig
Managing Editor: Jamie Snavely
Assistant Managing Editor: Carole Coulson
Typesetter: Kim Barger
Cover Design: Lisa Tosheff
Printed at: Yurchak Printing Inc.

Published in the United States of America by
Information Science Reference (an imprint of IGI Global)
701 E. Chocolate Avenue, Suite 200
Hershey PA 17033
Tel: 717-533-8845
Fax: 717-533-8661
E-mail: cust@igi-global.com
Web site: http://www.igi-global.com/reference

and in the United Kingdom by
Information Science Reference (an imprint of IGI Global)
3 Henrietta Street
Covent Garden
London WC2E 8LU
Tel: 44 20 7240 0856
Fax: 44 20 7379 0609
Web site: http://www.eurospanbookstore.com

Library of Congress Cataloging-in-Publication Data

Kalyuga, Slava.

Managing cognitive load in adaptive multimedia learning / Slava Kalyuga.

p. cm.

Includes bibliographical references.

ISBN 978-1-60566-048-6 (hardcover) -- ISBN 978-1-60566-049-3 (ebook)

1. Interactive multimedia. 2. Instructional systems--Design. 3. Cognitive learning. 4. Short-term memory. I. Title.

LB1028.55.K35 2008

371.33'467--dc22

2008007567

British Cataloguing in Publication Data
A Cataloguing in Publication record for this book is available from the British Library.

DEDICATION

To most important women in my life:
my wife Marika,
my daughter Maria,
my mother Olga,
my sister Larisa.

Table of Contents

Chapter II

Chapter III

Chapter IV

Section III:
Towards Cognitively Efficient Adaptive Multimedia

Foreword:
The Next Phase in Multimedia Learning

Multimedia learning refers to learning from words and pictures. The words can be spoken or printed and the pictures can be illustrations, photos, animation, or video. Examples of multimedia learning include paper-based environments such as text and illustrations, computer-based environments such as animation and narration, and live environments such as a narrated PowerPoint presentation. If you want to create effective learning environments for students or effective training environments for trainees, you need to understand how to use words and pictures to promote learning.

As summarized in the table, there have been three major phases in research on multimedia learning. First, in work dating back to the 1980s and earlier, the major focus was on determining whether adding pictures to text would improve student learning. Research on this topic included studies of the role of illustrations in text, placing graphic advance organizers before lessons, and using scientific visualizations to help explain scientific concepts. As showcased in *Multimedia Learning* (Mayer, 2001), my colleagues and I have found strong and consistent evidence for what I call the *multimedia effect*: People learn better from words and pictures than from words alone. Thus, the first major accomplishment of research on multimedia learning was the creation of a research base supporting the multimedia effect. You can think of this phase as Multimedia Learning 1.0, in which the main goal has been to test for whether there is a multimedia effect.

Phase	Focus	Initial Period	Research Question	Example
Multimedia Learning 1.0	Search for an effect	Pre-1990s	Do pictures help?	Multimedia effect
Multimedia Learning 2.0	Search for design principles	1990s	Which features of multimedia help?	Spatial contiguity principle
Multimedia Learning 3.0	Search for boundary conditions	2000s	Under what conditions do features of multimedia help?	Expertise reversal effect

Early work culminating in persistent evidence for the multimedia effect was encouraging because it suggested that instructional designers could improve student learning by incorporating graphics into their lessons. However, it was clear that all forms of multimedia instructional messages were not equally effective, so the next step in multimedia learning research was to determine which features of multimedia instructional messages improved student learning. As shown in the second line of the table, in work largely underway in the 1990s, the major focus was broadened to include research on determining the features of effective multimedia. This work lead to the creation of principles for multimedia design, many of which are highlighted in *The Cambridge Handbook of Multimedia Learning* (Mayer, 2005). Exemplary principles include the *spatial contiguity principle* (People learn better when printed words are placed near rather than far from corresponding pictures on the screen or page), *coherence principle* (People learn when better when extraneous material is excluded rather than included), *modality principle* (People learn better when words are spoken rather than printed), and *personalization principle* (People learn better when words are in conversational style rather than formal style). You can think of this phase as Multimedia Learning 2.0, in which the main goal has been to test research-based principles of multimedia design.

We are now entering a third phase in research on multimedia learning in which the goal is to identify the boundary conditions under which the multimedia design principles apply. As shown in the third line of the table, in work largely underway in the 2000s, the focus has broadened once again to include research on determining when and for whom the principles apply. An important example of this phase is reflected in the *expertise reversal effect* (Kalyuga, 2005)—the finding that multimedia design principles that improve learning for low-experience learners may be ineffective or even harmful for high-experience learners. For example, an important boundary condition for the spatial contiguity principle is that the effect of spatial contiguity is strong for learners with low domain knowledge but not for learners with high domain knowledge (Mayer, 2001). Importantly, the boundary conditions can be used to test—and if necessary modify—theories of multimedia learning. You can think of this phase as Multimedia Learning 3.0, in which the main goal has been to establish the boundary conditions for multimedia design principles.

The book you are reading represents an important product of this emerging third phase of research on multimedia learning. In particular, Slava Kalyuga expands the field of multimedia learning by focusing on the role of learner's prior knowledge. He shows how learning is improved when multimedia principles are adapted to the knowledge level of the learner. His thesis is that instructional designers need to know what the learner knows (through embedded assessments) and to modify the lesson accordingly (through adaptation of instruction). In short, different instructional methods should be used for low-knowledge learners and high-knowledge learners, or as an individual learner progresses from low- to high-knowledge in a domain. The challenge facing instructional designers is how to encourage learners to engage in productive cognitive processing during learning without creating cognitive overload. Slava Kalyuga shows how this goal can be achieved by being sensitive to the knowledge level of learners.

In short, the book you are holding is a prime example of Multimedia Learning 3.0—the newest phase in multimedia learning research. A commendable hallmark of the book is that the author takes an *evidence-based approach*—by basing the book on scientific research findings, and a *theory-based approach*—by basing the book on research-tested theories of how people learn from words and pictures. If you are interested in the latest trends in multimedia learning, then *Managing Cognitive Load in Adaptive Multimedia Learning* belongs on your bookshelf.

Richard E. Mayer
University of California, Santa Barbara

REFERENCES

Kalyuga, S. (2005). The prior knowledge principle. In Mayer, R. E. (Ed.). *The Cambridge handbook of multimedia learning* (pp. 325-338). New York: Cambridge University Press.

Mayer, R. E. (2001). *Multimedia learning.* New York: Cambridge University Press.

Mayer, R. E. (Ed.). (2005). *The Cambridge handbook of multimedia learning.* New York: Cambridge University Press.

Prof. Richard E. Mayer is professor of psychology at the University of California, Santa Barbara (UCSB) where he has served since 1975. He received a PhD in psychology from the University of Michigan in 1973. His research interests are in educational and cognitive psychology, with a current focus on multimedia learning and computer-supported learning. He is past-president of the Division of Educational Psychology of the American Psychological Association, former editor of the Educational Psychologist and former co-editor of Instructional Science, former chair of the UCSB Department of Psychology, and the year 2000 recipient of the E. L. Thorndike Award for career achievement in educational psychology. He was ranked number one as the most productive educational psychologist for the latest 10-year period in contemporary educational psychology. He is the author of 18 books and more than 250 articles and chapters, including Multimedia Learning (2001), The Cambridge Handbook of Multimedia Learning (editor, 2005), Learning and Instruction (2nd ed.) (2008), and E-Learning and the Science of Instruction (2nd ed.) (with R. Clark, 2008). (http://www.psych.ucsb.edu/people/faculty/mayer/index.php)

Preface

Since learning is mostly the work of mind, it is obvious that the design of effective multimedia learning environments should take into account how the human mind works and what are its cognitive limitations. Mental resources we rely on when learning and performing different tasks are very scarce due to limited capacity and duration of working memory, a major component of our cognitive system. Working memory becomes overloaded if more than a few chunks of information are processed simultaneously. Processing and short-term storage demands on working memory cause cognitive load. If this load exceeds working memory limits, the learning will inevitably suffer.

Another essential component of our cognitive architecture is long-term memory that does not have any set limitations both in capacity and duration. Domain-specific knowledge base in long-term memory and associated expertise considerably influence the operation of working memory. The learner prior knowledge is considered as a major means of reducing cognitive load and guiding high-level cognitive activities. Long-term memory knowledge structures and associated cognitive characteristics may significantly change the effectiveness of various multimedia presentations and instructional methods. Therefore, in order to be efficient, instructional presentation formats and methods need to be tailored to cognitive characteristics of individual learners.

This book describes theory- and research-based cognitive principles and design guidelines for managing cognitive load by adapting multimedia learning formats and instructional procedures to levels of learner task-specific expertise. The suggested approaches and techniques are based on contemporary knowledge of human cognitive architecture, cognitive load theory, cognitive theory of expertise, and, most importantly, on extensive empirical studies in controlled experimental conditions. The book strictly follows the evidence-based approach to its recommendations on how to handle cognitive load in multimedia learning.

The book has both a theoretical and practical orientations. It is aimed at those who have academic interests in research on multimedia learning and those with practical interests in designing or selecting effective multimedia learning environments. The intended audience includes academics, educational researchers in multimedia learning, educational technologists, designers of multimedia instruction and assessment systems, and educators. The book could also be used in university graduate and postgraduate courses in instructional psychology and ICT in education, multimedia learning and instructional design, educational technology, and cognition and instruction.

THE CHALLENGES

Although benefits of individualized information presentation formats and instructional procedures have been recognized for long time, most multimedia materials are designed in a fixed, static way. Often, by default, novice users or learners are assumed (implicitly, if not explicitly) as intended audience. However, recent studies of the expertise reversal effect (see Kalyuga, 2005; 2006; 2007 for recent overviews) have indicated that designs and techniques that are effective with novices can lose their effectiveness and even have negative consequences when used with more experienced users. The major multimedia design implication of these studies is that information presentation and design techniques need to change as users acquire more expertise in a domain.

In education, the idea of individualized instruction still remains a mainly unrealized dream because of a very complex nature of the problem (multiple learner characteristics, technical, organizational and other aspects). Lack of suitable online diagnostic techniques has also impeded the development of truly adaptive multimedia learning environments. For these reasons, issues of managing cognitive load by adapting instructions to individual learners, although universally recognized as extremely important, has been avoided by most research projects in the field of cognition and instruction. On the other side, developmental projects in the area of adaptive e-learning are focused mostly on technical issues of tailoring instructional content to learner preferences, interests, choices, history of previous on-line behavior etc., and are not based on learner fundamental cognitive characteristics and principles of cognitive psychology.

This book provides a review of the recent research base and design recommendations and partially fills this need. The purpose of this book is to provide theory- and research-based guidance on information presentation techniques for multimedia and e-learning environments that are best suitable for learners with different and changing levels of knowledge in a specific task domain. The term multimedia in this book refers to the information presentations that use both text (on-screen and/or spoken) and images (still and/or animated). The book focuses on principles and methods that have been extensively researched in recent years. It includes a comprehensive review of the relevant literature, discusses practical implications of the proposed principles and their limitations, and provides concrete examples.

Cognitive load theory provides the basic theoretical framework for the book. According to this theory, limited capacity of our working memory in processing unfamiliar information represents the major factor influencing the effectiveness and efficiency of information presentations and instructional materials. It has also been shown that extensive knowledge base in a specific domain reduces working memory limitations by allowing experts to process information more efficiently. In recent years, there have been many studies of interactions between cognitive load and expertise factors in learning. Multimedia design implications of these studies are the main content of this book.

The interactions between levels of learner prior knowledge and effectiveness of different instructional techniques and procedures that constitute the essence of the expertise reversal effect have been intensively investigated within a cognitive load framework since mid-90s. Although the effect was predicted and explained by cognitive load theory, empirical findings associated with the effect correspond well to general studies of Aptitude-Treatment Interactions (ATI) that were actively investigated in 1960-70s (e.g., Cronbach & Snow, 1977). The chapters of this book review many empirical studies of the expertise reversal effect in multimedia learning, their interpretation within the cognitive load framework, implications for the design of learner-tailored instructional systems, and some recent experimental projects that use these findings in realistic adaptive learning environments.

There are several recent books on instructional design in multimedia environments that are based on empirical research and cognitive theories of learning in a larger pool of multimedia design literature that mostly describes the best practice in the field or personal experience of the authors. Richard Mayer's *Multimedia Learning* (Cambridge University Press, 2001) provides a review of studies carried out at the University of California, Santa Barbara for over a decade. There is a chapter (*Individual Differences Principle*) in this book that provides a brief discussion of the role of learners' prior knowledge in effectiveness of multimedia presentations. Ruth Clark's and Richard Mayer's *E-Learning and the Science of Instruction* (Pfeiffer, 2003; the second edition was published in 2007) also includes some comments on differential effectiveness of selected instructional procedures relative to learners' experience. John Sweller's book, *Instructional Design in Technical Areas* (Australian Council for Educational Research Press, 1999) summarizes studies in cognitive load theory-based design principles, however mostly in paper-based instruction. The recently published *Cambridge Handbook of Multimedia Learning* edited by R. Mayer (Cambridge University Press, 2005) is, probably, the most comprehensive overview of the state-of-the-art in the field. It contains a chapter *Prior Knowledge Principle* that deals with expert-novice differences and provides a brief overview of the relevant studies and design recommendations. *Instructing and Testing Advanced Learners: A Cognitive Load Approach* (by S. Kalyuga; Nova Science Publishers, 2006) provides an overview of studies on expert-novice differences in multimedia learning (involving instructions with on-screen and audio text and diagrams), however, it is focused more on rapid assessment procedures and does not reflect the recent studies of more advanced forms of multimedia learning environments such as instructional animations and simulations. Therefore, this book is intended to add a new important adaptive multimedia learning dimension to available publications that offer cognitive theory-based design guidelines.

ORGANIZATION OF THE BOOK

The book is divided into three sections. The first section describes a general theoretical background and the empirical support for the adopted model of human cognitive architecture and cognitive load theory. Procedures for rapid on-line assessment of user expertise and evaluation of cognitive load are reviewed. This section of the book provides a theoretical framework for discussing cognitive load issues in multimedia learning, as well as general evaluation approaches and measurement instruments used in the following parts of the book. The second section of the book describes cognitively efficient evidence-based instructional techniques, procedures, and different forms of multimedia presentations for learners with different levels of task-specific expertise. It includes different multimedia design techniques appropriate for novice and advanced users in audiovisual presentations, interactive learning environments, animations, and instructional simulations. The third section discusses specific adaptive procedures and methods for dynamic online tailoring of multimedia presentations to levels of task-specific expertise and other cognitive characteristics of individual learners in complex adaptive interactive learning environments. Directions for future research in the field are outlined in the conclusion.

The book contains twelve chapters. A brief description of each of the chapters follows.

Chapter I provides an overview of a contemporary model of human cognitive architecture and its implications for performance and learning. Processing limitations of working memory, which becomes overloaded if more than a few chunks of information are processed simultaneously, influences significantly the effectiveness of performance, particularly in complex tasks. The role of learner prior domain-specific knowledge and associated levels of expertise are considered as means of reducing these limitations and guiding high-level knowledge-based cognitive activities. The available knowledge base is considered as the single most important cognitive characteristic that influences learning and cognitive performance. Understanding the key role of long-term memory knowledge base in our cognition is important to successful management of cognitive load in multimedia learning. This chapter provides a theoretical foundation for the analysis and evaluation of various means of managing cognitive load for learners with different levels of expertise described in the following chapters.

Chapter II provides an introduction to cognitive load theory as an instructional theory that considers instructional design implications of human cognitive architecture outlined in the previous chapter. Based on theoretically and empirically established instructional principles (usually referred to as cognitive load effects or multimedia learning principles), the theory makes specific prescriptions for managing cognitive load in learning and instruction. The chapter describes different types and sources of cognitive load (e.g., effective and ineffective load; intrinsic, extraneous, and germane load) that are associated with different instructional implications and cognitive load effects, design methods and techniques for dealing with potential cognitive overload. Cognitive load factors that could potentially influence efficiency of interactive multimedia applications are analyzed (e.g., levels of element interactivity, their spatial and temporal configurations, redundant representations, representational formats used for input parameters, levels of learner prior experience in a task domain). Basic assumptions of cognitive theory of multimedia learning are discussed.

Chapter III describes cognitive processes leading to the expertise reversal effect and its instructional implications, and provides a review of empirical evidence for the effect. Cognitive studies of expertise (reviewed in Chapter I) demonstrated that prior knowledge is the single most important learner characteristic that influences learning processes. Recently, it has been established that learning procedures and techniques that are beneficial for learners with low levels of prior knowledge may become redundant for more knowledgeable learners. This reversal effect is related to aptitude-treatment interactions (interactions between results of different instructional treatments and student aptitudes). Learner level of prior knowledge or expertise is the aptitude of interest in the expertise reversal effect. The effect is related to the cognitive overload of more knowledgeable learners due to processing redundant for these learners instructional components (as compared to information without redundancy). Therefore, instructional outcomes of different multimedia learning formats and procedures are relative to levels of learner task-specific expertise.

Chapter IV describes a cognitive load-based approach to rapid diagnostic assessment of learners' task-specific expertise that has been designed for online application in adaptive learning environments. Main implication of the expertise reversal effect is the need to tailor instructional techniques and procedures to changing levels of learner expertise in a domain. The availability and levels of acquisition of domain-specific knowledge structures represent the most important factor and critical parameter for adapting multimedia formats to individual learners. In order to design adaptive procedures capable of tailoring instruction in real-time, it is necessary to have online measures of learner expertise. Such measures should be rapid enough to be used in real time. At the same time, they need to have a sufficient diagnostic power to detect different levels of expertise. One of the reasons for low practical applications of the results of aptitude-treatment interaction studies were inadequate aptitude measures. Most of the assessment methods used in those studies were psychometric instruments designed for selection purposes (e.g., large batteries of aptitude tests based on artificially simplified tasks administered mostly in laboratory conditions). Another suggested reason was inability to apply such measures dynamically, in real time, as learners proceeded through a learning session. The idea of the rapid diagnostic approach and results of its initial application in several relatively well-defined task domains are presented in this chapter (with some directions of future research of this approach also indicated). Two possible ways of implementing the approach are described: the first-step method and the rapid verification method. They are based on evaluating knowledge structures that learners are able to activate rapidly and apply to a briefly presented problem situation, thus avoiding cognitive overload associated with alternative search-based solution methods.

Chapter V reviews some techniques that could be used for evaluating cognitive load. Availability of valid and usable measures of cognitive load is essential for providing support for cognitive load-related explanations of the effects predicted and described in cognitive load theory and for general evaluation of learning conditions. Besides, the evaluation of cognitive load provides another indicator of levels of learner expertise in addition to performance scores. As mentioned before, due to available schematic knowledge base, more knowledgeable learners are expected to perform their tasks with lower mental effort than novices. Even though simple subjective rating scales remain the most used measures of cognitive load imposed by instructional materials, new more sophisticated techniques are being developed, especially in multimodal environments associated with performance of complex cognitive tasks. The recent application of concurrent verbal reporting method for evaluating sources of potential cognitive overload associated with multimedia learning is described. This chapter reviews some traditional, as well as novel methods for measuring cognitive load, and approaches to using these measures for estimating instructional efficiency of learning conditions. Different possible ways of combining measures of performance and cognitive load into an integrated indicator of cognitive efficiency are discussed.

Chapter VI describes specific evidence-based methods for managing cognitive load in verbal and pictorial information representations. According to the forms of memory storage representations, there are verbal and pictorial representational modes, whereas according to forms of sensory input, there are auditory and visual information modalities. The chapter considers sources of cognitive load in different modes and modalities of multimedia information presentations. When learners process text and visuals that could not be understood in isolation, the process of integration of verbal and pictorial representations is required. When text and pictures are not appropriately located or synchronized in time, integrating these referring representations may increase working memory load and inhibit learning. Instructional design techniques dealing with such split attention situations may enhance learning. Reducing split-attention in on-screen text and graphics was one of the first and most commonly mentioned application of cognitive load theory. Using dual-mode presentations is considered as an alternative approach to dealing with split attention situations. The chapter discusses means for eliminating redundant components of presentations, coordinating verbal and pictorial information in space and time, segmenting presentations and other techniques, as well as interactions between instructional efficiency of different formats of multimedia presentations and levels of learner expertise in specific task domains.

Chapter VII analyzes different types of interactive learning environments according to levels of involved interactivity and levels of allowed learner control. Interactivity is an important feature of online environments. Sophisticated multimedia learning environments include various forms of interactivity and respond dynamically to learner specific actions. Such environments are active, learner-engaged forms of learning that are expected to promote deep cognitive processes and result in active construction and acquisition of new knowledge. Hypermedia learning environments represent an important online form of interactive multimedia that involve multiple representations, linked information network, and high levels of learner control (content control, sequencing of information, and the control of representational formats). General cognitively-based design guidelines for such environments could be derived from cognitive theories of multimedia learning and cognitive load theory. High levels of cognitive load in interactive learning environments could be caused by the large number of variables involved in corresponding cognitive processes; uncertainty and non-linear relationships between these variables; and temporary delays. In many situations, individual learners carry the burden of deciding when to use additional learning support (if available) and what forms of support to request. While more advanced learners could handle such burden, it may be beyond cognitive resources available to less experienced learners. Different levels of learner prior knowledge are important factor influencing the effectiveness of learning in interactive environments. Cognitive load framework can provide a suitable conceptualization for the general analysis of the conditions and methods for enhancing instructional efficiency of interactive multimedia learning environments. The cognitive aspects of learning in such environments are the main focus of this chapter. General issues in managing cognitive load in interactive learning are discussed, and some specific methods and techniques are suggested for reducing wasteful forms of cognitive load caused by interactive multimedia.

Chapter VIII considers cognitive load aspects of instructional efficiency of dynamic multimedia representations such as animations. According to cognitive theory of multimedia learning, different mental representations are constructed from verbal and pictorial information, and meaningful learning occurs only when the learner actively establishes connections between these representations. The cognitive theory of multimedia learning could also be effectively applied to dynamic visualizations such as animations. Cognitive processes involved in learning from dynamic visual representations are analyzed, and factors influencing cognitive load in animated and static visualizations are considered. The chapter describes the relationship between instructional effectiveness of animated and static visualizations and levels of learner task-specific expertise. According to the expertise reversal effect, continuous animations may be too cognitively demanding for novice learners due to a high degree of transitivity of these visualizations, on the one hand, and limited capacity and duration of working memory, on the other hand. Less knowledgeable learners may benefit more from a set of equivalent static diagrams. However, animations could be relatively more beneficial for more knowledgeable learners who have already acquired a sufficient knowledge base for dealing with issues of transitivity and limited working memory capacity. Optimal forms of tailoring visual dynamic representations to levels of learner expertise are suggested such as setting an appropriate level of visual dynamics and selectively using animations and static visualizations.

Chapter IX analyzes cognitive load issues in online instructional simulations and games. Practical use of software products and physical equipment usually does not lead to understanding of theoretical principles they try to convey because of high cognitive demands of familiarization with equipment and procedures, taking measurements, interpreting data, etc. Limited (if any) cognitive resources remain available for generalizations required for understanding the theory. Simulations may help to partially avoid these problems because they may eliminate the need for handling apparatus and simultaneously represent observable and theoretically predicted variables. Interactive visualizations of abstract knowledge are important benefits of simulations. Simulations may provide environments for exploring hypotheses and receiving immediate feedback, thus enhancing the development of critical thinking and problem-solving skills. However, high levels of working memory load could be responsible for instructional failures of many simulations. Many instructional simulations and games represent purely exploratory learning environments with limited guidance for learners. From cognitive load perspective, random search procedures that novice learners have to use in such environments may impose excessive levels of working memory load thus interfering with meaningful learning. Optimizing levels of instructional guidance represents the most important means of managing cognitive load and enhancing learning outcomes in such environments. The Chapter describes representational formats (symbolic and iconic representations) for input parameters and levels of instructional guidance as important factors that may differentially influence effectiveness of simulations for learners with various levels of prior knowledge. Concurrent verbal reports for evaluating sources of potential cognitive overload and other empirical data from studies of simulations in high-school science are used to support the theoretical model.

Chapter X provides an overview of theoretical frameworks and empirical evidence for the design of complex adaptive multimedia environments that are tailored to levels of user expertise and other relevant individual cognitive characteristics to optimize cognitive resources available for learning. A major instructional implication of the expertise reversal effect is the need to tailor dynamically instructional techniques, procedures, levels of instructional guidance to current levels of learner expertise. In multimedia online instructional systems, the levels of task-specific expertise may change noticeably as learners develop more experience in a specific task domain. Therefore, the tailoring process needs to be dynamic, i.e. to consider learner levels of expertise in real time as they gradually change during the learning sessions. Personalized adaptive multimedia environments provide individual learners or learner groups with experience that is specifically tailored to them. To achieve effective personalization, various information about the learner is required. Tailoring multimedia environments to individual learner cognitive characteristics is becoming a major means in achieving a true learner-centered experience for learners through their interaction with multiple content sources and presentation formats. The chapter suggests adaptive methodology that is based on previously described empirically established interactions between levels of learner expertise and formats of multimedia presentations (the expertise reversal effect), and on real-time monitoring of users' expertise using rapid cognitive diagnostic methods.

Chapter XI describes evidence-based methods for selecting appropriate levels of instructional support and tailoring instructional guidance to gradually changing levels of learner proficiency in a domain to optimize cognitive load. Within a cognitive load framework, providing optimal levels of instructional support is considered to be the main means of managing cognitive load in adaptive learning environments. Recent studies in expertise reversal indicate that instructional design principles that benefit low-knowledge users may disadvantage more experienced ones. This reversal in the relative effectiveness of different instructional methods is due to increase in cognitive load required for integration of presented supporting information with available knowledge base. The suggested procedures for adapting levels of instructional guidance have been developed in conjunction with empirically established interactions between levels of learner proficiency and instructional techniques. The chapter starts with the description of the processes and approaches to learning complex cognitive skills. The appropriate design models for learning complex skills are presented and different ways of varying levels of learner control in such models are reviewed. The relations between levels of learner expertise and optimal levels of instructional guidance are discussed and specific empirical studies of the expertise reversal for instructional guidance and sequencing of learning tasks are reviewed. The completion tasks and faded worked examples are specific instructional procedures used in the described studies for managing levels of instructional guidance in adaptive learning environments. Real-time monitoring of learner levels of expertise using rapid cognitive diagnostic methods has been used in some of those studies.

Chapter XII suggests different ways of constructing adaptive procedures for efficient cognitively-optimized learning in multimedia environments. The chapter describes adaptive procedures based on rapid diagnostic methods for evaluating ongoing levels of learner task specific expertise. Two specific approaches to the design of adaptive instruction are considered: adaptive procedures based on rapid measures of performance and adaptive procedures based on combined measures of performance and cognitive load (efficiency measures). Higher levels of expertise in a task domain are characterized not only by rapid and effective performance due to a well-organized knowledge base, but also by relatively effortless performance that does not require much cognitive resources and associated cognitive load. Using integrated indicators of cognitive efficiency based on multiple cognitive measures provides alternative adaptive procedures to those based only on performance indicators. The rapid diagnostic approach was successfully used for real-time evaluation of learner levels of expertise in adaptive online tutorials in the domains of linear algebra equations and vector addition motion problems in kinematics. Both first step diagnostic method and rapid verification technique were applied in corresponding adaptive procedures. According to the rapid assessment-based tailoring approach, the tutorials provided dynamic selection of levels of instructional guidance that were optimal for learners with different levels of expertise based on real-time online measures of these levels. In learner-adapted groups, at the beginning of training sessions, each student was provided with an appropriate level of instructional guidance according to the outcome of the initial rapid pretest. Then during the session, depending on the outcomes of the ongoing rapid tests, the learner was allowed to proceed to the next learning stage or was required to repeat the same stage and then take the rapid test again. At each subsequent stage, a lower level of guidance was provided to learner, and a higher level of the rapid diagnostic tasks was used at the end of the stage. The chapter also considers means of optimizing levels of learner control in adaptive task selection procedures.

The book concludes with the note that task-specific expertise is a stage in achieving higher levels of professional expertise that are associated with adaptive or flexible performance in new situations. Extending the described approaches and techniques to less structured domains and developing adaptive forms of expertise represents important directions for future research in this area.

REFERENCES

Clark, R. C., & Mayer, R. E. (2003/2007). E-learning and the science of instruction. San Francisco, CA: Pfeiffer.

Cronbach, L., & Snow, R. (1977). *Aptitudes and instructional methods: a handbook for research on interactions.* New York: Irvington.

Kalyuga, S. (2005). Prior knowledge principle. In R. Mayer (Ed.), *Cambridge Handbook of Multimedia Learning* (pp. 325-337). New York: Cambridge University Press.

Kalyuga, S. (2006). *Instructing and testing advanced learners: A cognitive load approach.* NY: Nova Science Publishers.

Kalyuga, S. (2007). Expertise reversal effect and its implications for learner-tailored instruction. *Educational Psychology Review, 19,* 509-539.

Mayer, R. E. (2001). *Multimedia learning.* Cambridge, MA: Cambridge University Press.

Mayer, R. E. (Ed.). (2005). *Cambridge handbook of multimedia learning.* New York: Cambridge University Press.

Sweller, J. (1999). *Instructional design in technical areas.* Melbourne: ACER.

Section I
Cognitive Load and Expertise in Learning and Performance

Chapter I
Human Cognitive Processes

INTRODUCTION

One of the major components of our cognitive architecture, working memory, becomes overloaded if more than a few chunks of information are processed simultaneously. For example, we all experience this cognitive overload when trying to keep in memory an unfamiliar telephone number or add two four-digit numbers in the absence of a pen and paper. Similar in nature processing limitations of working memory represent a major factor influencing the effectiveness of human learning and performance, particularly in complex environments that require concurrent performance of multiple tasks.

The learner prior domain-specific knowledge structures and associated levels of expertise are considered as means of reducing these limitations and guiding high-level knowledge-based cognitive activities. One of the most important results of studies in human cognition is that the available knowledge is a single most significant learner cognitive characteristic that influences learning and cognitive performance. Understanding the key role of long-term memory knowledge base in our cognition is important to the successful management of cognitive load in multimedia learning.

This chapter provides a general overview of our cognitive architecture and its implications for performance of cognitively-rich tasks and learning new information. It outlines major structural components of our cognitive systems and their functions in cognition. The role of our knowledge base and the nature of expertise are considered in more detail. This knowledge would serve as a theoretical foundation for the analysis and evaluation of various means of managing cognitive load for learners with different levels of expertise described in the following chapters.

MAIN FEATURES OF OUR COGNITIVE ARCHITECTURE

Current theoretical models of human cognitive architecture and available empirical evidence about its functioning in learning and performance indicate several major characteristics that underline operation of this system. These features could be associated with corresponding general principles that may govern all natural information processing systems (another example of a natural information processing system is evolution by natural selection in biology; see Sweller, 2003; 2004; Sweller & Sweller, 2006; van Merriënboer & Sweller, 2005, for more detailed descriptions of these principles and their general implications for the design of information presentations). Some of these features will be explained in more details in the following sections of this chapter.

The first feature defines our cognitive system as an essentially knowledge-based one. Our cognitive architecture includes a large store of organized information with effectively unlimited storage capacity and duration. Long-term memory as a repository of organized knowledge base represents that store of information. It contains a huge number of various schematic knowledge structures that effectively determine our capabilities to function successfully in complex environments. Generally, schemas are organized knowledge structures that are used for mentally categorizing and representing concepts and procedures in long-term memory. Most of our cognitive activities in everyday situations, professional life, learning, etc. are based on available domain- and task-specific knowledge base. We know what to do when buying things at a supermarket, eating at a restaurant, filling in a car. We easily understand fiction books we read, however certainly encounter huge problems when reading specialist books in unfamiliar domains. This is because we have a massive knowledge base for dealing with our natural and social environment in everyday life which is usually sufficient for understanding fiction books, but no specific knowledge in many professional domains.

The second feature of our cognitive architecture is a functional mechanism that drastically limits the scope of immediate changes to that store of organized knowledge. The concept of working memory represents this mechanism at a psychological level of analysis. Some models consider working memory as a separate component of information-processing system (e.g., Baddeley, 1986), while other models regard working memory as an activated part of long-term memory (e.g., Cowan, 2001). In any case, the essential common attribute of most working memory models is severe limitations in capacity and duration when dealing with novel information. Working memory provides temporary storage and transformation of verbal and pictorial information that is currently in the focus of our attention (e.g., constructing and updating mental representations of a situation or task).

If too many elements of information are processed simultaneously in working memory, its capacity may become exceeded causing cognitive overload. For example, according to Miller (1956) we cannot provide a temporary short-term storage for more than around seven units of information simultaneously. Processing limitations of working memory and associated cognitive load represent a major factor influencing the effectiveness of instruction in general and multimedia presentations in particular. It has been established (Baddeley, 1986) that there are two relatively independent sub-systems of working memory, one responsible for dealing with visual information and another one for dealing with auditory information. Therefore, as will be discussed further in this book, presenting related elements of information (e.g., pictures and related words) in alternative modalities (visual and auditory) may reduce cognitive load.

It should be noted that cognitive load is always associated with conscious information processing that takes place in working memory while performing a current cognitive task or episode. Therefore, the issue of cognitive overload is not the same as general information overload that is often mentioned these days due to abundance of available information people may have to deal with. While cognitive (working memory) overload occurs at a micro-level of cognition, information overload usually relates to a macro-level of cognition over longer periods of time. Because cognitive overload is associated with conscious information processing, it could also be different from perceptual overload that is traditionally considered in interface design and usability evaluation procedures. Cognitive load theory is dealing with factors that influence conscious information processing as we perform a specific task in real time on a scale from several to tens of seconds.

The third major characteristic of our cognitive system is its ability to organize complex situations or tasks, appropriately direct our attention, and coordinate different cognitive activities. Considering above mentioned severe working memory limitations within which those activities occur, it is a truly magnificent capability that makes our higher cognitive processes possible and effectively underlies our intellectual abilities. It is assumed that available knowledge structures are capable of performing this organizing and governing (executive) role. The concept of long-term working memory (Ericsson & Kintsch, 1995) provides theoretical and empirical underpinnings for this assumption. According to this theory, long-term memory knowledge structures associated with components of working memory may create a long-term working memory structure that is relatively stable and capable of holding large amounts of information for extended periods of time. These processes will be discussed in more detail in the next section of the chapter.

ROLE OF DOMAIN KNOWLEDGE IN COGNITIVE PROCESSES

Most human cognitive activities occur in specific domains rather than have a general and common to many domains value. Even such common activities as reading, writing, and speaking could also be considered as specific domains themselves. Correspondingly, such activities are based on and governed by mostly domain specific knowledge structures. In any specific area of human activity, available domain-specific knowledge structures allow rapid encoding and storage of large amounts of information in long-term memory. After sufficient practice, such encoding and retrieval processes could reach the speed comparable with that of working memory operations resulting in superior task performance in familiar and well learned task domains (the skilled memory effect, Ericsson & Staszewski, 1989).

For example, the short-term memory span is defined as an immediate serial recall capability measured by the number of randomly presented digits or other simple symbols that an individual can reproduce immediately after their presentation. According to Miller (1956) this span is usually seven plus-or-minus two units of information. However, people can increase their short-term memory span far beyond this limit by using familiar chunks of knowledge in long-term memory to encode new information in an easily accessible units (similar to how we often remember phone numbers by associating some groups of digits with familiar years, dates, address street numbers, etc.). Thus, long-term memory knowledge structures effectively determine the capacity of working memory. In the presence of the relevant organized knowledge base in long-term memory, working memory can effectively handle very large amounts of information, organize very complex environments, and govern very rich cognitive activities.

Although our cognitive system has limits on how much information it can process at any given time, ignoring the role of our knowledge base may produce various misunderstandings about actual implications of these limitations to our cognitive performance. They are usually based on ignoring the contribution of long-term memory knowledge structures to reducing working memory limitations and applying the classical Miller's rule of "magical number seven plus or minus two" too literally. For example, Csikszentmihalyi (1990) states that "...we can manage at most seven bits of information – such as differentiated sounds, or visual stimuli, or recognizable nuances of emotion or thought – at any one time, and that the shortest time it takes to discriminate between one set of bits and another is about 1/18 of a second [as suggested by Orme (1969) based on calculations of von Uexkull (1957)]. By using these figures one concludes that it is possible to process at most 126 bits of information per second, or 7,560 per minute, or almost half a million per hour. Over a lifetime of seventy years, and counting sixteen hours of waking time each day, this amounts to about 185 billion bits of information. It is out of this total that everything in our life must come - every thought, memory, feeling, or action. It seems like a huge amount, but in reality it does not go that far" (p.29). This may look like an impressive estimate, however, considering that a single chunk based on a high-level knowledge structure in long-term memory may encapsulate massive (effectively unlimited) amounts of information in the area of a person's expertise, no such calculations can provide any meaningful indication on the real human processing capabilities.

A simple example of long-term working memory functioning in everyday situations is reading a fiction book and being interrupted. When resuming the reading later, you would usually be able to continue without returning to the sections of the book that were read prior to the interruption. When reading a text, we construct and continuously update in our working memory a cognitive structure called a situation model of the text using our knowledge base in long-term memory. This situation model represents the current content of long-term working memory. Due to the association with a stable long-term memory knowledge base, this content is sufficiently stable, durable, and resistant to temporary interferences (Kintsch, 1998).

Situation models constructed from multimedia representations of text usually have a multidimensional nature (Zwaan, Magliano, & Graesser, 1995). Using methods for examining text-based models, it is possible to evaluate the level of representation (for example, immediate surface level or situation level that outlines the situational gist) developed using multimedia representation formats. For example, a hypermedia text presentation may provide too much information for a user to develop a situation model, while an optimal amount of information for developing a low-level surface representation (Rapp, Taylor, & Crane, 2003). It is practically possible to determine the content of a person's long-term working memory when dealing with a specific task situation, for example, by analyzing the content of concurrent (think-aloud) verbal reports. This method, however, is time consuming and difficult to use in online multimedia learning environments. Another possible approach (a rapid diagnostic approach) will be considered later in this book.

This "chunking" role of available knowledge structures explains the means by which we manage to acquire the enormous knowledge base in our long-term memory. Considering severe working memory limitations, it is a remarkable capability. However, most of the information in our long-term knowledge storage is reorganized information originated from other available sources rather than novel information discovered and constructed bit-by-bit individually. Such knowledge reconstruction processes mean that the information is not copied to the long-term memory store literally. Incoming parts of information need to pass through working memory, where the knowledge is actively reconstructed and integrated with available prior knowledge in long-term memory. Available knowledge structures in long-term memory guide this reconstruction process and make it relatively effortless and efficient. When suitable knowledge structures are not available (or only partly available) in long-term memory and not provided by external sources, or information is truly new, a major mechanism for problem solving and generating new information is random search followed by tests of effectiveness. Theories of human problem solving in unfamiliar situations (Newell & Simon, 1972) and corresponding empirical evidence support this feature of our cognition.

REDUCING COGNITIVE LOAD IN LEARNING AND PERFORMANCE

The general limitations of cognitive resources available for performing cognitive tasks were discussed by Kahneman (1973) in his capacity model of attention. According to this model, limited resources can be allocated flexibly to different stages and components of cognitive processing. Attentional resources used in everyday life match the demands. Only when substantial demands for attentional capacity are imposed by a task, the full pool of available resources up to the upper limit will be used. Working memory limitations represent an immediate direct reason for minimizing cognitive resources. Working memory is limited in duration and capacity when dealing with unfamiliar information, and it is easily overloaded if more than a few chunks of information are processed simultaneously (e.g., Baddeley, 1986; Miller, 1956; Peterson & Peterson, 1959).

For example, we experience this limitation when trying to dial an unfamiliar phone number that we have just heard (especially if it contains more than 7-8 digits). Prior knowledge structures held in long-term memory allow us to effectively reduce those limitations and eliminate working memory overload by encapsulating many elements of information into larger, higher-level units that could be treated as elements in working memory. If a subset of digits in the phone number in the above example coincides with some familiar number (e.g., your year of birth), the task would be noticeably simplified.

Similar cognitive-load-reduction effects could also be achieved by practicing skills until they can operate under automatic rather than controlled processing (Kotovsky, Hayes, & Simon, 1985; Shiffrin & Schneider, 1977). This prevents the cognitive system from becoming overloaded by processing demands. We can carry a meaningful conversation while searching for data on a computer when our computer skills are highly automated, but not when we learn how to use the device. A cognitive system with limited resources is most efficient when basic mental operations occur automatically, leaving resources for more sophisticated cognitive operations. "The central processor resembles a trouble-shooter in a number of respects. It appears to be responsive to indications that some lower-level process is experiencing difficulty. For example, walking is usually largely controlled by lower-level processes. However, if walking poses unusual problems (e.g. because of the limp or while descending very step steps), then the central processor can be used to facilitate walking by attending closely to the taking of each step" (Eysenck, 1982, p.46). Higher-level cognitive processes are relatively more general and non-automatic, while lower-level processes are relatively more specific and automatic. With practice and training, task performance involves relatively more automated lower-level processes. Higher-level cognitive processes are used to direct and sequence lower-level processes.

Long-term memory structures and levels of their acquisition define the characteristics of working memory: its content, capacity, and duration. Accordingly, the characteristics of learning and performance alter significantly with the development of learners' expertise in a specific domain. In the absence of relevant prior knowledge, novices are dealing with many new elements of information that may easily overload their working memories. These learners require considerable external support to build new knowledge structures in a relatively efficient manner. In contrast, experts may rely on retrieval and application of available long-term memory knowledge structures to handle situations and tasks within their area of expertise. There are no severe working memory limitations for knowledge-based performance of more proficient learners.

Acquisition and automation of schematic knowledge structures have been considered as the most significant factor in reducing cognitive overload in learning (Sweller, 1999; Sweller, van Merrienboer, & Paas, 1998). However, recent theoretical generalizations of the theory (Sweller, 2003; 2004; 2007) and empirical studies related to the expertise reversal effect (see Chapter III for an overview) emphasized the significance of their executive role in learning, which is associated with the engagement and coordination of different cognitive activities and directing learner attention to appropriate information. When dealing with tasks involving simple or automated cognitive processes (e.g. serial recall of numbers, letters, familiar words, etc.), the central executive was introduced as a separate controlling component of working memory (Baddeley, 1986).

As research tasks shifted from restricted laboratory-based stimuli (e.g., word lists, group of pictures, etc.) to real-world stimuli and how people comprehend complex, integrated information, this fixed executive has become more problematic. Realistic learning environments involve cognitive tasks that require extensive use of complex knowledge structures from long-term memory. A fixed central executive, although helpful in studying basic cognitive processes in simple, knowledge-lean cognitive situations, could not provide a comprehensive executive function in complex knowledge-rich cognitive activities. For example, it may lead to an infinite regress impasse when a higher-level executive is required to guide each lower-level one.

KNOWLEDGE BASE AND EXECUTIVE FUNCTION

Within the described cognitive architecture that is based on interacting working and long-term memory sub-systems, the executive function during complex cognitive processing could be provided by available domain-specific schematic knowledge base in long-term memory. This base could include both consciously applied explicit knowledge structures and well-practiced, highly-automated procedures and behavioral patterns that operate without a conscious control. In the absence of such domain-specific knowledge base, general random search strategies are applied to the situation or task. This assumption effectively excludes the need for a fixed central executive in complex cognition (Sweller, 2003).

Because knowledge structures held in long-term memory are capable of carrying out an executive guiding function during high-level cognitive processes, a central executive in such processes is not a fixed permanent processor in working memory similar to that proposed in Baddeley's (1986) model. The executive for high-level cognition could be considered as a virtual entity constructed for every specific situation or task. Appropriate knowledge structures are retrieved from long-term memory and combined to perform a specific function of managing incoming information streams (Kalyuga & Sweller, 2005).

According to this theoretical assumption, long-term memory knowledge structures in their executive role define the features and processes in working memory during complex knowledge-based cognitive activities. The theory of long-term working memory (Ericsson & Kintsch, 1995) effectively describes a mechanism of executive functioning of long-term memory knowledge base. Organized knowledge structures associated with active working memory components create a long-term working memory structure with characteristics that are different from those of working memory in knowledge-lean tasks. Long-term working memory has no set capacity limitations and is characterized by a relatively prolonged duration.

For example, in our everyday life, we are "experts" in handling many familiar situations, having mastered thousands of types of situations that are recognized, activated and used to govern our everyday activities (buying groceries, paying bills online, using a DVD player, etc.). Each type is associated with a set of cognitive representations (schemas) that are stored in long-term memory and provide an executive function when activated in a specific situation. Most of such knowledge structures for everyday situations are highly automated due to extensive practice and operate without a conscious control (Bargh & Chartrand, 1999).

When reading a written text, we construct and continuously update a mental model of the described situation. This situation model represents the current content of long-term working memory based on our prior knowledge (e.g., world knowledge and grammar rules). This model directs our attention and governs the reading process thus performing the executive function. An effective executive guidance of text search may be enhanced by knowledge of higher-level content representation means (e.g., text organizers such as the table of contents or index), without which the search could be a random activity (Rouet, 2006). For yet another example, in solving algebra equations, available schematic solution procedures and rules in long-term memory are activated when we approach a specific task. These procedures and rules make up the current content of long-term working memory that provides the executive guidance when performing solution steps in working memory.

In an impressive in-depth investigation of cognitive processes involved in an individual learning, Clement and Steinberg (2002) described the gradual process of acquisition of organized knowledge structures (or, as they called it, the evolution of mental models) in a specific domain of electrical circuits. The study was based on longitudinal concurrent verbal reports of the case study of one student. Although the results were not interpreted within the theoretical framework of the above described cognitive architecture, the provided analyses represent an excellent illustration of the guiding role of the learner prior knowledge in this process.

As could be assumed by the nature of our cognitive architecture, the change of the student mental model of the circuit operation occurred by small steps. Each step involved gradual refining and revision of previous stages of the model that could not explain certain empirical observations of the discrepancies in the circuit behavior. At each small modification stage, prior knowledge in the form of analogies guided the changes in the current explanatory model. One example of such analogies is air pressure in the inflated tire that causes air flow as an analogy of the electrical charge in a capacitor that causes current flow. Another example is the idea of pressure in the compressible electrical fluid as the analogy for current propulsion in circuits. The prior-knowledge-based guidance was complemented by external instructional guidance in the form of carefully selected observable events and discrepancies in the expected circuit behavior that lead to the model revision (Clement and Steinberg, 2002).

Similarly, when performing any complex cognitive task, we construct and continuously update a situation model, based on our prior schemas for the task and incoming information. This situation model directs our attention and governs our performance in real time. When no knowledge suitable for a task is available, we approach the task using mostly random search processes followed by tests of their effectiveness (e.g., see Newell & Simon, 1972 for a theory of human problem solving in unfamiliar situations). Such search processes require considerable resources of limited working memory and often cause cognitive overload resulting in slow or negligible learning (Sweller, 1988).

It is not surprising that our knowledge-based cognitive architecture has a general tendency of minimizing cognitive resources involved in task performance (a 'cognitive economy principle', see the following section). Using available knowledge structures is a more resource-efficient and, therefore, preferable means for governing cognitive activities than relying on alternative search procedures or resource-taxing chains of reasoning. Alternatively, direct instruction and external guidance can perform an executive role providing a partial substitute for the missing knowledge-based executive for novices by telling them exactly how to handle the situation or solve a task.

In learning processes, the executive role of available long-term memory structures or direct external instruction is essential for providing cognitively efficient guidance for the construction of new knowledge structures in working memory and their integration with available knowledge base. For example, when learning new electrical circuits, the activated prior knowledge of basic functional circuit components would direct learner attention to important parts of the circuits and their relations with new components. In this way, new information will be seamlessly integrated into available knowledge base. If learners do not have sufficient and active prior knowledge of basic parts, direct instruction should explicitly guide them through the necessary basics and help them to establish relationships between essential parts of the circuit.

The essence of our personality is also determined by the content of long-term memory. Our general goals that have been built over a long time, as well as a set of goals for any specific task situation are also included in our long-term memory knowledge base. In their executive role, these goals direct the person's attention and cognitive processes. The circularity and executive self-sufficiency of our cognitive system were noted by Sikszentmihalyi (1990): "Attention shapes the self, and is in turn shaped by it" (p. 34).

In the above examples of knowledge-based executive guidance, in the absence of appropriate knowledge structures in long-term memory, we would use random search processes. We will try to fit different behavioral patterns to handle unfamiliar situation in everyday life, apply various situational or linguistic schemes to understand a text written in unfamiliar genre or language, or randomly probe specific numbers or operations in trial-and-error attempts to solve an unfamiliar type of algebra equations.

The relative share of long-term memory knowledge structures and direct external guidance in a user's executive function for a task depends on the level of her/his expertise. While for novice learners, external guidance may possibly provide the only available source of executive function, for experts in the domain, all necessary knowledge structures could be available in long-term memory. At intermediate levels of expertise, these two sources of executive function need to complement each other in a balanced way. This balancing of the executive function when dealing with relatively new instructional situations is similar to optimizing learning within a zone of learner proximal development in the developmental framework of Vygotsky (1978). Accordingly, an executive function should be based on long-term memory knowledge necessary for dealing with familiar and previously learned components of incoming information, and on direct instructional guidance just required for dealing with unlearned, new units of information.

RESOURCE-EFFICIENCY IN OPERATION OF OUR COGNITIVE ARCHITECTURE

With the described characteristics, the operation of our cognitive system occurs in a way that tends to minimize cognitive resources involved in performance of a task. This general trend in cognitive functioning could be referred to as a cognitive economy principle. To achieve a resource-efficient cognitive operation, there is a certain hierarchy of priorities for the executive function. For example, using available knowledge structures is a more preferable option for governing cognitive activities than relying on alternative search procedures with associated effortful chains of reasoning. This tendency to minimize cognitive resources may even cause the system to select wrong knowledge structures for the executive role, e.g., misconceptions that may seem suitable for the task.

The structure of a cognitive system based on a large knowledge base in long-term memory is a resource-efficient one. The principle of minimizing cognitive (working memory) resources establishes the general tendency that determines the system functioning. We always tend to solve problems or behave based on some available knowledge rather than trying to search and test new solution steps. The survival and propagation of cognitive misconceptions of different kinds is a by-product of this generally very efficient cognitive system. This side-effect partly explains the notorious durability, perpetuation, and persistence of many explanatory misconceptions, especially in science-related phenomena ("alternative frameworks", "preconceptions", "phenomenological primitives"; see diSessa, 1993; Howard, 1987; Slotta, Chi, & Juram, 1995). Misconceptions are usually well-entrenched and simple structures, and they could require less working memory resources, be more "cognitively-economical" and preferable as an executive knowledge base. They often make newly presented scientific explanations incomprehensible without special pedagogical means of altering them.

On a more global level, it may also provide a cognitive base for explaining survival throughout the centuries of simplistic religious worldviews (e.g., various primitive myth-based pictures of the world's origin and structure), in spite evident empirical failures to support it and obvious lack of evidence behind it. Deeply entrenched in individual human knowledge base (usually from early years of life), this simplistic knowledge takes its priority over the more complex knowledge that would require extra cognitive resources and effort to be applied as an explanatory base.

Therefore, our knowledge-based cognitive system is both our blessing and curse. On the one side, it eventually allows us to achieve extraordinary levels of complexity and depth in describing and transforming surrounding world based on scientific models and theories of reality. On the other side, it often makes us addicted to simplified knowledge structures that are readily and uncritically accepted instead of being rejected in the process of cognitively uneconomical chains of reasoning that may refute simplistic solutions. Simplistic ideological schemes and fundamentalist religious beliefs have been able to take over large groups of people and societies in the history of mankind with often devastating consequences.

Elements of information comprise all input attributes that are encoded as memory traces in long-term memory. Some elements are encoded directly and automatically into long-term memory without conscious effortful processing in working memory, while others require such processing. In particular, substantial effortful processing is required for encoding relations among input attributes. Automatic cognitive operations require minimal resources and do not interfere with other cognitive operations. Mental operations that require considerable attentional capacity are called controlled or effortful processes (Schneider & Shiffrin, 1977; Hasher & Zacks, 1979).

Hasher & Zacks (1979) suggested two sources of the origin of automatic processes: heredity and practice. "It may be that the nervous system is wired in such a way that to maximize the processing of certain types of information. By this we mean that minimal experience is required for the acquisition of some automatic processes" (p.359). Among the investigated examples of processes for which we could be genetically predisposed are such fundamental aspects of the information processing as encoding the frequencies, spatial locations, and time of events.

Thus, memory processes occur along a continuum from effortful to automatic. The 'learned' automatic processes that develop through practice share some attributes with automatic processes for which we are presumably genetically prepared. For example, they occur without intention, not always give rise to awareness, do not interfere with other processes, and run to completion when activated. However, these two types of automatic processes differ in other respects. For example, genetically prepared automatic processes do not develop if given large amounts of practice. They require a person to attend to some information in order for them to be engaged (Hasher & Zacks, 1979; Posner & Snyder, 1970; Shiffrin & Schneider, 1977). "They may not be suppressed by conscious effort. They provide the person with new information that is subsequently available for a number of uses. Also, these processes may be part of the very early repertoire of the newborn as well as of the continuing repertoire of the elderly... [They are] relatively invulnerable to differences in motivation, education, early experience, culture, and intelligence" (Hasher & Zacks, 1979, p.362). The knowledge gained as output of automatic processes is accessible to consciousness and can provide executive guidance in specific situations and serve as retrieval cues for recall.

The class of genetically predisposed automatic processes could be associated with the recently described categories of knowledge that Geary (2002; 2005; 2007) called biologically primary knowledge. This knowledge is not learned consciously because we have evolved to acquire that knowledge easily and automatically. Learning a first language, recognizing faces, learning general problem solving techniques, or learning about basic social interactions fall into this category and effectively extend the basic categories of automatic cognitive processes considered by Hasher & Zacks (1979). Such knowledge is encoded directly into long-term memory without being consciously processed by working memory.

On the other side, we have not evolved to effortlessly and automatically acquire the biologically secondary knowledge, for example, much of the knowledge taught in educational institutions. To be acquired, this type of knowledge needs to be consciously and explicitly processed in working memory in effortful way. Cognitive load theory that is based on the relations between working and long-term memory primarily applies to biologically secondary rather than biologically primary knowledge (Sweller, 2007; Sweller & Sweller, 2006).

EVOLUTION OF OUR COGNITIVE ARCHITECTURE

Evolution of human cognitive architecture that undermines our learning capabilities is a subject of evolutionary educational psychology, a new branch of science that studies the application of evolutionary theory to the understanding of the human brain, mind, and its development (Geary, 2005). The distinction between biologically primary domains (knowledge and abilities as evolved cognitive components) and biologically secondary competencies (knowledge and abilities acquired through formal or informal training, such as reading and scientific reasoning) is a key point of evolutionary educational psychology.

Biologically primary domains include evolutionary significant folk knowledge and primary abilities that evolved to process and respond to specific forms of information in the environment that have been important for survival during the biological evolution. Examples are native languages, spatial abilities, facial processing, gesture processing, detecting features (e.g., movement) of members of the same species and features of typical prey or predators; "intuitive" understanding of how to engage in social interactions and how to hunt and avoid predators (Geary, 2005). These are abilities and forms of knowledge the human brain is (according to this theory) biologically predisposed to learn. Biologically primary domains are largely implicit and operate mostly automatically and below conscious awareness. For humans, folk knowledge can also be expressed explicitly.

Geary (2005) subdivided primary domains into three main areas. Folk psychology includes processing and manipulating the forms of social information essential for survival during human evolution (self, social interactions and relationships with other people). Folk biology involves categorizing local flora and fauna, decisions regarding the likely behavior of different species. Finally, folk physics includes mentally representing 3-dimensional space, guiding movement in this space, using physical materials for making tools, etc.

Biologically secondary domains are culture-specific domains based on the modification of primary abilities and explicit folk knowledge. For example, Geary (2005) describes the development of the base-10 formal mathematical number system which is based on such biologically primary competencies as implicit knowledge of small numbers, magnitude (implicit estimates of more than or less than), and "intuitive" understanding that successive counts increase quantity by one. Using these primary competencies, the biologically secondary components will include culture-specific system of number words; the number line; the creation of sets around 10 and their hierarchical organization; the extension of primary number knowledge to very large numbers; and procedural rules for complex operations.

Biologically secondary knowledge requires conscious, explicit, and effortful processes in working memory. In contrast to the biologically secondary domain, biologically primary knowledge is not learned consciously. We have evolved to acquire this knowledge easily and automatically. This knowledge is encoded directly into long-term memory without being consciously processed by working memory. This is how we learn, for example, a first language, skills in recognizing faces, general problem solving techniques, and basic social interactions (Geary, 2005; 2007).

Secondary competencies (including all human scientific, technological, and academic advances) initially emerged from primary domains. An essential condition of this emergence was the availability of the components of cognitive architecture that evolved to enable us to cope with variation and novelty. The most important of such components are conscious effortful processes in working memory. While for biologically primary domains, there are evolved brain systems that automatically focus our attention on relevant features (e.g., eyes, face scanning) and respond to information patterns that are essential for our biological survival, secondary abilities are heavily dependent on the explicit, conscious psychological mechanisms. Therefore, the explicit representation of novel information in working memory and manipulation of this information are vital for constructing secondary cognitive competencies. Working memory and controlled attention represent the key concepts for understanding how human can construct biologically secondary competencies (Geary, 2005).

Thus, form the evolutionary perspective, the most important function of working memory in our cognitive system is to cope with novel situations that cannot be handled by the implicit systems. Together with huge capacity and organization of our long-term memory, this function effectively defines adaptive advantages of human cognitive architecture. Also, unlike most other species, we have the ability to inhibit automatic execution of evolved implicit responses and engage explicit, controlled, and effortful problem solving in working memory. Since the ability to generate, maintain, and manipulate abstract mental representations is limited by working memory resources, these processes are effortful and inevitably generate a cognitive load.

Sweller (2003; 2004; 2007) investigated the analogy between our cognitive architecture and the evolution by natural selection as two examples of natural information processing systems. Evolution by natural selection involves a large store of genetic information that persists indefinitely and small random variations that are tested for effectiveness. Human cognitive architecture also includes a large store of information held in long-term memory that coordinates our cognitive activities and limited working memory that generates small alterations to long-term memory. Long-term memory determines cognitive characteristics of an individual (behavioral patterns, expertise, etc.) similar to the way the genome (genetic code) determines biological characteristics of a species. Both an existing genetic code and information in long-term memory guide behavior of the corresponding systems (biological and cognitive).

In addition, both evolution by natural selection and human cognitive architecture rely on randomness when faced with circumstances that require new ways of coordinating information. When these two systems deal with familiar information, there is a highly effective executive guidance (long-term memory or genome). If a new changed environment requires an alteration in biological activity, random mutation followed by effectiveness tests (natural selection) are the only available mechanisms. Similarly, random search processes in working memory are used to deal with new cognitive situations.

Thus, the processes used by evolution by natural selection strikingly resemble the processes of the human cognitive system. Based on these similarities, Sweller (2003) assumed that human cognitive architecture evolved in the same manner as all other human biological characteristics, with qualitatively similar properties. The major aspect of human cognitive architecture is the size of long-term memory. Most other intellectual differences between humans and other species (e.g., ability to learn and solve problems) stem from quantitative differences in long-term memory (Sweller, 2003; 2004).

As mentioned previously, if no knowledge structures are available in long-term memory to organize new information, learners try random combinations followed by the test of their effectiveness. As the number of elements increases, the number of possible combinations increases exponentially (a combinatorial explosion). Therefore, if elements must be combined randomly, the number of elements that can be considered at any time should be limited. Another evolutionary reason why the capacity of working memory is severely limited when dealing with new information is that these limitations ensure that each alteration to long-term memory is minor. Individual alterations to a genome are also slight because large random alterations are highly unlikely to permit survival (complex biological functions evolve over millions of years) (Sweller, 2003; 2004).

It has been noted previously that biologically secondary knowledge originated from biologically primary knowledge. Conscious cognitive processing of information in working memory was essential in this transition as a way to cope with irregular novelty in the environment. Then, abstract higher level secondary knowledge structures emerged from lower level components. Eventually, such processes resulted in contemporary scientific and technological knowledge base. The need for such multi-level secondary knowledge hierarchies could also be connected to general limitations of working memory. Abstract higher level knowledge representations in long-term memory might have emerged as a means for overcoming the combinatorial barrier. This barrier is associated with the above mentioned combinatorial explosion caused by the explicit integration of increasing number of lower level components (including explicitly expressed primary knowledge elements) within the limited capacity of working memory.

ROLE OF EXPERTISE IN COGNITIVE PROCESSING

The same multimedia instructional materials are processed differently by novices and experts in a specific task domain. For example, if an animated operation of a relatively new mechanical system (e.g., an engine) is presented to experienced mechanics, they would recognize familiar parts and understand how the whole system operates. On the other hand, mechanical apprentices may see only some individual familiar elements without understanding how they work together. Detailed multimedia instructions (for example, an animation of the engine operation with appropriately placed and synchronized narrated auditory explanations) would certainly help the novice learners to understand the operation of the engine. However, when the same detailed instructions are presented to the experienced technicians, they may find them unnecessary and frustrating, especially if they have to attend to the instructional details. The difference between these two groups of learners is in their domain-specific knowledge base which is the most important factor determining expert-novice differences in cognitive processing (see Chi, Glaser, & Farr, 1988, for an overview).

Cognitive studies of human expertise established that it is characterized not by superior strategies of problem solving or a larger capacity of working memory, but larger and better selection of organized domain-specific knowledge structures (schemas) in long-term memory. Such schematic knowledge representations allow us to categorize incoming information and act in appropriate ways. De Groot (1965; 1966) was the first to investigate the cognitive nature of expertise. He found that chess masters could recall many more pieces from briefly exposed real chess positions than novices. He explained these findings by the enormous amounts of knowledge about real game configurations and optimal moves that grandmasters can access in their long-term memory. Chase and Simon (1973) noticed that experts placed chess pieces on the board in groups that represented meaningful configurations. They also observed that the experts' superiority in recall of board configurations was not found on memory of random placements of the chess pieces.

In their overview of cognitive studies of expertise, Chi, Glaser, and Farr (1988) distinguished the following main characteristics of expert performance: domain-specificity; perception of problem situations by large meaningful patterns; high speed of performance; superior well-organized long-term memory knowledge base; deep-level and principle-based problem representations; thorough qualitative analysis of problems; and strong self-monitoring skills. Studies of experts' performance indicated that experts are able to efficiently interconnect different parts of their knowledge and switch between different levels of representations. For example, according to the Sternberg and Frensch's (1992) global/local architecture of expert cognition, when considering information from new domains, experts rely primarily on global level of processing. If information belongs to the expert's narrow area of expertise, he/she relies mostly on local processing that is often automated and characterized by minimal required processing resources.

As expertise develops, learned portions of procedures are transferred to a local processing system enabling experts to free global processing resources for dealing with new situations. Because it is difficult to reorganize an automated local procedure, experts may be inflexible in new situations. For example, performance of expert bridge players deteriorated more when new tasks required changing deep, abstract principles rather than surface features. Novices, on the other hand, were more affected by surface changes (Sternberg & Frensch, 1992). However, when domain-specific knowledge is missing, experts could still maintain a more structured approach than novices by making use of their abstract high-level knowledge. (Schraagen, 1993)

Research studies in the development of expert performance demonstrated that it required extensive deliberate practice at an appropriate and challenging level of difficulty in a specific domain (Ericsson & Charness, 1994; Ericsson, Krampe, & Tesch-Romer, 1993). High-level professional expertise includes many essential attributes such as professional attitudes, creative approaches to domain problem situations and systemic vision of the field, well-developed metacognitive strategies and skills (self-regulatory performance control) that allow experts to control their performance, assess their work, and predict its results. However, the most important common feature of expertise is the availability of a set of relevant domain-specific schematic knowledge structures that could be used in performing tasks in a specific domain. With experience in a domain, knowledge is organized into interconnected aggregate structures that explain the skilled performance of experts (Chi, Glaser, & Farr, 1988).

Thus, expertise is characterized first of all by the large amount of organized knowledge structures that experts can access. Schemas are a major type of organized knowledge structures in long-term memory that reflects prototypical features of objects, situations, and events, and allows us to categorize, understand, and use incoming information accordingly. Experts categorize tasks in their domains based on the general principles of the domain, whereas novices rely on surface features of each specific task (Schoenfeld and Hermann, 1982). When developed, schemas are initially associated with specific situations from which they were induced. With experience, they gradually become associated with general principles and organized into large groups.

For example, studies of problem solving in physics by individuals with different levels of expertise demonstrated that experts approached the problems in terms of the basic principles of physics, while novices heavily depended on surface features mentioned in each specific task (Chi, Feltovich, & Glaser, 1981). Different tasks with the same surface features (e.g., incline plane tasks) may require applying different principles (e.g., balance of forces or energy conservation, etc.). On the other hand, the presence of a specific surface feature alone does not determine the appropriate approach. Therefore, novices often fail in problem solving.

TASK-SPECIFIC EXPERTISE

High-level professional experts are also experts in solving most specific routine tasks in their domain. Task-specific expertise is an ability of a person to perform fluently in a specific class of tasks. It is a rather "narrow" definition of expertise in contrast to expertise in a professional domain. For example, a secondary school student could be an expert (in this narrow sense) in solving simple linear algebra equations of the type $ax + b = c$, although he or she is still very far away from becoming expert mathematician. However, task-specific expertise is a necessary prerequisite of the 'real' expertise.

In education and training, developing task-specific expertise is also an important condition of mastering specific subject domains and developing broader problem-solving skills in a domain. Such problem solving is generally considered as "cognitive processing directed at achieving a goal when no solution method is obvious to the problem solver" (Mayer & Wittrock, 1996, p. 47). In addition to domain knowledge and problem-solving strategies, problem solving includes self-regulation as an important component. Self-regulation is composed of metacognition (planning and self-monitoring) and motivation (effort and self-efficacy). A successful problem solver thus needs to have sufficient domain knowledge and problem-solving strategies, be able to plan and monitor problem-solving process, and be motivated to act (CRESST model of problem solving, O'Neil, 2002).

The availability of highly organized and automated domain-specific knowledge base is a common characteristic of both task-specific and broader professional expertise. In case of task-specific expertise, it is knowledge structures and procedures used in a specific class of tasks. A typical indicator of this expertise is the ability to rapidly retrieve and apply available advanced levels of knowledge structures in task-specific situations. Such advanced knowledge structures allow individuals to almost immediately jump to advance stages of solution (even provide final answers) by skipping some (or all) intermediate steps. Acquisition of organized task-specific knowledge structures eliminates the need to apply weak problem-solving methods (such as means-ends analysis or trial-and-error technique) when dealing with similar tasks from the same class. Strategically, it results in a shift from working backward from the goal using means-ends analysis and setting a set of sub-goals, to working forward from the initial state to the goal (a knowledge-based strategy).

For example, solving problems that require using complex online information databases includes identifying information needs, locating corresponding information sources, extracting and organizing relevant information from each source, synthesizing information from different sources. Expert problem solvers in such areas spend more time on defining the problem and more often activate their prior knowledge base, elaborate on the content, and regulate their cognitive processes. At the same time, experts and novices show little difference in how they search the Internet (Brand-Gruwel, Woperes, & Vermetten, 2005)

The importance of task-specific expertise is in freeing cognitive resources required for learning higher level tasks and developing flexible and transferable skills by acquiring well automated knowledge structures and procedures that guide performance of lower-level routine tasks. For example, many secondary school students experience notorious difficulties in understanding conventional concepts in mathematics. In many cases, such difficulties are caused by the students' failures to acquire well developed knowledge and skills in simpler prerequisite classes of tasks (e.g., basic algebra transformations, linear algebra equations, etc.). Such knowledge and skills would constitute task-specific expertise in those areas.

According to Anderson (1983), the process of skill learning occurs in several stages. Initially, the procedure is learned in the form of declarative knowledge. Then, the declarative information is transformed into a procedural form, and a set of procedures is acquired (the process of proceduralization). Finally, the skill becomes rapid and automatic. When knowledge becomes automated, conscious processing capacity can be concentrated on higher levels of cognition. Intensive training on certain procedural elements of a task can make them more automatic and free cognitive capacity for more creative cognitive processes such as transfer of training (Cooper & Sweller, 1987). Automated routine procedures enable learners to concentrate on dealing with unfamiliar situations.

By reorganizing our knowledge base as we acquire more expertise in a domain, we are able to effectively deal with information processing limitations of our cognitive architecture. Chunking many elements of information that need to be processed in working memory into a single unit using available long-term memory knowledge structures allow experts to effectively reduce working memory load. Such knowledge structures also allow experts to rapidly classify problem situations and retrieve appropriate schematic procedures for handling these situations. This is a more efficient problem solving method than employing cognitively demanding and inefficient search-based strategies that novices usually use. Experts approach routine tasks using knowledge-based forward-working strategies, while novices tend to work backward from the goal. However, when encountered with unfamiliar tasks, experts also work backward. On the other hand, when students' knowledge contains misconceptions, the knowledge-based forward reasoning could strengthen misconceptions and be harmful for learning.

ROLE OF TASK-SPECIFIC EXPERTISE IN LEARNING

Recent studies of the expertise reversal effect (see Chapters III; Kalyuga 2005; 2006; 2007, for recent overviews) have demonstrated that information or learning procedures that are beneficial for novice learners may become redundant for more knowledgeable learners. The expertise reversal effect can be related to research on aptitude-treatment interactions (e.g., Cronbach & Snow, 1977; Shute, 1992) that occur when different instructional treatments result in different learning outcomes depending on student aptitudes (knowledge, skills, learning styles, personality characteristics, etc.). In the expertise reversal effect, prior knowledge is the aptitude of interest.

The expertise reversal effect can be explained by assuming that for more knowledgeable learners, the redundant for them material or instructional guidance overloads working memory relative to information without redundancy. With redundant material, resources are required for cross-referencing presented and previously learned familiar information. Accordingly, the cognitive efficiency of multimedia presentations is relative to levels of learner task-specific expertise. When designing multimedia presentations, using appropriate procedures and removing redundant information at each level of user expertise, thus minimizing interfering cognitive processing, is necessary for optimizing cognitive resources.

For example, in a set of studies conducted with technical apprentices of a manufacturing company (Kalyuga, Chandler, & Sweller, 2000), detailed instructions in procedures for using specific types of diagrammatic representations (cutting speed nomograms) were used. Auditory explanations presented simultaneously with animated diagrams were cognitively optimal multimedia instructional formats for novice trainees. However, at higher levels of expertise achieved after a series of intensive training sessions, presenting a slightly different type of nomograms with detailed auditory explanations was suboptimal. Cognitive activities of these learners were based on well-learned schematic procedures. Explanations designed to support construction of schematic knowledge structures that had already been acquired by trainees were redundant and inefficient.

According to cognitive theories of multimedia learning (Mayer, 2001, 2005; Sweller, 1999), when text and pictures are not synchronized in space (located separately) or time (presented after or before each other), the integration process may increase cognitive load due to cross-referencing different representations. For example, related elements of text and diagram in Figure 1a are separated over distance. Their integration requires intense search processes and holding some elements of the diagram or segments of the text in working memory until other related elements or textual segments are attended and processed. These processes require additional resources and are likely to increase cognitive load.

Physically integrating verbal and pictorial representations may reduce this split-attention effect (Mayer & Gallini, 1990; Sweller, Chandler, Tierney, & Cooper, 1990). For example, Figure 1b demonstrates an integrated format for the instruc-

Figure 1. Split-attention (a) and integrated (b) formats for a diagram with textual explanations

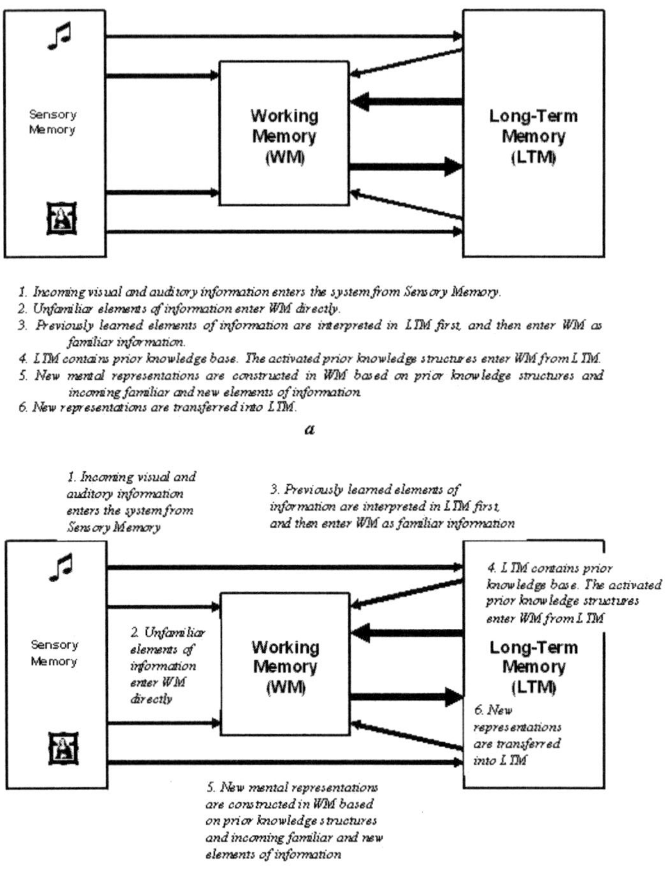

tional material in Figure 1a. However, recently established cognitive load effects in multimedia design for more advanced learners suggest eliminating non-essential redundant representations in multimedia formats and gradually reducing levels of instructional guidance (Kalyuga, 2005). In the example of Figure 1, rather than being integrated into the diagram, the textual explanations should be omitted altogether when used with more experienced learners. In this case, the diagram-only presentation (upper part of Figure 1a) would effectively provide a routine problem exercise for these learners that could be solved based on their available knowledge base. As learners gain more proficiency in the task domain, the relative share of problem-based practice and exploratory tasks should be increased.

Therefore, a cognitively-optimal design of multimedia presentations for novice learners usually requires eliminating situations when attention is split between multiple complementing information representations (e.g., on-screen text and diagrams). Sections of textual explanations could be embedded directly into the diagram in close proximity to relevant components of the diagram. Alternatively, dual-modality formats should be used with segments of narrated text presented simultaneously with the diagram (or relevant animation frames). Also, providing detailed instructional guidance by using plenty of fully worked-out examples at the initial stages of learning is required for novice learners (Sweller, et al., 1998). On the other hand, when instructing learners with relatively higher levels of task-specific expertise, instructional materials should be weeded of any components that are likely to be redundant for these learners due to their increased knowledge base.

Thus, studies of expert-novice differences have demonstrated that organized schema-based knowledge structures in long-term memory are the most critical factor influencing learning and proficient performance. These cognitive constructs effectively reduce or eliminate severe processing limitations of our cognitive system and fundamentally alter characteristics of our performance. They guide allocation of cognitive resources and significantly influence our perception of multimedia materials. Non-optimal multimedia formats may overload limited capacity of working memory. As a consequence, multimedia presentations that include information that is essential and appropriate for novices, may need to be re-designed by eliminating redundant information for more expert individuals in order to optimize cognitive resources.

FROM TASK-SPECIFIC TO ADAPTIVE EXPERTISE

The expertise reversal effect was investigated in relation to task-specific expertise as an ability to perform fluently in a specific class of tasks. Such fluent performance is based on well learned or automated knowledge structures related to conditions of their applicability. However, task-specific expertise is not an end in itself, but rather a stage in achieving higher levels of professional expertise. As was noted earlier, professional expertise is characterized by superior levels of professional accomplishments in a field. These levels of performance require many years of training and extensive deliberate practice organized at a challenging level of difficulty to allow steady skill refinements (Ericsson & Charness, 1994). Professional expert performance generally requires well-developed cognitive skills, well-organized high-level knowledge structures, and self-regulatory performance control or metacognitive strategies (Glaser, 1990). The acquisition of task-specific expertise in main classes of tasks within a domain is an important condition of higher level professional expertise in this domain. From a cognitive load perspective, this importance is related to freeing cognitive resources for learning higher level tasks and developing flexible and transferable skills.

A well organized knowledge base is a common essential characteristic of both task-specific and professional expertise. For task-specific expertise, this knowledge base includes concepts, strategies, and procedures (usually fully or partially automated) used in a specific class of tasks. Task-specific expertise may not be sufficient for successful performance in complex domains. In comparison to task-specific expertise, high-level professional expertise involves additional essential attributes, such as a systemic vision of the field, strategic processes based on higher level organized knowledge base, as well as developed metacognitive skills. These are important attributes for dealing with relatively new task situations that could not always be predicted in advance.

Adaptive expertise is characterized by flexibility in approaching new situations and environments, metacognitive abilities to monitor experts' own understanding and approaches to problem solving, continually question their current levels of expertise, change available procedures flexibly when required, and to create new procedures when the known approaches do nor work in new situations (Bransford, Brown, & Cocking, 1999; Hatano & Inagaki, 1986). An important feature of adaptive expertise is the ability to disengage irrelevant but well-learned prior knowledge structures in new situations. For example, adaptive experts may inhibit execution of entrenched schemas in favor of consciously applied higher level strategic schemas or effortful reasoning and problem solving. In order to withstand high levels of cognitive load involved in such processes, metacognitive skills in managing cognitive resources and self-managing cognitive load are required. Instructional means for developing such skills need further research.

Contrary to popular belief, abilities to adapt to new task situations and demands are unlikely to be based on some abstract universal problem solving skills that are usually described in rather unspecific, fuzzy, and mostly trivial ways. In such descriptions, these skills are not different from our default general problem solving heuristics (e.g., means-ends analysis). It is more likely that adaptive expertise is based on higher level schemas. Similar to other knowledge structures, these schemas could be learned directly in appropriately designed learning environments or acquired gradually by being inferred in the process of extensive problem-solving practice in the domain. Learning environments for developing adaptive expertise need to combine higher level general knowledge structures required for deep conceptual understanding of the field (e.g., principles, basic conceptual frameworks), practice in carrying out basic procedures in task-specific contexts, and variation in practice contexts for the development of flexible skills (Gentner & Stevens, 1983; Greeno & Simon, 1988; Hatano, 1982).

When novices learn new tasks in a domain, they require considerable instructional support to reduce cognitive overload. As these learners become more experienced in different classes of tasks within the domain, they may increasingly rely on available knowledge structures in long-term memory to handle situations within their areas of task-specific expertise without overloading working memory. As a consequence, cognitive resources become available for acquisition of important higher order knowledge structures and self- regulatory skills as essential characteristics of adaptive expertise. Developing adaptive expertise requires cognitive resources for dealing with flexible, non-routine and creative aspects of performance. Therefore, the acquisition of task-specific expertise in key classes of tasks within a domain is an important necessary condition for managing cognitive load during acquisition of higher level adaptive expertise.

FUTURE TRENDS IN THE STUDY OF HUMAN COGNITION

One of the most important contributions of cognitive science to the understanding of human learning, thinking, and problem solving is the discovery of the fundamental role of our knowledge base in these processes. Developing specific mechanisms of functioning of a knowledge base within the human cognitive architecture and constructing mental representations is an important trend in the study of human cognition relevant to the subject of this book. Within this perspective, especially significant is the relation of these mechanisms to duration- and capacity-constrained modes of conscious information processing. The previously mentioned theory of long-term working memory (Ericsson & Kintsch, 1995) is an example of an important recent development in this area. Even though this theory originated from attempts to explain skilled memory performance, it is essentially applicable to the whole range of human experience- and knowledge-based activities (including most everyday situations).

Another example of an important recent development is introduction of a new component, the episodic buffer, in the previously three-component working memory model (Baddeley, 2000). Even though the original model has been successful in describing and predicting human cognitive functioning in relatively simple and knowledge-lean situations, this model has encountered problems with more complex knowledge-based cognitive phenomena that are not captured by the original model.

The newly introduced buffer is a "limited capacity system that provides temporary storage of information held in a multimodal code, which is capable of binding information from the subsidiary systems, and from long-term memory, into a unitary episodic representation. Conscious awareness is assumed to be the principal mode of retrieval from the buffer. The revised model differs from the old principally in focusing attention on the processes of integrating information, rather than on the isolation of the subsystems. In doing so, it provides a better basis for tackling the more complex aspects of executive control in working memory" (p. 217).

Understanding evolutionary reasons behind the human cognitive architecture may provide important insights into the constraints and strengths of human learning processes (Sweller, 2004; 2007; Sweller & Sweller, 2006). The developing field of evolutionary educational psychology has made a clear distinction between biologically primary (developed throughout human evolution and genetically predisposed) and biologically secondary (created and acquired during the lifetime of a human being) knowledge. The first type of knowledge (e.g., first language, face recognition capabilities, small number counting, etc.) is acquired relatively effortlessly and rapidly, mostly without an explicit conscious processing and control. Working memory limitations and associated issues of cognitive load are not relevant when acquiring this type of knowledge. In contrast, the acquisition of biologically secondary knowledge is based on effortful conscious processing in limited capacity working memory. These processes that usually occur in different educational institutions and settings require specific methods for managing cognitive load in order to be efficient.

Another important research issue is facilitating the acquisition of expertise, especially transition from task-specific to adaptive and flexible forms of expertise. What are mechanisms of transfer of different types of knowledge (e.g., declarative and procedural knowledge)? How to enhance expert abilities to transfer different types of knowledge and skills to new situations using appropriate instructional methods and techniques? Although the problem of transfer has been around for quite a long period of time, the theory is still far from providing clear instructional recommendations.

INSTRUCTIONAL DESIGN IMPLICATIONS

Specific techniques for managing cognitive load will be considered in the following chapters of the book. At this stage, the general instructional design implications that flow from the human cognitive architecture could be outlined as following:

- a major goal of learning is acquisition of organized knowledge base in learner long-term memory and automation of basic routine components of this base;
- comprehension is the selection of an organized knowledge structure (schema) that allows assimilation of new information into something we know;
- if students have difficulties in understanding and learning new material, they most likely do not have appropriate knowledge base and, therefore, their working memories are overloaded;
- learners always search for schemas to make sense of new information; what is learned will always be assimilated in some sort of schemas, therefore, it is important to make learners' search for right schemas easier;
- avoid everything that stands in the way of learning and overloads learner working memory;
- draw learner attention to most important points of instruction;
- chunk information into meaningful groups and help student to link incoming information with prior knowledge base to overcome information-processing "bottleneck";
- build on top of students' existing knowledge: know what knowledge structures your students have and prime necessary knowledge before you start (e.g., using analogies, advance organizers);
- students' well entrenched preexisting misconceptions resist change and should be directly confronted;
- promote automation of basic and frequently required knowledge structures and routine skills (e.g., reading skills) to release cognitive resources for learning new complex information;
- present and sequence new information in a way that helps students to acquire new knowledge structures by reducing working memory overload (e.g., by using a dual mode format).

SUMMARY OF CHAPTER I

The purpose of this chapter was to describe major features of our cognitive architecture that are essential for learning new complex information structures and the design of efficient instruction. Our cognitive architecture is a knowledge-based system that includes a large store of organized information (long-term memory) with effectively unlimited storage capacity and duration. It defines the key role of available organized knowledge structures in human learning.

The second major component of our cognitive architecture is a conscious processing mechanism with limited capacity for dealing with novel information (working memory). This component provides temporary storage and processing of verbal and pictorial information that is in the focus of our attention. Working memory is the workspace for constructing and transforming our mental representations and new knowledge structures.

The organizing and executive role of long-term memory knowledge structures explains how we manage to acquire our huge knowledge base in the conditions of severe working memory limitations. New elements of information pass through working memory, where they are integrated with available prior knowledge. Available knowledge structures in long-term memory guide this integration process and make it relatively effortful and efficient. Long-term memory knowledge structures effectively define the content, capacity, and duration of working memory.

In the absence of relevant prior knowledge base, learners are dealing with many new elements of information in unguided random way that may cause cognitive overload. Acquisition of organized task-specific knowledge structures eliminates the need for learners to apply cognitively inefficient (even though effective in many situations) random problem-solving search when dealing with familiar task classes. Therefore, novice learners need sufficient external support to build new knowledge structures efficiently.

Thus, acquisition and automation of organized knowledge structures is the most significant factor in reducing cognitive overload in learning. These structures effectively reduce or eliminate severe processing limitations of our cognitive system, guide allocation of cognitive resources, and alter characteristics of our learning and performance.

REFERENCES

Anderson, J. R. (1983). *The architecture of cognition*. Cambridge, MA: Harvard University Press.

Baddeley, A. D. (1986). *Working memory*. New York: Oxford University Press.

Baddeley, A. (2000). The episodic buffer: a new component of working memory? Trends in *Cognitive Sciences 4 (11)*, 417-422.

Bargh, J. A., & Chartrand, T. L. (19990. The unbearable automaticity of being. *American Psychologist, 54*, 462-479.

Brand-Gruwel, S., Woperes, I., & Vermetten, Y. (2005). Information problem solving by experts and novices: analysis of a complex cognitive skill. *Computers in Human Behavior, 21*, 487-508.

Bransford, J.D., Brown, A.L., & Cocking, R.R. (Eds.). (1999). How people learn: Mind, brain, experience, and school. Washington, DC: National Academy Press.

Chase, W. G., & Simon, H. A. (1973). Perception in chess. *Cognitive Psychology, 4,* 55-81.

Chi, M. T. H., Feltovich, P., & Glaser, R. (1981). Categorization and representation of physics problems by experts and novices. *Cognitive science, 5,* 121-152.

Chi, M. T. H., Glaser, R., & Farr, M. J. (Eds.). (1988). *The nature of expertise.* Hillsdale, NJ: Erlbaum.

Clement, J. & Steinberg, M. (2002). Step-wise evolution of models of electric circuits: A "learning-aloud" case study. Journal of the Learning Sciences, 11, 389-452.

Cooper, G., & Sweller, J. (1987). The effects of schema acquisition and rule automation on mathematical problem-solving transfer. *Journal of Educational Psychology, 79,* 347-362.

Cowan, N. (2001). The magical number 4 in short-term memory: A reconsideration of mental storage capacity. *Behavioral and Brain Sciences, 24*, 87-114.

Cronbach, L. J., & Snow, R. E. (1977). *Aptitudes and instructional methods: A handbook for research on interaction.* New York: Irvington Publishers.

Csikszentmihalyi, M. (1990). *Flow: the psychology of optimal experience.* NY: Harper & Row.

De Groot, A. D. (1965). *Thought and choice in chess.* The Hague: Mouton.

De Groot, A. D. (1966). Perception and memory versus thought: Some old ideas and recent findings. In B. Kleinmuntz (Ed.), *Problem solving: Research, method, and theory* (pp. 19-50). New York: Wiley.

diSessa, A. A. (1993). Toward an epistemology of physics. *Cognition and Instruction, 10*, 105-225.

Ericsson, K. A., & Charness, N. (1994). Expert performance: Its structure and acquisition. *American Psychologist, 49*, 725-747.

Ericsson, K. A., & Kintsch, W. (1995). Long-term working memory. *Psychological Review,* 102, 211-245.

Ericsson, K. A., Krampe, R. T., & Tesch-Romer, C. (1993). The role of deliberate practice in the acquisition of expert performance. *Psychological Review, 100,* 363-406.

Ericsson, K. A, & Staszewski, J. J. (1989). Skilled memory and expertise: Mechanisms of exceptional performance. In D. Klahr & K. Kotovsky (Eds.), *Complex information processing: The impact of Herbert A. Simon* (pp. 235-267). Hillsdale, NJ: Erlbaum.

Eysenck, M. W. (1982). Attention and arousal: Cognition and performance. New York: Springer-Verlag.

Geary, D. (2002). Principles of evolutionary educational psychology. *Learning and Individual Differences, 12,* 317-345.

Geary, D. (2005). *The origin of mind: Evolution of brain, cognition, and general intelligence.* Washington, DC: American Psychological Association.

Geary, D. (2007). Educating the evolved mind: Conceptual foundations for an evolutionary educational psychology. In J. S. Carlson & J. R. Levin (Eds.), *Psychological perspectives on contemporary educational issues* (pp. 1-99). Greenwich, CT: Information Age Publishing.

Gentner, D., & Stevens, A. L. (Eds.) (1983). *Mental models.* Hillsdale, NJ: Erlbaum.

Glaser, R. (1990). The reemergence of learning theory within instructional research. *American Psychologist, 45,* 29 - 39.

Greeno, J. G., & Simon, H. (1988). Problem solving and reasoning. In R. C. Atkinson, R. Herrnstein, G. Lindzey, & R. D. Luce (Eds.), *Stevens' handbook of experimental psychology.* New York: Wiley.

Hasher, L. & Zacks, R. T. (1979). Automatic and effortful processes in memory. *Journal of Experimental Psychology: General, 108,* 356-388.

Hatano, G. (1982). Cognitive consequences of practice in culture specific procedural skills. *Quarterly Newsletter of the Laboratory of Comparative Human Cognition, 4,*15 - 18.

Hatano, G, & Inagaki, K. (1986). Two Courses of Expertise. In H. Stevenson, H. Azuma, and K. Hakuta (Eds.), *Child Development and Education in Japan.* New York: Freeman.

Howard, R. W. (1987). *Concepts and schemata: Introduction.* London: Cassel Educational.

Kahneman, D. (1973). *Attention and effort.* Englewood Cliffs, NJ: Prentice-Hall.

Kalyuga, S. (2005). Prior knowledge principle. In R. Mayer (Ed.), *Cambridge Handbook of Multimedia Learning* (pp. 325-337). New York: Cambridge University Press.

Kalyuga, S. (2006). *Instructing and testing advance learners: A cognitive load approach.* Hauppage, NY: Nova Science.

Kalyuga, S., Chandler, P., & Sweller, J. (2000). Incorporating learner experience into the design of multimedia instruction. *Journal of Educational Psychology, 92,* 126-136

Kalyuga, S., & Sweller, J. (2005). Rapid dynamic assessment of expertise to improve the efficiency of adaptive e-learning. *Educational Technology, Research and Development, 53,* 83-93.

Kintsch, W. (1998). *Comprehension: A paradigm for cognition.* New York: Cambridge University Press.

Kotovsky, K., Hayes, J. R., & Simon, H. A. (1985). Why are some problems hard? Evidence from Tower of Hanoi. *Cognitive Psychology, 17,* 248-294.

Newell, A., & Simon, H. A. (1972). *Human problem solving.* Englewood Cliffs, NJ: Prentice-Hall.

Mayer, R. E. (2001). *Multimedia learning.* New York: Cambridge University Press.

Mayer, R. E. (Ed.). (2005). *Cambridge Handbook of Multimedia Learning.* New York: Cambridge University Press.

Mayer, R., & Gallini, J. (1990). When is an illustration worth ten thousand words? *Journal of Educational Psychology, 82,* 715-726.

Mayer, R. E., & Wittrock, M. C. (1996). Problem-solving transfer. In D.C. Berliner and R.C. Calfee (Eds.), *Handbook of educational psychology* (pp. 47-62). New York: Simon and Schuster Macmillan.

Miller, G. A. (1956). The magical number seven, plus or minus two: Some limits on our capacity for processing information. *Psychological Review, 63,* 81-97.

O'Neil Jr., H. F. (2002). Perspectives on computer-based assessment of problem solving. Computers in Human Behavior, 18, 605-607.

Orme, J. E. (1969). *Time, experience, and behavior.* London: Lliffe.

Peterson, L., & Peterson, M. (1959). Short-term retention of individual verbal items. *Journal of Experimental Psychology, 58*, 193-198.

Posner, M. I., & Snyder, C. R. R. (1975). Attention and cognitive control. In R. L. Solso, (Ed.). Information *processing and cognition: The Loyola Symposium.* Hillsdale, N.J.: Erlbaaum.

Rapp, D. N, Taylor, H. A., & Crane, G. R. (2003). The impact of digital libraries on cognitive processes: psychological issues of hypermedia. *Computers in Human Behavior, 19*, 609-628.

Rouet, J.-F. (2006). *The skills of document use: From text comprehension to Web-based learning.* Mahwah, NJ: Erlbaum.

Schneider W., & Shiffrin, R. (1977). Controlled and automatic human information processing: I. Detection, search and attention. *Psychological Review, 84*, 1-66.

Schoenfeld, A. H., & Hermann, D. J. (1982). Problem perception and knowledge structure in expert and novice mathematical problem solvers. *Journal of Experimental Psychology: Learning, Memory & Cognition, 8*, 484-494.

Schraagen, J. M. (1993). How experts solve a novel problem in experimental design. Cognitive Science, 17, 285-309.

Shiffrin, R. M., & Schneider, W. (1977). Controlled and automatic human information processing: II. Perceptual learning, automatic attending and a general theory. *Psychological Review, 84,* 127-190.

Shute, V. J. (1992). Aptitude-treatment interactions and cognitive skill diagnosis. In J. W. Regian & V. J. Shute (Eds.), *Cognitive approaches to automated instruction* (pp. 15-47). Hillsdale, NJ: Lawrence Erlbaum Associates

Slotta, J. D., Chi, M. T. H., & Juram, E. (1995). Assessing students' misclassifications of physics concepts: An ontological basis for conceptual change. *Cognition and Instruction, 13*, 373-400.

Sternberg, R. J., & Frensch, P. A. (1992). On being an expert: A cost-benefit analysis. In R. Hoffman (Ed.), *The psychology of expertise: Cognitive research and empirical AI* (pp. 191-203). New York: Springer-Verlag.

Sweller, J. (1988). Cognitive load during problem solving: Effects on learning. *Cognitive Science*, 12, 257-285.

Sweller, J. (1999). *Instructional Design in Technical Areas.* Melbourne: ACER.

Sweller, J. (2003). Evolution of human cognitive architecture. In B. Ross (Ed.), *The psychology of learning and motivation, Vol. 43* (pp. 215-266). San Diego, CA: Academic Press.

Sweller, J. (2004). Instructional design consequences of an analogy between evolution by natural selection and human cognitive architecture. *Instructional Science, 32*, 9-31.

Sweller, J. (2007). Evolutionary biology and educational psychology. In J. S. Carlson & J. R. Levin (Eds.), *Psychological perspectives on contemporary educational issues* (pp. 165-175). Greenwich, CT: Information Age Publishing (in press).

Sweller, J., Chandler, P., Tierney, P., & Cooper, M. (1990). Cognitive load and selective attention as factors in the structuring of technical material. *Journal of Experimental Psychology: General, 119,* 176-192.

Sweller, J., & Sweller, S. (2006). Natural information processing systems. *Evolutionary Psychology, 4*, 434-458.

Sweller, J., van Merriënboer, J., & Paas, F. (1998). Cognitive architecture and instructional design. *Educational Psychology Review, 10*, 251-296.

Van Merriënboer, J. & Sweller, J. (2005). Cognitive load theory and complex learning: Recent developments and future directions. *Educational Psychology Review, 17,* 147-177.

von Uexkull, J. (1957). *Instinctive behavior.* London: Methuen.

Vygotsky, L. S. (1978). *Mind in society.* Cambridge, MA: Harvard University Press.

Zwaan, R. A., Magliano, J. P., & Graesser, A. C. (1995). Dimensions of situation model construction in narrative comprehension. *Journal of Experimental Psychology: Learning, Memory, and Cognition*, 21, 386-397.

Chapter II
Cognitive Load Theory

INTRODUCTION

Cognitive load theory is a learning and instruction theory that describes instructional design implications of human cognitive architecture outlined in the previous chapter. Based on these theoretically and empirically established instructional consequences (usually referred to as cognitive load effects or principles), the theory makes specific prescriptions on managing cognitive load in learning and instruction. The theory distinguishes several different types or sources of cognitive load (e.g., effective and ineffective load; intrinsic, extraneous, and germane load) that are associated with different instructional implications and cognitive load effects. This chapter analyzes cognitive load factors that could potentially influence efficiency of interactive multimedia applications (e.g., levels of element interactivity, spatial and temporal configurations of instructional presentations, redundant representational formats, levels of learner prior experience in a task domain). Basic assumptions of cognitive theory of multimedia learning are discussed. The chapter starts with the description of the sources of cognitive load followed by an overview of the major cognitive load effects.

THE CONCEPT OF COGNITIVE LOAD

Cognitive load could be generally defined as the demand for working memory resources required for achieving goals of specific cognitive activities in certain situations (e.g., instructional episodes or learning tasks). Ideally, these are cognitive resources required for information processing by a specific person (or persons with similar cognitive characteristics) when the individual is fully committed to the task. Thus, cognitive load is a theoretical concept reflecting the interactions between the information structures and learner cognitive characteristics. An actual amount of resources invested in a cognitive activity depends on many factors, including levels of motivation, attitudes, and other personality characteristics.

The actual invested amount of cognitive resources (actual cognitive load) should be distinguished from ideally required resources (required cognitive load). Actual cognitive load can not exceed the amount of ideally required cognitive load. Because of its dependency on multiple factors, the theoretical usability of the concept of actual load is relatively limited at this stage of the development of cognitive load theory and its practical applications. In practice though, this is the load that we usually measure using different cognitive load measurement methods (see Chapter V for an overview). It is assumed that the measured actual load reflects the level of required cognitive load. Therefore, the concept of required ideal cognitive load that is abstracted from many influencing factors (e.g., it implies fully motivated and committed learners) will be the main focus of the following theoretical discussion.

Another important point is that cognitive load is not an objective, depersonalized feature of external information presentations or tasks. It is always related to cognitive processes and characteristics of a specific individual. The word "cognitive" immediately implies relation to individual human cognition. For example, complexity of information (e.g., the level of interactivity between elements of information and even what constitutes an element of information) is always relative to a specific person or a group of learners with similar cognitive characteristics. This issue has become especially important and pronounced in studies of the expertise reversal phenomena (interactions between cognitive load effects and levels of learner expertise in a domain). However, it is equally essential for any other cognitive load phenomena.

ESSENTIAL (EFFECTIVE) COGNITIVE LOAD

There are various sources of cognitive load in multimedia environments. Most obvious ones that we clearly experience when learning complex materials are associated with cognitive activities of establishing key connections between related elements of presented information in working memory and integrating them with available knowledge base in accordance with specific instructional goals. These cognitive activities result in modified or new knowledge structures in long-term memory. They also essentially signify comprehension of the situation and generation of knowledge-based response actions. This cognitive load is usually referred to as intrinsic cognitive load, since it is caused by internal intellectual complexity of the task or material. The magnitude of the essential cognitive load is determined by the degree of interactivity between individual task elements relative to the level of learner expertise in a specific task domain.

An element of information for a particular person is determined by her/his long-term memory knowledge base. For example, for a novice learner of a second language, each letter in a printed word could be a separate element of information. For a more experienced and knowledgeable in this language person (e.g., a native speaker), whole printed words or even certain combinations of words could be regarded as elements of information. These elements will be treated as single units when processed in working memory.

When task elements need to be processed simultaneously (even if the number of elements is relatively small), the material is high in element interactivity and can require a high intrinsic cognitive load. For example, understanding a whole electronic circuit is much more difficult than figuring out the type of each individual element of this circuit. Even if all elements of the circuit are well known to a person in isolation, when combined in the circuit they become interconnected and need to be considered simultaneously as a whole in order to understand the operation of the circuit. Once the interactions of the components of the circuit have been learned, corresponding lower-level knowledge structures become the elements of a higher-order structure that can further act as a single element. If the learner encounters this configuration of components in a new circuit, cognitive processing would require much less cognitive effort.

Because intrinsic cognitive load is essential for achieving specific learning goals (comprehending a situation, performing a task, constructing new higher-level knowledge structures, achieving flexibility of such structures sufficient for transfer in relatively new task situations, etc.), it is vital to provide all the necessary resources to accommodate the intrinsic cognitive load without exceeding limits of working memory capacity. If essential cognitive load required for achieving a specific learning goal exceeds cognitive capacity of a learner, it needs to be appropriately managed. For example, the initial goal could be divided in a series of sub-goals each of which requires less essential processing that is within capacity of the learner working memory. Accordingly, the instructional material should be segmented into smaller units.

Alternatively, essential interactions between elements of information could be eliminated from consideration at the initial stages of learning followed by the fully interactive materials (an isolated-interactive elements effect). For example, students could learn first the names of each element of a circuit without considering interrelationships between different elements. The resulting outcome will be rote learning without real understanding of the whole system. However, it may help in creating a rudimentary knowledge structure that could ease cognitive load during the subsequent stage of learning relationships between elements.

The management of the essential cognitive load may also require its increase rather than reduction if this load is at low levels. If the learning task is too simple for a learner and much cognitive capacity remains unused, nothing or little will be learned. In such situations, techniques for increasing essential cognitive processing could be used. For example, more challenging learning goals could be set that involve more complex cognitive activities with higher levels of element interactivity. Other methods may involve preventing uncontrolled reduction of essential cognitive processing, for example, when learners attempt to spontaneously rely on available simplistic knowledge structures (misconceptions) in guiding their cognitive activities.

EXTRANEOUS (NON-ESSENTIAL) COGNITIVE LOAD

In contrast to the essential and relevant load, extraneous cognitive load ("bad", unproductive, non-constructive load) is associated with a diversion of cognitive resources on activities irrelevant to performance and learning. This load is caused by cognitive activities that a user is involved in because of external design-related factors (e.g., poor interface design, multimedia presentation format, or task sequencing). The design features that impose extraneous cognitive load could take various forms (direct instruction, demonstrations, animations, simulations, exploratory environments etc.), use various modes (e.g., verbal and/or pictorial) and modalities (e.g., visual and/or auditory), illicit cognitive activities with different sequences and sizes of steps.

For example, when related textual, graphical, or audio elements of information are separated over distance or time, their integration might require intense search processes and recall of some elements until other elements are attended and processed. Segments of text need to be held in working memory until corresponding components of a diagram are located, attended, and processed; or images need to be maintained in active state until corresponding fragments of the text are found, read, and processed. Such processes need additional resources and might significantly increase demands on working memory. Searching for suitable solution steps when solving unfamiliar problems may also involve keeping a large number of interacting statements in working memory and require significant cognitive resources that become unavailable for other essential cognitive activities. These cognitive demands are irrelevant to the learning and/or performance goals and should be considered as an extraneous cognitive load.

The following are examples of most typical instructional situations that cause extraneous cognitive load:

1. Separated (in space and/or time) related representations that require users to perform extensive search and match processes (spatial or temporal split-attention situation)
2. An excessive step-size or rate of information change that introduces too many new elements into working memory and/or introduces them too fast to be successfully incorporated into long-term memory structures (excessive information situation).
3. An insufficient externally provided guidance that does not compensate for limited available knowledge thus forcing users to search for solutions using random procedures (induced search situation).
4. User knowledge base overlaps with provided external guidance thus requiring learners to mentally co-refer different representations of the same information (redundancy situation).

The intrinsic and extraneous cognitive load result in the total cognitive load imposed on the cognitive system. For efficient performance and/or learning, total cognitive load should not exceed working memory capacity of a learner (which is obviously dependent on her/his level of task-specific expertise). When a task does not require high levels of intrinsic cognitive load (e.g., because it is low in element interactivity relative to the current level of learner expertise), total cognitive load may not exceed working memory capacity. In this case, the extraneous cognitive load imposed by poor design may not do much harm.

In contrast, when the task is characterized by a high degree of element interactivity relative to the person level of expertise, it might require a high level of intrinsic cognitive load to comprehend the situation. In this case, an additional extraneous cognitive load caused by an inappropriate design can leave insufficient cognitive resources for efficient learning because total cognitive load may exceed the learner working memory capacity. The available cognitive resources may be inadequate for sustaining the required level of total cognitive load. Elimination or reduction of extraneous cognitive load by improving the design of presentation formats or instructional procedures may be critical for learning.

In correspondence with the above distinction between sources of extraneous cognitive load, the general guidelines for minimizing cognitive load in multimedia applications suggest providing learners with direct access to required knowledge base, avoiding diversion of learner cognitive resources on redundant and/or irrelevant cognitive activities, managing step-size and rate of information changes, and eliminating spatial and temporal split of related sources of information.

It should be noted that the differences between extraneous and intrinsic cognitive load are relative to cognitive characteristics of a learner, first of all to available domain-specific knowledge base or levels of learner expertise. Some components of cognitive load that are essential (intrinsic) for understanding instructional message by novice learners, should be considered as extraneous (irrelevant) load for relatively more experienced learners, and vice versa. For example, trying to understand a direct instruction that describes in details an electrical circuit could represent intrinsic load for novice learners and extraneous load for more experienced learners who are familiar with the circuit. It is also possible that required intrinsic load itself may exceed working memory capacity limitations for a particular learner. This excessive intrinsic load would then cause the disruption of learning processes and effectively become a form of extraneous load for the learner.

GERMANE COGNITIVE LOAD

At the beginning, cognitive load theory was focused exclusively on means of reducing or eliminating extraneous cognitive load. It was obvious however that, when dealing with most usual content in educational settings, no meaningful learning could occur without cognitive load. The concept of germane cognitive load was initially introduced into cognitive load theory to separate useful, learning-relevant demands on working memory from irrelevant and wasteful forms of cognitive processing (Sweller, van Merriënboer, & Paas, 1998). Although, according to this general definition, intrinsic cognitive load should be regarded as the most important part of this overall relevant load, germane cognitive load has been traditionally associated with various auxiliary cognitive activities that are intentionally designed with the purpose of fostering learning. For example, prompting learners to engage in explicit self-explanations when learning from worked examples or to imagine procedures described in instructional materials (without looking at the instruction) is expected to enhance learning in comparison with just studying such direct instruction materials.

With this approach, germane cognitive load is caused by various additional learner activities designed to enhance learning outcomes or increase levels of learner motivation. Such activities would obviously increase total cognitive load, however, they contribute to learning (unless the total cognitive load exceeds working memory capacity). Although useful for instructional design implications, the concept of germane cognitive load needs to be applied cautiously. Loose manipulations of this concept may diffuse and devalue cognitive load framework and blend cognitive load approach with essentially any other instructional theory or method by providing universal explanatory framework. Indeed, any effective evidence-based instructional technique or procedure could be hypothetically attributed to increased germane cognitive load. However, without direct empirical evidence of actual increases of this type of load, such speculations would have little if any value. Unfortunately, no investigators have yet managed to differentially measure different types of cognitive load to actually prove such claims.

Figure 2 depicts possible configurations of different types of cognitive load that can take place in various instructional situations. When a learner actually attends to the learning elements, attempts to establish connections between them and construct a coherent mental representation in working memory, the invested mental effort represents an essential cognitive load (intrinsic and/or germane; light area in Figure 2). On the other side, the irrelevant cognitive load (dark area) represents invested cognitive resources that are not essential for achieving instructional goals and are invoked by the instructional design features of specific material or learning tasks. The bold rectangle in Figure 2 represents a learner's effective working memory capacity (that is always relative to her/his level of expertise in a specific task domain). If all three types of load combined together are within this capacity (Figure 2, a), the total cognitive load is under control and no instructional modification could be necessary in this situation.

In a situation when the total load exceeds working memory limits (Figure 2, b), the first obvious step should be directed at reducing extraneous load as much as possible, at least, to get the total load within the accepted capacity limits. If this is not possible, reducing essential load could be the next re-design action. If, on the other side, extraneous load has been successfully reduced or eliminated (Figure 2, c) the available resources should be effectively used by increasing essential load. Because this load is essential for comprehending the material and constructing new knowledge structures, it is vital to maximize its level within limits of working memory capacity. If these capacity limits are exceeded (Figure 2, d), essential load should be appropriately reduced. Canceling some additional cognitive activities designed to enhance germane load would be an obvious course of actions in this case.

In some situations, the learning task could be difficult for learners and cause cognitive overload even if no extraneous or germane loads are involved (Figure 2, e). Sometimes, the level of intrinsic cognitive load that is acceptable for more knowledgeable learners could be overwhelming for novices exceeding the limits of their working memory resources (and thus effectively becoming a form of extraneous load). A number of specific techniques and procedures were developed to manage the exceeding levels of intrinsic load for novices (e.g., segmenting or partitioning the original task, artificially reducing structural complexity of the task on initial phases of learning, etc.). However, such techniques and procedures could become redundant for experts who may need to unnecessarily divert their resources on performing all the required activities.

Similarly, instructional methods for enhancing levels of germane load may produce cognitive overload for less experiences learners (Figure 2, d), thus effectively converting germane load for experts into extraneous load for novice learners. Such situations could be regarded as forms of the previously mentioned expertise rever-

Figure 2. Possible configurations of different types of cognitive load: (a) Total load within working memory capacity; (b) overload with excessive extraneous load; (c) unused working memory capacity; (d) overload with excessive germane load; (e) overload with excessive intrinsic load

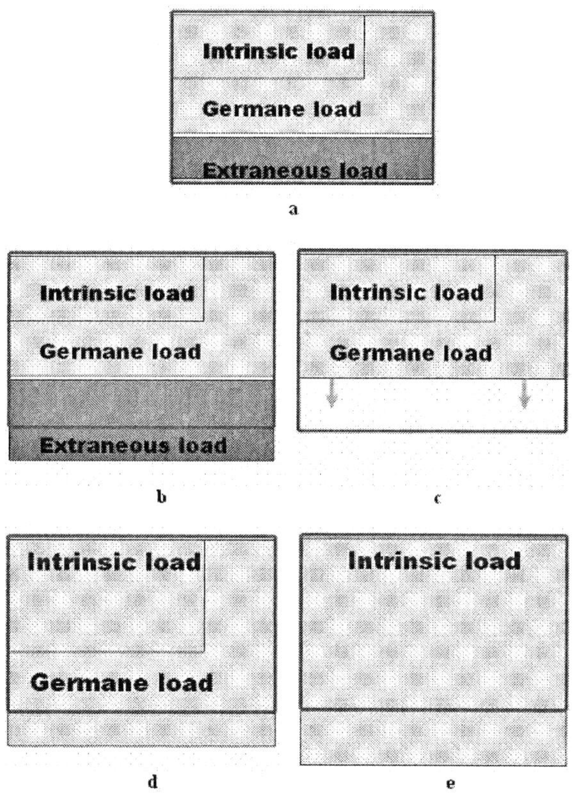

sal effect (more details about the effect will be provided in the following chapter). Thus, not only the magnitude, but also the type of experienced cognitive load may depend on levels of learner task-specific expertise.

COGNITIVE LOAD EFFECTS

Research within cognitive load framework substantially increased our understanding of limitations of human learning processes and the changes in these processes that occur with acquisition of expertise in a domain. Cognitive load effects are theoretically predicted and empirically established stable relationships between instructional procedures, learner characteristics, and learning outcomes. According to cognitive load theory, the extraneous cognitive load may not influence learning significantly when essential cognitive load required for achieving instructional goals is within cognitive capacity of the learner (relative to her/his level of task-specific expertise). In this case, the total cognitive load does not exceed working memory capacity and there is no cognitive overload.

However, when the required essential cognitive processing demand is high, an additional extraneous cognitive load caused by an inappropriate design can be harmful to learning because total cognitive load may exceed working memory capacity. Insufficient cognitive resources would be available for essential processing. In this situation, the extraneous cognitive load imposed by the instructional design may be critical for learning. In order for learning to occur, extraneous cognitive load should be reduced. Examples of some cognitive load techniques for dealing with excessive levels of extraneous cognitive load that are applicable in complex multimedia learning environments are briefly described in the following sections.

WORKED EXAMPLES EFFECT

The cognitive load approach originated at the beginning of 1980s from the studies of human learning during performance of problem-solving tasks. Sweller Mawer, and Howe (1982) used simple number tasks similar to the following one: get from number 31 (initial state) to the number 3 (goal state) by using only two operators, multiplying by 3 and subtracting 69. The solution of this task requires sequential application of alternating multiplication and subtraction operators: 31 X 3 = 93; 93 - 69 = 24; 24 X 3 = 72; 72 - 69 = 3. Even though the general solution procedure for this task, as well as many others similar tasks of this class, was rather simple (multiply, subtract, multiply, subtract, etc. until the required number is reached), it was very difficult for students to figure it out. They repeatedly continued applying random search procedures task after task.

According to cognitive load theory, solving problems using weak strategies such as means-ends analysis is associated with significant extraneous load that could be detrimental for learning. Such strategies include many cognitive components such as determining differences between problem states, finding solution moves to reduce those differences, considering chains of sub-goals, etc. Keeping many of these components simultaneously active in working memory may impose a significant cognitive load. This load would prevent essential cognitive processing associated with constructing organized knowledge structures (schemas), thus interfering with learning (Cooper & Sweller, 1987; Lewis & Anderson, 1985; Owen & Sweller, 1985; Sweller & Cooper, 1985).

An alternative instructional method to conventional problem solving could be studying a worked example that provides all the appropriate solution steps for a problem. While studying the worked example, learners attend simultaneously only to one problem state and an associated solution step. This process requires significantly less working memory capacity thus reducing extraneous cognitive load and facilitating learning (worked example effect). In multiple experimental studies in mathematics-related task domains, using relatively more worked examples instead of solving equivalent conventional problems lead to better learning outcomes (including transfer performance) achieved faster and with less wasteful cognitive load (Cooper & Sweller, 1987; Paas, 1992; Sweller & Cooper, 1985; Zhu & Simon, 1987).

SPLIT ATTENTION EFFECT

Many multimedia presentations include diagrams or pictures with related on-screen textual explanations. If neither explanations nor pictures can be understood separately, the statements in the explanatory text need to be mentally coordinated with corresponding elements in a picture in order for an integrated cognitive structure to be built. Such mental coordination processes require additional cognitive resources that are not directly related to learning. Wasting substantial working memory resources on such search and match processes may inhibit learning even if the instruction takes the form of a worked example. Similar problems could occur in temporal split-attention situations when corresponding words and pictures are presented successively rather than simultaneously.

These searching and coordinating processes could be reduced significantly if each textual statement is located near its matching parts on the picture, similar to the way embedded textual segments are used in comics and cartoons for children. Reduced split attention is obviously one of the reasons for the popularity of comics and cartoons among younger children. Considering that reading textual segments could impose high intrinsic cognitive load on them, reducing any form of extraneous load is essential. Physically integrating textual explanations with the related pictorial information actually improved learning performance significantly in geometry, kinematics, electrical engineering and other task areas (split-attention effect) (Chandler & Sweller, 1991; Tarmizi & Sweller, 1988; Ward & Sweller, 1990).

Online learning environments place great cognitive demands on learners due to nonlinear nature and heterogeneity of presented information. For example, reading could be more difficult in a nonlinear 'hypertext" environment than in a traditional linear paper-based format. Many interlinked short texts and segments should be integrated and reconciled thus placing an excessive cognitive load on a reader. Multiple representations of information (text, pictures, video, etc.) in hypermedia environments may also cause significant split attention problems. Techniques that could reduce these problems include integrating the text into the graphic on the screen, avoiding covering or separating related sources of information that must be integrated for learning, and designing space for guidance or feedback close to problem statements (both being visible).

THE REDUNDANCY EFFECT

An important condition for the split-attention effect to occur is the interdependency between different sources of information, when either source cannot be understood on its own without attending to the related ones. In some instructional situations, however, individual sources of pictorial and textual information could be understood separately. If such sources of information are physically separated, learners may simply ignore unnecessary information and attend only to a single sufficient source. However, if they are physically integrated (with the intention to handle an assumed split-attention situation) learners could be actually forced to attend and process redundant information. Such additional processing may impose extraneous cognitive load that is non-essential and interferes with learning. In this situation, elimination rather than integration of such redundant sources of information could produce better learning outcomes (Chandler & Sweller, 1991).

Thus, if a source of information (textual or graphical) is fully intelligible on its own, then any additional redundant sources of information should be removed from the instructional materials rather than integrated into it (redundancy effect). As a simple example, placing guiding notes for driving directions in addition to arrows (Figure 3a) would not make the directions easier to understand. Simple lines indicating the driving route are self-explanatory and most easy to understand and use (Figure 3b).

Repeatedly occurring examples of redundancy situations could be found in maps, street directories, pie-charts, and instructional manuals. For example, traditional instructional manuals for various software applications usually require learners to simultaneously pay attention to explanations and instructions in the manual (in many cases, illustrated by screenshots or pictures), to the actual computer screen, and enter data or commands using the computer keyboard. The learner is placed into a split-attention situation that may result in a high level of extraneous cognitive load.

One effective way of dealing with this situation is initially eliminating the essentially redundant hardware and placing graphical representations of the computer screen (e.g., using screenshots) and keyboard in the manual with textual instructions embedded into the diagrams at appropriate locations. Such self-contained manuals proved to be effective for novice computer users dealing with highly interactive components of instruction (Sweller & Chandler, 1994; Chandler & Sweller, 1996). No differences were found when the learning materials involved low element interactivity.

Figure 3. Redundant (a) and non-redundant (b) ways of presenting driving directions

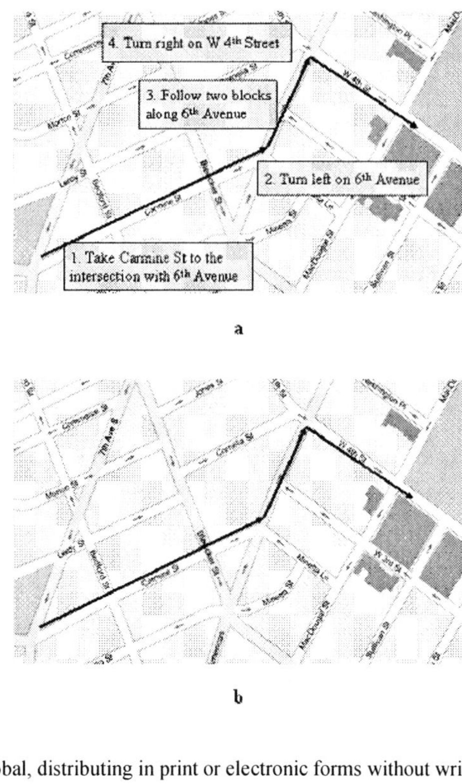

An alternative way of dealing with the above mentioned split attention situation is eliminating the printed manual and placing integrated instructions on the screen. In this case, the role of computer at the initial stages of learning would only be turning on-screen pages. In both cases, the computer would be used in more interactive modes of learning at the following stages. By that time, learners would already have acquired initial knowledge of the application and would be able to handle potentially high levels of cognitive load.

THE MODALITY EFFECT

Physically integrating related and non-redundant sources of information is a means of reducing or eliminating split attention and associated extraneous cognitive load. Another possible means of dealing with potential cognitive overload is presenting one of the sources of information in an auditory form. This technique (modality effect) is based on engaging another processing channel in working memory and effectively expanding its available capacity. The amount of information that can be simultaneously processed using both auditory and visual channels may exceed the amount of information processed in a single channel. Instructional materials that present information using dual or multiple modalities (for example, a visual diagram accompanied by an auditory text) can be more efficient than equivalent single modality formats. Students learn better when words are presented as narration rather than as on-screen text, and prefer listening to explanations of complex materials (e.g. diagrams or animations) rather than reading such explanations in print.

The modality effect is also one of the principles of cognitive theory of multimedia learning (Mayer, 2001; 2005) that will be discussed in more details in the next section. However, it has a clear cognitive load explanation and, in fact, it was generated within the framework of cognitive load theory using instructional materials with relatively high levels of element interactivity (geometry problems in Mousavi, Low & Sweller, 1995; electrical wiring diagrams and tables in Tindall-Ford, Chandler, & Sweller, 1997). Instructional implications of this effect for the design of multimedia learning will be considered in the next part of the book.

As an important means of dealing with split-attention situations, the modality effect has a similar condition of its applicability to that of split-attention effect: the source of information presented in an auditory modality should not be a redundant one. Otherwise, a redundancy effect could be applied similar to single-modality instructional presentations: rather than being presented in an alternative modality, the redundant instructional information should be removed. For example, when a diagram is self-contained, any additional verbal explanations could unnecessarily distract learner attention, waste cognitive resources, and generate extraneous cognitive load irrespective whether they are presented in integrated visual format or using auditory modality.

COGNITIVE THEORY OF MULTIMEDIA LEARNING

Multimedia learning in general is defined as learning from words (printed such as on-screen text or spoken as a narration) and pictures (static such as diagrams, illustrations, maps or dynamic as animations, video, interactive simulations) (Mayer, 2001). Cognitive theory of multimedia learning is based on three major assumptions: dual-channel, limited-capacity, and active processing. Current models of working memory consider its capacity distributed between separate auditory and visual processing channels. For example, the "separate stream hypothesis" proposed by Penney (1989) assumed independent processing of auditory and visually presented verbal items in working memory.

Dual coding theory of Paivio (1990) also suggested that information can be encoded, stored and retrieved from two different systems, one for verbal information, another for images. For example, in Baddeley's (1986) theory of working memory these systems were identified as a phonological loop and visuospatial sketchpad. The phonological loop processes auditory information (verbal or written material in an auditory form), while the visuospatial sketchpad deals with visual information such as diagrams or pictures. These two sub-systems contribute additively to total memory capacity.

Therefore, if information is coded in both verbal and pictorial coding systems, memory for the information will be enhanced. Active processing assumes that learning requires active selecting (paying attention to certain auditory and/or visual sensory inputs), organizing (constructing coherent verbal and/or pictorial representations) and integrating (merging) of constructed cognitive representations with existing knowledge base. Active processing of multimedia materials requires selecting words, selecting images, organizing words, organizing images, and integrating them together. These processes are partially guided by activated prior knowledge (Mayer & Moreno, 2003).

A related cognitive model of multimedia learning (Schnotz and Bannert, 2003) explains how information from different external representations is integrated. The model consists of a descriptive and a depictive branches of processes. The descriptive branch includes processes of symbol analysis that construct a surface representation and then a propositional representation of the text. The depictive branch includes analog structure mapping processes that construct a visual image and then a mental model of the external picture. In addition to pure text comprehension theories, this model considers the visual image generated from the external picture or diagram as a source of information for the construction of the mental model. Thus, the resulting mental model is the representation that integrates propositions from the text base, pictorial elements from the visual image, and general world knowledge. This model is constructed in a step-by-step continuous process within the limits of available working memory resources that results in a coherent structure representing jointly text and pictures.

Although similar in some respects, the above two cognitive models of multimedia learning are different. In Mayer's cognitive theory of multimedia learning, the distinction between the "verbal-auditory channel" and the "visual-pictorial channel" is based on a combination of sensory modalities and representational formats. In Schnotz and Bannert's model, the descriptive and depictive branches are explicitly specialized for processing information represented in specific formats irrespective of the perceptual modality. This approach corresponds more closely to the distinction of verbal and visuospatial components of working memory.

Also, Mayer's model assumes that processing in both channels results in two, verbal and visual, mental models that are initially processed independently. Referential connections between the models are constructed only at the next stage of processing. In contrast, Schnotz and Bannert (2003) assume only one modality-unspecific referential mental model constructed from interacting elements of the visual image and the propositional representation. Interrelating these two processing branches, however, requires working memory resources for coordinating processes (Dutke & Rinck, 2006). The above two versions of the cognitive theory of multimedia learning provide theoretical frameworks for describing and explaining the effects of using multimedia representations in learning and instruction.

COGNITIVE OVERLOAD IN MULTIMEDIA LEARNING

Mayer and Moreno (2003) described several types of situations in multimedia learning that can cause excessive cognitive load. They also offered corresponding means of managing cognitive load in these situations. The first type of overload is when one processing channel is overloaded with essential demands. For example, split attention between different forms of visual representations (diagrams or animations with separated explanatory text) may cause this type of overload in the visual channel. Off-loading the channel is suggested as an appropriate cognitive load management method in this situation. For example, presenting words as narration would reduce demands on visual channel (modality effect).

The second type of overload occurs when both channels are overloaded with essential processing demands. For example, when information is complex (due to high intrinsic load or high element interactivity) and presented at a high pace rate, there could be not enough time for learners to properly select, organize, and integrate this information. An effective cognitive load management technique in this situation is segmenting the content into smaller chunks and allowing learners to control the pace of their presentation (segmentation effect, Mayer & Chandler, 2001). Another suggested method of dealing with this type of overload is pre-training. This method provides prior instruction about the names and behavior of the components of a complex system before the whole system is learned. Learning both components and causal links between them simultaneously could be very cognitively demanding. Pre-training method breaks this process up into two separate stages (Mayer, Mathias, & Wetzell, 2002; Pollock, Chandler, & Sweller, 2002).

The next type of cognitive overload occurs when one or both channels are overloaded by non-essential processing demands imposed by extraneous materials, such as background music, pictures, video-clips, etc. even though they are related to the topic. In this case, a suitable cognitive load management technique is weeding or eliminating interesting but extraneous material in order to make the presentation concise and coherent (coherence effect; Mayer, Heiser, & Lonn, 2001; Moreno & Mayer, 2000). Another method for dealing with this type of cognitive overload is signaling that provides cues on how to select and organize the material, for example, by stressing key words in text, adding headings to the text, highlighting essential parts of visualizations with arrows, flashings, highlights, etc., or adding a content map (signaling effect; Mautone & Mayer, 2001).

Another type of cognitive overload can take place when one or both channels are overloaded by the combination of essential and extraneous cognitive load. For example, this situation may occur when separated graphics (or animations) and text require extraneous load for their processing. Integrating presentations by aligning words and pictures is an effective method for dealing with this type of situations (split-attention effect, Sweller, Chandler, Tierney, & Cooper, 1990; or spatial contiguity effect; Mayer, 2001). Another example of this type of load is simultaneous presentation of graphics (animations), narration, and on-screen text. The learner needs to reconcile on-screen and narrated explanations that may cause extraneous cognitive load (multimedia redundancy effect, Kalyuga, Chandler, & Sweller, 1999; Mayer et al., 2001). Getting rid of redundant onscreen text would eliminate this source of cognitive overload.

Finally, cognitive overload may also take place when there is a need to hold information temporarily in working memory in addition to essential processing. This situation may happen, for example, during successive presentation of related narration and animation. Synchronizing the presentation of corresponding pictorial and auditory elements of information may eliminate this extraneous load (temporal contiguity effect; Mayer & Anderson, 1991; 1992; Mayer & Sims, 1994). Segmenting the presentation into small units that often alternate between narration and animation (few seconds each) may also reduce this source of extraneous load (Moreno & Mayer, 2002).

Individual differences that have been found to influence the learning outcomes in multimedia learning include levels of learner prior knowledge (Mayer, 2001), visualizer/verbalizer learning preferences (Leutner & Plass, 1998; Plass et al., 1998), spatial and verbal abilities (Jonassen and Grabowski, 1993; Mayer, 2001; Pellegrrino, Alderton, & Shute, 1984). According to cognitive studies of expert-novice differences, levels of learner prior knowledge is the most important factor that influences learning. In most cases, prior knowledge would override the influence of other individual differences. The role of this factor in cognitive load theory will be considered in detail in the following chapter.

FUTURE TRENDS IN COGNITIVE LOAD THEORY

Differentiation of types of cognitive load requires further theoretical and empirical investigation including the development of appropriate measurement instruments (this issue will be discussed later in Chapter V of this book). Important directions are managing intrinsic load, developing clear concept and understanding of the nature and role of germane cognitive load in learning and instruction, and studying the interaction between germane, intrinsic, and extraneous types of load. For example, Schnotz, Cierniak, Pierolt, and Rasch (2007) suggested that germane load is constrained by intrinsic load. For example, it is possible to solve a very difficult task without deep reflection associated with germane cognitive load, however it is not possible to reflect deeply about a very easy task. Germane cognitive load includes additional activities beyond simple task performance (e.g., intentional application of specific learning strategies, metacognitive regulation of learning, abstraction of general patterns). Therefore, learning depends on the interaction between intrinsic and germane cognitive load.

Cognitive load effects have been investigated mostly in technical domains (mathematics, science, technical education, etc.) with relatively well defined problems. It is important to continue to extend the theory into more poorly specified task areas that are typical for social sciences and humanitarian disciplines (history, literature, economy, etc.), as well as many complex tasks in practical domains (management, health care, education, etc.). For example, foreign (second) language acquisition remains an important domain for cognitive load research. There have been a number of recent applications of cognitive load principles to the instructional design in this area (Diao, Chandler, & Sweller, 2007; Diao & Sweller, 2007). Moussa, Ayres, and Sweller (2007) investigated a redundancy effect in second language learning. They established that when learning a foreign language, the simultaneous presentation of oral and written material may inhibit learning. The conclusion was that in many situations, we can learn more about a language by reading alone rather than by reading and listening.

One of the important research trends in cognitive load theory is examining cognitive load effects in complex multimodal environments that include not only written text, narration, and graphics, but also less traditional information delivery means such as gestures, dynamic visualizations, three-dimensional virtual environments, etc. It will take the field closer to investigating cognitive load phenomena in complex real world settings that are usually less predictable, high-intensity, high-load, multi-source, and real-time environments. Examples of such settings are managing emergency responses in street and air traffic control systems, health care, high-energy industrial and research equipment, etc..

Another important research trend is investigating cognitive load consequences and implications for collaborative learning environments. It is important to establish conditions under which learning in such environments becomes more efficient than individual learning. There has been a recent explosion in the interest towards collaborative learning environments. They certainly have a great potential as vehicles for effective learning in natural conditions of social interactions in which we have evolved to function effectively. However, positive learning and performance results are not always found in such environments, and learner cognitive overload could be one of reasons for this. In terms of evolutionary educational psychology (Chapter I), these environments represent natural conditions for the acquisition of biologically primary knowledge. Acquiring secondary knowledge structures within constrains of individual working memory capacity may require a set of additional conditions to enhance cognitive effectiveness and efficiency of collaborative learning environments.

For example, Kirschner and Paas (2007) suggested that enhancing the effectiveness of collaborative learning requires considering the limited working memory capacity, the complexity of the task, and the cognitive transaction costs caused by the demands of communicating and coordinating knowledge between the group members in such environments. It is believed that group-based learning could be potentially more effective than individual learning when the task demands exceed the cognitive resources of a single individual together with the cognitive demands associated with the communication and coordination of the knowledge. Further research requires developing instruments for measuring group cognitive load; determining the levels of task complexity at which it could be more effective to assign tasks to groups rather than to individuals; and determining the relations between the task complexity and learner levels of expertise in effective collaborative learning environments (Kirschner & Paas, 2007).

MULTIMEDIA INSTRUCTIONAL DESIGN IMPLICATIONS

For efficient performance and/or learning, total cognitive load imposed on cognitive system should not exceed limited working memory capacity. The total cognitive load is composed of intrinsic, extraneous, and (if involved) germane cognitive load. When a task does not require high levels of intrinsic cognitive load (e.g., because it is low in element interactivity relative to the current level of learner expertise), the extraneous cognitive load imposed by a poor instructional design may not do much harm because the total cognitive load would not exceed working memory capacity.

In contrast, when the task is characterized by a high degree of element interactivity relative to the learner level of expertise, it may require a heavy intrinsic cognitive load to comprehend the situation. In this case, an additional extraneous cognitive load caused by an inappropriate design can leave insufficient cognitive resources for efficient performance and/or learning because total cognitive load may exceed the learner working memory capacity. The available cognitive resources may be inadequate for sustaining the required level of total cognitive load. Elimination or reduction of extraneous cognitive load by improving the design of presentation formats or task procedures may be critical for learning.

In correspondence with the previously mentioned sources of extraneous cognitive load, the general guidelines for minimizing this type of cognitive load in multimedia applications suggest providing learners with direct access to required knowledge base, avoiding diversion of learner cognitive resources on redundant and/or irrelevant cognitive activities, managing step-size and rate of information presentation, and eliminating spatial and temporal split of related sources of information.

In the most general form, the main instructional implication of cognitive load theory could be expressed as the need to avoid anything that gets in the way of learning. Some specific design implications in respect to multimedia learning include:

- enrich printed text with visual representations;
- present visualizations and corresponding textual explanations simultaneously rather than successively to avoid temporal split-attention;

- present related sources of information close to one another on screen (e.g., embed the text into the graphic, avoid covering or separating information that must be mentally integrated for learning, design space for guidance or feedback close to problem statements);
- avoid irrelevant graphics, stories, interesting but irrelevant details, irrelevant sounds and music, nonessential words and lengthy text;
- use visual representations explained by audio narration rather than on-screen text;
- use animated visualizations with brief audio narrations rather than on-screen textual explanations;
- present static or animated visualizations with narration-only instead of duplicating the narration with onscreen text.

When designing an instructional guidance on how to use the hardware that involves material with high levels of element interactivity, a self-contained instruction that does not require the use of the computer or other hardware could be superior to instructional formats that involve continual interactions with the hardware. The following chapters will further explain some of the above recommendations (see also Clark & Mayer, 2003; Mayer, 2005 for more details).

SUMMARY OF CHAPTER II

Research in cognitive science substantially widened our understanding of mental processes involved in competent performance, limitations of our cognitive system, the role of learner prior knowledge, and changes in these processes that occur with the acquisition of expertise in a domain.

The essential cognitive load is associated with cognitive resources directed towards achieving certain learning objectives. When essential cognitive load is involved, the learner attends to the learning elements, attempts to establish connections between them and construct a coherent mental representation in working memory. Because this load is essential for comprehending the material and constructing new knowledge, it is vital to maximize its level within limits of working memory capacity. On the other side, the irrelevant extraneous cognitive load represents invested cognitive resources that are not essential for achieving learning goals and are caused by the instructional design features of specific learning tasks.

Major sources of excessive extraneous cognitive load that may inhibit performance and learning with multimedia applications are spatially and/or temporally split elements of information that need to be integrated for understanding; an excessive step-size and/or rate of information presentations that introduce too many new elements of information into working memory too fast to be organized and comprehended; insufficient user support or guidance for lower prior knowledge learners; excessive redundant support overlapping with available knowledge structures of more experienced learners.

The cognitive theory of multimedia learning is based on three assumptions: (1) the dual-channel assumption about two information processing channels (a visual channel and a verbal channel); (2) the active processing assumption that considers learners as active information processors; and (3) the limited working memory capacity assumption. Based on this theory, a series of evidence-based principles for effective multimedia learning design has been suggested.

REFERENCES

Baddeley, A. D. (1986). *Working memory.* New York: Oxford University Press.

Chandler, P., & Sweller, J. (1991). Cognitive load theory and the format of instruction. *Cognition and Instruction, 8,* 293-332.

Chandler, P., & Sweller, J. (1996). Cognitive load while learning to use a computer program. *Applied Cognitive Psychology, 10*, 1-20.

Clark, R. C., & Mayer, R. E. (2003). E-learning and the science of instruction. San Francisco, CA: Pfeiffer.

Cooper, G., & Sweller, J. (1987). The effects of schema acquisition and rule automation on mathematical problem-solving transfer. *Journal of Educational Psychology, 79,* 347-362.

Diao, Y., Chandler, P., & Sweller, J. (2007). The effect of written text on comprehension of spoken English as a foreign language. *The American Journal of Psychology, 120*, 237-262.

Diao, Y. & Sweller, J. (2007). Redundancy in foreign language reading comprehension instruction: Concurrent written and spoken presentations. *Learning and Instruction, 17,* 78-88.

Dutke, S., & Rinck, M. (2006). Multimedia learning: Working memory and the learning of word and picture diagrams. *Learning and Instruction, 16*, 526-537.

Kirschner, F., & Paas, F. (2007, March). *When Collaborative Learning Becomes More Efficient Than Individual Learning.* Paper presented at the International Conference on Cognitive Load Theory, Sydney, UNSW.

Kalyuga, S., Chandler, P., & Sweller, J. (1999). Managing split-attention and redundancy in multimedia instruction. *Applied Cognitive Psychology, 13*, 351-371.

Lewis, M. W., & Anderson, J. R. (1985). Discrimination of operator schemata in problem solving: learning from examples. *Cognitive Psychology, 17*, 26-65.

Mautone, P. D., & Mayer, R. E. (2001). Signaling as a cognitive guide in multimedia learning. *Journal of Educational Psychology, 93*, 377-389.

Mayer, R. E. (2001). *Multimedia learning.* New York: Cambridge University Press.

Mayer, R. E. (Ed.). (2005). *Cambridge Handbook of Multimedia Learning.* New York: Cambridge University Press.

Mayer, R., & Anderson, R. (1991). Animations need narrations: An experimental test of a dual-coding hypothesis. *Journal of Educational Psychology, 83*, 484-490.

Mayer, R., & Anderson, R. (1992). The instructive animation: Helping students build connections between words and pictures in multimedia learning. *Journal of Educational Psychology, 84*, 444-452.

Mayer, R. E., & Chandler, P. (2001). When learning is just a click away: Does simple user interaction foster deeper understanding of multimedia messages? *Journal of educational Psychology, 93*, 390-397.

Mayer R. E., Heiser, J., & Lonn, S. (2001). Cognitive constraints on multimedia learning: When presenting more material results in less understanding. *Journal of Educational Psychology, 93,* 187-198.

Mayer, R. E., & Moreno, R. (2003). Nine ways to reduce cognitive load in multimedia learning. Educational Psychologist, 38, 43-52.

Mayer, R. E., Mathias, A., & Wetzell, K. (2002). Fostering understanding of multimedia messages through pre-training: Evidence fro a two-stage theory of mental model construction. *Journal of Experimental Psychology: Applied, 8*, 147-154.

Mayer, R. E., & Sims, V. K. (1994). For whom is a picture worth a thousand words? Extensions of a dual-coding theory of multimedia learning. *Journal of Educational Psychology, 86*, 389-401.

Moreno, R., & Mayer, R. E. (2000). A coherence effect in multimedia learning: The case for minimizing irrelevant sounds in the design of multimedia instructional messages. *Journal of Educational Psychology, 92*, 117-125.

Moreno, R., & Mayer, R. E. (2002). Verbal redundancy in multimedia learning: When reading helps listening. *Journal of Educational Psychology, 94*, 156-163.

Mousavi, S. Y., Low, R., & Sweller, J. (1995). Reducing cognitive load by mixing auditory and visual presentation modes. *Journal of Educational Psychology, 87*, 319-334.

Moussa, J., Ayres, P., & Sweller, J. (2007, March). Cognitive Load and the Impact of Spoken English on Learning English as a Foreign Language. Paper presented at the International Conference on Cognitive Load Theory, Sydney, UNSW.

Owen, E., & Sweller, J. (1985). What do students learn while solving mathematics problems? *Journal of Educational Psychology, 77*, 272-284.

Paas, F. (1992). Training strategies for attaining transfer of problem solving skill in statistics: A cognitive load approach. *Journal of Educational Psychology, 84*, 429-434.

Paivio, A. (1990). *Mental representations: A dual-coding approach.* New York: Oxford University Press.

Penney, C. G. (1989). Modality effects and the structure of short-term verbal memory. *Memory and Cognition, 17*, 398-422.

Pollock, E., Chandler, P., & Sweller, J. (2002). Assimilating complex information. *Learning and Instruction, 12*, 61-86.

Schnotz, W., & Bannert, M. (2003). Construction and interference in learning from multiple representation. *Learning and Instruction, 13*, 141-156.

Schnotz, W., Cierniak, G., Pierolt, G., & Rasch, T. (2007, March). *Constraints on Germane Cognitive Load.* Paper presented at the International Conference on Cognitive Load Theory, Sydney, UNSW.

Sweller, J., & Chandler, P. (1994). Why some material is difficult to learn? *Cognition and Instruction, 12*, 185-233.

Sweller, J., Chandler, P., Tierney, P., & Cooper, M. (1990). Cognitive load and selective attention as factors in the structuring of technical material. Journal of Experimental Psychology: General, 119, 176-192.

Sweller, J., & Cooper, G. A. (1985). The use of worked examples as a substitute for problem solving in learning algebra. *Cognition and Instruction, 2*, 59-89.

Sweller, J., Mawer, R. & Howe, W. (1982). The consequences of history-cued and means-ends strategies in problems solving. *American Journal of Psychology, 95*, 455-484.

Sweller, J., van Merriënboer, J., & Paas, F. (1998). Cognitive architecture and instructional design. *Educational Psychology Review, 10*, 251-296.

Tarmizi, R., & Sweller, J. (1988). Guidance during mathematical problem solving. *Journal of Educational Psychology, 80*, 424-436.

Tindall-Ford, S., Chandler, P., & Sweller, J. (1997). When two sensory modes are better than one. *Journal of Experimental Psychology: Applied, 3*, 257-287.

Ward, M., & Sweller, J. (1990). Structuring effective worked examples. *Cognition and Instruction, 7*, 1-39.

Zhu, X., & Simon, H. (1987). Learning mathematics from examples and by doing. *Cognition and Instruction, 4*, 137-166.

Chapter III
The Expertise Reversal Effect

INTRODUCTION

Cognitive studies of expertise that were reviewed in Chapter I indicated that prior knowledge is the most important learner characteristic that influences learning processes. Recently, it has been established that learning procedures and techniques that are beneficial for learners with low levels of prior knowledge may become relatively inefficient for more knowledgeable learners due to cognitive activities that consume additional working memory resources. This expertise reversal effect could be related to aptitude-treatment interactions (interactions between learning outcomes of different instructional treatments and student aptitudes) that were actively investigated in 1960-70s. The learner level of prior knowledge or level of expertise is the aptitude of interest in this case. The effect is explained by the cognitive overload that more knowledgeable learners may experience due to processing redundant for these learners instructional components (as compared to information without redundancy). As a consequence, instructional outcomes of different multimedia learning formats and procedures are always relative to levels of learner task-specific expertise.

This chapter describes cognitive processes that cause expertise reversal effect and major instructional implications of this effect. The chapter provides a review of empirical evidence obtained in the original longitudinal studies of the effect, the expertise reversal for methods of enhancing essential cognitive load, and expertise reversal phenomena when learning from textual and hypertextual materials. The chapter also describes relations between the expertise reversal effect and studies of Aptitude-Treatment Interactions. Additional empirical evidence for the effect in other areas will be described in the following chapters in Section 2 of the book.

LEVELS OF EXPERTISE AND IMBALANCES OF EXECUTIVE FUNCTION

As described in Chapter I, long-term memory structures provide executive guidance in performing high-level cognitive tasks. In the absence of such structures, external information may also provide necessary guidance. An executive imbalance occurs when externally provided information conflicts with existing knowledge-based guidance, thus distracting from fluent execution of appropriate cognitive processes. Therefore, well ordered and balanced (optimized) executive function assumes that the external information entering working memory fits and complements available knowledge-based executive structures.

If challenges of the task significantly exceed the available learner knowledge base, the task could cause cognitive overload and anxiety. On the other hand, when these challenges are too low relative to the available knowledge and skills, the task will be easy and boring for the learner. A well fitted task that provides challenges just above the level of learner available experience would provide the best motivating power. Paying unnecessary attention to information that could otherwise be processed automatically and effortlessly would reduce cognitive resources required for other more complex cognitive activities that may indeed require effortful conscious processing in working memory. Such unnecessary diversion of attention may also be a de-motivating factor in learning.

The expertise reversal effect has been initially predicted within the cognitive load theory framework as a form of redundancy effect. This form of redundancy occurs when information that is beneficial for novice learners becomes redundant for more knowledgeable learners due to acquired higher level of expertise in a task domain (Kalyuga, Chandler, & Sweller, 1998). For example, when related text and pictures are separated in space the integration process is expected to increase cognitive load. Physically integrating verbal and pictorial representations may reduce or eliminate this load (split-attention effect). However, for more advanced learners, eliminating non-essential redundant textual explanations was expected to be more effective. For more knowledgeable learners, processing the redundant material (especially if it is embedded into the pictures without the possibility to ignore it) may overload working memory relative to information without redundancy.

The expertise reversal effect was then observed with different presentation modalities and levels of instructional guidance. It became clear that this is a different kind of redundancy. It occurs when external information becomes redundant relative to learner internal knowledge structures, and additional cognitive resources are required for cross-referencing presented and previously learned information. For example, detailed narrated directions in using specific types of diagrams that were presented concurrently with the animated diagrams were effective for novice learners (Kalyuga, Chandler, & Sweller, 2000). However, after a number of intensive training sessions, when the same learners achieved higher levels of task-specific expertise, presenting a different version of these diagrams with detailed narrated explanations inhibited learning. At this higher level of expertise, learner cognitive activities were based on previously acquired knowledge structures. External explanations were redundant and required cross-referencing of presented explanations and available knowledge base.

Using essential and removing redundant information and procedures as learner acquire more task-specific expertise, thus reducing or eliminating interfering cognitive processing, is important for optimizing cognitive resources. For novice learners, cognitively-optimal instructional designs reduce situations when attention is split between multiple complementing representations. Such designs are achieved by integrating these representations, placing them in close proximity of each other, or using dual-modality formats with segments of narrated verbal information presented simultaneously with visual representations. For more experienced learners, cognitively-optimal designs could be achieved by eliminating redundant sources of information rather than integrating them with essential representations.

COGNITIVE EXPLANATIONS OF THE EXPERTISE REVERSAL EFFECT

Executive imbalances occur when there are misfits between externally provided information and existing knowledge-based guidance. In a situation where no executive guidance is provided for dealing with new elements of incoming information by either of these providers, users have to resort to general search strategies. Such strategies are very inefficient as learning means. Such situations happen, for example, when minimally guided performance environments are used with users who have insufficient levels of prior knowledge in this task domain. On the other hand, there could be an overlap between long-term memory knowledge structures and external providers of the executive function when both of them are available for dealing with the same units of information.

Although several different (internal and/or external) representations for the same cognitive processes could generally coexist, only a single central executive could actually guide cognitive activities. Therefore, a user would have to relate and cross-reference the overlapping components of the central executive function. For example, it may be necessary to "dismantle" some well-learned and even partially automated long-term memory structures. This process of reconciling the related components of available long-term memory knowledge base and externally provided guidance would likely impose an additional working memory load. Consequently, less capacity could be available for new knowledge acquisition and performance improvement, resulting in a phenomenon that has been referred to as the expertise reversal effect (Kalyuga, Ayres, Chandler, & Sweller, 2003).

In other words, presenting experienced learners with detailed guidance that they do not need any more may hinder their performance relative to other similar experienced learners who have not been presented with such detailed instructions. Therefore, as levels of learner expertise in a domain increase, relative effectiveness of different designs may reverse. Presentations formats that are optimal for novices may hinder relative performance of more experienced learners. A major design implication of this effect is that information presentation formats and levels of instructional guidance need to be tailored to different levels of learner expertise in a specific task domain.

The cognitive overload caused by an unbalanced executive function could lower the level of learner motivation, thus providing an additional complementing explanation of the expertise reversal effect. Eysenck, (1982) noted that "the most striking omission from the great majority of information-processing theories is any serious consideration of the dynamic interrelationship among motivation, emotion and cognition" (p. 1). The situation has not changed substantially since then. In cognitive load theory, motivational factors have not been considered until very recently (Paas, Tuovinen, van Merrienboer, & Darabi, 2005).

Miller, Galanter, and Pribram (1960) and Neisser (1976) investigated the role of goals in cognitive regulation of human behavior. Goals represent an essential part of a learner knowledge base. As an important part of the executive function provided by LTM components in cognitive processing, the goals play a major role in determining the direction of attention. From this perspective, balancing external guidance with learner internal goal structures is important for maintaining high levels of motivation. Most of the effects of goals on behavior are mediated by attentional mechanisms.

There is a close relationship between motivational states and operation of working memory, as well as between motivational and attentional processes. Motivational states determine the contents of attention. Attentional mechanisms essentially provide the link between the motivational and cognitive aspects of human learning and performance (Eysenck, 1982), since motivation is effectively a major controller of our attention (Simon, 1967). When learning is motivated by consciously chosen personal goals, the learners experience a sense of control and meaningfulness of their experience. Thus, the learner goal structure is an essential part of her/his knowledge base that provides executive regulation of cognition.

Understanding and processing any source of information always depend on available relevant knowledge base of the learner. As was mentioned in Chapter I, a learner domain-specific knowledge base, or level of her/his domain-specific expertise, is the major factor influencing learning and problem solving. This knowledge base determines what constitutes an element of information and the intensity of interaction between elements in learning. Therefore, some sources of information might be redundant for more experienced learners and generate unnecessary extraneous cognitive load for these learners when processed. The same sources of information could be essential for less experienced learners. In this case, they need to be integrated or presented in dual-modality formats rather than omitted to reduce an unnecessary working memory load. Thus the relation between the split-attention and redundancy effects may reverse as learner expertise develops.

Kalyuga et al. (1998) demonstrated experimentally that the level of learner expertise relates split-attention to redundancy. With novice electrical apprentices, the split-attention rather than the redundancy effect was obtained when learning from wiring diagrams with accompanying textual explanations. Students learned poorly from a diagram alone, better from a diagram with separated diagram and text, and best from a physically integrated diagrams and text. After extensive training in the domain, when the same learners became more experienced in the same task domain, an interaction effect was obtained: the effectiveness of the integrated diagram and text condition decreased while the effectiveness of the diagram alone condition increased. Eventually, after even more additional training, substantial differences between an integrated diagram and text condition and a diagram alone condition were obtained (the redundancy effect). Diagram-alone materials were easier to process but generated a higher level of performance on the subsequent tests. Textual explanations that were essential for novices became redundant for more knowledgeable learners.

Although the expertise reversal effect has only been studied in individual learning, it could also take place in group settings, for example, in collaborative learning environments. In such environments, with increased levels of participants' expertise, gradually diminishing detailed support (e.g., external representations or scripts on how to interact, collaborate, and solve problems) should be presented to the groups. Also, the level of group control over the means of support (what and when they want to use) could be increased with higher levels of participants' expertise (Kester & Paas, 2005).

OPTIMIZATION OF COGNITIVE LOAD IN INSTRUCTION

As was noted in the section on executive functioning of available knowledge structures, the simultaneous use, cross-referencing, and integration of knowledge-based and instruction-based executive guidance dealing with the same units of information may generate an additional source of extraneous cognitive load. As a result, cognitive resources available for meaningful learning will be decreased. Using essential instructional guidance and removing redundant components as the level of learner task-specific expertise gradually increases is the process of *optimization of cognitive load* in learning. This process reduces extraneous and enhances essential cognitive load. Optimization of cognitive load assumes not only presenting appropriate information and instructional guidance at the appropriate time, but also timely removal of unnecessary redundant information as learner levels of learner expertise increase.

For example, direct instruction in the form of worked examples may represent optimal instructional formats for novice learners because they substitute for missing executive knowledge structures. At intermediate levels of task-specific expertise, a mix of examples for supporting construction of new knowledge structures and problem solving practice for exercising and strengthening previously acquired knowledge components could provide an optimal instructional procedure. For example, it could be realized as a series of completion tasks or faded examples. At higher levels of expertise, problem-solving or exploratory learning environments based on using available knowledge structures could be cognitively optimal instructional methods.

Thus, optimizing cognitive load should be based on tracking changes in domain-specific knowledge base as learners acquire more expertise in a specific task domain and accordingly tailoring specific instructional techniques. Understanding cognitive mechanisms that influence efficiency of multimedia information presentations is essential for optimizing cognitive load. However, to be able to dynamically select multimedia formats optimal for individual learners, it is also necessary to have suitable methods for collecting information about learner levels of expertise in a domain suitable for real-time applications.

The following sections briefly review specific empirical findings on the expertise reversal effect. The magnitude of the effect could be estimated by effect size differences that are computed by subtracting the effect size for the high-knowledge learners from the effect size for the low-knowledge learners (e.g., Mayer, 2001). This method was also used in a brief review chapter in the Cambridge Handbook of Multimedia Learning (Mayer, 2005) where the effect was called "prior knowledge principle" (Kalyuga, 2005).

EXPERTISE REVERSAL EFFECT AND APTITUDE-TREATMENT INTERACTIONS

The research on expertise reversal effect could be related to general studies of aptitude-treatment interactions (Kalyuga, 2007; Kalyuga et al., 2003; Fletcher & Tobias, 2005). Those studies were initiated more than 40 year ago by Cronbach (1967). The aptitude was defined broadly as "a complex of personal characteristics that accounts for an individual's end state after a particular educational treatment, i.e., that determines what he learns, how much he learns, or how rapidly he learns...Aptitude, pragmatically, includes whatever promotes the pupil's survival in a particular educational environment..." (p. 23). Relevant aptitudes include knowledge, skills, learning styles, personality characteristics, etc.

Aptitude-treatment interactions (ATIs) occur when different instructional treatments result in differential learning rates depending on student aptitudes (e.g., Cronbach & Snow, 1977; Lohman, 1986; Mayer, Stiehl, & Greeno, 1975; Shute & Gluck, 1996; Snow, 1989, 1994; Snow & Lohman, 1984). ATIs are domain-specific, i.e. they may vary for different subject domains. For example, Tallmadge and Shearer (1969) demonstrated triple interactions between instructional methods, subject matters, and individual characteristics. Learners for whom one instructional method was optimal for one subject domain perform best with another instructional method in a different domain, however the results were not replicated with another set of domains (Tallmadge & Shearer, 1971).

Learner prior knowledge is the aptitude of interest in the context of the expertise reversal effect. Tobias (1976) reviewed a series of studies in the domain of medical education that consistently demonstrated interactions between prior familiarity with the domain and instructional treatments in programmed learning environments. In unfamiliar domains, detailed and consistent instructional support provided to learners (for example, appropriate sequencing of material according to instructional objectives, overt responding, feedback, etc.) produced significantly better results than reading the materials. On the other side, no differences were found for familiar materials. It was suggested that prior achievement (as defined by pretest scores) was an important variable in ATI research. An inverse relationship existed between prior achievement and optimal instructional strategies in a variety of task domains: the higher the level of prior achievement, the lower the level of instructional support required for learners and vice versa.

Tobias (1976) indicated that low prior familiarity may invoke similar cognitive processes in a variety of task domains, thus predicting a similar optimal instructional strategy. Due to relatively clear definition and meaning of prior achievement (familiarity or, as me may claim today, prior knowledge) as determined by detailed pretests, ATIs involving prior achievement could be investigated more easily and produced more convincing results than more imprecisely defined aptitudes and abilities. Pre-training learners in a task domain could allow easy manipulation of this variable (what actually was realized in the previously described longitudinal studies of the expertise reversal effect). Developing operational definitions of low and high prior achievements was noted as a important research task (Tobias, 1976).

Except for the levels of prior achievement, there was no consistent empirical support found for aptitude-treatment interactions with other categories of aptitudes (Bracht, 1970). Even though there was a clear general trend indicating that high-level ability students succeeded with little assistance, while low-level ability students benefited from various forms of guidance, Cronbach and Snow's (1977) concluded that "no aptitude by treatment interactions are so well confirmed that they can be used directly as guides to instruction" (p. 492). One of the suggested possible reasons was inadequate aptitude measures that were designed for selection purposes (large batteries of aptitude tests based on artificial simplified tasks administered mostly in laboratory conditions). Another suggested reason was inability to apply such measures dynamically, as learners proceeded through a learning session, thus ignoring practice effects.

Therefore, ATI research had no significant influence on classroom instruction and was difficult to use for guiding development of practically useful adaptive instructional systems (Boutwell & Barton, 1974; Federico, 1980; 1999; Tobias, 1989). In the ATI approach, differences in aptitudes were studied and instructional treatments selected without taking into account differences in associated cognitive processes. Aptitudes were measured by using mostly psychometric tools unsuitable for diagnosing, evaluating, and facilitating ongoing cognitive processes involved in knowledge acquisition (Federico, 1980). Cognitive processes involved in knowledge construction should be determined in order to select optimal instructional techniques to increase effectiveness and efficiency of instruction. Instructional support should be defined in terms of cognitive processes required of students, rather than merely in terms of external attributes of instructional methods (Tobias, 1989).

Developing clear operational definitions of low and high prior achievement levels was noted as an important research task. "...It may become possible to use level of prior achievement adaptively; that is, students with high prior familiarity in a given area may be assigned to an instructional treatment, with minimal instructional support, or to a forward-ranching sequence. On the other hand, students with low prior achievement may require maximal instructional support each step of the way. Such adaptation to individual differences would be a notable step towards individualizing the method of instruction rather than merely the instructional rate" (Tobias, 1976, p. 72). Developing means to realize this approach is essentially what studies in cognitive load framework have been trying to achieve in recent years.

Tobias (1982; 1989) suggested that problems with replicating ATI results could be due to two implicit assumptions of ATI research. One was that different instructional methods would require different types or frequencies of cognitive macroprocesses (instructional episodes or units larger than the immediate content of working memory). Another assumption was that the student characteristics are differentially related to such macroprocesses. The research provided little support for these assumptions. Different macroprocesses are neither automatically elicited by instructional methods nor necessarily correlated with student characteristics. There were few differences in learners' use of macroprocesses across alternative modes of instruction, unless they were specifically manipulated in experiments. Also, there was little relationship between macroprocesses used by students and their individual characteristics, especially levels of prior domain-specific knowledge.

Tobias (1989) noted that the low relations with prior knowledge were especially surprising because prior knowledge is strongly related to learning outcomes and it usually correlates highly with measures of general ability and other cognitive characteristics. It was suggested that better consistency in replicating the effect could be achieved by training or prompting students in using the cognitive processes that are presumed to be elicited by specific instructional methods. Students' actual use of cognitive processes that are required or stimulated by a specific instructional method should not be assumed. The learners' actual application of specific cognitive processes should be evaluated by using diagnostic tools (e.g., "think aloud" protocols and other forms of free or stimulated self-reporting).

EMPIRICAL LONGITUDINAL STUDIES OF THE EXPERTISE REVERSAL EFFECT

A series of longitudinal studies was specifically designed to investigate interactions between different cognitive load effects and levels of learner expertise in controlled experimental conditions (see Kalyuga, 2006 for a more detailed overview). The general design of those studies included training the same samples of participants from novice to more advanced state of knowledge in specific task areas. Their levels of performance and mental effort were measured at different stages along the way to see changes in relative effectiveness and efficiency of different instructional techniques at different levels of learner expertise.

Intensive training sessions using the same evidence-based instructional methods and procedures for all participants were conducted between the experimental stages to increase learner task-specific expertise. The task domains were restricted to specific narrow classes of tasks in electrical and mechanical engineering to allow sufficient increases in learner levels of expertise within a few weeks or months. At the same time, the selected tasks also allowed a gradual increase in complexity by raising the number of task elements or parameters within the same set of general principles and solution approaches. It was necessary in order to expand training over these periods of time without making the tasks too simple and trivial for learners.

If sources of information that require mental integration for understanding are separated in space or time, the processes involved in visual search-and-match or cross-referencing may substantially increase the burden on working memory and inhibit learning. Physically integrated (embedded) formats were demonstrated to be an effective alternative to such "split-source" instructions (split-attention effect, Chandler & Sweller, 1991; Mayer & Anderson 1991; 1992; Mayer & Gallini, 1990; Sweller, Chandler, Tierney, & Cooper, 1990; Tarmizi & Sweller, 1988; Ward & Sweller, 1990). As was mentioned earlier, the split-attention situations may also be managed by using different modalities. The integration of the verbal auditory and pictorial visual information may not overload working memory if its capacity is effectively expanded by using a dual-mode presentation (modality effect; Mayer, 1997; Mayer & Moreno, 1998; Mousavi, Low, & Sweller, 1995; Tindall-Ford, Chandler, & Sweller, 1997).

However, if sources of information are intelligible in isolation, the elimination rather than integration of a redundant source would be a preferable technique (redundancy effect; e.g., Chandler & Sweller, 1991; Mayer, Heiser, & Lonn, 2001). Whether information is redundant depends on the level of expertise of the learner. What is essential for a novice could be redundant for more knowledgeable learners or even for the same learners at later stages of instruction. As a consequence, integrated presentation formats that are effective for novices could be ineffective for more expert learners. Similar to visual, auditory explanations may also become redundant when presented to more experienced learners.

Kalyuga, Chandler, and Sweller (1998) demonstrated that the relation between the split-attention and redundancy effects reverses as learner gains more expertise. With novice learners, the split-attention effect was obtained: students learned best from textual explanations that were embedded into the wiring diagrams. After extensive training in the domain, the effectiveness of the integrated diagram and text condition decreased while the effectiveness of the diagram alone condition increased. After additional intensive training, substantial differences between an integrated diagram and text condition and a diagram alone condition were observed (Figure 4). For experts, diagram-alone materials were easier to process (according to subjective ratings of learning difficulty) and generated a higher level of performance on the subsequent tests. Textual explanations that were essential for novices became redundant for more knowledgeable learners.

Kalyuga, Chandler, and Sweller (2000; 2001) and Kalyuga, Chandler, Tuovinen, and Sweller (2001) obtained more evidence for the interaction between different

Figure 4. An interaction between instructional formats and levels of learner expertise according to Kalyuga, Chandler, and Sweller (1998): (a) Test scores; b) difficulty ratings

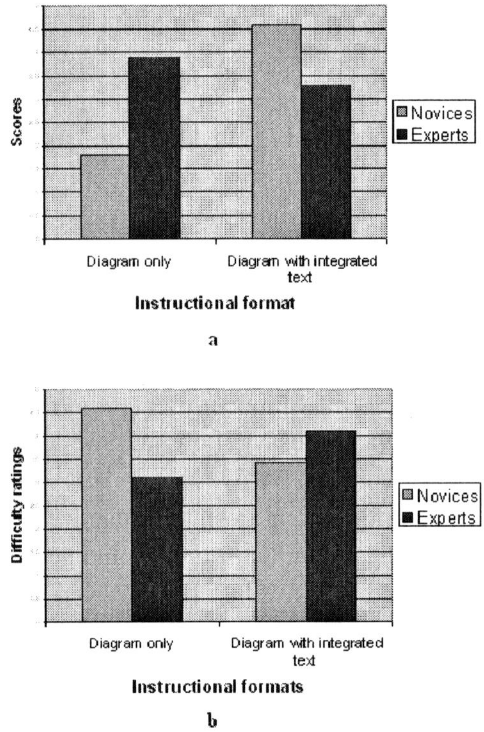

instructional methods and levels of learner task-specific expertise. Patterns of results were similar to those shown in Figure 4. The techniques for reducing extraneous cognitive load (integrating sources of information or using dual-modality formats in a split-attention situation, using worked examples instead of conventional problem solving) were effective for novice learners. For more knowledgeable learners, such instructional techniques became ineffective and often resulted in negative rather than positive or neutral effects.

For example, narrated explanations presented concurrently with on-screen animated diagrams that were effective for novices (modality effect), became redundant and reduced relative learning outcomes as learners became more knowledgeable in the task domain (Kalyuga et al., 2000). The relative advantage of the narrated diagram format gradually disappeared while the diagram-alone condition became more effective. After several intensive training sessions, the diagram only group outperformed the diagram with narrated text group, effectively reversing the results of the first stage. Subjective ratings of learning difficulty supported a cognitive load explanation of the results.

Kalyuga, Chandler, Tuovinen, and Sweller (2001) demonstrated that the superiority of worked examples over problem-solving practice (according to worked example effect in cognitive load theory) disappeared as trainees acquired more experience in the task domain of programming logic controllers. In another experiment with tasks on writing Boolean switching equations for relay circuits, there was no difference between conditions initially (the trainees had some limited familiarity with the task domain), however, after intensive training in the domain, the learning of relatively more complex tasks with greater numbers of elements in the circuits was better supported by problem solving than by worked-out examples.

Kalyuga, Chandler, and Sweller (2001, Experiment 2) compared worked-out examples with an exploratory-based instruction on writing switching equations for relay circuits (learners designed different circuits using an interactive on-screen template and then wrote equations for those circuits). Although initially the worked-out examples group outperformed the exploratory one, as the level of learner expertise increased after a series of intensive example- and problem-based training sessions, the exploratory group progressed better and eventually outperformed the worked examples group. Tuovinen and Sweller (1999) compared worked examples with an exploratory-based instruction on how to use a database program in a cross-sectional study. Novice students benefited more from worked examples, with no differences found between conditions for higher knowledge students.

The expertise-related redundancy (in presentation formats or instructional guidance) that was demonstrated in these studies was different from the redundancy effect that had been previously obtained using mostly novice learners. In the expertise reversal effect, the redundant source of information is redundant only relatively to the learner knowledge base rather than to other external sources of information. Accordingly, the integration of this subjectively redundant information with learners' schemas rather than with other presented sources of information causes an additional cognitive load that may interfere with learning. Therefore, the expertise reversal effect is a form of redundancy only in a wider sense when the learner knowledge base is also included in the list of sources of information. This effect is not an example of the redundancy effect in a narrow sense that considers only external sources of information.

EXPERTISE REVERSAL FOR METHODS OF ENHANCING ESSENTIAL COGNITIVE LOAD

If specific techniques for engaging learners into additional cognitive activities designed to enhance germane load (e.g., explicitly self-explaining or imagining content of worked examples) cause total cognitive load to exceed learner working memory limitations, the germane load would effectively become a form of extraneous load that may inhibit learning. This especially applies to novice learners who lack relevant schematic knowledge structures in long-term memory that could effectively increase cognitive resources due to the chunking effect. More knowledgeable learners may have sufficient resources for effectively accommodating additional germane load and enhancing their learning outcomes.

Cooper, Tindall-Ford, Chandler, and Sweller (2001) demonstrated that imagining procedures and concepts (e.g., related to using spreadsheets) may produce better instructional outcomes than simply studying worked examples. They obtained this effect with students who had appropriate knowledge base to construct and run corresponding mental representations. However, the imagining procedure produced a negative effect for low-knowledge students thus demonstrating an expertise reversal effect. When studying worked examples, novices construct their schematic knowledge structures for interacting elements. More knowledgeable learners already have such knowledge structures and studying worked examples is a redundant activity for these learners. They may benefit more from additional practice provided by imagining corresponding procedures.

These results were replicated by Ginns, Chandler, and Sweller (2003) with the complexity of learning material as an additional experimental factor. In according with cognitive load predictions, the study demonstrated that low prior knowledge students learning structurally complex materials (university students learning HTML code) benefited more from studying worked examples than from imagining them. On the other hand, more knowledgeable students dealing with less complex materials (secondary school students studying geometry materials) reached higher levels of learning as measured by transfer tests when imagining rather than studying examples.

These results were further supported by the study of Leahy and Sweller (2005) with primary school students learning to read a bus timetable (Experiment 1) or temperature graphs (Experiment 2). The same students were used initially as novices, and two weeks later as relative experts in a domain. In Experiment 1, the study condition was more effective for novice learners than the imagination condition, whereas a reversed pattern was observed when students became more experienced in this task domain. In Experiment 2, which allowed a greater spread between low and high element interactivity materials, the same pattern of results was replicated with stronger effects.

McNamara (1995) demonstrated that many learners are better at retaining information that they generate themselves than information generated for them (a generation effect). For example, working out the solution of a math problem could produce better learning outcomes than reading the solution. It was found, however, that low- and average-prior-knowledge learners benefited more from the generation effect than high-prior-knowledge students. The expertise reversal in relation to germane cognitive load could be a possible explanation of this effect.

EXPERTISE REVERSAL IN TEXTUAL AND HYPERTEXTUAL MATERIALS

Several studies demonstrated the expertise reversal effect in learning from text and hypertext. Yeung (1999) compared two instructional formats of incorporating definitions of unfamiliar words into textual material. One was a traditional glossary placed at the end of the whole text. Another format integrated unfamiliar words' definitions into the space above the line of text directly above the defined word. According to cognitive load theory, traditional glossaries could produce a split-attention effect due to extra effort necessary for locating the required definition in the glossary, comprehending and remembering it while finding their way back to the original word in the text being read.

Secondary school students learned better from the integrated definition format than from the traditional glossary format (as measured by comprehension scores). However, the university students demonstrated better comprehension scores with the glossary format. The results were explained by the increased cognitive load caused by the need for more knowledgeable student to process redundant for them information (as measured by the time students spent on referencing a definition). The use of integrated definitions could have a positive or negative effect on learning depending on levels of learner prior knowledge.

Although texts are usually linear in structure, mental representations (situation models) constructed based on these texts are not linear. However, using non-linear texts do not improve the situation models; on the contrary, they may decrease the quality of situation models. A possible reason could be a high cognitive load involved in reading non-linear texts and managing navigation in such environments. Amadieu, Tricot, and Marine (2007) suggested that non-linear texts may improve situation model for more experienced learners with relatively high levels of prior knowledge that are based on large number of schemas. The non-linear structure should also be compatible with learner prior knowledge structure in order to be beneficial for these learners.

The main characteristics of a hypertext are semantically interrelated elements of information (nodes and links) and a non-linear organization of information when the reader can choose his/her own path. There is no consistent empirical evidences in regards to a positive effect of hypertext on learning (Amadieu & Tricot, 2006 ; Chen & Rada, 1996 ; Dillon & Gabard, 1998). However there is a general consensus that processing hypertext usually requires significant levels of cognitive effort, may cause disorientation and associated cognitive overload with reduced levels of learning and performance.

Calisir and Gurel (2003) investigated the interaction between text structure (traditional linear text, hierarchical hypertext, and mixed hypertext) and learner prior knowledge in reading comprehension. In linear text condition, knowledgeable learners had higher reading comprehension scores than non-knowledgeable learners. Domain knowledge may have helped these learners to understand and conceptualize the structure of the text. There was no significant difference between knowledgeable and non-knowledgeable learners in the hierarchical and the mixed conditions. The structures of the hierarchical and mixed texts may have compensated for the lack of a conceptual structure of the domain. It is a likely explanation especially considering that non-knowledgeable learners in the mixed condition had higher scores than non-knowledgeable learners in the linear condition.

Shapiro (1999) studied the relationship between learner prior knowledge and interactive overviews as a method of organizing and structuring presented material in hypermedia-based learning environments. The study found that such external structuring aid (in fact, a form of external instructional guidance) was more beneficial for novices than for learners with higher levels of prior knowledge in the domain. The suggested reason for the absence of advantages for more knowledgeable learners was a redundancy effect caused by the need to process unnecessary sources of information. These findings are in correspondence with earlier results of Eylon and Reif (1984) who found that presenting well structured hierarchical organization of material is essential for low ability learners but not for high ability learners.

Generally, the above studies suggested that a hierarchical hypertext could be an appropriate instructional format for non-knowledgeable learners under conditions when this format reflects the organizational structure of the task domain better than the traditional linear text. Otherwise, the traditional text should be considered as a default preferable instructional format for these learners.

FUTURE TRENDS IN THE INVESTIGATION OF THE EXPERTISE REVERSAL EFFECT

Further studies are needed in expertise reversal phenomena involving different instructional methods for enhancing germane cognitive load. Investigating cognitive load aspects of the acquisition of adaptive expertise would lead to issues of expertise reversal in this area. Would an expertise reversal effect be observed with instructional methods facilitating the development of adaptive expertise (e.g., those based on applying higher level strategic schemas, effortful reasoning and problem solving, metacognitive skills in self-managing cognitive resources)?

Tobias (1989) suggested that including affective variables in research could achieve better consistency in replicating the aptitude-treatment interactions. For the same reasons, this suggestion could also be applicable to the research on expertise reversal effect. Cronbach and Snow (1977) noted that ATI studies indicated that well motivated students (with preferences for learning independently) tended to benefit from instructions that provided more freedom and challenge for the learner to structure the task. Research should incorporate affective components that initiate and maintain focused cognitive processes leading to more consistent interactions between these processes, instructional methods, and learner cognitive characteristics.

Affective computing is one of the most active research areas in computer science. It aimed at developing means to equip computers with capabilities of registering, interpreting, and generating affect features in order to improve the intelligence of computers and quality of human-computer interactions and communication. Affective computing research and development use such technologies as emotional speech recognition, facial expression, body gesture and movement, multimodal systems, affect understanding and generating (e.g., see Paiva, Prada, & Picard 2007; Tao & Tan, 2005). Establishing connections between affective variables and cognitive load, and using methods of affective computing could enhance capabilities of multimedia environments in tailoring learning to cognitive characteristics of individual learners.

Investigating effects of variable learner support and guidance relative to the levels of learner experience in a task domain represent an important direction of further extension of the research on expertise reversal effect. For example, adaptive interface scaffolding in computer-assisted learning assumes that a schema support could be faded in and out as a function of the learner experience with the computer. Computer-controlled fading needs well-developed specifications of suitable levels of support for learner with different levels of knowledge as well as means for evaluating levels of learner understanding (Chalmers, 2003). Guided learner-tailored scaffolding may combine advantages of learner- and system-controlled learning environments when learners control the fading procedure with the help of the system (Jackson, Krajcik, & Soloway, 1998). This approach will be further described in Section III of the book.

MULTIMEDIA INSTRUCTIONAL DESIGN IMPLICATIONS

The major instructional design implication of the expertise reversal effect is that instructional techniques and procedures need to change with alterations in levels of expertise and be tailored to levels of learner prior knowledge. Dynamically adaptive learning environments represent the best solution to the problem. This implication will be further discussed in Section III of the book.

In general terms, the lower the level of a learner prior knowledge in a specific task domain, the more instructional support and guidance should be provided to the learner. Using more worked-out examples and other forms of direct instruction for novice learners would represent an effective instructional approach. As levels of learner knowledge increase, worked examples could be faded and more problem-solving practice and guided exploratory environments could be included in instruction.

For similar reasons, learner choices over instructional options need to be limited for novice learners. On the other hand, more control over instructional methods and content could be allowed in more advanced courses when learners have sufficient related prior knowledge and skills. When the level of learner prior knowledge is not known, most important well guided instructional methods should be used as default options. In any case, learners need to always have the options to progress at their own pace and to review prior topics/lessons.

SUMMARY OF CHAPTER III

Over the long period of time, substantial empirical evidence has been obtained for interactions between different instructional methods and levels of learner task-specific expertise (the expertise reversal or prior knowledge effect). It has been found that many previously developed techniques for reducing extraneous cognitive load (e.g., integrating sources of information or using dual-modality formats in a split-attention situation, using worked examples instead of conventional problem solving) were effective for relatively novice learners. For more knowledgeable learners, such instructional techniques became ineffective and often resulted in negative rather than positive or neutral effects.

This chapter reviewed some empirical findings related to the expertise reversal effect and presented a theoretical explanation of the effect within a cognitive load framework. The effect has been consistently replicated in many studies with a large range of instructional materials and participants either as a full reversal (with significant differences for both novices and experts) or, more often, as a partial reversal (with a non-significant difference for either novices or experts, but with a significant interaction).

In cognitive load theory, the expertise reversal effect is associated with imbalances between learner organized knowledge base and provided instructional guidance. Two major types of such imbalances are described. One is caused by an insufficient learner knowledge base that is not complemented by appropriate instructional guidance (especially at the initial stages of novice learning). Another type of imbalances is caused by overlaps between available knowledge of more advanced learners and provided instructional guidance. The need for higher knowledge learners to integrate and cross-reference redundant instructional guidance with available knowledge structures that relate to the same situations may consume additional cognitive resources. Minimazed instructional guidance would allow these learners to take advantage of their knowledge base in the most efficient way.

The expertise reversal effect is considered as a logical extension of the aptitude-treatment interaction approach. Although levels of learner prior knowledge were considered within that approach, few research studies and instructional design recommendations demonstrated explicitly how to use the ATI approach in practice. Aptitudes and instructional treatments were investigated without taking into account specific cognitive processes elicited by investigated instructional treatments.

In order to balance the executive function and optimize cognitive load, instructional guidance should be provided at the appropriate time, while unnecessary support removed as learners progress to more advanced levels of proficiency in a specific task domain. Adaptive learning environments that dynamically tailor levels of instructional support to changing individual levels of learner expertise in a domain have the best potential for optimizing cognitive load. The approaches to designing such environments will be considered in the following chapters of this book.

REFERENCES

Amadieu, F. & Tricot, A. (2006). Utilisation d'un hypermédia et apprentissage : deux activités concurrentes ou complémentaires ? *Psychologie Française, 51,* 5-23

Amadieu, F., Tricot, A., & Mariné, C. (2007). Knowledge diversity effect on cognitive load, disorientation and comprehension in a non-linear learning. Paper presented at the *Cognitive Load Theory Conference*, Sydney Australia, 24-26 March.

Boutwell, R., & Barton, G. (1974). Toward an adaptive learner-controlled model of instruction: a place for the new cognitive aptitudes. *Educational Technology, 14,* 13-18.

Bracht, G. (1970). Experimental factors related to aptitude-treatment interactions. *Review of Educational Research, 40,* 627-645.

Calisir, F. & Gurel, Z. (2003). Influence of text structure and prior knowledge of the learner on reading comprehension, browsing and perceived control. *Computers in Human Behavior, 19,* 135-145.

Chalmers, P. A. (2003). The role of cognitive theory in human-computer interface. *Computers in Human Behavior, 19*, 593-607.

Chandler, P., & Sweller, J. (1991). Cognitive load theory and the format of instruction. *Cognition and Instruction, 8,* 293-332.

Chen, C., & Rada, R. (1996). Interacting with hypertext: A meta-analysis of experimental studies. *Human-Computer Interaction, 11*, 125-156.

Cooper, G., Tindall-Ford, S., Chandler, P., & Sweller, J. (2001). Learning by imagining procedures and concepts. *Journal of Experimental Psychology: Applied, 7,* 68-82.

Cronbach, L. (1967). How can instruction be adapted to individual differences. In R. Gagne (Ed.), *Learning and individual differences* (pp. 23-39). Columbus, OH: Merrill.

Cronbach, L. & Snow, R. (1977). *Aptitudes and instructional methods: a handbook for research on interactions*. New York: Irvington.

Dillon, A., & Gabbard, R. (1998). Hypermedia as an educational technology: A review of the quantitative research literature on learner comprehension, control, and style. *Review of Educational Research, 68*, 322-349.

Eylon, B., & Reif, F. (1984). Effects of knowledge organization on task performance. *Cognition and Instruction, 1,* 5-44.

Eysenck, M. W. (1982). Attention and arousal: Cognition and performance. New York: Springer-Verlag.

Federico, P-A. (1980). Adaptive instruction: trends and issues, In R. Snow, P-A Federico & W. Montague, *Aptitude, learning, and instruction: Vol. 1, Cognitive process analyses of aptitude* (pp. 1- 26). Hillsdale, NJ: Erlbaum.

Federico, P-A. (1999). Hypermedia environments and adaptive instruction. *Computers in Human Behavior, 15*, 653-692.

Fletcher, J. D. & Tobias, S. (2005). The multimedia principle. In R. E. Mayer(Ed.), *Cambridge Handbook of Multimedia Learning* (pp. 117-133) New York: Cambridge University Press.

Ginns, P., Chandler, P., & Sweller, J. (2003). When imagining information is effective. *Contemporary Educational Psychology, 28*, 229-251.

Jackson, S. L., Krajcik, J., & Soloway, E. (1998). The design of guided learner-adaptable scaffolding in interactive learning environments. *CHI Conference Papers*, 187-194.

Kalyuga, S. (2005). Prior knowledge principle. In R. Mayer (Ed.), *Cambridge Handbook of Multimedia Learning* (pp. 325-337). New York: Cambridge University Press.

Kalyuga, S. (2006). *Instructing and testing advanced learners: A cognitive load approach.* New York: Nova Science Publishers.

Kalyuga, S. (2007). Expertise reversal effect and its implications for learner-tailored instruction. *Educational Psychology Review* (in press)

Kalyuga, S., Ayres, P., Chandler, P., & Sweller, J. (2003). Expertise reversal effect. *Educational Psychologist, 38,* 23-31

Kalyuga, S., Chandler, P., & Sweller, J. (1998). Levels of expertise and instructional design. *Human Factors, 40,* 1-17.

Kalyuga, S., Chandler, P., & Sweller, J. (2000). Incorporating learner experience into the design of multimedia instruction. *Journal of Educational Psychology, 92,* 126-136

Kalyuga, S., Chandler, P., & Sweller, J. (2001). Learner experience and efficiency of instructional guidance. *Educational Psychology, 21,* 5-23.

Kalyuga, S., Chandler, P., Tuovinen, J., & Sweller, J. (2001). When problem solving is superior to studying worked examples. *Journal of Educational Psychology, 93,* 579-588.

Kester, L., & Paas, F. (2005). Instructional interventions to enhance collaboration in powerful learning environments. *Computer in Human Behavior, 21,* 689-696.

Leahy, W., & Sweller, J. (2005). Interactions among the imagination, expertise reversal, and element interactivity effects. *Journal of Experimental Psychology: Applied, 11,* 266-276.

Lohman, D.F. (1986). Predicting mathemathanic effects in the teaching of higher-order thinking skills. *Educational Psychologist, 21,* 191-208.

Mayer, R. E. (1997). Multimedia learning: Are we asking the right questions? *Educational Psychologist, 32,* 1-19.

Mayer, R. E. (2001). *Multimedia learning.* Cambridge, MA: Cambridge University Press.

Mayer, R. E. (Ed.). (2005). *Cambridge Handbook of Multimedia Learning.* New York: Cambridge University Press.

Mayer, R., & Anderson, R. (1991). Animations need narrations: An experimental test of a dual-coding hypothesis. *Journal of Educational Psychology, 83*, 484-490.

Mayer, R., & Anderson, R. (1992). The instructive animation: Helping students build connections between words and pictures in multimedia learning. *Journal of Educational Psychology, 84*, 444-452.

Mayer, R., & Gallini, J. (1990). When is an illustration worth ten thousand words? *Journal of Educational Psychology, 82,* 715-726.

Mayer R. E., Heiser, J., & Lonn, S. (2001). Cognitive constraints on multimedia learning: When presenting more material results in less understanding. *Journal of Educational Psychology, 93,* 187-198.

Mayer, R., & Moreno, R. (1998). A split-attention effect in multimedia learning: Evidence for dual-processing systems in working memory. *Journal of Educational Psychology, 90*, 312 - 320.

Mayer, R., Stiehl, C., & Greeno, J. (1975). Acquisition of understanding and skill in relation to subjects' preparation and meaningfulness of instruction. *Journal of Educational Psychology, 67,* 331-350.

McNamara, D. S. (1995). Effects of prior knowledge on the generation advantage: calculators versus calculation to learn simple multiplication. *Journal of Educational Psychology, 87,* 307-318.

Miller, G. A., Galanter, E. H., & Pribram, K. (1960). *Plans and the structure of behavior.* New York: Holt.

Mousavi, S. Y., Low, R., & Sweller, J. (1995). Reducing cognitive load by mixing auditory and visual presentation modes. *Journal of Educational Psychology, 87,* 319-334.

Neisser, U. (1976). *Cognition and reality.* San Francisco: Freeman.

Paas, F., Tuovinen, J. E., van Merrienboer, J. J. G., & Darabi, A. A. (2005). A motivational perspctive on the relation between mental effort and performance. *Educational technology, Research and Development, 53*, 25-34.

Paiva, A., Prada R., & R. W. Picard (Eds.) (2007), *Affective Computing and Intelligent Interaction. Lecture Notes in Computer Science, Volume 4738*. Berlin: Springer-Verlag.

Shapiro, A. M. (1999). The relationship between prior knowledge and interactive overviews during hypermedia-aided learning. *Journal of Educational Computing Research, 20*, 143-167.

Shute, V. J., & Gluck, K. A. (1996). Individual differences in patterns of spontaneous online tool use. *The Journal of the Learning Sciences, 5*, 329-355.

Simon, H. A. (1967). Motivational and emotional controls of cognition. *Psychological Review, 74*, 29-39.

Snow, R. E. (1989). Aptitude-treatment interaction as a framework for research on individual differences in learning. In P.L. Ackerman, R.J. Sternberg, & R. Glaser (Eds.), *Learning and individual differences. Advances in theory and research* (pp. 13-59). New York: W. H. Freeman.

Snow, R. (1994). Abilities in academic tasks. In R. Sternberg and R. Wagner (Eds.), *Mind in context: Interactionist perspectives on human intelligence* (pp. 3-37). Cambridge, MA: Cambridge University Press.

Snow, R., & Lohman, D. (1984). Toward a theory of cognitive aptitude for learning from instruction. *Journal of Educational Psychology, 76*, 347-376.

Sweller, J., Chandler, P., Tierney, P., & Cooper, M. (1990). Cognitive load and selective attention as factors in the structuring of technical material. *Journal of Experimental Psychology: General, 119,* 176-192.

Tallmadge, C. K., & Shearer, J. W. (1969). Relationships among learning styles, instructional methods, and the nature of learning experiences. *Journal of Educational Psychology, 60*, 222-230.

Tallmadge, C. K., & Shearer, J. W. (1971). Interactive relationships among learner characteristics, types of learning, instructional methods, and subject matter variables. *Journal of Educational Psychology, 62*, 31-38.

Tao, J., & Tan, T. (2005). Affective computing: A review. In J. Tao., T. Tan & R. W. Picard (Eds.), *Affective Computing and Intelligent Interaction. Lecture Notes in Computer Science, Volume 3784* (pp. 981-995). Berlin: Springer-Verlag.

Tarmizi, R., & Sweller, J. (1988). Guidance during mathematical problem solving. *Journal of Educational Psychology, 80*, 424-436.

Tindall-Ford, S., Chandler, P., & Sweller, J. (1997). When two sensory modes are better than one. *Journal of Experimental Psychology: Applied, 3*, 257-287.

Tobias, S. (1976). Achievement treatment interactions. *Review of Educational Research, 46*, 61-74.

Tobias, S. (1982). When do instructional methods make a difference? *Educational Research, 11(4),* 4-9.

Tobias , S. (1989). Another look at research on the adaptation of instruction to student characteristics. *Educational Psychologist, 24*, 213-227.

Tuovinen, J., & Sweller, J. (1999). A comparison of cognitive load associated with discovery learning and worked examples. Journal of Educational Psychology, 91, 334-341.

Ward, M., & Sweller, J. (1990). Structuring effective worked examples. *Cognition and Instruction, 7*, 1-39.

Yeung, A. S. (1999). Cognitive load and learner expertise: split attention and redundancy effects in reading comprehension tasks with vocabulary definitions. *Journal of Experimental Education, 67,* 197-221.

Chapter IV
Assessment of Task-Specific Expertise

INTRODUCTION

Main implication of the expertise reversal effect is the need to tailor instructional techniques and procedures to changing levels of learner expertise in a specific task domain. In order to design adaptive procedures capable of tailoring instruction in real-time, it is necessary to have online measures of learner expertise. Such measures should be rapid enough to be used in real time. At the same time, they need to have sufficient diagnostic power to detect different levels of task-specific expertise.

One of the previously mentioned reasons for low practical applicability of the results of studies in Aptitude-Treatment Interactions were inadequate aptitude measures. Most of the assessment methods used in those studies were psychometric instruments designed for selection purposes (e.g., large batteries of aptitude tests based on artificially simplified tasks administered mostly in laboratory conditions). Another suggested reason was unsuitability of those methods for dynamic, real-time applications while learners proceeded through a single learning session.

This chapter describes a rapid diagnostic approach to the assessment of learner task-specific expertise that has been intentionally designed for rapid online application in adaptive learning environments. The method was developed using an analogy to experimental procedures applied in classical studies of chess expertise mentioned in Chapter I. In those studies, realistic board configurations were briefly presented for subsequent replications. With the described diagnostic approach, learners are briefly presented with a problem situation and required to indicate their first solution step in this problem situation or to rapidly verify suggested steps at various stages of a problem solution procedure.

The idea of the method and results of its initial application in several relatively well-defined task domains are presented in this chapter. In the following sections of the book, some other examples of the rapid diagnostic techniques will be provided. Specific applications of the rapid diagnostic approach to the adaptive dynamic selection of learning tasks and multimedia instructional formats that are optimal for learners with different levels of expertise will be considered in Section 3 of the book.

ASSESSMENT OF DOMAIN-SPECIFIC KNOWLEDGE

The research on expertise emphasizes the importance of diagnosing domain-specific knowledge structures. Levels of learner expertise could be best evaluated using interviews and think-aloud protocols. However, these methods are not suitable for real-time, on-line adaptation of multimedia formats to dynamically changing levels of expertise. Traditional educational tests either have limited diagnostic capabilities or are too time-consuming. For example, multiple-choice items usually do not provide information about actual solution steps and strategies used by students. These test rather measure the ability of students to solve the problems by any means, with the same scores allocated for expert-like knowledge-based solutions as for novice-like search-based (e.g., trial-and-error) results.

There have been attempts to develop specific techniques and assessment tasks for evaluating organized schematic knowledge structures, for example, by requesting students to group presented tasks into clusters on the basis of similarity or to categorize tasks after hearing only part of the text. Different computer-based problem-solving environments were used to assess learners' knowledge and skills (Baker & Mayer, 1999). Other 'exotic' assessment tasks asked students to provide answers to problems when relevant task-specific content words had been replaced by nonsense words, identify which information within problems is necessary and sufficient for solution; or to classify problems in terms of whether the text of each problem provides sufficient, missing or irrelevant information for solution ('text editing') (Low & Over, 1992).

In order to evaluate deep differences in knowledge about concepts due to expertise, concept-explanation tasks were used (Chi, Feltovich, & Glaser, 1981; Van de Wiel, Boshuizen, Schmidt, & Schaper, 1999; Nievelstein, van Gog, Boshuizen, & Prins, in press). Concept-explanation tasks require participants to tell everything they know about a concept in a short period of time (usually 2-3 minutes). For example, using this method Boshuizen and Schmidt (1992) and Van de Wiel, Boshuizen, and Schmidt (2000) demonstrated medical experts' 'encapsulation' of lower level concepts under higher level, more abstracted concepts. Both electronic computerized and manual versions of concept mapping and card sorting tasks can be used as knowledge structure elicitation techniques (Hoeft, Jentsch, Harper, Evans, Bowers, & Salas, 2003).

All the above methods provide useful diagnostic information about levels of learner expertise and could be used in appropriate learning situations. However, they are hardly usable in online learning environments for real-time tailoring of instruction to levels of learner expertise. As a result, no appropriate, cognitively oriented diagnostic methods are available to be used in adaptive procedures for user-tailored multimedia learning. In order to tailor dynamically instructional methods to changing levels of learner task-specific expertise, rapid online methods of cognitive diagnosis are required. Such diagnostic instruments should be capable of detecting different levels of expertise. They should also be rapid enough to provide the diagnostic information in real time, during a single instructional session.

RAPID DIAGNOSTIC ASSESSMENT APPROACH

It was noted previously that our knowledge base is a single most important factor influencing learning and performance. Another important feature of our cognitive architecture mentioned in Chapter I was related to its processing limitations. Processing capabilities of working memory are severely limited in duration and capacity when dealing with unfamiliar elements of information (Baddeley, 1997; Miller, 1956). For example, using such limited resources on processing irrelevant information or on establishing essential connections between unnecessarily separated in space or time sources of information may substantially slow down learning. Well organized schematic knowledge structures that experts hold in their long-term memory allow them to effectively expand working memory capacity in comparison to novices and successfully deal with such situations.

The available long-term memory knowledge base allows experts to encapsulate great amounts of information in larger chunks that are treated as single elements in working memory, thus minimizing its limitations. Therefore, long-term memory knowledge structures effectively define the main characteristics of working memory such as its content, capacity, and duration. Accordingly, the evaluation of limitations and the content of working memory when an individual approaches a problem could be used for evaluating levels of expertise in the task domain. In other words, characteristics of working memory could be used to determine relevant components of knowledge base held in long-term memory. Rapid evaluation of specific task-activated knowledge structures essentially means accessing and monitoring current content of working memory or, more accurately, long-term working memory, since we are dealing with knowledge-based cognitive performance.

As noted in Chapter I, long-term memory knowledge structures associated with current components of working memory form a long-term working memory structure (Ericsson & Kintsch, 1995). For example, when reading a text, we construct and continuously update a model of the text in working memory using our knowledge base of a specific domain or everyday situations, depending on the nature of the text. This model represents the current content of long-term working memory. Due to the association with our knowledge base, this content is more stable and durable than random individual components of working memory (Kintsch, 1998). It is practically possible to determine the content of a person's long-term working memory when dealing with a specific task situation, for example, by analyzing the content of concurrent (think-aloud) verbal reports.

Thus, the available knowledge structures in long-term memory define working memory processing capabilities during knowledge-based cognitive activities and effectively determine the current content of long-term working memory. Therefore, tracing this content may provide indicators of levels of acquisition of corresponding long-term memory knowledge structures and, consequently, levels of expertise in the corresponding classes of tasks. Concurrent verbal protocols could be used to obtain such information, although this method is time consuming and, therefore, is hardly suitable for real-time use in adaptive instructional systems.

Alternatively, such information could be obtained by observing how learners approach briefly presented tasks. Based on their extensive and well structured knowledge base, more experienced learners would immediately see the task within their higher-level knowledge structures. Novices may only be able to identify some random lower-level components. Organized knowledge base in long-term memory is the main factor determining such differences. Learners with more and better organized knowledge could be able to retrieve appropriate higher level solution schemas. Thus, a diagnostic assessment of expertise suitable for real-time environments could be developed if we were able to rapidly determine if and how learners use their knowledge structures while approaching a specific problem or situation. This method could have a potential diagnostic power approaching that of the concurrent verbal reports, but could be administered considerably faster.

The idea of this approach was instigated by experimental procedures used in classical studies of chess expertise by De Groot (1965) and Chase and Simon (1973). In those studies, professional chess masters performed considerably better than weekend players in reproducing briefly presented chess positions taken from real games (with no differences for random configurations of chess figures). Schematic knowledge base of effective moves for a huge number of different real game configurations held in grand masters' knowledge base allowed them to reproduce realistic positions by large familiar chunks rather than by individual chess figures.

Initially, the same approach was literally applied in an educational context by asking learners to reproduce briefly presented (for several seconds) real task statements in a pilot study using coordinate geometry tasks. However, no significant correlation was actually found between learners' performance in reproducing diagrams and more traditional measures of knowledge. The following attempts were based on the solution moves rather than on the problem states (Kalyuga & Sweller, 2004). When a student solves a task in a familiar domain, her or his immediate approach to this task is likely to be based on available task-relevant knowledge structures. This knowledge is rapidly activated, and a corresponding sufficiently stable and durable long-term working memory structure is created. It allows sufficient time for evaluating such structure in a suitably designed diagnostic procedure.

Thus, the general idea of the rapid diagnostic approach is to determine the highest level of organized knowledge structures (it could be procedural as well as conceptual structures) a student applies rapidly to a task or situation she or he encounters. For example, consider a complex electronic system composed of many interconnected modules each of which represents a complex system itself. If there is a technical fault in this system, troubleshooting approaches of novice- and expert-level technicians could be quite different.

An expert has a large base of organized knowledge about the system and appropriate fault-finding procedures. Due to extensive practice with the system, he or she has direct knowledge about causes of many specific types of faulty situations. If a specific situation is recognized as a typical one, such knowledge is retrieved immediately and applied to fixing the problem. Such a rapid specific response to the task situation could be immediately observable reaction of this person. In this case, we are essentially dealing with fully or partially automated knowledge base that directly guides the technician's cognitive (and physical) performance.

If this person is encountered with a relatively new situation for which he or she has no readily available response, the knowledge of the system needs to be used for analyzing and finding a possible cause of the malfunction. The expert approach in this situation would be most likely based on the top-down approach. High-level knowledge of the whole system will be activated to pinpoint the likely faulty component based on the interaction between the system parts. Then, the expert will gradually move to a lower level component for identifying possible defective parts (or directly applying knowledge of specific faulty situations with this component, if available). In this relatively non-standard novel case, the observable behavior will reflect a top-down approach based on applying high-level knowledge first.

Novice-level technicians may also recognize some simple situation for which they may have already acquired corresponding response rules, although these rules may still not be in an automated state of application. The beginning technicians or apprentices may consult their records or available manuals for typical standard troubleshooting actions. In a more complex and non-standard situation, they most likely will act randomly by trying to check individual components for possible contributions to the problem. Such random trials or search for available rules will be observable cognitive activities when these individuals first approach the situation.

At different intermediate levels of expertise, the immediate responses would represent some mixtures of the above extreme situations with intermediate levels of knowledge structures applied. For example, a better known sub-component of the whole system could be analyzed in a top-down way, however, relevant lower level components could still be searched in a random manner. At each level of expertise, the immediate rapid reaction of a person when approaching a complex problem situation will reflect the highest available level of organized domain- or task-specific knowledge base. This knowledge will provide the basis for constructing corresponding long-term working memory structures that could be captured in a properly designed diagnostic assessment procedure.

FIRST-STEP DIAGNOSTIC METHOD

The general idea of the rapid assessment approach was realized in the first-step diagnostic method. According to this method, learners are presented with selected tasks for a limited time and asked to rapidly indicate their first step toward solution of each task (Kalyuga, 2003; Kalyuga & Sweller, 2004). For more experienced learners, their well learned higher level solution procedures (that in many cases include automated lower level steps) would allow these learners to rapidly generate advanced steps of the solution skipping some intermediate steps (Blessing & Anderson, 1996; Sweller, Mawer, & Ward, 1983).

Using the example of the chess game that was investigated in many classical cognitive studies of expertise, the chess grand masters know the best move for each of the remembered typical game configurations. Their knowledge base contains a corresponding move for each such configuration. Therefore, a rapid test of chess expertise could be based on presenting typical game configurations for brief periods of time and asking players to rapidly indicate their first moves. We could expect different responses based on the levels of player expertise. The first-step diagnostic assessment method is, to some extent, similar to this approach.

According to the previously mentioned characteristics of expert performance, the first step would involve different cognitive operations for individuals with different levels of expertise in a specific task domain. More knowledgeable learners presumably should be better able to retrieve appropriate higher level solution schemas than less knowledgeable learners. Thus, the method may allow capturing the content of long-term working memory when a learner approaches the task. An expert may provide immediately the final answer to the problem or retrieve a higher level knowledge of the situation to start her/his solution. A less knowledgeable person may indicate the very first operation according to detailed step-by-step solution rules remembered or borrowed from an available manual, or retrieve an intermediate level knowledge for analyzing the situation. Finally, a novice may start a random search for solution, for example, by using a trial-and-error technique.

Therefore, different first-step responses would reflect different levels of acquisition of corresponding task-specific knowledge structures. Skipping some intermediate levels of knowledge or procedural operations when performing the first subjectively significant solution move would indicate a higher level of proficiency. An expert may have corresponding knowledge structures and operations automated or well learned to be able to apply that knowledge or perform operations without using much conscious working memory resources.

The first-step diagnostic method was used (both in paper-based and online computer-based formats) to diagnose secondary school students' knowledge of procedures for solving linear algebra equations, simple coordinate geometry tasks, and arithmetic word problems (Kalyuga & Sweller, 2004; Kalyuga, 2006 C). Experimental results indicated significant correlations (in the range from 0.72 to 0.92) between performance on these diagnostic tasks and more traditional measures of knowledge that required lengthy complete solutions of similar problems. Test times were reduced by factors of up to 4.9 in comparison with traditional test times. The first-step diagnostic method was significantly less time consuming in comparison with traditional tests and sensitive to underlying knowledge structures.

EXAMPLE OF USING FIRST-STEP METHOD IN ALGEBRA

In order to use the method in a specific task domain, it is necessary first to establish the set of schematic procedures involved in knowledge-based solutions in this class of tasks. For simple linear algebra equations, e.g. $\frac{2x+3}{2} = 4$, the sequence of main solution steps is: 1) multiplying both sides of the equation by 2 to obtain $2x + 3 = 8$; 2) subtracting 3 from both sides of the equation to obtain $2x = 5$; 3) dividing both sides of the equation by 2 to obtain the solution $x = \frac{5}{2}$.

Solving the original equation would require the sequential applications of these schematic steps to corresponding sub-tasks. If a learner has some of these schemas well learned, she or he could perform the corresponding operations mentally without writing them down. This learner may omit some intermediate stages of the solution by integrating several separate steps, thus indicating a higher level of expertise in comparison with a learner who explicitly carries out each intermediate step.

In the above example, a student who knows the procedure for multiplying out the denominator but has not had sufficient practice in applying this procedure may write as the first step: $\frac{2x+3}{2} * 2 = 4 * 2$. A student who has practiced this procedure previously, may write immediately $2x + 3 = 8$. Another student with more experience in solving linear equations may immediately start subtracting 3 from both sides of the equation, $2x + 3 - 3 = 8 - 3$, as the first operation this person would write down on paper as her or his first step. If this learner has the schema for this procedure well practiced before, he or she may write the first solution step as $2x = 5$. A learner who is highly experienced in this narrow task domain may have the entire solution procedure well practiced and would be able to write the final answer, $x = \frac{5}{2}$, immediately as her or his first step.

Accordingly, a possible scoring procedure may allocate higher scores for more advanced performances. For example, a score 1 could be allocated for providing immediate first step of multiplying out the denominator in the above example; a score 2 for writing down the result of this procedure as a first step; a score 3 for writing down the subtraction operation as a first step; a score 4 for indicating the results of this operation, etc. A high-level expert capable of producing immediately the final answer would receive a top score of 6.

The rapid assessment test in this class of tasks could be designed as a series of tasks representing different levels of task complexity (e.g., $\frac{3x+2}{4} = 2$; $4x + 1 = 3$; $5x = 7$). Then, each task could be presented to a student for limited time and the student asked to indicate immediately her or his first step toward the solution (instead of providing a complete solution in a traditional test). For example, the following instructions to students were used by Kalyuga and Sweller (2004):

On each of the following pages, you will see an equation.

For each equation, you have to type a single one-line step that you would normally do first when solving the equation on paper.

*For example, when asked to solve the equation 2(3x – 1) = 1, some people would first write 2*3x – 2* 1= 1, others could start from 6x – 2 = 1 or 6x = 3, and some might even write the final answer (x = 1/2) as the first step.*

If, when you are given an equation, you do not know how to solve it, click the button "Don't know". You will be allowed no more than one minute to type your answer.

RAPID VERIFICATION DIAGNOSTIC METHOD

In an alternative rapid diagnostic assessment method, learners could be presented with a series of potentially possible steps at various stages of the solution procedure, and asked to rapidly verify the correctness of these steps instead of generating the steps themselves. This rapid verification method is easier to implement in online learning environments. It is also easier to use with relatively poorly defined tasks with a very large number of possible solution steps or when these steps could not be specified exactly in advance (e.g., when the solution procedure requires drawing graphical representations).

For example, the previously considered chess game situations usually allow a large number of potential moves. A possible alternative approach to a rapid test of chess expertise may be based on presenting a real game configuration for a brief period of time, followed by displays of several possible (both suitable and unsuitable) moves for this configuration, one display at a time. A player should rapidly verify the suitability of each of these moves.

Both correct and incorrect steps reflecting various stages of the solution procedure should be presented for verification, and students may respond by clicking on displayed buttons or pressing specified keys on the computer keyboard (e.g., correct, incorrect, or don't know). For example, consider the following vector addition motion task: *A crane is moving horizontally at 3 m/s. A load is being lifted at 1 m/s. What is the velocity of the load relative to the ground?* For this task, each solution verification window may include a diagrammatic and/or numerical representation of a possible (correct or incorrect) solution step and buttons "Right", "Wrong", and "Don't know" for students to click on (see Figure 5 for an example of a suggested incorrect step). The "Don't know" button is included as the third answer option in order to reduce a possible guessing effect.

Although the rapid verification method uses a recognition test format for verifying suggested solution steps, this method is different from traditional recognition tests measuring knowledge of shallow task characteristics. With the rapid verification method, learners need to recognize intermediate steps in a solution procedure, and these steps have to be rapidly constructed and integrated first using available knowledge base. These processes involve much more complex cognitive activities than those involved in traditional recognition tests, and require sufficient levels of expertise.

The rapid verification method was first validated using sentence comprehension tasks and indicated a significant correlation of 0.63 between performance on rapid verification tasks and traditional measures of reading comprehension, with test time reduced by factor of 3.7 (Kalyuga, 2006 B). In the rapid test, a sequence of gradually increasing in complexity sentences was developed (simple to composite

Figure 5. A suggested incorrect solution step for a rapid verification diagnostic task

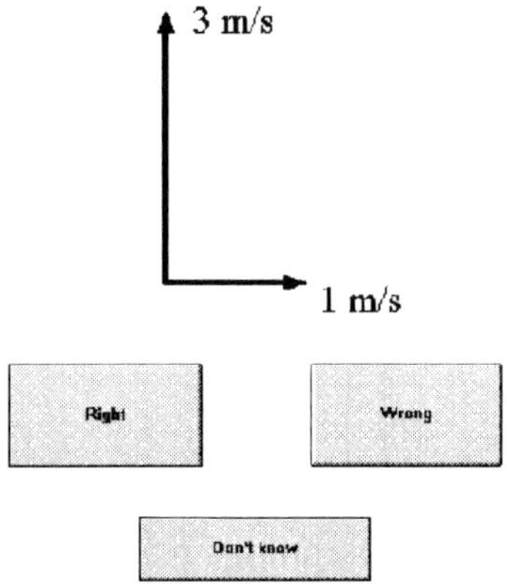

and to multiple-embedded sentences). Each sentence was displayed for a limited time sufficient for reading the sentence, and four simple statements were presented sequentially on the computer screen for rapid verification.

Another study used task domains of kinematics (vector addition motion problems similar to that presented in Figure 5) and mathematics (transforming graphs of linear and quadratic functions). Students' rapid online test scores were compared with results of observations of the same students' problem solving steps using video-recordings and concurrent verbal reports. Traditional paper-based tests were used for the purpose of evaluating concurrent validity of the rapid verification method. In these tests, the same students were required to provide complete solutions of tasks similar to those in the rapid verification procedure. The students' on-paper actions and think-aloud verbalizations were recorded (Kalyuga, 2008).

A student's performance on traditional tasks was assessed as the number of correct solution steps that the student completed continuously within a short period of time (usually 10-20 seconds) of starting the solution. This score was determined based on the analysis of both visual and audio recordings of the student's actions. The steps that were preceded by long chains of reasoning and required more time did not count even if they were eventually completed correctly, because these steps were not based on immediately available knowledge of solution procedures in long-term memory. In order to determine actual time reductions associated with rapid method in comparison with traditional tests, self-paced tasks were used in both tests. Results indicated significant correlations (respectively .71 and .75), with reductions of testing times in rapid tests by factors of 3.2 and 3.5 (Kalyuga, 2008).

Also, in both conditions, due to the available schematic knowledge base, more knowledgeable learners were expected to perform their tasks with lower mental effort than novices. Therefore, the evaluation of cognitive load was also included in the procedure to provide another indicator of levels of learner expertise in addition to the test performance scores. Simple subjective rating scales were used to measure cognitive load imposed by instructional materials (e.g., see Chapter V; Paas, Tuovinen, Tabbers, & van Gerven, 2003 for overviews). The measures of cognitive load in the rapid and traditional assessment procedures were also highly correlated (correspondingly, .67 and .82).

EXAMPLE OF USING RAPID VERIFICATION METHOD IN KINEMATICS

A typical task in the class of vector addition motion problems requires adding two vectors that are positioned at a certain angle to each other. The following task is an example of such tasks: *A sea wave is travelling at 8 m/s towards the beach. A swimmer moves at 3 m/s in a direction perpendicular to the direction of the wave. What is the velocity of the swimmer relative to the ground?* During the rapid verification test, students were presented with a set of possible intermediate solution steps and asked to rapidly verify the correctness of these steps. More knowledgeable learners presumably should be better able to rapidly construct, integrate, and recognize intermediate solution moves than less knowledgeable learners.

For example, a person who knows that a vector approach should be applied, but who has not practiced graphical addition of vectors, may be able to verify correctly a diagram with two perpendicular vectors as a valid step toward the solution. An individual, who has more experience with vectors, may rapidly verify perpendicular vectors with numerical values assigned to the length of each vector. Another person who is familiar with the vector addition procedure may verify immediately a diagram representing the graphical addition of these vectors. Someone with more experience in adding vectors might be able to rapidly verify a numerical expression for the Pythagorean Theorem. A learner with substantial experience in solving this class of tasks may be even able to verify a numeric expression representing the final answer without a diagram present.

Each textual task statement was followed by five suggested solution steps (correct or incorrect) for rapid verification. The first verification subtask for each task provided vector graphs indicating only directions of movements. The second verification subtask provided vector graphs with velocity values indicated next to them. For example, for the previously mentioned task that described a situation with perpendicular directions of movements, vector graphs indicating perpendicular directions of movements with corresponding velocity values were provided. The third verification subtask, in addition to the vectors and their values, graphically represented the vector addition operation.

For example, for the fourth task (*A boat is traveling at 5 m/s. A passenger runs across the deck at 5 m/s in a direction of 120° relative to the direction of motion of the boat. What is the velocity of the passenger relative to the water?),* the third verification subtask (incorrect step) is presented in Figure 6. The fourth verification subtask provided all necessary graphical information and indicated a numerical expression for calculating the length of the resulting vector. For example, for the above (120° angle) task, a simple expression V = 5 m/s was placed next to the diagram (60° angles and equal sides in two equilateral triangles were also indicated on the diagram). Finally, the fifth verification subtask included a numerical answer (an integer or surd) with no graphics provided. The values of angles between vectors were intentionally selected as 0°, 180°, 90°, 120°, or 60° in order to make calculations possible without using trigonometry.

Students were instructed that each task in the test would be displayed for a limited time and that following each task, several possible (both correct and incorrect) solution steps would be presented one at a time. Tasks were displayed for 15 seconds each. This time was established in pre-experimental trials as sufficient for reading and comprehending task statements. Students were also told that most of presented possible solution steps were intermediate stages on a way to the solution, but some suggested steps could even indicate final answers.

Figure 6. Snapshot of the rapid response window for a vector addition motion task. Reprinted from Kalyuga (2008). Copyright © 2008 American Psychological Association. Used with permission.

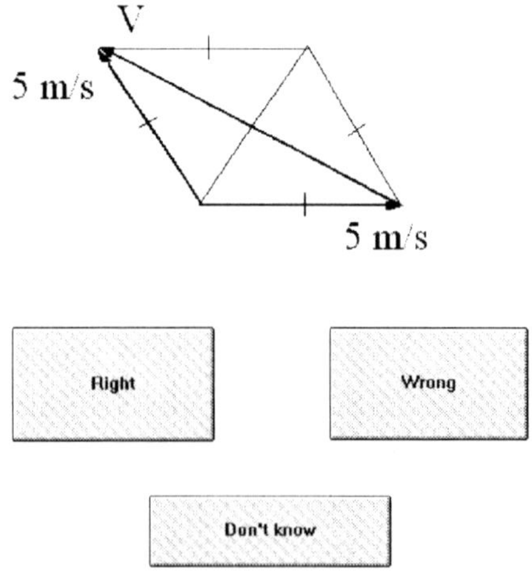

For each suggested step, students had to immediately verify if this step could be a correct step leading to the solution (or providing the final answer). Each solution verification window included a diagrammatic and/or numerical representation of a possible solution step and the buttons "Right", "Wrong", and "Don't know" for students to click on. Limiting the allowed verification response time to several seconds by automatically switching to the next verification window or task could forcefully interrupt genuine verification responses, thus invalidating results. Therefore, before the commencement of the rapid test, the participants were 'coached' in responding sufficiently rapidly using exercises with tasks from a different area. During those exercises, the students had received a sense of what was considered a rapid response (if a student did not respond within a set short time interval, she or he was asked to respond faster next time).

Scores allocated for correct responses to different verification subtasks depended on the level of the subtasks. For example, the first subtask required learners to verify the application of only one step (a graphical representation of vectors), and a score 1 was allocated for a correct response. On the other hand, the fifth subtask required learners to verify the result of the application of five sequential procedural steps, and a score 5 was allocated for a correct response. Null scores were always allocated for incorrect responses and "Don't know" entries.

EXAMPLE OF USING THE RAPID VERIFICATION METHOD FOR GRAPH TRANSFORMING TASKS

The tasks of transforming graphs of linear and quadratic functions in mathematics required students to transform a provided graph of the basic line $y = x$ into graphs of more complex lines, for example, $y = -2x + 3$ and $y = \frac{1}{3}x - 2$ (see Figure 7 for an example of a task's statement). The subsequent tasks asked students to transform a provided graph of the basic line $y = x^2$ into graphs of more complex quadratic functions, for example, $y = -\frac{1}{3}x^2$ and $y = 2(x - 2)^2$. The tasks required application of two or three of the following operations: flipping a graph because of the minus sign in front of x or x^2 (the negative slope); squeezing (expanding) a graph toward (from) the y-axis according to the value of the coefficient in front of x or x^2 (whether it is more or less than 1); and horizontal/vertical shifting.

In the rapid diagnostic test, each task statement was presented for 10 seconds (this time was established in pre-experimental trials as sufficient for comprehending very brief task statements) and was followed by four suggested solution steps for rapid verification. Students were instructed that most of the suggested steps were supposed to be intermediate steps on a way to the solution, but some suggested steps could indicate final answers. Figure 8 shows an example of an incorrect final step

Figure 7. Snapshot of the statement for a graph transformation task

This is a graph of the line y = x.

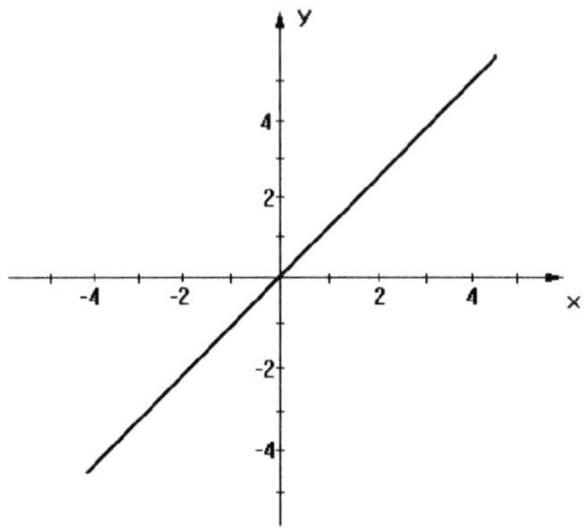

Transform it into a graph of the line $y = \frac{1}{3}x - 2$.

for the task represented in Figure 7. Some verification subtasks indicated results of the application of only one operation, while other subtasks indicated results of the application of several operations (e.g., flipping, expanding, and shifting in Figure 8).

The scoring procedure in this task domain was different from that used in the previous example. For the vector addition tasks, verification subtasks for each solution stage, except the final numerical answer, showed explicitly the fixed sequence of prior steps that students would normally perform. For example, a diagram representing the graphical addition of vectors would show the vectors themselves with assigned numerical values. In contrast, in this task domain, verification subtasks showed only results of the application of a possible combination of prior steps. An individual student might not necessarily solve a graph transformation task using this specific combination of steps. For example, when constructing a graph of the line $y = ⅓x - 2$, one student could first expand the line $y = x$, then shift the expanded line downwards. Another student would prefer to shift the original line first and then expand it.

Therefore, in this task domain, a suggested step that a learner needs to verify does not necessarily represent an exact specific sequence of operations she or he would actually perform when solving the task in normal conditions. In this situation, the verification process is likely to be performed by locating a feature that would immediately exclude the suggested step from a list of possible correct steps. For example, noticing that a flipped line is depicted for a function with a positive slope

Figure 8. Snapshot of a rapid response window for a graph transformation task

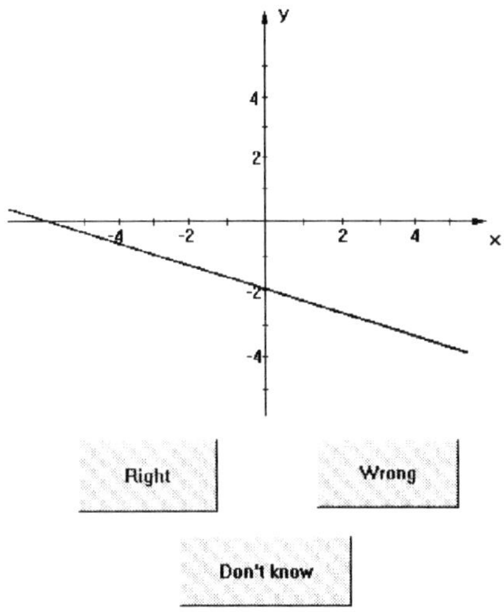

(e.g., in the example of Figure 8), or that an expanded line is depicted when the squeezing operation is required, or that a shift is made in a wrong direction, would immediately flag an incorrect step. Because locating a single incorrect operation could be sufficient for the verification purpose, the scoring procedure in this task domain allocated a score 1 for each correctly verified step (instead of the cumulative scoring approach used in the previous example in kinematics).

FUTURE TRENDS IN DIAGNOSIS OF EXPERTISE

The above described validation studies suggested a sufficiently high degree of concurrent validity for the first-step and rapid verification methods. All the described cases represented domains associated with sufficiently well-structured tasks. An important direction of further studies in this area is extending the rapid diagnostic approach (both first-step and rapid verification methods) to different task domains, especially those involving poorly structured problems and using multiple representational formats. For example, tasks with different possible graphical representations of situations, or problems with multiple possible routes to solutions. In such domains, only a limited number of situations or steps representing different possible states or levels of solution procedures could be selected and included into rapid verification subtasks.

For instance, in medical diagnosis tasks, a sequence of progressively more advanced stages of testing different hypotheses (including both correct and incorrect steps) could be presented for rapid verification. Because of the variety of possible solution paths in this case, a simple scoring procedure should be applied. In further research, the generality and limits of usability of the method, especially in poorly structured and complex task domains need to be established.

Studies of problem solving in physics by individuals with different levels of expertise demonstrated that experts approached the problems in terms of the basic principles of physics, while novices heavily depended on surface features of each specific task (Larkin, McDermott, Simon, & Simon, 1980). For example, in the case of an object being balanced on an inclined plane, the experts saw it as an example of a class of problems requiring a balance-of-forces approach, while novices saw it as an inclined planes problem type. Different incline plane tasks may require different approaches (based on balance of forces, energy conservation, etc.), and the presence of the inclined plane alone does not determine the appropriate approach.

The results of those studies may serve as a framework for cognitive analysis of specific task domains in science and developing relevant rapid diagnostic instruments. Based on a student's ability to adopt a proper solution approach from the very first steps in the solution process (or to verify correctly a series of presented steps) it could be possible to rapidly make a qualified judgment about the learner's level of expertise in the corresponding class of tasks. Correlations with results of conventional cognitive diagnoses will indicate the extent to which such tests are a valid measure of expertise, and the time savings will indicate their usefulness for adaptive online learning environments.

Technical systems in electronics and electrical engineering usually include many components that are complex systems themselves. Domain experts are able to immediately see higher level integrated structures in such systems and analyze them using a top-down approach, while novices at best can see only some isolated lower level components. The rapid assessment of expertise could be based on presenting, for a limited time, a series of diagrammatic representations of selected electronic circuits ordered according to levels of their structural complexity and types of components involved. These representations should be complemented with some specific input signal patterns (for example, diagrams of a simple halve-wave rectification circuit with one rectifier, a full-wave rectification circuit with two rectifiers, etc., all with a standard a.c. voltage input). Then participants will be required to indicate or verify the circuit outcomes at a level they can figure out immediately. An expert who has appropriate higher level knowledge structures for the whole system might be able to determine the overall system outcome immediately. A less knowledgeable person will have to analyze subsystems or even individual components separately, and at best could determine quickly the outcomes of only the first subjectively meaningful component she/he encounters.

In the currently available form, the rapid diagnostic approach (both the first-step and rapid verification methods) could be more suitable for measuring level of expertise of relatively advanced learners rather than for the thorough cognitive diagnosis of novice learners. These learners may have knowledge deficits of types that could not be anticipated in advance to select relevant possible solution steps for verification or to program the scoring engine (e.g., linguistic comprehension problems, insufficient factual knowledge, lack of basic metacognitive planning and monitoring skills). Most of these types of knowledge are usually taken for granted when dealing with more experienced learners. Applying the approach to diagnosing knowledge structures of novice learners require additional research and also depends on above mentioned extension of the approach to relatively poorly defined task domains and skills.

Another closely related area of important future research is investigating applicability of rapid diagnostic tools for evaluating components of adaptive expertise. The general idea of the rapid diagnostic approach is to determine the most advanced (generalized) level of knowledge structures a person is capable of applying rapidly to a new task or situation. When an adaptive expert encounters a new situation for which he or she has no available schema, general conceptual knowledge of the system may be used (a top-down approach). With the rapid diagnostic method, from the initially reported application of higher level knowledge, it may be possible to identify a top-down expert approach. On the other side, a search for available rules will be reported when routine experts first approach the situation. At intermediate levels, the immediate actions will reflect the highest available level of knowledge. Thus, from a learner's ability to adopt a corresponding top-down approach from the very beginning of the solution process, it might be possible to rapidly make a qualified judgment about the learner's type of expertise.

MULTIMEDIA INSTRUCTIONAL DESIGN IMPLICATIONS

The rapid diagnostic approach was designed to be used in adaptive online learning environments for real-time tailoring of instructional procedures and techniques to changing levels of learner expertise in a specific task domain. These diagnostic tests need to be embedded into adaptive multimedia instructional sessions as means of evaluating current levels of learner knowledge. Specific approaches and examples of such applications of the rapid diagnostic methods will be considered in Section III of the book.

SUMMARY OF CHAPTER IV

Generally, the application of the rapid diagnostic approach involves three major stages. The first stage is conducting a cognitive analysis of the task domain and developing a student model that describes a full set of organized knowledge structures that guide cognitive processing in a specific task area (e.g., see Mislevy, Steinberg, Breyer, Almond, & Johnson, 2002, for an example of cognitive analysis for assessment purposes in the field of dental hygiene). The second stage is development of the corresponding task model or a pattern of tasks necessary to obtain evidence about above cognitive structures. Finally, the third stage involves developing the evidence model that defines specific variables to evaluate, a scoring procedure (an evaluation method), and a specific statistical model to be applied to the collected data (Mislevy et al., 2002).

Developing and using a first-step diagnostic test in a specific task domain includes 1) establishing a sequence of possible main intermediate stages in the solution procedure; 2) for each stage, selecting tasks that require gradually increasing number of representative solution steps; 3) for each task, presenting the task statement to a learner for a limited time sufficient to read and understand the statement; 4) asking learners to rapidly indicate (write down or type in) their first step leading to the solution of the task; 5) selecting a progressively increasing (cumulative) scoring procedure that reflects the number of skipped steps in the first-step response: the more advanced is the response, the higher the allocated score, with one unit added for each level of advancement.

Developing and using a rapid verification diagnostic test in a specific task domain includes the following steps: 1) for a specific task, establishing a sequence of possible main intermediate stages in the solution procedure; 2) for each stage, selecting representative (either correct or incorrect) problem solution steps; 3) presenting the original task statement to a learner for a limited time sufficient to read and understand the statement; 4) presenting a series of the selected intermediate solution steps to learners, one at a time, with the requirement to quickly verify if each of the suggested steps could lead to a complete solution of the task; 5) selecting a scoring procedure depending on the uniqueness of the solution sequence for the task. If there is only one possible solution path, a progressively increasing, or cumulative, scoring procedure should be used (the more advanced is a correctly verified step, the higher the allocated score, with one unit added for each level of advancement). If the solution sequence includes a range of possible solution paths, a simple scoring procedure should be applied (a score 1 is assigned for each correctly verified step).

REFERENCES

Baddeley, A. (1997). *Human memory: Theory and practice.* East Sussex, UK: Psychology Press.

Baker, E. L., & Mayer, R. E. (1999). Computer-based assessment of problem solving. *Computers in Human Behavior, 15*, 269-282.

Blessing, S. B., & Anderson, J. R. (1996). How people learn to skip steps. *Journal of Experimental Psychology: Learning, Memory, and Cognition, 22*, 576-598.

Boshuizen, H. P. A., & Schmidt, H. G. (1992). On the role of biomedical knowledge in clinical reasoning by experts, intermediates and novices. *Cognitive Science, 16*, 153-184.

Chase, W. G., & Simon, H. A. (1973). Perception in chess. *Cognitive Psychology, 4,* 55-81.

Chi, M. T. H., Feltovich, P., & Glaser, R. (1981). Categorization and representation of physics problems by experts and novices. *Cognitive science, 5,* 121-152.

de Groot, A. D. (1965). *Thought and choice in chess.* The Hague: Mouton.

Ericsson, K. A., & Kintsch, W. (1995). Long-term working memory. *Psychological Review,* 102, 211-245.

Hoeft, R. M., Jentsch, F. G., Harper, M. E., Evans III, A. W., Bowers, C. A., & Salas, E. (2003). TPL-KATS concept map: a computerized knowledge assessment tool. Computers in Human Behavior, 19, 653-657

Kalyuga, S. (2003). Rapid assessment of learners' knowledge in adaptive learning environments. In Hoppe, U., Verdejo, F., & Kay, J. (Eds.), *Artificial intelligence in education: Shaping the future of learning through intelligent technologies* (pp. 167-174). Amsterdam: IOS Press.

Kalyuga, S. (2006 A). *Instructing and testing advanced learners: A cognitive load approach.* New York: Nova Science Publishers.

Kalyuga, S. (2006 B). Rapid assessment of learners' proficiency: A cognitive load approach. *Educational Psychology, 26*, 613-627.

Kalyuga, S. (2006 C). Rapid cognitive assessment of learners' knowledge structures. *Learning and Instruction, 16*, 1-11.

Kalyuga, S. (2008). When less is more in cognitive diagnosis: A rapid assessment method for adaptive learning environments. *Journal of Educational Psychology* (in press).

Kalyuga, S., & Sweller, J. (2004). Measuring knowledge to optimize cognitive load factors during instruction. *Journal of Educational Psychology, 96,* 558-568.

Kintsch, W. (1998). *Comprehension: A paradigm for cognition*. New York: Cambridge University Press.

Larkin, J., McDermott, J., Simon, D., & Simon, H. (1980). Models of competence in solving physics problems. *Cognitive Science, 4,* 317-348.

Low, R., & Over, R. (1992). Hierarchical ordering of schematic knowledge relating to area-of-rectangle problems. *Journal of Educational Psychology, 84*, 62-69.

Miller, G. A. (1956). The magical number seven, plus or minus two: Some limits on our capacity for processing information. *Psychological Review, 63,* 81-97.

Mislevy, R. J., Steinberg, L. S., Breyer, F. J., Almond, R. G., & Johnson, L. (2002). Making sense of data from complex assessments. *Applied Measurement in Education, 15,* 363-389.

Nievelstein, F., van Gog, T., Boshuizen, H. P. A., & Prins, F. J. (in press). Expertise-related differences in ontological and conceptual knowledge development in the legal domain. *European Journal of Cognitive Psychology.*

Paas, F., Tuovinen, J., Tabbers, H., & van Gerven, P. (2003). Cognitive load measurement as a means to advance cognitive load theory. *Educational Psychologist, 38,* 63-71.

Sweller, J., Mawer, R., & Ward, M. (1983). Development of expertise in mathematical problem solving. *Journal of Experimental Psychology: General, 12*, 639-661.

Van de Wiel, M. W. J., Boshuizen, H. P. A., & Schmidt H. G. (2000). Knowledge restructuring in expertise development: Evidence from pathophysiological representations of clinical cases by students and physicians. *European Journal of Cognitive Psychology, 12(3)*, 323-355.

Van de Wiel, M. W. J., Boshuizen, H. P. A., Schmidt, H. G. & Schaper, N. C. (1999). The explanation of clinical concepts by expert physicians, clerks, and advanced students. *Teaching and Learning in Medicine, 11*, 153-163.

Chapter V
Evaluation of Cognitive Load

INTRODUCTION

Availability of valid and usable measures of cognitive load involved in learning is essential for providing support for cognitive load-based explanations of the effects predicted and described in cognitive load theory as well as for general evaluation of learning conditions. Besides, the evaluation of cognitive load may provide another indicator of levels of learner expertise in addition to performance scores. As mentioned before, due to the available schematic knowledge base, more knowledgeable learners are expected to perform their tasks with lower mental effort than novices.

Even though simple subjective rating scales remain the most often used measures of cognitive load imposed by instructional materials, new more sophisticated techniques are being developed, especially in multimodal environments associated with performance of complex cognitive tasks. This chapter provides a brief overview of traditional, as well as some novel methods for measuring and evaluating cognitive load. Some recently developed approaches to using these measures in estimating instructional efficiency of learning environments are also discussed.

APPROACHES TO EVALUATING COGNITIVE LOAD IN LEARNING AND INSTRUCTION

There are analytical (e.g., based on mathematical models) and empirical approaches to evaluation of cognitive load (Xie & Salvendy, 2000). Empirical approaches to measuring cognitive load could be divided into two major categories associated with direct/indirect and objective/subjective dimensions. Accordingly, there are direct objective measures (e.g., dual-task methodology, eye tracking techniques, or brain activity measures such as fMRI); indirect objective measures (physiological measures such as cardiovascular indicators, EEG, behavioral measures such as linguistic indices or interaction features, and learning outcome measures); direct subjective measures (self-reported stress level); and indirect subjective measures (self-reported mental effort) (Brünken, Plass & Leutner, 2003). Task or performance-based measures (e.g. primary task measures, dual task measures) and self-reports (subjective self-rating scales such as unidimensional Likert-type scales and multi-dimensional scales, e.g., NASA TLX) are mostly posterior indicators of cognitive load. Most of other measures of cognitive load are concurrent measures that are collected during the task performance.

One of the first methods for evaluating cognitive load that was used within a cognitive load framework was based on constructing and studying computational models (Sweller, 1988). It is possible to model cognitive processes in terms of elementary cognitive operations. For example, production rule models can be used that are based on condition-action (or *if-then*) pairs where specific cognitive actions take place when corresponding conditions are in place. By counting the number of active conditions in learner working memory, it is possible to estimate the level of working memory load required for performing specific cognitive tasks. Instruction processing times were also used as indicators of cognitive load (Sweller, Chandler, Tierney, & Cooper, 1990) before more directly related techniques were developed or adopted, and applied to instructional situations. In most of recent research studies within a cognitive load framework, subjective ratings and the dual-task technique have been used.

Subjective measures (e.g., Hill, Lavecchia, Byers, Bittner, Zaklad, & Christ, 1992), psychophysiological measures (Beatty, 1982; Paas, van Merrienboer, & Adam, 1994), and the secondary-task method (Bloem & Damos, 1985) are major empirical methods used for measuring mental workload. Subjective rating scales are capable of providing valid and reliable estimates of perceived mental load in a non-intrusive way (Gopher & Braune, 1984; Nygren, 1991; Paas et al., 1994). In most studies using subjective scales, cognitive load has been assessed retrospectively after learning based on the assumption that learners are capable of reflecting on their cognitive processes and report their mental effort during learning (i.e., there is a direct relation between subjective measures and actual load). An important advantage of this approach is its simplicity and practicality due to non-intrusiveness into actual cognitive processes.

Van Gog and Paas (2007) suggested that process-tracing techniques may allow the tracing of actual cognitive processes that occur during learning and problem solving, thus providing direct measures of these processes and contributing to deeper understanding of cognitive load factors. Process-tracing techniques may include verbal reports (e.g., concurrent and cued retrospective reporting) and eye tracking procedures. Concurrent verbal reports could be effectively used for evaluating cognitive load, however they are obviously not suitable under very high cognitive load conditions and when learning tasks are presented in audio format. Preliminary studies indicated that cued retrospective reports were as effective as concurrent reports (Van Gog, Paas, & van Merriënboer, & Witte, 2005). Both these methods are more informative about actual cognitive processes than free retrospective reports that are prone to the loss of essential information. Eye tracking techniques could be successfully used for investigating learner attention shifts by using patterns of fixations and mesuring their duration and pupil dilation (Van Gog & Paas, 2007; Van Gog et al., 2005).

In studies of human-computer interactions in hypermedia systems, there is a general tendency of moving from a quantitative analysis approach to a qualitative approach (Card, Moran, & Newell, 1983). Using contemporary computer-based technologies for tracking data for these purposes is becoming a very interesting empirical research method. By studying data tracks, it is possible to infer details of learner interactions and experiences within learning environments. By combining auditory and visual tracking data, it is possible to elicit information about cognitive load-related problems learners encounter in the process of learning.

Card et al. (1983) distinguished between several types of tracking tools. Customized tracking is provided by programming means used to collect specific information such as chronological lists (logs) of student actions regarding navigation, progress in the program, etc. Records of written products allow distributing real-time comments on relevant aspects of programs that depend on student verbal articulating abilities and could be imprecise, reflecting student perceptions rather than actual use of the program. Interaction histories provide textual logs or graphic displays of learners' moves and reflect actual use rather than student perception of it. Online recorders copy student spoken comments (e.g., their think-aloud notes regarding specific program features) onto a computer memory system and are also dependent on learners' communication skills and perceptions. Finally, real-time playback tools record screen actions taken by students with possible reflective verbal annotations of those records by students or prompt questions-answer sessions with the researcher. The last tool integrates features of several previous instruments (records of actual behavior and students' perceptions). The below section on the evaluation of cognitive load using concurrent verbal reports describes the application of this type of tools for qualitative evaluation of levels of cognitive load involved in learning from computer-based training programs.

EVALUATION OF COGNITIVE LOAD USING RATING SCALES AND DUAL-TASK TECHNIQUE

Subjective ratings of cognitive load are based on the assumption that people are able to introspect their cognitive processes. This assumption may not always be true, for example, in case of automatic processes that occur on a subconscious level (although such processes do not require working memory resources anyway). Ratings of subjective mental effort associated with learning instructional materials have been used in most of studies within a cognitive load framework (starting from Paas and Van Merrienboer, 1994a; 1994b) as they are easy to implement and do not intrude on primary task performance. Furthermore, previous research in evaluating mental workloads (e.g., in conditions of multitasking) indicates that various subjective measures of mental load are sufficiently reliable and correlate highly between themselves and with objective measures (Braarud, 2001; Moray, 1982; O'Donnell & Eggemeier, 1986; Eggemeier, 1988).

Subjective ratings in cognitive load studies have been usually collected using Likert-type scales, with participants asked to estimate how easy or difficult were instructions to understand (perceived task difficulty) or how much mental effort they invested into learning by choosing a number on the scale, ranging from 1 (extremely easy; least effort) to 7 or 9 (extremely difficult; most effort). Seven or nine point scales have been usually used. An example of an online cognitive load rating scale is provided in Figure 9.

Figure 9. Screenshot of an online cognitive load rating scale tool

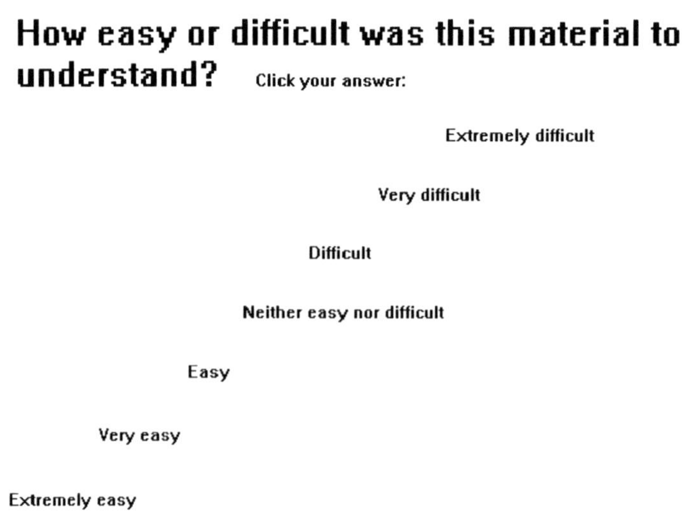

Previous research has indicated that such simple measures could be sufficiently sensitive to variations in cognitive load conditions (see Paas, Tuovinen, Tabbers, & van Gerven, 2003 for an overview). As there is no an absolute scale for subjective ratings of mental effort, they are more useful for comparing cognitive load levels involved in alternative applications or interface designs with the same set of users. They could be used for evaluating cognitive load imposed by a single application as levels of expertise of the same users increase. These methods could also be used for comparing cognitive load imposed by sequential versions of an application in the iterative process of the redesign of components that could contribute to increased cognitive load conditions. The same users could be asked to rate mental effort involved in using the application after each modification stage. Such instruments are less useful for evaluating a single application with different users.

Although cognitive studies indicate that subjective ratings of task difficulty or mental effort have been successfully used to measure cognitive load in many realistic and experimental educational settings (Paas et al., 2003), there could be potential problems with this method. For example, participants' subjective interpretations of the rating scale could vary. Therefore, alternative methods such as dual-task or secondary-task methodology based on more objective indicators have been developed and applied in cognitive load studies.

In general, a dual-task methodology is based on the assumption about the existence of one limited central processing mechanism (Moray, 1967; Bourke, Duncan & Nimmo-Smith, 1996). The degree of interference with the performance of secondary task serves as the indicator of the cognitive demands of the primary task (Kahneman, 1973). The dual-task technique uses performance on simple secondary tasks as indicators of cognitive load associated with performance on main tasks (Brünken, Steinbacher, Plass, & Leutner, 2002; Chandler & Sweller, 1996; Marcus, Cooper, & Sweller, 1996; van Gerven, Paas, van Merriënboer, & Schmidt, 2006). Various simple responses can be used as secondary tasks, for example, reaction times to some events (e.g., a computer mouse click), counting backwards, recalling the previous letter seen on the screen of a separate computer while encoding the new letter appearing after a tone sounded. An important requirement is that a secondary task should affect the same working memory processing system (visual and/or auditory) as the primary task; otherwise, it may not be sensitive to changes in actual cognitive load.

The usability of dual-task techniques for measurement of cognitive load in multimedia learning were studied by Brünken, Plass, and Leutner (2003, 2004) and Brünken et al. (2002). In these studies, the secondary task represented a simple visual-monitoring task requiring learners to react (e.g., press a key on the computer keyboard) as soon as possible to a color change of a letter displayed in a small frame above the main task frame. Reaction time in the secondary monitoring task was used as a measure of cognitive load induced by the primary multimedia presentation. The secondary task used by Chandler and Sweller (1996) consisted of recalling the previous letter seen on the screen of a separate computer while encoding the new letter appearing after a tone sounded. The studies demonstrated the applicability of the dual-task approach to measurement of cognitive load experienced by each individual user.

EVALUATION OF COGNITIVE LOAD USING CONCURRENT VERBAL REPORTS

Evaluation of cognitive load characteristics of a single multimedia application could also be based on concurrent verbal reports (think-aloud protocols) with audio and video tracking of participants' verbalizations and on-screen actions. The generated qualitative verbal data would reflect cognitive load caused by different types of sources and expressed through the participants' own language. Verbal data from think-aloud interviews should be coded using rubrics based on expected learners' or users' verbal expressions or remarks for different types of cognitive load (see examples below). For each rubric, sample keywords and phrases could be set and serve as a coding scheme for classifying participants' remarks. Of course, only a rough correspondence to the sample words and phrases in each of the categories of cognitive load might be established. Verbal data from the protocols could be analyzed by screening digital recordings of each interview on a computer using the samples of expected responses. Digital recordings may include audio and screen captures from the participant's computer obtained with specialized recording software (for example, TechSmith Camtasia Studio or similar applications).

Similar to any application of verbal report-based methods (Ericsson & Simon, 1993), before commencing the procedure, participants need to be coached in how to think aloud. The moderator should instruct them to think out loud at all times. It could be emphasized that it is of particular interest to investigators to know what participants find clear and what they find unclear. At any time, if participants get quiet, the moderator should ask them to keep talking. Participants need to be given only a brief general overview of what the specific application is about, and not instructed on the specifics of how it should be used. Participants should be asked to follow whatever information is available on the screen and perform corresponding learning tasks. Throughout the session, general probes could be used by the moderator to elicit relevant remarks. However, to avoid biasing the results, the probes should not explicitly mention *difficulty* and *effort*. The following questions could be used as possible non-leading probes (with related cognitive load aspects of performance indicated in brackets):

What is your strategy for learning (performance, task solution)? (Does the participant need more guidance? Is he or she trying to randomly search for an answer?)

What are you learning? What is familiar to you? What is unfamiliar? (Does the participant have required knowledge? Does he or she already know this material?)

What information are you paying most attention to? What do you ignore? Why?

What do you think of the amount of information and the way it is presented? Is it too much information? Too little? Too fast? Too slow? (Does anything distract the participant from learning or performance? Are there too many things to learn or to attend, are they changing too quickly?)

What is going on the screen? How easy or hard is it to keep track of things? (Does the participant have to quickly switch her or his attention between different things? Does the participant have to temporarily hold many items of information in working memory?)

Analysis of concurrent verbal reports for indicators of cognitive load requires locating relevant words, remarks, and expressions and relating them to various sources of cognitive load. The following rubrics could be used for this purpose, with possible samples of participants' remarks:

- Does the application provide sufficient explanations (guidance)?
  (can't get an idea, too complex to understand, don't know what to do, need some hints)
- Are participants involved in extensive random search (e.g. trial-and-error) processes?
  (let's try and see, just enter anything, play with numbers)
- Does the application activate relevant prior knowledge?
  (don't know anything about it, never heard about it, it doesn't ring a bell, thought it was something else)
- Does the application explain things that are already known?
  (know this stuff, we did it differently, studied this before)
- Do the unnecessary explanations distract from learning new information?
  (it is annoying, need to go through this again, it doesn't tell me anything new)
- Are too many new elements of information introduced too quickly?
  (can't catch it, the information is changing too fast, slow down!)

- Does the application proceed by too large step-sizes?
  (plenty of new things, can't grasp it all, a lot of unknown information)
- Does the application include related verbal and/or pictorial components that need to be attended or studied simultaneously and are located in different parts of the display or not synchronized in time?
  (jumping across the screen, it is over there, this has already changed earlier)
- Does the understanding of the interrelated components require extensive co-referencing and temporary holding much of information in memory?
  (need to go back to the diagram or text, it's too much to remember, already forgot about that).

MEASURES OF INSTRUCTIONAL EFFICIENCY

Performance scores and mental effort ratings could be used for interpreting and comparing instructional efficiency of different learning environments. For example, consider four hypothetical experimental conditions. In one condition, average performance score is P = 4 (out of 20) and average rating of mental effort is M = 8 (out of 9). For the second condition, the indicators are correspondingly P = 4 and M = 2. The third condition resulted in P = 17 and M = 2, and the fourth condition averaged P = 17 and M = 8. The first two conditions both resulted in poor performance outcomes, however the first group performed poorly even with a high level of invested mental effort. Therefore, even though both these conditions were ineffective, the first condition was also very inefficient. Both last two conditions resulted in good performance outcomes, however, the group in the third condition did so with relatively low level of mental effort, while the fourth condition required plenty of effort to reach higher levels of performance. Therefore, even though both these conditions were effective, the third condition was also instructionally very efficient, while the fourth condition was not efficient.

Therefore, it is important that the cognitive load approach considers learning and instruction in terms of efficiency rather than mere effectiveness. In other words, it evaluated learning results in terms of cognitive cost (cognitive resources spent, mental effort invested, or cognitive load imposed) of achieving instructional effects. With a sufficiently high level of motivation, students could eventually learn from any, even primitive or poorly designed, learning environments. The whole point of investing considerable human and financial resources into the design and development of sophisticated high-tech interactive multimedia learning environments is to achieve returns in terms of efficiency: learning faster and without mental stress.

The efficiency becomes a key feature of contemporary instructional systems. Measures of subjective load indicators and performance scores could be used to generate instructional efficiency indicators. Cognitively-supported learning environments are expected not only to be instrumental in achieving desired instructional effects, but achieving them efficiently, with optimal expenditures of cognitive resources and instructional time. The efficiency approach allows measures of cognitive load to be combined with measures of performance in order to derive information on the relative efficiency of instructional conditions and to estimate the cognitive cost of learning. High efficiency learning occurs under conditions of low cognitive load and high test performance, and low efficiency occurs under high cognitive load and low test performance.

According to Paas and van Merriënboer's (1993) procedure, efficiency values can be calculated, for example, by converting cognitive load and performance measures into *z*-scores (*R* and *P* correspondingly) and combining those scores using the formula:

$$E = \frac{P - R}{\sqrt{2}}$$

The denominator $\sqrt{2}$ is used in this formula in order to make the graphical interpretation of the formula more straightforward by representing the cognitive load and performance *z*-scores in a cross of axes. The relative efficiency of an instructional condition as a point (R, P) on the diagram can be measured as the distance from this point to the line of zero efficiency (P = R; or $E = 0$) and calculated using the above formula. The high efficiency area (relatively lower cognitive load with higher performance) with $E > 0$ is above this line. The low efficiency area (higher cognitive load with lower performance) with $E < 0$ is located below this line (for more details, see Paas & Van Merriënboer, 1993).

In the earlier work by Paas and van Merrienboer (1994a), relative condition efficiency was calculated with the mental effort and the performance scores on the post-instruction test. Kalyuga, Chandler, and Sweller (1999) combined the subjective mental effort ratings for the training session with the performance scores on the test to determine the relative condition efficiency. Paas & van Gog (2007) reported results of a review of 38 papers using instructional efficiency measures. Most of studies used assessment of mental effort during the learning phase combined with post-training test performance scores. Only 4 of reviewed papers used the original measure of instructional efficiency that combined test performance scores and mental effort ratings for the test phase.

Paas and van Gog (2007) noted that the original instructional efficiency measure reflected the learner expertise acquired in the instruction phase and should be used when it is difficult to disentangle the contribution of different instructional factors to the mental effort involved in the learning phase. For example, in studies that aim at increasing investment of useful effort during learning (i.e., increasing germane cognitive load) to enhance learning outcomes, the use of the modified instructional efficiency measure that relies on effort during learning could be questionable and/or misleading.

Several new approaches to measures of instructional efficiency of learning conditions have been recently suggested. In a new version of the efficiency formula suggested by Salden, Paas, Broers, and van Merriënboer (2004) and Tuovinen and Paas, (2004), the efficiency is calculated on the basis of three dimensions, for example, two test performance measures (test time and performance scores) and a test mental effort measure.

The mental effort rating (R) of a task could also be combined with the performance measure on the same task (P) using the formula E = P/R. This definition is different from that suggested by Paas and van Merriënboer (1993) not only by the appearance of the formula. In the original efficiency studies, efficiency indicators were calculated after experiments had been completed. The efficiency was effectively defined as the difference between *z*-scores for performance and mental effort ratings, and the means and standard deviations based on experimental data were used to calculate these *z*-scores. Thus, the efficiency could only be estimated after the performance and rating data were collected from the whole set of participants.

By using the above ratio formula, the efficiency indicator could be calculated in real time during the instructional session, when it is not possible to obtain *z*-scores yet. Nevertheless, the efficiency indicator defined as P/R, has similar general features to those of the previously used construct in that efficiency is higher if similar levels of performance are reached with less effort or, alternatively, higher levels of performance are reached with the same mental effort invested (Kalyuga & Sweller, 2005). Also, this definition is consistent with the common sense understanding of efficiency as an effect relative to the resources spent on obtaining the result.

With the ratio formula, for each task level, a critical level of instructional efficiency could be defined. For example, Kalyuga and Sweller (2005) defined it as Ecr = Pmax/Rmax, which is Ecr = Pmax/9 in case of the 9-point rating scale, where Pmax is the maximum performance score for the given task level. Cognitive performance of a learner in a task was considered as efficient (and the learner was regarded as competent), if E > Ecr (see Figure 10). If E ≤ Ecr, cognitive performance was considered as relatively inefficient and the learner was regarded as less competent. Although these values of the critical efficiency levels were selected arbitrarily based on common sense considerations, they could be further refined or adjusted experimentally.

The rationale for such levels was based on the general assumption that, if someone invests maximum mental effort in a task but does not display the maximum level of task performance, his or her cognitive performance should not be regarded as efficient (e.g., point A in Figure 10). On the other hand, if someone performs at the maximal level with less than a maximal mental effort, his or her cognitive performance should be regarded as efficient (e.g., point B). All other (non-extreme) cases (e.g., points (R1, P1) and (R2, P2)) should be judged relative to the critical level. Similar to Paas and van Merriënboer's (1993) approach, the proposed definition is based on a simplifying assumption of a linear relation between performance and mental effort. This assumption may not hold well when, for example, performance approaches asymptotic levels.

Another approach to defining the efficiency of instructional conditions may combine traditional or rapid test scores for evaluating levels of learner expertise with subjective ratings of mental effort using a simple qualitative definition of efficiency based on certain set thresholds of performance and mental effort {Kalyuga,

Figure 10. Graphical representation of learner cognitive efficiency according to Kalyuga & Sweller (2005). Copyright © 2005 Association for Educational Communication Technology. Used with permission.

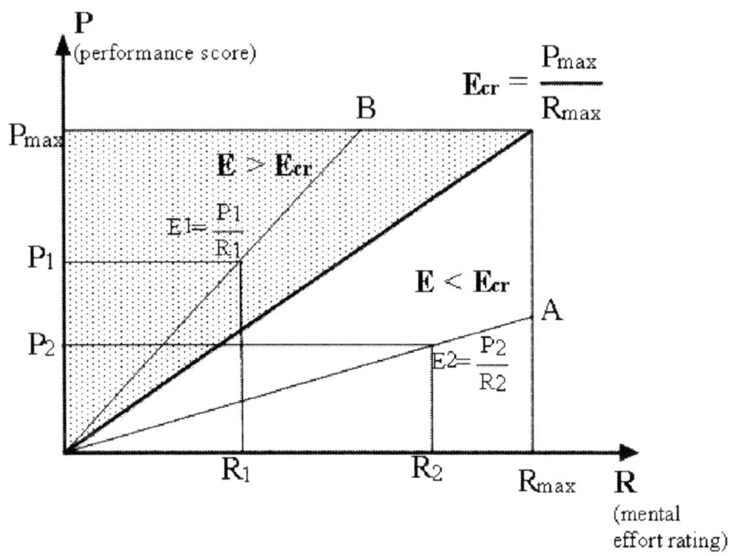

Note: E = Efficiency, Ecr = a critical level of Efficiency, Pmax = the maximum performance score, Rmax = the maximum mental effort rating

2006). For example, a learner's performance in a class of tasks could be considered as efficient if, in a rapid verification task corresponding to this class of tasks, she or he correctly verifies all the suggested solution steps at least up to a certain set level (for example, up to, but not including, the final numerical answer) and rates the task difficulty below the average value (i.e., less than 5 for a 9-point rating scale).

MEASURES OF INSTRUCTIONAL INVOLVEMENT

The amount of mental effort invested in a learning task could also reflect the learner's level of motivation. However, it could not measure the motivation because due to limited cognitive resources, the learner attention could also be focused outside the learning task. The real measure of motivation should take into account not only the invested mental effort but also the associated performance results. Paas, Tuovinen, van Merrienboer, and Darabi (2005) suggested that when learner involvement is higher, more mental effort is likely to be invested which should result in higher performance. The instructional involvement score, I, could be computed in the same two-dimension coordinate system of z-scores for performance (P) and mental effort (R) as that is used for calculating instructional efficiency, but using the formula $I = (P+R)/\sqrt{2}$. Graphically, the formula represents the distance from point (R, P) to the line $P = -R$.

When this formula was applied to the data from experiments investigating interactions between levels of learner prior knowledge and efficiency of exploratory or problem-solving vs worked out learning environments (Kalyuga, Chandler, & Sweller, 2001; Kalyuga, Tuovinen, Chandler, & Sweller, 2001), the results indicated that the exploration (problem solving) practice tended to provide greater involvement that the worked example practice, with the strongest effect for higher-prior-knowledge students (in accordance with the expertise reversal effect). Even though the expertise reversal effect has been explained in terms of cognitive efficiency, a motivational perspective may offer another explanation. According to this approach, more advanced learners are not motivated enough to invest mental effort in well explained and structured learning tasks designed for novices (Paas, Tuovinen, van Merrienboer, & Darabi, 2005).

To obtain a combined graphical interpretation of measures of instructional efficiency and instructional involvement, the location of the point (R, P) should be evaluated against both critical lines $P = R$ (the line of zero efficiency $E = 0$) and $P = -R$ (the line of zero involvement $I = 0$). The best instructional conditions correspond to the upper quadrant of these intersecting lines, and the worst instructional conditions correspond to the bottom quadrant. As Paas, Tuovinen, van Merrienboer, and Darabi (2005) noted, sometimes verbal labels of task difficulty are used to measure the amount of mental effort instead of mental effort (e.g., as in Kalyuga et al., 1999). According to Paas and van Merrienboer (1994), mental effort is determined by the level of task difficulty, learner characteristics, and task-learner interactions. As long as the task is not too easy or too difficult, ratings of task difficulty may correlate highly with ratings of invested mental effort. If, however, the learner perceives the task as too easy or difficult, he/she may not wish to invest much mental effort in it resulting in reduced learning. Therefore, when using the motivational approach, it is necessary to use rating scales related to invested mental effort.

Approaches that combine mental efficiency and motivational perspectives could also be used in adaptive methodologies for the dynamic selection of learning tasks as an alternative to the efficiency only-based approach which has not yet demonstrated expected advantages (see Section III of the book for descriptions of some preliminary studies on using efficiency indicators in adaptive learning environments). Some initial research on effectiveness of adapting computer-based instruction to levels of learner motivation was conducted by Song and Keller (2001).

FUTURE TRENDS IN EVALUATION OF COGNITIVE LOAD AND EFFICIENCY

Finding usable objective techniques and developing instruments that are capable of distinguishing between different types of cognitive load are important and very challenging directions of current research in the field (e.g., Cierniak, 2007; DeLeeuw & Mayer, 2007). It is highly desirable to be able to measure not only overall cognitive load but obtain individual scores for intrinsic, extraneous and germane load. For example, Opfermann, Gerjets, and Scheiter (2007) suggested using different rating scales for this purpose. For example, for evaluating the level of intrinsic cognitive load in specific learning tasks in the domain of probability theory, the following question was used: *How easy or difficult do you consider probability theory at this moment?* The level of extraneous load was estimated using learner ratings on the questions *How easy or difficult is it for you to work with the learning environment? How easy or difficult is it for you to distinguish important and unimportant information in the learning environment? How easy or difficult is it for you to collect all the information that you need in the learning environment?* etc. Finally, for collecting ratings of germane cognitive load, the following question was used: *How easy or difficult was it for you to understand the contents?* (Opfermann et al., 2007).

Research in new approaches to measuring cognitive load may also provide more reliable objective, though unobtrusive, and real-time dynamic indicators.

Since learners in complex multimedia environments often adapt their behavior to changes in cognitive load, multimodal behavior patterns could also serve as indicators of cognitive load. For example, the redundancy and complementing nature of multimodal input, features of speech and gesture input could serve as potential multimodal indices of cognitive load. Research studies indicate that learners tend to use more redundant sources in their input when tasks are easy and less redundant input when tasks are hard. On the other side, they tend to use more complementary sources when tasks are hard and less complementary sources when tasks are easy (Chen, Ruiz, Taib, Yin, Choi, & Shi, 2007).

Characteristics of human speech can also represent an effective means for the insight into learner cognitive state. Such tools could potentially be used for automatic real-time evaluation of cognitive load of a learner through his/her speech utterances and for adapting the learning system behaviour accordingly (Jameson, Kiefer, Müller, Großmann-Hutter, Wittig, & Rummer, 2006). Potential types of speech characteristics that could be used for this purpose are pitch and pitch dynamics, spectral features, phonetic characteristics, linguistic features (e.g. pause rate). For example, some preliminary studies indicated that the pause rate and the rate of pitch peak could serve as potential indicators of levels of cognitive load in speech-only data (e.g., the pause rate is higher when the level of cognitive load is higher; and the rate of pitch peak is higher when the level of cognitive load is higher) (Chen et al., 2007). Much more research is needed to investigate behavioural patterns associated with different types of cognitive load in tasks incorporating multimodal features and performance under time pressure.

To further validate the efficiency as an integrated indicator of performance and cognitive load, it is necessary to test its generality and limits of usability in other, especially less structured, tasks areas. Alternative measures of cognitive load need to be investigated in conjunction with rapid diagnostic techniques, for example, dual-task techniques that use performance on simple secondary tasks as indicators of cognitive load associated with performance on primary tasks. Various criteria of efficient performance need to be evaluated in dynamic online instructional systems for tailoring instructional methods to changing levels of learner expertise (see Section III for descriptions of some preliminary findings in this area).

MULTIMEDIA INSTRUCTIONAL DESIGN IMPLICATIONS

The evaluation of general usability characteristics of computer-based multimedia or online applications are traditionally aimed at ensuring that interface components are understandable and recognizable (e.g., have clear meanings and interpretations, employ a simple and consistent color-coding scheme, use recognizable and consistent metaphors, simple and clear language, and provide help if required), and are functionally efficient (have clear functional roles, provide fast feedback and response times, are easy to recover from errors, and provide clear exit paths). Evaluating cognitive load characteristics of multimedia applications involved in intellectually complex task performances should become an important part of the usability studies. Experience accumulated in this area is very limited, and most research studies have been conducted using traditional paper-based instructional formats and very rough cognitive load measures like subjective rating scales or response times on secondary tasks as indicators of cognitive load.

An important implication of the reviewed approaches and techniques is that the evaluation of cognitive load could be embedded into multimedia instructional systems, together with the performance-based assessment of levels of learner task-specific expertise. These indicators could be effectively used to achieve optimal and appropriate adjustments of instructional methods and presentation formats to cognitive load conditions and characteristics of individual learners. Some possible approaches to using and combining these measures in adaptive learning environments will be considered in Section III of the book.

SUMMARY OF CHAPTER V

In most studies within a cognitive load framework, cognitive load has been assessed using subjective rating scales based on the assumption that there is a direct relation between learner self-report measures and actual levels of cognitive load. An important advantage of this technique is its simplicity and practicality due to non-intrusiveness into actual cognitive and learning processes.

The dual-task technique uses performance on simple secondary tasks as indicators of cognitive load associated with performance on main tasks. Various simple responses can be used as secondary tasks, for example, reaction times to some events (e.g., computer mouse clicks), counting backwards, tracking the color of a letter seen on the top of the screen, etc. An important requirement of the method is that a secondary task should affect the same working memory processing system (visual or auditory) as the primary task.

Concurrent verbal reports (think-aloud protocols) with audio and video tracking of participants' verbalizations and on-screen actions could also be used for evaluating cognitive load characteristics of multimedia instructional applications. The generated qualitative verbal data would reflect cognitive load caused by different types and sources of cognitive load. Such data would be expressed through the learners' verbal utterances or remarks that could be classified as corresponding to the sample words and phrases in each of the categories of cognitive load. Verbal data from the protocols could be analyzed by screening digital computer-based records of each interview using the samples of expected responses.

The efficiency becomes a key feature of contemporary instructional environments. They are expected not only to be instrumental in achieving desired instructional effects, but achieving them efficiently, with optimal expenditures of cognitive resources and instructional time. Performance scores and mental effort ratings could be used for evaluating and comparing instructional efficiency and motivational involvement of students in different learning environments.

The efficiency approach allows measures of cognitive load to be combined with measures of performance in order to derive quantitative information on the relative efficiency of instructional conditions and estimate the cognitive cost of instruction. High efficiency occurs under conditions of low cognitive load and high test performance, and low efficiency occurs under high cognitive load and low test performance. Evaluations of cognitive load and indicators of instructional efficiency could be embedded into multimedia instructional systems in order to appropriately tailor instructional methods and presentation formats to cognitive load conditions and characteristics of individual learners.

REFERENCES

Beatty, J. (1982). Task-evoked papillary responses, processing load, and the structure of processing resources. *Psychological Bulletin, 91*, 276-292.

Bloem, K. A., & Damos, D. L. (1985). Individual differences in task performance and subjective estimation of workload. *Psychological Reports, 56*, 311-322.

Braarud, P. O. (2001). Subjective task complexity and subjective workload: Criterion validity for complex team tasks. *International Journal of Cognitive Ergonomics, 5*, 261-273.

Brünken, R., Plass, J., & Leutner, D. (2003). Direct measurement of cognitive load in multimedia learning. *Educational Psychologist, 38*, 53-61.

Brünken, R., Plass, J. L., & Leutner, D. (2004). Assessment of cognitive load in multimedia learning with dual-task methodology: Auditory load and modality effects. *Instructional Science, 32, 115*-132.

Brünken, R., Steinbacher, S., Plass, J., & Leutner, D. (2002). Assessment of cognitive load in multimedia learning using dual-task methodology. *Experimental Psychology, 49*, 109-119.

Card, S., Moran, T., & Newell, A. (1983). The psychology of human-computer interaction. Hillsdale, NJ: Lawrence Erlbaum Associates.

Chandler, P., & Sweller, J. (1996). Cognitive load while learning to use a computer program. *Applied Cognitive Psychology, 10*, 1-20.

Chen, F., Ruiz, N., Taib, R., Yin, B., Choi, E., & Shi, Y. (2007). Cognitive load measurement through multimodal behavior patterns. Paper presented at International Conference on Cognitive Load Theory, 26-28 March, 2007, Sydney, UNSW.

Cierniak, G. (2007). Subjective and objective load measures: Subjective load ratings vs. dual-task methodology. Paper presented at International Conference on Cognitive Load Theory, 26-28 March, 2007, Sydney, UNSW.

DeLeeuw, K. E., & Mayer, R. E. (2007). A comparison of measures of cognitive load. Paper presented at International Conference on Cognitive Load Theory, 26-28 March, 2007, Sydney, UNSW.

Eggemeier, F. T. (1988). Properties of workload assessment techniques. In P. A. Hancock & N. Meshkati (Eds.), *Human mental workload* (pp. 41-62). Amsterdam: Elsevier.

Ericsson, K. A., & Simon, H. A. (1993b). Protocol analysis: Verbal reports as data. Cambridge, MA: MIT Press.

Gopher, D., & Braune, R. (1984). On the psychophysics of workload: Why bother with subjective measures? *Human Factors, 26*, 519-532.

Hill, S. G., Lavecchia, H. P., Byers, J. C., Bittner, A. C., Zaklad, A. L., & Christ, R. E. (1992). Comparison of four subjective workload rating scales. *Human Factors, 34*, 429-439.

Jameson, A., Kiefer, J., Müller, C., Großmann-Hutter, B., Wittig, F., & Rummer, R. (2006). Assessment of a User's Time Pressure and Cognitive Load on the Basis of Features of Speech. *Journal of Computer Science and Technology* (in press).

Kahneman, D. (1973). *Attention and effort.* Englewood Cliffs, NJ: Prentice-Hall.

Kalyuga, S. (2006). Assessment of Learners' Organized Knowledge Structures in Adaptive Learning Environments. *Applied Cognitive Psychology, 20*, 333-342.

Kalyuga, S., Chandler, P., & Sweller, J. (1999). Managing split-attention and redundancy in multimedia instruction. *Applied Cognitive Psychology, 13*, 351-371.

Kalyuga, S., Chandler, P., & Sweller, J. (2001). Learner experience and efficiency of instructional guidance. *Educational Psychology, 21,* 5-23.

Kalyuga, S., Chandler, P., Tuovinen, J., & Sweller, J. (2001). When problem solving is superior to studying worked examples. *Journal of Educational Psychology, 93*, 579-588.

Kalyuga, S., & Sweller, J. (2005). Rapid dynamic assessment of expertise to improve the efficiency of adaptive e-learning. *Educational Technology, Research and Development, 53*, 83-93.

Marcus, N., Cooper, M., & Sweller, J. (1996). Understanding instructions. *Journal of Educational Psychology, 88*, 49-63.

Moray, N. (1982). Subjective mental workload. *Human Factors, 24*, 25-40.

Nygren, T. E. (1991). Psychometric properties of subjective workload measurement techniques: Implications for their use in the assessment of perceived mental workload. *Human Factors, 33*, 17-33.

O'Donnell, R. D., & Eggemeier, F. T. (1986). Workload assessment methodology. In K. R. Boff, L. Kaufman, & J. P. Thomas (Eds.), *Handbook of perception and human performance* (Vol. 2, Chapter 42, pp. 1-49). New York: Wiley.

Opfermann, M., Gerjets, P., & Scheiter, K. (2007). Online measurement of different types of cognitive load with an adjusted version of NASA-TLX. Paper presented at International Conference on Cognitive Load Theory, 26-28 March, 2007, Sydney, UNSW.

Paas, F., Tuovinen, J., Tabbers, H., & van Gerven, P. (2003). Cognitive load measurement as a means to advance cognitive load theory. *Educational Psychologist, 38*, 63-71.

Paas, F., Tuovinen, J. E., van Merrienboer, J. J. G., & Darabi, A. A. (2005). A motivational perspctive on the relation between mental effort and performance. *Educational technology, Research and Development, 53*, 25-34.

Paas, F., & van Gog, T. (2007). Revisiting the original construct of instructional efficiency in educational research. Paper presented at International Conference on Cognitive Load Theory, 26-28 March, 2007, Sydney, UNSW.

Paas, F., & van Merriënboer, J. J. G. (1993). The efficiency of instructional conditions: An approach to combine mental-effort and performance measures. *Human Factors, 35*, 737-743.

Paas, F., & van Merriënboer, J. J. G. (1994a). Variability of worked examples and transfer of geometrical problem-solving skills: A cognitive-load approach. *Journal of Educational Psychology, 86*, 122-133.

Paas, F., & van Merriënboer, J. J. G. (1994b). Instructional control of cognitive load in the training of complex cognitive tasks. *Educational Psychology Review, 6*, 351-371.

Paas, F. G. W. C., van Merrienboer, J. J. G., & Adam, J. J. (1994). Measurement of cognitive load in instructional research. *Perceptual and Motor Skills, 79*, 419-430.

Salden, R. J. C. M., Paas, F., Broers, N. J., & van Merriënboer, J. J. G. (2004). Mental effort and performance as determinants for the dynamic selection of learning tasks in air traffic control training. *Instructional Science, 32,* 153-172.

Song, S. H., & Keller, J. M. (2001). Effectiveness of motivationally adaptive computer-assisted instruction on the dynamic aspects of motivation. *Educational Technology, Research and Development, 49*, 5-22.

Sweller, J. (1988). Cognitive load during problem solving: Effects on learning. *Cognitive Science*, 12, 257-285.

Sweller, J., Chandler, P., Tierney, P., & Cooper, M. (1990). Cognitive load and selective attention as factors in the structuring of technical material. *Journal of Experimental Psychology: General, 119,* 176-192.

Tuovinen, J. E., & Paas, F. (2004). Exploring multidimensional approaches to the efficiency of instructional conditions. *Instructional Science, 32*, 133-152.

Van Gerven, P. W. M., Paas, F., van Merriënboer, J. J. G., & Schmidt, H. G. (2006). Modality and variability as factors in training the elderly. *Applied Cognitive Psychology, 20*, 311-320.

van Gog, T., & Paas, F. (2007). Process tracing techniques to investigate cognitive processes and cognitive load. Paper presented at International Conference on Cognitive Load Theory, 26-28 March, 2007, Sydney, UNSW.

Van Gog, T., Paas, F., Van Merriënboer, J.J.G., & Witte, P. (2005). Uncovering the problem-solving process: cued retrospective reporting versus concurrent and retrospective reporting. *Journal of Experiment Psychology: Applied, 11*, 237-244.

Xie, B., & Salvendy, G. (2000). Prediction of mental workload in single and multiple task environments. *International Journal of Cognitive Ergonomics, 4*, 213-242.

SUMMARY OF SECTION I

This section of the book presented an overview of major theoretical issues and empirical evidence that are essential for understanding main implications of a cognitive load theoretical framework for the design of multimedia learning. Implementing cognitive design principles in multimedia learning environments involves reducing extraneous cognitive load by avoiding diversion of cognitive resources on activities and tasks that are not directly related to learning, for example, on searching and locating appropriate components in pictures and/or text, or attending to unnecessary details. It is also important to prevent uncontrolled reduction of essential (intrinsic and germane) cognitive load in learning. An essential part of enhancing learners' self-regulation abilities is developing their skills in managing cognitive resources.

Substantial empirical evidence has been obtained for interactions between different instructional methods and levels of learner task-specific expertise (the expertise reversal effect or prior knowledge effect). It was found that many techniques for reducing extraneous non-essential cognitive load (such as integrating sources of information or using dual-modality formats in a split-attention situation, using worked examples instead of conventional problem solving) were effective for relatively novice learners. For more knowledgeable learners, such instructional techniques may become ineffective. In many situations, these techniques resulted in negative rather than positive or neutral effects when used with more experienced learners. This effect has been consistently replicated in many studies with a large range of instructional materials and participants. A theoretical interpretation of the effect within a cognitive load framework was presented in this part of the book.

The most important implication of the expertise reversal effect is that the design of effective and cognitively efficient multimedia environments needs to be tailored to changing levels of learner task-specific expertise. Such adaptive learning environments may optimize cognitive resources available for comprehending multimedia messages and constructing appropriate organized knowledge base. For example, multimedia systems may include several different interaction modes that present the same information differently to different learners or to the same learners at different stages of development of their expertise in the domain.

Dynamic adaptive instructional systems require rapid online methods for evaluating levels of learner expertise. A rapid diagnostic approach has been developed for real-time monitoring of levels of learner task-specific expertise in a domain by capturing authentic domain-specific knowledge structures involved in processing presented information. This diagnostic approach has the potential for developing more rapid and sensitive knowledge tracing techniques than traditional measures.

It could be used to increase the accuracy of information about levels of learner knowledge and expertise contained in instructional systems' student models.

The new rapid diagnostic methods together with techniques for evaluating levels of cognitive load will be applied in the following sections of the book as means of tailoring multimedia environments to levels of learner expertise.

Section II
Managing Multimedia Cognitive Load for Novice and Expert Learners

Chapter VI
Managing Cognitive Load in Verbal and Pictorial Representations

INTRODUCTION

Chapter VI describes specific evidence-based methods for managing cognitive load in verbal and pictorial information representations. According to the major forms of memory storage, there are verbal and pictorial representational modes, whereas according to major forms of sensory input, there are auditory and visual information modalities. The chapter will consider sources of cognitive load involving different modes and modalities of multimedia information presentations.

When learners process text and visuals that could not be understood in isolation, the process of integrating verbal and pictorial representations is required for comprehension. When text and pictures are not appropriately located close to each other or not synchronized in time, integrating these referring sources of information may increase working memory load and inhibit learning. Instructional design techniques dealing with such split attention situations may enhance learning. Reducing split-attention in paper-based and on-screen text and graphics was one of the first and most commonly mentioned applications of cognitive load theory. Using dual-mode presentations that involve different processing channels of human cognitive system is an alternative approach to dealing with split attention situations.

This chapter discusses means for coordinating verbal and pictorial sources of information in space and time, eliminating redundant components of presentations, segmenting instructional presentations in units that could be processed with less cognitive load, and other techniques. The chapter also describes interactions between instructional efficiency of different formats of multimedia presentations and levels of learner expertise in specific task domains.

COGNITIVE LOAD IN PICTORIAL REPRESENTATIONS

According to classical work of Larkin and Simon, (1987), an essential advantage of pictorial representations over verbal representations is their capability to provide a more direct access to information. More stimulus features may be represented by pictures in a more compact and cognitively economical and efficient way than by verbal formats. In contrast to verbal information that usually needs to be processed sequentially, visual information is relational in nature and its elements can be encoded simultaneously. According to some recent studies (e.g., Carlson, Chandler, & Sweller, 2003), pictorial representations may reduce cognitive load imposed by intrinsically complex materials (i.e., materials with high levels of element interactivity) compared to the written information. Thus pictorial representations may free required cognitive resources and allow students to redirect these resources to solving complex tasks.

This advantage of pictorial representation has been observed during learning as well as problem solving. For example, Goolkasian (2000) studied the effect of presentation formats on human reasoning processes and showed a consistent advantage of pictures. The advantage was considerable for the acquisition of the externally presented material, however it was much less pronounced when participants were reasoning from material stored in their memory. Problem solving and extracting information from pictured material was quicker than from verbally presented material.

Pictures may also facilitate learning and reasoning because they act as external memory aids that allow freeing up processing resources of working memory (Hegarty & Just. 1993). Together with dual channel processing hypothesis of cognitive theory of multimedia learning (Mayer, 2001) and modality effect of cognitive load theory (Tindall-Ford, Chandler, & Sweller, 1997), these ideas explain why both pictures and spoken words (especially when materials are presented across sensory modalities) have advantage over printed or on-screen words.

Some empirical studies have had difficulties with replicating all predictions of cognitive theory of multimedia learning (Brunken, Plass, & Leutner, 2004; Dutke & Rinck, 2006; Goolkasian, 2000; Lowe, 2003; Moreno & Duran, 2004; Schnotz & Bannert, 2003). The nature of the representations characteristic for different knowledge domains may be essential in predicting the differences in expected results. The studies of R. Mayer and his colleagues in cognitive theory of multimedia learning were conducted in science knowledge areas with well-defined and unambiguous depictive concrete representations for specific content. Others domains may not have accepted representational systems, or such representations could be less developed and ambiguous.

The pictorial representations may also vary from very abstract (e.g., a formulae representing a chemical structure) to concrete representations (e.g., car brake system or bike pump used in many studies of Mayer and his colleagues). Concrete representations show mostly inherent and relatively easily recognizable characteristics of reality. On the other side, when dealing with an unfamiliar abstract representational system, learners may experience difficulties and higher levels of cognitive load.

Therefore, the learner's prior knowledge of the abstract representational conventions is an important factor influencing learning from multimedia materials (Lowe, 2003). Acquiring prior knowledge of accepted representational systems and cultural conventions is essential for learning and performing in many domains (Kozma & Russel, 2005). In such domains, extraneous cognitive load could be reduced by using techniques developed within cognitive load theory if learners have prior knowledge of a specific representational system. Otherwise, the visual representations may in fact increase cognitive load and inhibit learning. For example, contrary to expectations based on the modality principle, providing narrated audio explanations to visual diagrams may increase cognitive load if learners do not have prior knowledge sufficient for understanding symbolic representational conventions used in the diagram (unless the explanations specifically address these conventions).

REDUCING SPLIT-ATTENTION IN ON-SCREEN TEXT AND GRAPHICS

When novice learners process text and visuals that could not be comprehended in isolation, they need to integrate mentally related components of verbal and pictorial representations. When text and pictures are not synchronized in space (e.g., separated at different locations on the screen) or time (presented after or before each other), cross-referencing of different representations may increase working memory load and inhibit learning. Physically integrating verbal and pictorial representations may eliminate or reduce this problem. This integration could be accomplished by directly embedding sections of onscreen text into the diagram in close proximity to relevant components of the diagram, or by presenting segments of narrated text simultaneously with the diagram or relevant animation frames (a split-attention effect, Chandler & Sweller, 1991; Sweller, Chandler, Tierney, & Cooper, 1990; Tarmizi & Sweller, 1988; or contiguity effect, Mayer & Anderson 1991; Mayer & Gallini, 1990).

The split-attention effect occurs when instructional material requires learners to split their attention unnecessarily between two or more sources of information. Physical integration of related sources of information that are separated over space or time decreases extraneous cognitive load by reducing search and co-referencing processes involved in conventional split source instructional formats. For example, in the case of instruction on using cutting speed nomograms in training technical apprentices to control cutting machinery, an illustration of the integrated instructional format is presented in Figure 11.

Mayer (1989) and Mayer & Gallini (1990) found that instructions consisting of separate text and unlabelled diagrams were less effective than diagrams that contained labels that clearly connected text and diagrams. The labeled diagrams could be considered as a form of physical integration of the diagram and text, as both techniques reduced the search processes. In fact, physically embedded printed textual narratives have been used successfully for long time in comics and cartoons for children thus demonstrating their effectiveness. However, until recently, this technique has rarely been used in general instructional design practice.

Studies by Mayer and Anderson (1991, 1992), Mayer and Sims (1994) on temporal contiguity principle in animated instructional presentations provide an example of a temporal split-attention effect. Animation and related narration were more effective when presented simultaneously rather than sequentially. The sequential presenta-

Figure 11. Integrated diagram-and-text format of instruction

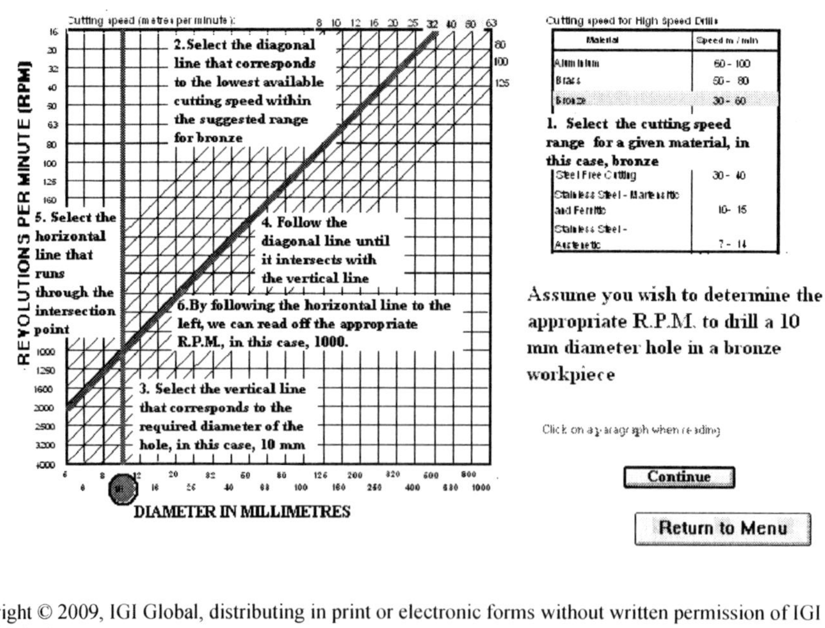

tion formats requires additional working memory resources for holding elements of pictorial representations until corresponding verbal explanations appear on the screen or, alternatively, keeping the verbal information in working memory until the corresponding animated pictures are displayed.

In pictorial representations, much of the needed information is presented at a single location and little search is required: each element is close to other related elements. When textual information is embedded into corresponding diagrams or presented concurrently in an auditory format, the advantages of pictorial representations effectively extend to the combined materials. However, the instructional benefits of diagrams may depend on learners' knowledge and expertise in a specific domain. Highly knowledgeable or high-ability learners may comprehend well both a textual segment alone and a diagram alone. Since switching between processing text and a diagram requires additional cognitive resources (even in the integrated format), these learners are able to reduce this cognitive load by switching less often and holding representations with fewer chunks in working memory due to available knowledge base (Hegarty & Just, 1989).

REDUCING COGNITIVE LOAD IN ONSCREEN OR PRINTED TEXT

A number of studies investigated relative effectiveness of different forms of textual-only representations of information for learners with different levels of expertise in a specific domain. McNamara, Kintsch, Songer, and Kintsch (1996) found that adding additional explanations to an instructional science text that were intended to increase text coherence were beneficial only for low-knowledge readers. High-knowledge readers benefited more from the original, minimally coherent textual format.

McNamara et al. (1996) explained their results based on the high-knowledge readers' more active engagement in the processing of the minimally coherent text format. However, these results could also be considered as an example of the expertise reversal effect within a cognitive load framework. In similar situations that were used in studies within the cognitive load framework (e.g., Kalyuga et al.,1998; Yeung, Jin, & Sweller, 1998), expert learners actually reported lower ratings of cognitive load in the minimal instructional formats as compared to formats with extended explanations. Such extended explanations clearly contained redundant for these learners information that required additional cognitive resources for its processing.

For example, Yeung et al. (1998) compared two instructional formats for incorporating definitions of unfamiliar words into textual materials. One was a traditional glossary placed at the end of the whole text. Another format integrated unfamiliar words' definitions into the space above the line of text directly above the defined word. According to cognitive load theory, traditional separate glossaries could produce a split-attention effect due to additional cognitive effort necessary for their processing. It includes locating the required definition in the glossary, comprehending and remembering this definition while finding the way back to the original word in the text being read.

Results of the experiments indicated that 5th Grade students (relative novice readers) learned better from the integrated definition format than from the traditional glossary format (as measured by comprehension scores). On the other hand, the university students (relative expert readers) demonstrated better comprehension scores with the separate glossary format. The results were explained by the increased cognitive load caused by the need for more knowledgeable student to process redundant for them information (as measured by the time students spent on referencing a definition). Thus, the use of integrated definitions could have a positive or negative effect on learning depending on levels of learner prior knowledge.

In another set of experiments, Yeung et al. (1998) compared the above two instructional format with 8th grade students. In one experiment, lower-ability students from remedial ESL classes were involved in the study. In another experiment, higher-ability students were selected for participation in the study. The same reversed pattern of results was obtained. Relative novices in the domain benefited from the integrated instruction, while more experienced learners achieved better results from the traditional, separate glossary format. In a replication study with 5th and 8th grades secondary school and university students, Yeung (1999) again compared the above two instructional formats of incorporating definitions of unfamiliar words into text. As expected, the comprehension scores indicated that novices learned better from the integrated definition format than from the traditional glossary format, and the university students demonstrated better comprehension with the separate glossary format.

MANAGING COGNITIVE LOAD IN DUAL-MODALITY (AUDIO-VISUAL) PRESENTATIONS

When textual information is presented in an auditory form, mental integration of this information with pictures may not overload working memory. In this situation, working memory capacity may be effectively increased by using combined resources of the visual and auditory channels of sensory and working memory that may exceed the processing capacity of a single channel. Such dual-modality presentations could be used to reduce extraneous cognitive load caused by split-attention. Mayer and his associates (see Mayer, 2001 for an overview) have conducted a number of controlled experimental studies that demonstrated the superiority of dual-modality instructions by comparing alternative instructional formats (see also Chapter II for a brief review of relevant studies).

For example, Mayer and Anderson (1991) compared an animation depicting the operation of a bicycle tire pump with simultaneous audio text; the audio text only without an animation; the animation only without audio text; and a control condition with no formal training. According to the post-training test results measuring the number of creative and detailed solutions on the problem-solving tasks, the first experimental condition produced the best results. Mayer & Anderson (1992) and Mayer & Sims (1994) compared simultaneous and sequential presentations of the related audio and visual information and demonstrated that dual-mode instructions were superior only when presented in the simultaneous form (the temporal contiguity effect).

Cognitive load measures were not used in the above experiments that were generated within the framework of cognitive theory of multimedia learning. Based on cognitive load theory, Tindall-Ford, Chandler, & Sweller (1997) predicted a modality effect based on the idea of extending effective working memory capacity. The prediction was empirically supported by experimental studies in training technical apprentices in the area of electrical engineering. Measures of cognitive load using subjective rating scales were collected in that series of experiments and corroborated the cognitive load-based hypothesis. Learning from dual-mode instructions (inspecting electrical wiring diagrams and listening to simultaneous auditory explanations) produced better post-test performance than equivalent single-mode presentations (wiring diagrams with printed textual explanations). Importantly, dual-mode instructions also imposed less cognitive load as reported by trainees themselves.

Dual-modality presentations often show superiority over alternative single-mode formats only when special means for attracting student attention to the relevant components of the diagram are used (cueing or signaling effect) (Jeung, Chandler, & Sweller, 1997; Mayer & Moreno, 2002; 2003). Even when learning from text-only presentations, results are better when the text includes cues (using headings, emphasizing or highlighting key information, etc.) about the organization of the material. With multimedia presentations, the effectiveness often depends on the availability of indicators of the most important components of presentations that are being currently explained verbally (e.g., by using flashing or highlighted elements).

For more experienced learners, some sources of information (text or visuals) may become redundant due to available knowledge base. When onscreen text is embedded into a diagram or narrated when the diagram is presented, it is not possible to avoid processing the redundant information and integrating it with available knowledge structures in long-term memory. These processes consume cognitive resources that become unavailable for constructing higher levels of knowledge. Eliminating redundant verbal or pictorial information could be the best design decision when dealing with more experienced learners. Thus, the effectiveness of different instructional formats may depend on levels of domain-specific expertise of the intended learners (in accordance with the expertise reversal effect).

R. Mayer and his associates studied learning from text and graphics with different text and illustration formats using learners with different levels of prior knowledge in specific domains. The experiments indicated that using graphics usually enhanced learning outcomes for students with low prior knowledge levels, but not those with higher prior knowledge levels. In his major review of the multimedia learning studies, Mayer (2001) called the effect an individual differences principle. It was attributed to the ability of high-knowledge learners to use their knowledge base to compensate for missing instructional guidance. Advantages of multimedia presentations disappeared with increases in learner levels of prior knowledge.

For example, Mayer and Gallini (1990) and Mayer, Steinhoff, Bower, and Mars (1995) demonstrated that spatially integrated instructional formats were more effective for low-knowledge learners rather than for high-knowledge learners. As learners' knowledge in a domain increases, positive learning effects of such formats disappeared. Kalyuga et al. (1998) found that more experienced technical apprentices learned new versions of a familiar class of wiring diagrams more effectively from the diagrams alone rather than from diagrams with integrated detailed explanations. Additional instructional explanations were redundant for these learners and generated extraneous cognitive load (as reported by learners' subjective ratings of cognitive load).

Using dual-modality presentations with narrated rather than on-screen text represents an excellent alternative to direct physical integration of text and diagrams due to an effective working memory capacity extension (Mayer, 1997; Mayer & Moreno, 1998; Mousavi, Low, & Sweller, 1995; Tindall-Ford, Chandler, & Sweller, 1997). For more knowledgeable learners, however, narrated explanations may become redundant and reduce learning effectiveness similar to physically embedded on-screen text..

For example, Kalyuga et al. (2000) trained technical apprentices in reading specific charts used to set up cutting machines. In dual-modality instructional presentations, when a button corresponding to a procedural step was clicked on, an auditory narration of an explanation of this step was delivered through headphones instead of being displayed as an identical visual text next to the diagram. Replacing on-screen textual explanations of procedural steps with corresponding narrated explanations was beneficial for novice learners (thus demonstrating a modality effect). Interactive diagram-only presentations (that provided student-controlled on-screen highlights of lines, numbers and other components of the chart) were the least effective for these inexperienced learners.

Following the initial learning phase, all learners went through a series of common intensive training sessions and became more experienced in the task domain. When they were trained again in more advanced types of charts using different experimental instructional formats, the advantage of auditory narrations disappeared. After more intensive training in the domain, an interactive diagram-only presentation format became more beneficial than the diagram with narrated explanations, with relatively less cognitive load imposed on learners as measured by subjective rating scales. The pattern of results in this set of experiments (Figure 12) is typical for many studies of the expertise reversal effect.

Another example of using dual-modality presentation formats for reducing cognitive load was provided in a recent study of After-Action Review (AAR) procedures in a computer-based collaborative problem solving environments (O'Neil &

Figure 12. An interaction between instructional designs and levels of learner expertise in Kalyuga, Chandler, & Sweller (2000): (a) Test performance scores; b) difficulty ratings

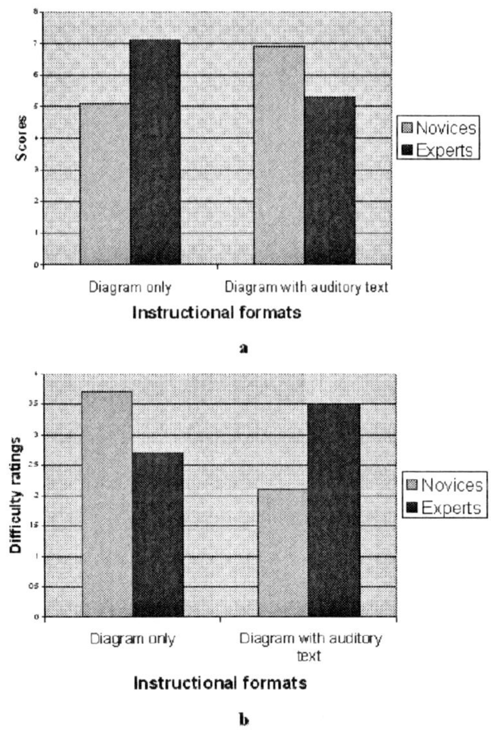

Chuang, 2007). The researchers proposed to present part of verbal feedback using auditory modality, so that visual channel and audio channel were both engaged in a complementary manner without being overloaded at any given time. The study compared the effect of this complementary audio plus visual text AAR with visual text only AAR on team performance in online searching and mapping tasks. The results indicated that the audio/visual text feedback significantly improved student content understanding and communication scores. Therefore, when providing extensive textual feedback, cognitive load could be reduced by presenting some parts of information in the audio channel.

MULTIMEDIA REDUNDANCY EFFECT

When auditory textual explanations of a diagram are presented concurrently with the same on-screen text, learners may need to mentally relate corresponding visual and auditory components of the explanations. Such cognitive activities may require additional working memory resources. Elimination of a redundant source of information may enhance learning in this situation. Kalyuga, Chandler, & Sweller (1999) compared three formats of multimedia instructions explaining how to read a diagram: 1) visual text only located next to the animated diagram; 2) auditory text only presented concurrently with the same animated diagram; and 3) simultaneously presented visual and auditory text together with the same animated diagram (see Figure 13 for a screenshot of visual components of the first and third presentation formats). The results demonstrated the advantage of using diagram with auditory text over the diagram with visual text (modality effect), but they also demonstrated that the auditory text only experimental condition outperformed visual plus auditory text group.

Thus, duplicating textual explanations using different modalities may actually inhibit learning. This is a case of a multimedia redundancy effect (redundancy effect in multimedia learning). Subjective ratings of cognitive load indicated that presenting on-screen textual explanations of the diagram together with the same auditory explanations actually imposed additional cognitive load. This effect often occurs during PowerPoint presentations when large amounts of textual information are presented on the screen and simultaneously narrated by the presenters. In this situation, audience needs to relate the on-screen explanations with the presenter's oral explanations (often also paying attention to additional graphical information presented on the screen). These processes may require excessive working memory resources that become unavailable for learning.

Using instructions on the formation of lighting storms, Mayer, Heiser, & Lonn (2001) demonstrated that learners who received narrations with concurrent

Figure 13. Snapshot of the visual-only format of instruction used in Kalyuga, Chandler, & Sweller (1999)

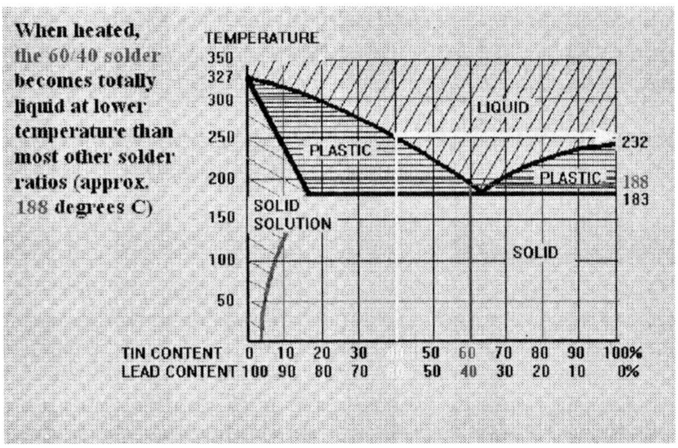

animations performed better on post-instruction retention and transfer tests than students who learned from animation with concurrent narration and on-screen text that summarized or duplicated the narration. Lower transfer performance was also demonstrated when interesting but irrelevant details were added to the narration, or interesting but irrelevant video clips were inserted during or before the presentation. The inserted irrelevant details may have activated inappropriate prior knowledge that unnecessarily consumed additional processing resources of working memory.

In a series of three experiments, Kalyuga, Chandler, and Sweller (2004) studied the effects of using the same on-screen and auditory textual information. In the first two experiments, a non-concurrent presentation of auditory and visual explanations of a diagram proved superior to a concurrent presentation of the same auditory and visual explanations. The effect was significant only when instruction time was limited. Simultaneous presentations overloaded working memory by the need to relate both modes resulting in neither mode being processed adequately (unrestricted instruction time might have partially compensated for the unavailable processing resources). In contrast, with sequential presentations, both modes were studies without overloading working memory. The second presentation was effectively used as a form of repetition facilitating the positive effects of the first presentation. Evidence for the cognitive load-related nature of the effect was provided by subjective rating scales. The concurrent presentation formats were subjectively perceived by the learners as more demanding than non-concurrent presentations.

These results were in line with previous studies of verbal redundancy in multimedia learning (Kalyuga, Chandler, & Sweller, 1999, 2000; Mayer, Heiser, & Lonn, 2001; Moreno & Mayer, 2002). When, in addition to the narrated explanations of animated diagrams, learners received simultaneous on-screen text containing the same explanations, the visual information channel might have become overloaded. The third experiment in Kalyuga et al. (2004) showed that, under similar conditions, a concurrent presentation of auditory and visual text without any diagrams present was also worse than auditory-only text (even though the influence of repeated presentations of the text and visual split attention was excluded in this experiment). However, Moreno and Mayer (2002) demonstrated that when no visual diagrams were involved, concurrent presentations of the same auditory and visual text produced better results than auditory-only text.

This difference in results could be due to the size of textual segments that were processed continuously without a break. In Kalyuga et al. (2004) study, the text was continuously presented to participants as a single large chunk (of around 350 words) from the beginning to the end without any breaks. The process of referencing, reconciling and integrating visual and auditory components of information might have imposed a heavy working memory load, thus inhibiting learning. This cognitive load could be reduced when the text is presented in several consecutive small segments with appropriate breaks between them. Such breaks may allow learners to consolidate partial mental models constructed from each segment of the text before moving to the next one. In fact, such text presentation formats were used in Moreno and Mayer (2002) experiments.

EMPIRICAL STUDY OF THE EFFECT OF SEGMENTATION ON MULTIMEDIA REDUNDANCY

According to the above assumption, the size of textual segments that are processed continuously without a break may influence the conditions of applicability of the multimedia redundancy effect. To test this assumption, an experiment was designed (Kalyuga, unpublished study) to investigate whether concurrent presentation of the same audio and visual text by small portions instead of one large uninterrupted chunk would improve learning outcomes (a segmentation effect).

On-screen textual explanations with concurrent auditory narration of the same text were presented in two formats: 1) as a single chunk continuously narrated from the beginning to the end; and 2) as a sequence of small portions of the text with time breaks between them. Participants were 20 undergraduate university students, native English language speakers without prior knowledge of the specific topic described in the text. The participants were randomly allocated to two groups corresponding to the two instructional formats that were delivered through a laptop computer. All participants were tested individually. Each participant spent about 10 min working at the computer.

The training materials were based on a section of text (344 words) about pre-stressed concrete adopted from a popular science and technology book. The text did not require any specialized prerequisite knowledge, although learners had to build a complex mental model to be able to understand the explanations and answer post-instruction test questions. Both formats contained identical narrations of the same sections of text presented via headphones. The same explanations were also visually presented on the screen when corresponding auditory explanations were delivered.

In the partitioned format, the text was divided into six segments. Each segment contained a logically completed part of the description. After a segment had been articulated and the corresponding visual text disappeared from the screen, learners were allowed a break of 10 seconds before the next segment appeared on the screen. It could be assumed that the break was used by learners to think over the last segment of the text. In the uninterrupted text format, learners were allowed 60 seconds at the end of the whole text presentations before the test phase started. Thus the total instruction time was identical for both groups. After studying the instructions, subjective ratings of task difficulty were collected from all participants electronically on the computer. A 7-point scale was used with participants being asked "*How easy or difficult was this text to understand?*" A cognitive load rating ranging from 1 (extremely easy) to 7 (extremely difficult) was collected for each participant.

Performance test consisted of a series of eight multiple-choice questions. The questions were directly concerned with the factors described in the instruction, and correct answers required understanding of relations between those factors. The following are examples of some questions: *Why is water added to cement? Why is it usually not recommended to continue construction next day after pouring wet concrete into a building foundation? Why are steel cables stretched when producing pre-stressed concrete?* Four alternatives were provided for each multiple-choice question. Up to 45 seconds were allowed for each of the eight questions with a clock provided on the screen to indicate remaining time. The responses to each multiple-choice item were electronically recorded, judged as either correct or incorrect, providing a score out of eight for each participant.

The independent variable in this study was the instructional format (uninterrupted or partitioned presentation of the text). The dependent variables were subjective ratings of mental effort, M=3.4, SD=.7 for the uninterrupted text, M=2.4, SD=1.0 for the partitioned text; test performance scores on multiple-choice items, M=5.0, SD=0.7 for the uninterrupted text, M=5.7, SD=1.0 for the partitioned text (maximum possible test score was 8); and instructional efficiency measures calculated using Paas & van Merriënboer (1993) formula, M=-0.65, SD=.74 for the uninterrupted text, M=.0.65, SD=1.15 for the partitioned text (actual range for instructional efficiency was from -1.89 to 1.99).

The statistical analysis indicated marginally significant differences for multiple-choice items, $t(18) = 1.91$, $p=0.07$; significant differences for subjective ratings of mental load, $t(18) = 2.65$, $p < .05$, and for instructional efficiency, $t(18) = 3.00$, $p < .01$. The instructional format based on the partitioned presentation of text was significantly more efficient than the uninterrupted text format. Effect size using pooled standard deviations was 0.80 for the multiple choice items, 1.03 for subjective ratings of mental load, and 1.13 for instructional efficiency. All these values are much larger than the 1/3 standard deviation commonly required for clinical significance in education.

Thus, as text was partitioned into logically completed segments (with time breaks between them), performance of the narration with concurrent visual text group improved. These results indicate that the size of the textual fragments processed without time breaks may significantly influence working memory load imposed by redundant verbal information. When text is presented by easily managed sequential portions with sufficient temporal breaks between them, a concurrent presentation of identical on-screen and auditory textual material might not cause deleterious effects on learning similar to those caused by an uninterrupted presentation of the same text as a whole unit.

As with other cognitive load effects, processing redundant multimedia information may overload working memory only when learners are dealing with intrinsically complex information. Uninterrupted presentations of long textual descriptions may definitely contribute to this complexity by forcing learners to relate and reconcile many elements of auditory and visual information within limited time scope. Segmenting the text may eliminate negative effects of verbal redundancy.

REDUCING VISUAL COGNITIVE LOAD IN INTERACTIVE DYNAMIC REPRESENTATIONS

Interactive dynamic representations are a special type of instructional visual representations, most commonly implemented as instructional simulations. Use of simulations in education (especially in science education) has increased significantly in recent years, however has not yet produced expected strong contributions to improving students' learning outcomes. Recent research suggests that although interactive visualizations in general can enhance learning under some conditions (Schnotz & Rasch, 2005; Tversky, Morrison, & Betrancourt, 2002), static visualizations may result in better learning outcomes under different conditions (Schnotz, Böckler, & Grzondziel, 1999). This section addresses the questions of why, under what conditions, and for whom are instructional simulations effective. The approach is based on the assumption that a major reason for lower than expected instructional effectiveness of simulations is that they are not always consistent with the nature of human cognitive architecture and limitations of our cognitive system.

Cognitive load theory provides a suitable theoretical framework for investigating cognitive conditions of instructional effectiveness of simulations, optimizing cognitive load imposed by visual representations in simulations and studying the impact of learner expertise. High levels of working memory load could be responsible for failures to demonstrate clear instructional advantages by many instructional simulations. One of the main factors that may contribute to cognitive load in interactive simulations is related to the representation of the content of the visual information and how well this representation supports relevant cognitive processes and assists in managing visual cognitive load. Representational formats for input parameters and levels of instructional guidance could be important factors that may differentially influence effectiveness of simulations for learners with various levels of prior knowledge in a task domain.

Complementing traditional symbolic (e.g., verbal and numerical) representational formats for input parameters used in instructional simulations with iconic (pictorial) versions may enhance instructional effectiveness of simulations, especially for novice learners. Iconic representations contain concrete graphics to represent the various elements of the physical environment (e.g. flames to represent temperature, weights to represent pressure, etc.). In another dimension, traditional exploratory-based simulations could be complemented by worked-out versions of simulations as a form of incorporating components of direct instructional guidance into simulated learning environments.

There is preliminary empirical data from studies that compared different formats of simulations for learning gas laws in high-school chemistry to support these assumptions (Kalyuga & Plass, 2007; Lee, Plass, & Homer, 2006; Plass, Homer, Milne, Jordan, & Kalyuga, 2006). Adding iconic representations to symbolic information in instructional simulations would obviously require some additional processing resources. On the other hand, such iconic representations would eliminate or reduce resources needed for interpreting and storing meanings of symbolic information in working memory, thus delivering overall cognitive benefits.

Figure 14 shows a fragment of a possible modification in the instructional simulation for exploring the relationships between main characteristics of an idealized gas by controlling pressure, volume, and the temperature of the gas by moving sliders (adapted from Kalyuga & Plass, 2007; Plass et al., 2007). In addition to the word "temperature" next to the slider (a symbolic representation of the concept of temperature), there is a representation of the temperature in the form of burners below the gas container that change in number as the value of the temperature changes. Pressure is represented in the form of weights that are displayed on top of the cylinder containing the gas, and volume is represented by the position of the indicator connected to the piston and volume slider. Buttons for fixing (locking) parameter values are also represented as locks in open (green) or closed (red) states. In the original non-modified symbolic-only version, all these iconic representations were absent and locking facilities were depicted as simple radio-buttons.

The burners, weights, and the size of the container below the piston are directly associated with temperature, pressure, and volume respectively. Although adding iconic representations would lead to a visually more complex display, it is nevertheless can induce less extraneous load because the added representations externally represent information that the learner would otherwise have to hold internally in her/his working memory. Therefore, a display with a higher visual complexity and

Figure 14. Modified version of visual representations in a gas laws simulation. Adapted from Kalyuga & Plass (2007); Plass, Homer, Milne, Jordan, & Kalyuga (2006).

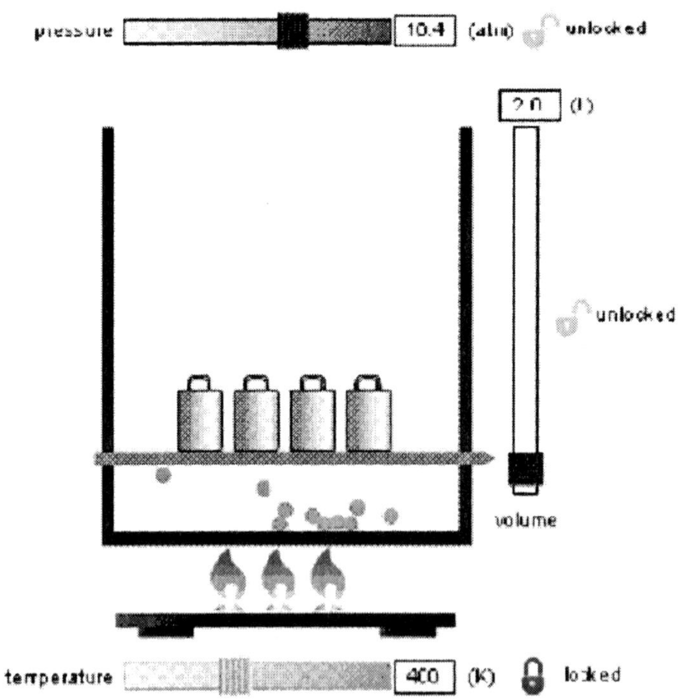

additional representations could be less difficult to understand than one with a lower complexity because the added information enables learners to better relate the new information to their prior knowledge.

Lee, Plass, & Homer (2006) investigated an interaction between two different modes of visual representations in the gas law simulation for middle-school chemistry students and different levels of learners' prior science knowledge. Essential gas characteristics were presented either in a traditional symbolic form only, or by adding iconic information to the symbolic representations. The study indicated that whereas low prior knowledge learner benefited more from added iconic representations than from symbolic format only (effect size 1.59), high prior knowledge learners benefited more from symbolic only representations than from added iconic ones (effect size 1.27).

It is likely that iconic representations were redundant for these learners and could interfere with their knowledge-based cognitive processes. It should be noted that the expertise reversal effect was observed only with materials that had manageable levels of intrinsic cognitive load, at least for more knowledgeable learners (for example, simulations that considered only two parameters at a time). For high complexity materials with excessive levels of intrinsic cognitive load for all participants (for example, simulations in which all three parameters were considered simultaneously), iconic representations were beneficial for all learners.

Thus, the level of learner prior knowledge in a domain is an important factor that contributes to cognitive load effects in interactive simulations. In accordance with the expertise reversal effect, the suggested iconic additions to simulations may be effective for novice learners, but could become less effective as learner levels of expertise increase. A number of studies in individual differences in learning from text and visual displays (e.g., Hegarty & Just, 1989; Lowe, 1993; Schnotz, 2002; Schnotz, Picard, & Hron, 1993) have also demonstrated that the instructional advantages of diagrams depend on student domain-specific knowledge and experience. Less knowledgeable learners may have difficulty in inferring meaning from purely symbolic representations because the limited capacity of their working memory.

As described in Chapter I, acquiring sufficient prior knowledge base in a specific task domain could reduce working memory overload associated with cognitive processing of presented information and thus enhance learning. As experience in the domain increases, limited duration and capacity of working memory could become less important because many relevant schematic representations may already be held in long-term memory. The available knowledge structures may require integration with displayed (and now redundant for these more knowledgeable learners) graphics thus imposing an extraneous cognitive load for more experienced learners and eliminating or even reversing a positive learning effect.

EMPIRICAL INVESTIGATION OF COGNITIVE LOAD IN INSTRUCTIONAL SIMULATIONS

As discussed in the previous section, learners with lower levels of prior knowledge in a task domain are expected to benefit more from simulations with added iconic representations of visual information than from symbolic-only representations, but there may be no differences between formats for learners with higher levels of prior knowledge. A series of studies was conducted to test these assumptions in school computer labs during regular class hours in intact classes (Kalyuga & Plass, 2007). All simulations were designed using Macromedia Flash software and delivered online through desktop PCs.

Thirty 11-12 grades students from high school science classes participated in the study. Pre-test scores indicated that participants' prior knowledge of gas laws area of chemistry was low (mean total score 4.45 out of 16). Instructional materials included two versions of a simulation: (1) simulation with symbolic-only representations of input parameters; (2) simulations with added iconic representations for temperature, pressure, and volume (see Figure 13 for a fragment of instructional presentation with added iconic components). The experimental procedure included an initial pre-test of learners' knowledge, an instructional session, and a final post-test.

Pre-test of prior knowledge consisted of 9 items. Three short-answer questions tested general knowledge of situations that involve gas features. Prior knowledge of relations between gas characteristics was assessed using 6 multiple-choice questions. At the *instructional phase*, students were instructed to manipulate the temperature, volume, and pressure of the gas, and observe the resulting change of the other properties of the gas. Before they started to explore the simulation, students had been advised to do some exercises with changing different variables by moving sliders.

General guidelines for exploring the system were also provided. For example, when exploring a system with many variables, a good strategy is to change only one variable to observe its effects on another variable. Students were advised to lock one of the variables and explore how changing one of the remaining variable would affect the other unlocked variable. For example, exploring the following questions was suggested: *How the gas pressure changes when you change the volume with constant temperature? How will it change if you double the volume?* In both versions of the simulation, students were advised to take all the time they needed to study the material and not proceed to the test before they had explored the simulations thoroughly.

Post-test included 16 items. 10 multiple-choice questions composed a comprehension test which included 2 questions on knowledge of basics of kinetic theory, 3 questions on qualitative relations between pressure, volume, and temperature, 3 questions on quantitative relationships, and 2 questions that tested knowledge of graphical representations of relationships. Transfer test consisted of 6 short-answer questions that required explaining different phenomena and real life situations using the learned gas laws. Two of these were questions on applying knowledge to explain real-life phenomena, 2 questions required applying knowledge to predict phenomena, and 2 questions required applying knowledge to suggest solutions to some real-life problems.

In both pre- and post-tests, scoring procedures for multiple-choice questions allocated a score 1 for a correct answer; short-answer questions were scored independently by two graders according to the specified scales (for most questions, the scores were 0 for no answer or completely incorrect answer, 1 for some elements of a correct answer indicated, 2 for most elements of a correct answer indicated, and 3 for a complete correct answer).

The independent variable was the type of representation of visual information (iconic vs. symbolic). The dependent variables under analysis were differences between the final and initial test z-scores (calculated separately for multiple-choice and short-answer scores) as indicators of the relative gains in learners' knowledge due to the instructional session. Because pre- and post- tests were structurally different, standardized z-scores were used as indicators of students' relative standing and changes in performance (Table 1).

Although there were no statistically significant differences between the treatments, the effect size of 0.29 (using a pooled standard deviation value) for the short-answer questions indicated a possible small-to-medium effect favoring the iconic format

Table 1. Means and standard deviations for less and more knowledgeable learners

	Less knowledgeable learners		More knowledgeable learners	
	symbolic N=15	iconic N=15	symbolic N=35	iconic N=27
short answers				
M	-.10	.15	.06	-.08
SD	1.55	.97	.93	1.24
multiple-choice				
M	.09	.00	-.02	.02
SD	1.17	1.09	.92	.78

over the symbolic format for transfer tasks. Thus, adding iconic representations to simulations could have possible positive effect on transfer performance for novice learners.

The second study was conducted with relatively more knowledgeable learners (pre-test mean total score 8.03 out of 16). Sixty two 11-12 grades (age range 16-18) students participated in this study. By the time of the experiment, students had studied some material related to gas laws and, therefore, were relatively more knowledgeable in the topic. The experimental procedure was identical to that used in the previous study. Results indicated that there were no significant differences between the treatments. For short-answer questions, results showed a possible reversed tendency for means (effect size .14) to that obtained in the previous study: iconic group performed relatively worse than symbolic group. These results provide preliminary empirical evidence that adding iconic representations do not seem to influence performance scores for relatively more knowledgeable learners (with a possible reversed tendency for transfer tasks).

FUTURE TRENDS IN THE DESIGN OF AUDIOVISUAL MULTIMEDIA PRESENTATIONS

With the explosion of multimedia images, digital video, and hypermedia systems, together with the advances in networks and information technology, the impact of multimedia on our life increases dramatically. From personal multimedia mobile devices to multimedia information technologies in business, education, healthcare and other areas of human activity, multimedia changes the way learners interact with information.

The design of adaptive multimedia interfaces need to focus on how to make the interaction between information and learners smarter based on knowledge of human cognitive processes. Intelligent interfaces need to have the capability to adapt to the learner cognitive characteristics, to provide appropriate feedback, personalized interaction and intelligent visualization of information. Taking into account levels of learner prior knowledge in specific task areas should be an essential requirement in designing adaptive audiovisual multimedia presentations.

Adaptive graphics design that is based on understanding of individual learner cognitive capabilities may enhance learning by providing appropriate external or distributed representations of information. Such representations need to be sensitive to the real-time cognitive demands of learning in the context of the available cognitive resources, and adapt the form of the presentation according to the individual levels of task-specific expertise and experience with the system.

MULTIMEDIA INSTRUCTIONAL DESIGN IMPLICATIONS

Several major instructional design principles could be derived from the reviewed studies of cognitive load effects in audiovisual multimedia learning environments:

- Presenting the same information simultaneously in different modalities may cause cognitive overload
- When using audio narration to explain graphics or animations, do not duplicate the same explanations as on-screen text
- Verbal explanations could be duplicated when learners need time to process text (e.g., second language learning) and the text is segmented into small sections.

Many computer display design principles are, in effect, mirror the above cognitive load implications. For example, the proximity compatibility principle states that when two or more sources of information must be mentally integrated to complete the task, parts of the information should be displayed close together. The principle of multiple resources recommends designing information display using different modalities, e.g., audition and vision (Wickens, Lee, Liu, & Gordon-Becker, 2003).

SUMMARY OF CHAPTER VI

Learning processes are usually facilitated when the text is accompanied by pictures. Pictures and diagrams are more efficient information representations than text because they provide a more efficient form of organizing this information by indexing it by location (Larkin & Simon, 1987). Much of the needed information is conveniently (and cognitively efficiently) presented at a single location. Little search is required since each element may be located beside any number of other elements. Integrating verbal explanations into pictorial representations or using dual-modality presentations could effectively extend these benefits of pictures to combined verbal-pictorial formats. However, the instructional benefits of diagrams as well as integrated formats depend on student knowledge and expertise in a specific task domain. More experienced learners may benefit most from single-modality, pictorial-only or verbal-only, representations.

When auditory textual explanations of a diagram are presented concurrently with the same on-screen text, learners may need to mentally relate corresponding visual and auditory components of instruction. Such cognitive activities may require additional working memory resources. Duplicating textual explanations using different modalities may actually inhibit learning (redundancy effect in multimedia learning). Elimination of a redundant source of information may enhance learning in this situation.

As was the case with other cognitive load effects, processing redundant information may overload working memory only when learners are dealing with intrinsically complex information (i.e., materials with high levels of element interactivity). When processing uninterrupted presentation of long textual descriptions, learners may be forced to relate and reconcile many elements of auditory and visual information within limited time scope. Segmenting the text may eliminate negative effects of verbal redundancy.

High levels of working memory load could be responsible for failures to demonstrate clear instructional advantages of many interactive dynamic visual representations (such as instructional simulations). Representational formats for input parameters could be important factors that differentially influence effectiveness of instructional simulations for learners with different levels of prior knowledge. There has been preliminary empirical evidence indicating that learners with lower levels of prior knowledge may benefit more from simulations with added iconic representations of information than from traditional symbolic-only (verbal and numerical) representations. On the other hand, there may be no differences between formats for learners with higher levels of prior knowledge. The following chapter will continue describing means of managing cognitive load in interactive multimedia learning environments.

REFERENCES

Brünken, R., Plass, J. L., & Leutner, D. (2004). Assessment of cognitive load in multimedia learning with dual-task methodology: Auditory load and modality effects. *Instructional Science, 32, 115*-132.

Carlson, R., Chandler, P., & Sweller, J. (2003). Learning and understanding science instructional material. *Journal of Educational Psychology, 95*, 629-640.

Chandler, P., & Sweller, J. (1991). Cognitive load theory and the format of instruction. *Cognition and Instruction, 8,* 293-332.

Dutke, S., & Rinck, M. (2006). Multimedia learning: Working memory and the learning of word and picture diagrams. *Learning and Instruction, 16*, 526-537.

Goolkasian, P. (2000). Pictures, words, and sounds: ·From which format are we best able to reason? *The Journal of General Psychology, 127,* 439-459.

Hegarty, M., & Just, M. A. (1989). Understanding machines from text and diagrams. In H. Mandl & J. Levin (Eds.), *Knowledge acquisition from text and picture* (pp. 171-194). Amsterdam: North Holland.

Hegarty, M., & Just, M. A. (1993). Constructing mental models of machines from text and diagrams. *Journal of Memory and Language, 32*, 717-742.

Jeung, H., Chandler, P., & Sweller, J. (1997). The role of visual indicators in dual sensory mode instruction. *Educational Psychology, 17*, 329-343.

Kalyuga, S., Chandler, P., & Sweller, J. (1998). Levels of expertise and instructional design. *Human Factors, 40*, 1-17.

Kalyuga, S., Chandler, P., & Sweller, J. (1999). Managing split-attention and redundancy in multimedia instruction. *Applied Cognitive Psychology, 13*, 351-371.

Kalyuga, S., Chandler, P., & Sweller, J. (2000). Incorporating learner experience into the design of multimedia instruction. *Journal of Educational Psychology, 92*, 126-136

Kalyuga, S., Chandler, P., & Sweller, J. (2004). Effects of redundant on-screen text in multimedia technical instruction. *Human Factors, 46*, 567-581.

Kalyuga, S., & Plass, J. (2007). Managing cognitive load in instructional simulations. In M. B. Nunes & M. McPherson (Eds.), Proceedings of the IADIS International Conference E-Learning 2007, July 6-8, 2007, Lisbon, Portugal (Volume 1, pp. 27-34). International Association for Development of the Information Society (IADIS) Press.

Larkin, J. H., & Simon, H. A. (1987). Why a diagram is (sometimes) worth ten thousand words. *Cognitive Science, 11*, 65-99.

Lee, H., Plass, J.L., & Homer, B.D. (2006). Optimizing cognitive load for learning from computer-based science simulations. *Journal of Educational Psychology, 98*, 902-913.

Lowe, R.K. (1993). Constructing a mental representation from an abstract technical diagram. *Learning and Instruction, 3*, 157-179.

Lowe, R.K. (2003). Animation and learning: Selective processing of information in dynamic graphics. *Learning and Instruction. 13*, 157-176.

Mayer, R. E. (1989). Systematic thinking fostered by illustrations in scientific text. *Journal of Educational Psychology, 81*, 240-246.

Mayer, R.E. (1997). Multimedia learning: Are we asking the right questions? *Educational Psychologist, 32*, 1-19.

Mayer, R. E. (2001). *Multimedia learning.* Cambridge, MA: Cambridge University Press.

Mayer, R., & Anderson, R. (1991). Animations need narrations: An experimental test of a dual-coding hypothesis. *Journal of Educational Psychology, 83*, 484-490.

Mayer, R., & Anderson, R. (1992). The instructive animation: Helping students build connections between words and pictures in multimedia learning. *Journal of Educational Psychology, 84*, 444-452.

Mayer, R., & Gallini, J. (1990). When is an illustration worth ten thousand words? *Journal of Educational Psychology, 82,* 715-726.

Mayer R. E., Heiser, J., & Lonn, S. (2001). Cognitive constraints on multimedia learning: When presenting more material results in less understanding. *Journal of Educational Psychology, 93,* 187-198.

Mayer, R. E., & Moreno, R. (1998). A split-attention effect in multimedia learning: Evidence for dual processing systems in working memory. *Journal of Educational Psychology, 90*, 312–320.

Mayer, R. E., & Moreno, R., (2002). Animation as an aid to multimedia learning. *Educational Psychology Review, 14*, 87–99.

Mayer, R. E., & Moreno, R. (2003). Nine ways to reduce cognitive load in multimedia learning. *Educational Psychologist, 38*, 43–53.

Mayer, R. E., & Sims, V. K. (1994). For whom is a picture worth a thousand words? Extensions of a dual-coding theory of multimedia learning. *Journal of Educational Psychology, 86*, 389-401.

Mayer, R. E., Steinhoff, K., Bower, G., & Mars, R. (1995). A generative theory of textbook design: Using annotated illustrations to foster meaningful learning of science text. *Educational Technology Research and Development, 43*, 31-43.

McNamara, D., Kintsch, E., Songer, N.B., & Kintsch, W. (1996). Are good texts always better? Interactions of text coherence, background knowledge, and levels of understanding in learning from text. *Cognition and Instruction, 14*, 1-43.

Moreno, R., & Durán, R. (2004). Do multiple representations need explanations? The role of verbal guidance and individual differences in multimedia mathematics learning. *Journal of Educational Psychology, 96*(3), 492-503.

Moreno, R., & Mayer, R. E. (2002). Verbal redundancy in multimedia learning: When reading helps listening. *Journal of Educational Psychology, 94*, 156-163.

Mousavi, S. Y., Low, R., & Sweller, J. (1995). Reducing cognitive load by mixing auditory and visual presentation modes. *Journal of Educational Psychology, 87*, 319-334.

O'Neil, H. F., & Chuang, S. S. (2007). An Audio/Text After-Action Review in a Computer-Based Collaborative Problem Solving Task. National Center for Research on Evaluation, Standards, and Student Testing (CRESST), University of California, Los Angeles.

Paas, F., & van Merriënboer, J. J. G. (1993). The efficiency of instructional conditions: An approach to combine mental-effort and performance measures. *Human Factors, 35*, 737-743.

Plass, J., Homer, B., Milne, C., Jordan, T., & Kalyuga, S. (2006). Molecules and Minds: Optimizing Cognitive Load in Simulations for Science Education. Paper presented at *the 2006 Research Conference of the Institute of Educational Sciences (IES), US Department of Education,* 15 – 16 June, 2006, Washington, DC.

Schnotz, W. (2002). Towards an integrated view of learning from text and visual displays. *Educational Psychology Review, 14*, 101-120.

Schnotz, W., & Bannert, M. (2003). Construction and interference in learning from multiple representation. *Learning and Instruction, 13*, 141-156.

Schnotz, W., Böckler, J., & Grzondziel, H. (1999). Individual and co-operative learning with interactive animated pictures. *European Journal of Psychology of Education, 14*, 245-265.

Schnotz, W., Picard, E., & Hron, A. (1993). How do successful and unsuccessful learners use text and graphics? *Learning and Instruction, 3,* 181-199.

Schnotz, W., & Rasch, T. (2005). Enabling, facilitating, and inhibiting effects of animations in multimedia learning: Why reduction of cognitive load can have negative results on learning. *Educational Technology Research and Development, 53*, 47-58.

Sweller, J., Chandler, P., Tierney, P., & Cooper, M. (1990). Cognitive load and selective attention as factors in the structuring of technical material. *Journal of Experimental Psychology: General, 119,* 176-192.

Tarmizi, R., & Sweller, J. (1988). Guidance during mathematical problem solving. *Journal of Educational Psychology, 80*, 424-436.

Tindall-Ford, S., Chandler, P., & Sweller, J. (1997). When two sensory modes are better than one. *Journal of Experimental Psychology: Applied, 3(4)*, 257-287.

Tversky, B., Morrison, J.B., & Betrancourt, M. (2002). Animation: Can it facilitate? *International Journal of Human Computer Studies, 57*, 247-262

VanLehn, K., Graesser, A. C., Jackson, G. T., Jordan, P., Olney, A., & Rose, C. P. (2007). When are tutorial dialogues more effective than reading? *Cognitive Science, 31*, 3-62.

Wickens, C.D., Lee, J., Liu, Y., & Gordon-Becker, S.E. (2003) *An Introduction to Human Factors Engineering* (2nd ed.) Upper Saddle Hill, N.J.: Prentice Hall.

Yeung, A. S., Jin, P., & Sweller, J. (1998). Cognitive load and learner expertise: Split attention and redundancy effects in reading with explanatory notes. *Contemporary Educational Psychology, 23,* 1-21.

Yeung, A. S. (1999). Cognitive load and learner expertise: split attention and redundancy effects in reading comprehension tasks with vocabulary definitions. *Journal of Experimental Education, 67,* 197-221.

Chapter VII
Managing Cognitive Load in Interactive Multimedia

INTRODUCTION

Most sophisticated multimedia learning environments include various interactivity features. Interactive multimedia learning environments respond dynamically to learner specific actions. Such environments support active, learner-engaged forms of learning that are expected to promote deep cognitive processes and result in active construction and acquisition of new knowledge.

Spector, Christensen, Sioutine, and McCormack (2001) noted that interactivity is the most critical feature of technology-enhanced learning environments. They summarized the relevant conclusions addressed in the research literature in this area as follows:

1. "Doing goes hand-in-hand with learning: learners learn what they do.
2. As learning environments provide more and more opportunities for active learner participation, they tend to promote learning; too many opportunities for interaction, however, can lead to confusion and disorientation.
3. Cognitive engagement with the subject material is vital for learning.
4. Opportunities for reflection generally improve learning.
5. Informative feedback is a necessary part of meaningful cognitive engagement; advanced learners may be able to generate their own feedback (a metacognitive skill)" (p. 522).

Hypermedia learning environments represent an online form of interactive multimedia. Hypermedia environments usually involve multiple representations, hyperlinked information networks, and high levels of learner control. In typical hypermedia environments, learner control may include content control, sequencing of information, and the control of representational formats. Research on instructional effectiveness of such environments has produced rather ambiguous results (Chen & Rada, 1996; Dillon & Gabbard, 1998).

Usually interactive (including hypermedia) learning environments are designed by professional computer programmers without applying relevant instructional design guidelines. General cognitively-based design guidelines for such environments could be derived from cognitive theories of multimedia learning and cognitive load theory (e.g., see Mayer, 2005 for a recent comprehensive overview of the field). However, as noted by Scheiter, Gerjets, Vollmann, and Catrambone (2007), these instructional theories have explicitly addressed mostly system-controlled learning environments. In such environments, information is presented to learners in the same predefined order that cannot be skipped and learners cannot choose from different representational formats. On the other hand, different levels of learner prior knowledge have been noted for long time as an important factor influencing the effectiveness of learning in interactive environments (Gay, 1986).

From a cognitive load point of view, observed learner physical activity within an interactive environment may not necessarily result in essential cognitive processes and effective (if any) learning. Instead, it may impose additional processing demands on learner limited cognitive resources and thus hinder learning. Mixed results from research on effectiveness of interactivity and learner control in instruction support this concern. Analyses of associated cognitive processes and structures are required to understand the role of interactivity in learning.

High levels of cognitive load in interactive learning environments could be caused by the large number of variables involved in corresponding cognitive processes; uncertainty and non-linear relationships between these variables; and associated temporal delays. In many situations, individual learners carry the burden of deciding when to use additional learning support (if available) and what forms of support to request. While more advanced learners could handle such a burden, it may be beyond cognitive resources available to less experienced learners.

Thus, a cognitive load framework is potentially capable of providing a suitable conceptualization for the analysis of the conditions and the development of methods for enhancing instructional efficiency of interactive multimedia learning environments. The cognitive load aspects of learning in interactive multimedia learning environments are the main focus of this chapter.

INTERACTIVE LEARNING ENVIRONMENTS

Before considering how the available means for managing cognitive load may apply to interactive learning environments, a suitable classification scheme for such environments needs to be established. The main defining feature of interactive learning environments is their responsiveness to learners' actions. Another dimension that is important for distinguishing between different interactive learning environments is related to the concept of learner control (Kalyuga, 2007).

While most sophisticated interactive systems usually allow some level of learner control, this is not a defining feature of interactive environments. For example, there are simple interactive environments that may not allow a learner control, e.g., fully system-controlled environments that respond by providing automatic feedback on all learners' entries. Even relatively complex interactive learning environments could be entirely system-controlled, for example, adaptive tutoring systems that automatically tailor instructional procedures and formats of information presentation to learner responses. On the other hand, all learner-controlled environments are interactive ones, since they always respond to the learners' actions, at least in regard to the controlled parameters. Therefore, the level of learner control represents an important feature or dimension of an interactive learning environment.

In general, the learner control could be exercised over different aspects of information processing. It is possible to distinguish between learner control over information delivery means, forms of information representations, and the content of information. The information delivery control may include pacing (changing the rate of delivery) and sequencing (changing the order of delivery). The control over representational forms includes the ability to select different forms of presentation (e.g., modality and dynamics of presentations, angles of viewing, visual cues). The control of content ranges from selecting the amount of presented information (e.g., simple vs extended feedback, hints, or help), segmenting information into suitably sized units (e.g., zooming in or out), to actually selecting the units or elements of information to be learned (e.g., navigational control, selecting content from a menu, etc.).

Since the defining feature of interactive environments is their responsiveness, they could be classified based on different types of responses to learner activities. Two important dimensions for describing such responses are their flexibility and dependence on learner previous activities. Accordingly, the environmental responses could be 1) fixed (predetermined) and independent of the history of learner previous behavior; 2) flexible (variable) and independent of the history of learner previous behavior; 3) adapted or tailored to the history of learner previous behavior with a fixed set of options; and 4) dynamic and iteratively tailored to the history of learner previous behavior with a flexible set of options (Table 2).

Table 2. Main characteristics and levels of interactivity

		Flexibility of responses	
		Fixed	Variable
Dependence on learner previous activities	Independent of previous behavior	*Feedback level*	*Manipulation level*
	Dependent on previous behavior	*Adaptation level*	*Communication level*

The lowest level, the feedback level of interactivity, is associated with providing a pre-defined feedback on specific learners' actions (solution steps, questions, local search queries, answers, etc.). The feedback could be immediate or delayed; simple, corrective (e.g., "correct" or "incorrect") or extended, explanatory (e.g., principle-based explanations, word references, glossaries, etc.); with or without a learner control (e.g., an automatic feedback or feedback on demand). These features could be grouped in a range of different combinations from simple automatic feedback to extended on-demand feedback.

The next level of interactivity, the manipulation level, involves real-time on-line change or transformation of information in response to learners' actions. The manipulation level provides flexible, variable responses, although not tailored to the learner previous behavior. This level of interactivity may involve different degrees of learner control (e.g., moving objects by using a click-and-drag technique, rotating an object, manipulating a simulation by entering specific values for input parameters, selecting answer options for web search queries etc.), although it could also be fully system-controlled, for example, worked-out simulations or dynamic visualizations (animation, rotation, etc.) that demonstrate the process to the learner as responses to her/his actions.

Another level, the adaptation level of interactivity, involves responses that are tailored to the learner previous behavior, even though they are selected from a fixed pool of options. Adaptive interactive e-learning environments dynamically tailor the real-time selection of learning tasks, instructional procedures and formats based on the information about learner current and past actions and online behavior. As other levels, adaptive interactive environments could be either system-controlled (automatic adaptation) or learner-controlled (for example, advisory systems that suggest possible options for learners to select from). This level is actually the main focus of this book.

Finally, the top level, the communication level of interactivity, is represented by dynamic online learning environments that involve flexible, non-predetermined responses to learners live queries that may be refined in an iterative process. This level may include features of the previous levels, for example, dynamic feedback, manipulation, real-time personalized task selection and information tailoring. Examples of this level of interactivity are online prompting for and submitting self-explanations or predictions for next procedural steps. This level of interactivity could be implemented using online communication channels between learners and between learners and instructors.

Complex interactive multimedia learning environments usually include several (or even all) of the above levels of interactivity. In such environments, students can also exercise different levels of control up to the full control of the content. For example, intelligent cognitive tutors (Anderson, Corbett, Koedinger, & Pelletier, 1995) are sophisticated interactive learning environments that involve different types of feedback and hints on each problem solution step, as well as adaptive procedures for task selection based on student problem-solving performance. Feedback and hints could be either requested on-demand or system-generated, and sequenced with a gradual increase in the level of provided details.

COGNITIVE LOAD IN INTERACTIVE LEARNING ENVIRONMENTS

Interactivity features implemented in multimedia learning environments may both go along and against essential characteristics of human cognitive architecture. The process of managing cognitive load in such environments is aimed at making such features work in the right direction, i.e. using interactivity features as a means of optimizing cognitive load. Different types of interactivity provide means for managing various sources of cognitive load.

The feedback level of interactivity may assist in balancing the executive function between knowledge-based and instruction-provided guidance. Koedinger and Aleven (2007) refer to this guidance-balancing problem as the assistance dilemma. According to the feedback principle (Moreno & Mayer, 2007), novice learners learn better with explanatory rather than with only simple corrective feedback. Within a cognitive load framework, the explanatory feedback is capable of providing external instructional guidance in place of missing internal long-term memory structures. A similar general conclusion about the usefulness of extended feedback provided in response to learner problem-solving errors is supported by research involving cognitive tutors (Koedinger & Aleven, 2007).

With lower levels of learner control (e.g., no control or delivery level control – pacing and sequencing), it is only possible to provide external guidance retroactively in response to certain learner actions or on demand. To balance the guidance more flexibly by providing or withdrawing information as levels of learner expertise in a task domain change, higher levels of learner control (e.g., control of representation formats or content) are required. For example, learners could be allowed to limit the representational format to pictorial-only mode. This may eliminate redundant verbal explanations that could otherwise overload limited WM processing capacity for more experienced learners. However, relying on learners' own decisions in selecting external guidance on-demand (feedback, hints, etc.) may not necessarily be more effective that using a system-controlled provision of guidance (Koedinger & Aleven, 2007), especially for novice learners. For example, system-controlled worked-out animated procedures (a manipulation level of interactivity) may provide effective external guidance for learners with lower levels of prior knowledge.

Adaptation level of interactivity could be effectively used for balancing executive guidance as well as the rate of information presentation. By adapting instructional procedures and techniques to levels of learner task-specific expertise, an optimal level of instructional guidance could be provided at each level of expertise. For example, fully worked-out procedures or direct guidelines could be provided to novice learners at the initial stages of the skill acquisition process to facilitate construction of new knowledge. In adaptive interactive environments, as learners acquire more experience in a specific task domain, detailed explanations are gradually taken away and a relative share of problem-solving practice or exploration is increased. For instance, worked examples could be gradually faded and replaced with completion tasks that require completing remaining steps of the procedure (Atkinson & Renkl, 2007; Renkl & Atkinson, 2003). As learners reach higher levels of task-specific expertise, problem-solving practice or exploratory learning environments could be used to learn relatively new procedures in this task domain. When used with low-knowledge learners, such environments need to be supplemented with appropriate scaffolding to provide sufficient instructional guidance.

Interactive exploratory learning environments could be very cognitively demanding for novice learners because of a heavy working memory load. Such environments may generate a cognitive overload for novice learners and thus result in poor learning outcomes. Using a sequence of worked examples together with structurally similar problem solving practice may reduce this source of cognitive overload. However, as learner experience in a domain increases, processing a redundant worked example and integrating it with previously learned schematic knowledge structures may generate a higher cognitive load than learning in an interactive exploratory environment. For more advanced learners, such interactive exploratory practice may facilitate further schema refinement and automation.

For example, Kalyuga, Chandler, Tuovinen, and Sweller (2001) demonstrated that as learners became more experience in a specific technical domain (writing simple programmable logic controller code for relay circuits of different levels of complexity), the superiority of learning worked-out procedures disappeared. In the interactive problem-solving learning environment, learners were required to compose a program for the displayed circuits by dragging provided separate components of the program into appropriate positions in the program table and then check the correctness of his program by clicking on a "Check" button. In the worked examples condition, all steps in programming corresponding circuits were presented. As learner expertise in the domain increased, the relative improvement in performance of the problem-solving group was superior to the worked example group.

Kalyuga, Chandler, and Sweller (2001) compared direct (worked example-based) instruction with an interactive exploratory learning environment on constructing switching equations for relay circuits. In the exploratory environment, an interactive screen-based template allowed learners to construct different circuits by clicking on thin contour lines and symbols of input elements. After a suitable circuit had been constructed, the learners were asked to write a switching equation for this circuit (Figure 15).

Figure 15. A problem based on a circuit constructed with the interactive screen-based template

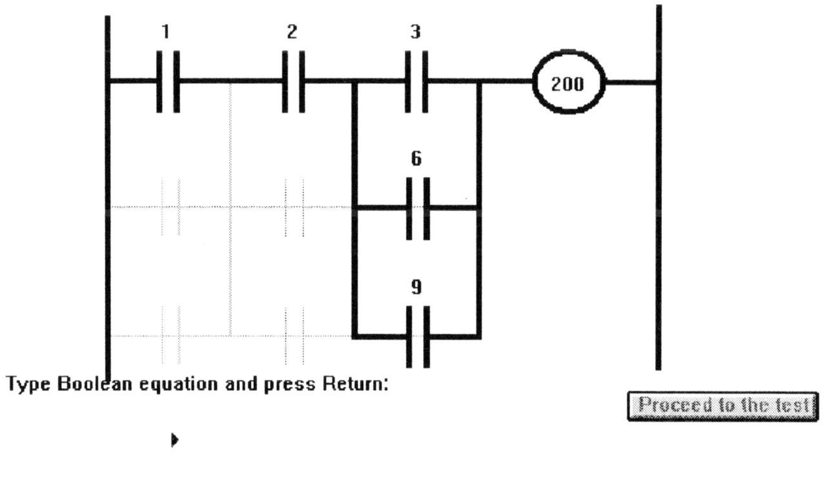

The exploratory-based learning environment resulted in better learning outcomes than worked examples for learners who became more experienced in the domain after a series of training sessions (Figure 16). Subjective ratings of cognitive load supported the cognitive load explanation of the effect, however only for relatively more complex tasks with numerous options to explore (there were no differences between the instructional procedures for simpler tasks with lower levels of element interactivity).

Sufficient levels of instructional guidance should be provided to learners when they lack necessary task-specific knowledge base to serve in the executive role to prevent unproductive and instructionally inefficient search activities. However, embedding worked-out examples into interactive learning environments that already provide extended feedback and hints may not improve (could even inhibit) learning. Such worked examples could be redundant and require additional cognitive resources on co-referencing and reconciling them with other provided means of instructional support. Interactive environments that provide extended hints at

Figure 16. An interaction between instructional designs (worked examples vs. exploratory learning) and levels of learner expertise according to Kalyuga, Chandler, & Sweller (2001): a) Test performance scores; b) difficulty ratings

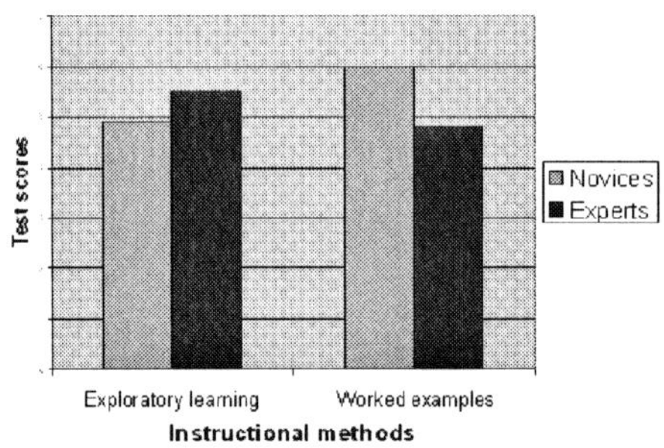

a

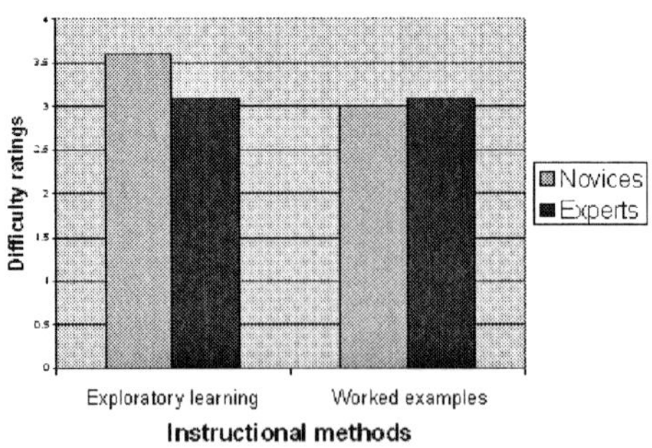

b

the student request are effectively transformed into a form of annotated worked examples (Koedinger & Aleven, 2007).

The level of learner prior knowledge has been consistently demonstrated to influence the effectiveness of interactivity in dynamic multimedia learning environments (Lowe 2004; Schnotz & Rasch, 2005). Computational knowledge-tracing methods (Anderson et al., 1995) or rapid diagnostic assessment techniques (Kalyuga, 2006a) could be used for real-time evaluation of levels of learner task-specific expertise and tailoring levels of guidance in adaptive online environments. Available evidence indicate that adaptive learning environments using either of these diagnostic methods produce better learning outcomes than equivalent non-adaptive learning environments (see Koedinger & Aleven, 2007, for a review of effectiveness of mastery learning with model-tracing intelligent adaptive tutors; Kalyuga, 2006b; Kalyuga & Sweller, 2005 for effectiveness of adaptive rapid assessment-based tutors; the latter type of tutors in some task areas will be described in Section III of this book).

Interactive learning environments that implement a communication level of interactivity may increase essential (e.g., germane) cognitive load by prompting learners for self-explanations and predictions. The self-explanation technique requires learners to explain explicitly suggested solution steps or actions based on their knowledge of the domain. The prediction method requires learners to predict the next procedural step before it is demonstrated or described. Although these techniques could be implemented at lower levels of interactivity (e.g., by using prompts after describing each procedural step), the communication level of interactivity may also provide means for effective verification and evaluation of student responses and for providing appropriate feedback.

REDUCING EXTRANEOUS COGNITIVE LOAD IN INTERACTIVE LEARNING

The design of interactive multimedia learning environments may impose excessive extraneous cognitive load that disrupts learning. Some possible examples (e.g., providing feedback with redundant information that could unbalance executive guidance for learners with higher levels of prior knowledge) were mentioned above. Interestingly, the extraneous load could be imposed by the same types of interactivity that otherwise may help in managing essential load. For example, feedback messages may create split-attention situations when they appear far from the original task or in a separate window that cover the learner responses. Feedback messages may also provide an excessive amount of information.

By engaging learners into manipulating several interrelated parameters, the manipulation-level interactivity may also cause split-attention situations (e.g., when observing concurrent changes in different locations on the screen or keeping track of sequential events or states of a manipulated object in working memory), processing excessive amounts of information, or high rates of its introduction. Designing effective facilities for controlling and tracking sequential changes in interactive dynamic visualizations could reduce the level of extraneous load. Communication-level environments may also involve learners in processing, coordinating, and integrating excessive amounts of information from different sources in their working memory.

Extraneous cognitive load in interactive multimedia learning environments could be reduced by using various techniques for enhancing levels of learner control. For example, appropriate pacing and sequencing of information may help in reducing temporal split attention, as well as the rate and amount of information processed in working memory simultaneously (pacing principle, Moreno & Mayer, 2007). Pacing may also need to be supplemented with segmenting materials into smaller sections, especially for learners with insufficient levels of prior knowledge (Mayer & Chandler, 2001). Selecting appropriate modes of information presentation and appropriate visual cues for display may assist in reducing spatial split attention and directing learner attention to essential information components.

Scanlon and O'Shea (1988) demonstrated that novice learners were not able to use effectively both equations and diagrammatic representations in an interactive tutoring system when solving problems in kinematics. They suggested that the use of multiple representations may inhibit non-expert students' learning and that careful use of alternative representations is required with such learners. These novice learners could learn more productively from instructions that allow them to process one representation at a time and move orderly from one representation to another instead of alternating between different representations.

With content control (e.g., segmenting the content, selecting and sequencing the segments), the amount of provided information could be balanced according to learners' needs and their available knowledge base. Content control methods could often be effective only for relatively more experienced learners who have a sufficient knowledge base in the task domain. Pre-training could be used to compensate for the missing prior knowledge base in interactive learner-controlled environments (the pre-training principle, Moreno & Mayer, 2007).

COGNITIVE LOAD IN INTERACTIVE HYPERMEDIA LEARNING

Learner cognitive characteristics may influence the instructional effectiveness of hypermedia learning environments. Scheiter, Gerjets, Vollmann, and Catrambone

(2007) investigated individual differences associated with differences in information utilization strategies, cognitive load, and problem-solving performance. Using cluster analysis, they identified several groups according to learner self-reported characteristics. For example, the learner group with high prior knowledge preferred condensed worked examples to elaborated ones; the group with high prior knowledge and positive attitudes preferred modular to molar worked examples; the meta-cognitive active group reflected longer on the example selection page.

In complex interactive hypermedia environments, it could be difficult for learners to maintain goals in working memory while searching for relevant information. The search processes may consume resources that would become unavailable for constructing relevant knowledge structures. Variety of possible navigational choices may cause learner disorientation and distraction (Gerjets & Scheiter, 2007) and may also increase extraneous cognitive load.

The level of learner prior domain-specific knowledge is an important factor influencing the effectiveness of hypermedia learning environments. Learner prior knowledge provides a foundation for knowledge-based information search and selection, and for separating essential from non-essential information (Alexander & Jetton, 2003; Chen, Fan, & Macredie, 2006; Gall & Hannafin, 1994). Learners with lower levels of prior knowledge need adequate forms of instructional support to be provided to them. Unsupported hypermedia environments could be suitable mostly for relatively more experienced learners with sufficient levels of prior knowledge. The available knowledge base would guide these learners in their exploration of the environment (Gerjets & Scheiter, 2007).

Spiro and Jehng (1990) suggested that the efficient interactive exploration in complex nonlinear hypertext and hypermedia environments could be based on traversing the information space along several intersecting dimensions. With this approach, learners study the same content material from a variety of different perspectives. The provided pre-determined dimensions for exploration may effectively prevent extensive random search activities that usually impose heavy working memory loads, thus potentially reducing extraneous cognitive load irrelevant to learning. From a cognitive load perspective, such guided traversing with partially directed exploration in hypermedia learning environments could be used with relatively more advanced learners. Jacobson and Spiro (1995) suggested that in order to be effective, the multidimensional traversing (crisscrossing) in hypertext and hypermedia learning environments needs external support facilities such as explicit modeling and scaffolding. Jacobson and Spiro (1995), Spiro and Jehng (1990) demonstrated that only advanced learners appropriately supported by instructional scaffolding may profit from crisscrossing multiple representations in ill-structured domains.

Simons and Klein (2007) studied how embedded scaffolds and student achievement levels influence learning in a problem-based hypermedia learning environment (an inquiry project on designing and planning a balloon trip around the world for seventh grade students). Three conditions were investigated: (1) exploratory problem-based environment without scaffolding; (2) an optional scaffolding condition; and (3) a compulsory scaffolding condition that required all students to study all included scaffolds. Results indicated that no scaffolding condition was significantly worse than both scaffolding conditions; high prior achieving students benefited more from the exploratory problem-based environment than low prior achieving student. Analyses of student project notebooks revealed that students in the compulsory scaffolding condition made more directly relevant entries, thus demonstrating qualitative differences in favor of compulsory scaffolds.

In a review of the effectiveness of multiple external representations in hypertext/hypermedia systems, Tergan (1997) noted that there were certain rationales favoring multiple representations, such as corresponding to principles of encoding specificity and encoding variability, supporting the construction of context-indexed mental representations, providing conditions for multimodal cognitive processing and for individualizing instruction. However, the number of representations or perspectives used in an instructional environment does not automatically improve learning outcomes. Sufficient instructional scaffolding is required, especially for novice learners who may face increased cognitive load while integrating several representations and establishing interrelationships between them. Tergan (1997) concluded that cognitive characteristics of the learners, the task at hand, and the specific instructional methods used for supporting cognitive processing are the most important factors influencing learning.

Wenger and Payne (1996) also suggested that processing hypertext as a coherent entity may impose working memory load that exceed cognitive limitations of the learners' processing system. Learners may become cognitively overloaded by crisscrossing hypermedia environments and establishing appropriate mental links and connection. To prevent a potential cognitive overload, appropriate instructional guidance and support should be provided to the learners.

An effective way of organizing information presentations in hypermedia learning environments in order to reduce cognitive load, especially for novice learners, is using different forms of organizers. They include advance organizers, outline organizers, post organizers (summaries), graphic organizers (e.g., spatial displays of verbal information), continuous organizers (continuously updated organizers that contain references to the past, current, and future information) (Chalmers, 2003). Concept maps may also be useful for relatively more experienced learners, however they may provide excessive levels of load for novice learners (Diaz, Gomes, & Correia, 1999).

Thus, the level of learner prior domain-specific knowledge is a major factor that may influence learning in non-linear hypertext or hypermedia learning environments (Dillon & Gabbard, 1998; Shapiro & Niederhauser, 2004). Studies of the role of prior knowledge in learning from hypertext have generally indicated that low prior knowledge learners benefit more from well structured linear texts. Even though higher prior knowledge learners are usually expected to benefit from non-linear environments and network structures (e.g., Spiro, Feltovich, Jacobson & Coulson, 1991; Spiro & Jehng, 1990; Jacobson, 1994; Jacobson & Levin, 1995), the sufficient positive evidence in support of this suggestion still needs to be accumulated. Also, specific conditions of effectiveness of these environments need to be established and refined.

EXPERTISE REVERSAL IN HYPERTEXT AND HYPERMEDIA LEARNING ENVIRONMENTS

It is usually believed that, in contrast to novice learners, high prior knowledge learners may not encounter disorientation and cognitive overload in hypertext and hypermedia learning environments because they could use flexible and deep navigational strategies based on their available knowledge base. Expertise reversal effect in learning in such environments could imply providing high levels of structure and instructional guidance for novices, for example, using linear or hierarchical hypertext structures that have low requirements for the navigation control. On the other hand, reduced levels of guidance should be used with experts for whom non-linear structures could adequately support deep processing.

In their overview of cognitive load issues in hypertext environments, DeStefano and LeFevre (2007) noted that the general assumption about the role of prior knowledge in learning from hypertext was that high prior knowledge learners may be able to process and make sense of unordered segments of text. They may also be able to handle interruptions in reading by connecting these segments to existing knowledge structures without overloading working memory. Available abstract schemas of more experienced learners may support inferences, elaborations of new information, and retrieval of relevant knowledge from long-term memory.

Learners with lower levels of prior knowledge may experience cognitive overload in hypertext and hypermedia environments that could inhibit learning outcomes. For example, Shin, Schallert, and Savenye (1994) compared high- and low-prior knowledge second-graders using either full or limited access versions of hypertext. Navigation facilities in the limited access hypertext were restricted. The results demonstrated no difference between these versions for students with higher levels of prior knowledge in the topic. For low prior knowledge learners, however, the more structured limited access version of hypertext was more beneficial.

Calisir and Gurel (2003) investigated the interaction between linear text and two versions of hypertext (a very well structured hierarchical version and a slightly less structured mixed format) and learner prior knowledge in the domain of productivity management. While for non-knowledgeable learners, both hypertext structures were significantly better than linear text, the results tended to reverse for more knowledgeable learners (although differences were not statistically significant). In this study, the linear text actually represented a poorly structured instructional format. Available domain knowledge may have helped more knowledgeable learners to understand the linear text by compensating for the missing structure of the text.

There was no significant difference between knowledgeable and non-knowledgeable learners in the better structured hierarchical and mixed conditions. In this study, the well structured hierarchical and mixed forms of hypertext enhanced comprehension for less-knowledgeable learners. These formats may have provided sufficient external executive guidance instead of the missing internal conceptual structure of the domain. Balcytiene (1999) also found that readers with low levels of prior knowledge benefited more from highly structured hypertext than from traditional text when learning to identify pieces of art. For learners with higher levels of prior knowledge in the domain, no difference was observed.

Shapiro (1999) developed interactive overviews as advanced organizers for structuring presented textual descriptions in hypermedia-based learning environments in the domain of elementary zoology and ecology. The study demonstrated that such external structuring means produced significant benefits for learners with low prior familiarity with the domain, however made little difference for learners with higher levels of prior familiarity. More knowledgeable learners were capable of imposing a structure on the hypermedia-based materials using their knowledge base and did not need to spend their cognitive resources on processing unnecessary and redundant for them overviews.

Potelle and Rouet (2003) compared different levels of structural organization of a hypertext environment in the area of social psychology provided by 1) a hierarchical map that represented the most explicit structure of the content, 2) a less structured semantic network map, and 3) an unstructured alphabetical list of topics without explicit hierarchical relations. The results indicated that readers with low levels of prior domain-specific knowledge learned most from the hierarchical map than other two structures, while high-knowledge readers learned equally from all three environments.

Amadieu, Tricot, and Marine (2007) investigated effects of the knowledge diversity (associated with different types of experience) on learning from hypermedia environments. They suggested that having only one type of experience may not help in dealing with new situations. On the other hand, a diversity of experiences would enhance the construction of abstract schemas. The study demonstrated that the knowledge diversity actually lead to higher comprehension performance and decreased disorientation associated with information search (as a source of extraneous cognitive load in non-linear learning environments).

The domain knowledge diversity is associated with deeper and more abstract schemas that improve comprehension in non-linear learning environments. It was also suggested that, if the hypermedia environment does not fit learner available knowledge structures, providing a conceptual map that could be modified by the learners may enhance learning. (Amadieu, Tricot, & Marine, 2007). It should be noted that Paas and van Merriënboer (1994) also demonstrated that comparing different cases (which is an effective way of increasing knowledge diversity) enhanced transfer performance.

Thus, the available evidence indicates that low-knowledge learners generally benefit more from well structured information representations either in hypertext/hypermedia or traditional text environments. At the same time, differently structured environments make no differences for high-knowledge learners. Indeed, no dramatic positive effects of non-linear structures or network-based conceptual maps for more knowledgeable learners have been demonstrated (e.g., Amadieu, Tricot, & Marine, 2007; Calisir & Gurel, 2003; Potelle & Rouet, 2003; Shin et al., 1994). The magnitude of cognitive load in learning always depends on the structure of instructional material relative to learners' different levels of prior knowledge and skills. Therefore, in order to predict the effectiveness of hypertext or hypermedia environments for novice and expert learners, it is important to take into account the specific nature of the content. For some materials, a well structured hypertext/hypermedia environment may demonstrate explicitly the structure of the material better than a traditional linear environment and thus be more beneficial even for novice learners.

FUTURE TRENDS IN COGNITIVELY OPTIMIZED INTERACTIVE LEARNING ENVIRONMENTS

In addition to the level of learner prior domain-specific knowledge, other learner cognitive characteristics may also significantly influence instructional effectiveness of interactive learning environments. One candidate is the level of self-regulation skills such as metacognitive strategies and levels of motivation (Azevedo & Cromley, 2004). Another relevant characteristic is associated with epistemological beliefs that determine the level of invested effort into comparing and contrasting different sources of required information and reflecting on the validity and usefulness of information (Jacobson & Spiro, 1995).

Students with more advanced metacognitive and self-regulation skills are more independent learners. Interactive learning environments could be effective not only in developing domain-specific knowledge and skills, but also in significantly enhancing learner metacognitive and self-regulation skills. For example, interactive metacognitive tutors can help learners to acquire advanced metacognitive skills by providing effective means for understanding learning processes, modeling metacognition, representing and tracing metacognitive knowledge, and assessing metacognitive skills (Azevedo, Cromley, Winters, Moos, & Greene, 2005; Azevedo & Hadwin, 2005).

Scheiter et al. (2007) noted that some learner cognitive characteristics can compensate for the lack of others. For example, cognitive and meta-cognitive strategies could compensate for the lack of positive attitudes towards a subject. However, using the cognitive and meta-cognitive strategies still enabled solving isomorphic rather than transfer problems. More powerful diagnostic tools than traditional questionnaires (e.g., eye-tracking techniques, think-aloud protocols) should be used to reliably establish the relationships between different learner cognitive characteristics and information processing strategies (Gay & Mazur, 1993).

Some recent technological innovations in communication systems could be used to manage cognitive load in interactive learning environments. For example, collaboration supporting and promoting facilities can help to structure the learning tasks in collaborative learning environments and set up a shared knowledge construction space. Indexed knowledge bases (e.g., embedded glossaries or online digital libraries) can provide students with source material and background information. Asynchronous communication environments allow learners to manage rate and amount of information processed at one time. Rich online visual representations of the learning task may reduce extraneous cognitive load and enhance essential load by providing common contexts and support.

Dynamic visualizations may allow students to represent their ideas and knowledge in cognitively efficient graphical formats such as dynamic concept maps and diagrams, thus reducing required working memory resources. These techniques may reduce randomness in computer-mediated collaborative environments and provide sufficient cognitive support for participants, thus reducing extraneous load and enhancing essential processing. As new technologies for tracking student interactions in real time are developed, more support functionality will be integrated into communication-based interactive learning environments to provide higher levels of interactivity and customized scaffolding to learners.

Most current educational online interactive applications are still not sufficiently learner-centered. When using provided interactive tools and navigational features, learners often lose sight of the learning goals and look for stimulating rather than learning-relevant material. Implementing appropriate adaptive and personalized techniques would reduce the intrinsic complexity of the dynamic interactive learning applications and provide the learners with optimal content and activities they need for successful learning.

MULTIMEDIA INSTRUCTIONAL DESIGN IMPLICATIONS

Interactive multimedia learning environments could be improved to better match the nature of human cognition by using appropriate types of interactivity and levels of learner control, and by taking into account levels of learner prior knowledge in a specific task domain.

The following general guidelines could be used in designing interactive learning environments:

- direct guidance should be provided to low-prior knowledge learners at the appropriate time or on-demand using various forms of worked-out procedures, feedback, and hints;
- unnecessary or redundant scaffolding should be timely removed as learners progress through the task domain;
- step-size and rate of presentation need to be learner-controlled to ensure that the capacity of working memory is not exceeded;
- split-attention situations should be eliminated or reduced by appropriately controlling presentation formats;
- content presentation formats and delivery features need to be tailored to changing cognitive characteristics of individual learners.

SUMMARY OF CHAPTER VII

Most of the approaches and techniques used in interactive multimedia learning environments may generate both essential and unnecessary cognitive processes, and contribute to both reduction and increase in extraneous cognitive load. Therefore, interactivity and learner control may help, but may also hinder learning. Specific conditions of their effective application, in particular those related to learner cognitive characteristics, should be taken into account in each case rather than relying rigidly on a set of fixed principles. The general approach is to facilitate interactivity that generates essential cognitive processing relevant to knowledge construction without increasing non-essential extraneous processing load.

The instructional effectiveness of interactive learning environments depends on levels of learner expertise in specific task domains. For example, interactive instructional hypertext and hypermedia learning environments could be very cognitively demanding for novice learners because of a heavy working memory load, and thus result in poor learning outcomes. Therefore, when used with low-knowledge learners, interactive learning environments need to be supplemented with appropriate scaffolding to provide sufficient instructional guidance. Alternatively, linearly sequenced traditional forms of instruction may also eliminate some sources of cognitive overload in interactive learning.

However, as learner experience in a domain increases, external guidance could to be gradually omitted and a relative share of problem-solving or exploratory activities increased. In these conditions, interactive environments may facilitate further schema refinement and automation, as well as development of flexible knowledge and skills. Adaptive interactive learning environments that change the nature of interactivity as learners acquire more experience in the domain may provide the optimal solution.

Structural characteristics and processing limitations of human cognition represent a major factor defining the efficiency of learning in interactive environments and need to be taken into account when designing and evaluating such environments. The level of learner expertise is the most significant factor influencing these limitations and learning outcomes. Adaptive interactive learning environments may allow efficient dynamic tailoring of the nature and levels of interactivity to changing cognitive characteristics of individual learners.

REFERENCES

Alexander, P. A., & Jetton, T. L. (2003). Learning from traditional and alternative texts: New conceptualization for an information age. In A. Graesser, M. Gernsbacher, & S. Goldman (Eds.), *Handbook of discourse processes* (pp. 199-241). Mahwah, NJ: Erlbaum.

Amadieu, F., Tricot , A., & Marine, C. (2007). Knowledge diversity effect on cognitive load, disorientation and comprehension in non-linear learning. Paper presented at International Conference on Cognitive Load Theory, 26-28 March, 2007, Sydney, UNSW.

Anderson, J. R., Corbett, A.T., Koedinger, K. R., & Pelletier, R. (1995). Cognitive tutors: Lessons Learned. *The Journal of the Learning Sciences, 4*, 167-207.

Atkinson, R. K., & Renkl, A., (2007). Interactive example-based learning environments: Using interactive elements to encourage effective processing of worked examples. *Educational Psychology Review, 19,* 375-386.

Azevedo, R. & Cromley, J.G. (2004). Does training on self-regulated learning facilitate students' learning with hypermedia? *Journal of Educational Psychology, 96*, 523-535

Azevedo, R. & Hadwin, A. (2005). Scaffolding self-regulated learning and metacognition – Implications for the design of computer-based scaffolds. *Instructional Science, 33*, 367-379.

Azevedo, R, Cromley, J. G., Winters, F. I., Moos, D.C., & Greene, J.A. (2005). Adaptive human scaffolding facilitates adolenscents' self-regulated learning with hypermedia. *Instructional Science*, 33, 381-412.

Balcytiene, A. (1999). Exploring individual processes of knowledge construction with hypertext. *Instructional Science, 27*, 303-328.

Calisir, F. & Gurel, Z. (2003). Influence of text structure and prior knowledge of the learner on reading comprehension, browsing and perceived control. *Computers in Human Behavior, 19*, 135-145.

Chalmers, P. A. (2003). The role of cognitive theory in human-computer interface. *Computers in Human Behavior, 19*, 593-607.

Chen, S. Y., Fan, J.-P., & Macredie, R. D. (2006). Navigation in hypermedia learning systems: Experts vs. novices. *Computers in Human Behavior, 22*, 251-266.

Chen, C., & Rada, R. (1996). Interacting with hypertext: A meta-analysis of experimental studies. *Human-Computer Interaction, 11*, 125-156.

DeStefano, D., & LeFevre, J-A. (2007). Cognitive load in hypertext reading: A review. *Computers in Human Behavior, 23*, 1616-1641.

Diaz, P., Gomes, M. J., & Correia, A. P. (1999). Disorientation in hypermedia environments: Mechanisms to support navigation. *Journal of Educational Computing Research, 20*, 93-117.

Dillon, A., & Gabbard, R. (1998). Hypermedia as an educational technology: A review of the quantitative research literature on learner comprehension, control, and style. *Review of Educational Research, 68*, 322-349.

Gall, J. E., & Hannafin, M. J. (1994). A framework for the study of hypertext. *Instructional Science, 22*, 207-232.

Gay, G. (1986). Interaction of learner control and prior understanding in computer-assissted video instruction. *Journal of Educational Psychology, 78*, 225-227.

Gay, G., & Mazur, J. (1993). The utility of computer tracking tools for user-centered design. *Educational Technology, April*, 45-59.

Gerjets, P., & Scheiter, K. (2007). Learner control in hypermedia environments. *Educational Psychology Review, 19*, 285-307.

Jacobson, M. J. (1994). Issues in hypertext and hypermedia research: Toward a framework for linking theory-to-design. Journal of Educational Multimedia and Hypermedia, 3(2), 141-154.

Jacobson, M. J., & Levin, J. A. (1995). Conceptual frameworks for network learning environments: Constructing personal and shared knowledge spaces. *International Journal of Educational Telecommunications, 1(4)*, 367-388.

Jacobson, M. J., & Spiro, R. J. (1995). Hypertext learning environments, cognitive flexibility, and the transfer of complex knowledge: An empirical investigation. Journal of Educational Computing Research, 12, 301-333.

Kalyuga, S. (2006a). *Instructing and testing advance learners: A cognitive load approach.* New York: Nova Science.

Kalyuga, S. (2006b). Assessment of learners'organized knowledge structures in adaptive learning environments. *Applied Cognitive Psychology, 20*, 333-342.

Kalyuga, S. (2007). Enhancing instructional efficiency of interactive e-learning environments: A cognitive load perspective. *Educational Psychology Review, 19*, 387-399.

Kalyuga, S., & Sweller, J. (2005). Rapid dynamic assessment of expertise to improve the efficiency of adaptive e-learning. *Educational Technology, Research and Development, 53*, 83-93.

Kalyuga, S., Chandler, P., & Sweller, J. (2001). Learner experience and efficiency of instructional guidance. *Educational Psychology, 21,* 5-23.

Kalyuga, S., Chandler, P., Tuovinen, J., & Sweller, J. (2001). When problem solving is superior to studying worked examples. *Journal of Educational Psychology, 93*, 579-588.

Koedinger, K., & Aleven, V. (2007). Exploring the assistance dilemma in experiments with cognitive tutors. *Educational Psychology Review, 19*, 239-264.

Lowe, R. (2004). Interrogation of a dynamic visualization during learing. *Learning and Instruction, 14*, 257-274.

Mayer, R. E. (Ed.). (2005). *Cambridge Handbook of Multimedia Learning.* New York: Cambridge University Press.

Mayer, R. E., & Chandler, P. (2001). When learning is just a click away: Does simple user interaction foster deeper understanding of multimedia messages? *Journal of educational Psychology, 93*, 390-397.

Moreno, R., & Mayer, R. (2007). Interactive multimodal learning environments. *Educational Psychology Review, 19*, 309-326.

Paas, F., & van Merriënboer, J. J. G. (1994a). Variability of worked examples and transfer of geometrical problem-solving skills: A cognitive-load approach. *Journal of Educational Psychology, 86*, 122-133.

Potelle, H., & Rouet, J. F. (2003). Effects of content representation and readers' prior knowledge on the comprehension of hypertext. *International Journal of Human-Computer Studies, 58*, 327-345.

Renkl, A., & Atkinson, R. K. (2003). Structuring the transition from example study to problem solving in cognitive skills acquisition: A cognitive load perspective. *Educational Psychologist, 38,* 15-22.

Scanlon, E., & O'Shea, T. (1988). Cognitive economics in physics reasoning: Implications for designing instructional materials. In H. Mandl & A. Lesgold (Eds.), *Learning issues for intelligent tutoring systems* (pp. 258-286). New York: Springer-Verlag.

Scheiter, K., Gerjets, P., Vollmann, B., & Catrambone, R. (2007). Learner characteristics, learner Activities, and cognitive load patterns in hypermedia learning. Paper presented at International Conference on Cognitive Load Theory, 26-28 March, 2007, Sydney, UNSW.

Schnotz, W., & Rasch, T. (2005). Enabling, facilitation, and inhibiting effects of animations in multimedia learning: Why reduction of cognitive load can have negative results on learning. *Educational Technology, Research and Development, 53*, 47-58.

Shapiro, A. M. (1999). The relationship between prior knowledge and interactive overviews during hypermedia-aided learning. *Journal of Educational Computing Research, 20*, 143-167.

Shapiro, A., & Niederhauser, D. (2004). Learning from Hypertext: Research issues and findings. In D. Jonassen (Ed.), Handbook of Research for Educational Communications and Technology (pp. 605-620). Hillsdale, NJ: Lawrence Erlbaum Associates.

Shin, E. C., Schallert, D. L., & Savenye, W. C. (1994). Effects of learner control, advisement, and prior knowledge on young students' learning in a hypertext environment. *Educational Technology Research and Development, 42*, 33-46.

Simons, K. D., & Klein, J. D. (2007). The impact of scaffolding and student achievement levels in a problem-based learning environment. *Instructional Science, 35*, 41-72.

Spector, M. J., Christensen, D. L., Sioutine, A. V., & McCormack, D. (2001). Models and simulations for learning in complex domains: using causal loop diagrams for assessment and evaluation. *Computers in Human Behavior, 17*, 517-545.

Spiro, R. J., Feltovich, P. J., Jacobson, M. J., & Coulson, R. L. (1991). Knowledge representation, content specification, and the development of skill in situation-specific knowledge assembly: Some constructvist issues as they relate to cognitive flexibility theory and hypertext. *Educational Technology, 31* (9), 22-25.

Spiro, R. J., & Jehng, J. (1990). Cognitive flexibility and hypertext: Theory and technology for the nonlinear and multidimensional traversal of complex subject matter. In D. Nix & R. Spiro (Eds.), Cognition, education, and multimedia: Exploring ideas in high technology. Hillsdale, NJ: Lawrence Erlbaum Associates.

Tergan, S. (1997). Multiple views, contexts, and symbol systems in learning with hypertext/hypermedia: a critical review of research. *Educational Technology*, July-August, 5-18.

Wenger, M. J., & Payne, D. G. (1996). Comprehension and retention of non-linear text: Considerations of working memory and material-appropriate processing. *American Journal of Psychology*, 93-130.

Wouters, P., Tabbers, H., & Paas, F. (2007). Interactivity in video-based models. *Educational Psychology Review, 19*, 327-342.

Chapter VIII
Managing Cognitive Load in Dynamic Visual Representations

INTRODUCTION

According to dual-coding theory, when learning concrete concepts, adding pictorial representations could be superior to verbal-only descriptions (Clark & Paivio, 1991; Sadoski & Paivio, 2001). This theory assumes existence of two additive sub-systems in human cognitive architecture that process verbal and pictorial information. Accordingly, people learn better when information is encoded verbally and visually rather than in one mode only. Information that has been encoded using two different modes can also be retrieved from memory more easily.

The cognitive theory of multimedia learning provides detailed theoretical arguments that effectively support this view and also apply it to dynamic visualizations such as instructional animations. According to cognitive theory of multimedia learning, different mental representations are constructed from verbal and pictorial information, and meaningful learning occurs only when learner actively establishes connections between these representations (Mayer, 2001; Mayer, & Moreno, 2003; Mayer & Sims, 1994).

This chapter discusses the strengths and weaknesses of dynamic visualizations and the relationship between instructional effectiveness of dynamic and static diagrams and levels of learner task-specific expertise. It has been mentioned previously that instructional formats that are effective for low-knowledge learners could be ineffective, or even deleterious, for high-knowledge learners and vice versa (the expertise reversal effect). Significant interactions between levels of learner expertise and instructional procedures have been found in many situations. Such an interaction may also exist between dynamic and static visualizations. For example, novice learners may benefit more from traditional static diagrams than from dynamic visual representations (e.g., animated diagrams), while more knowledgeable learners may benefit more from animated rather than static diagrams.

This assumption has a viable theoretical rationale. According to cognitive load theory, continuous animations and video may be too cognitively demanding for novice learners. Associated processing difficulties could be due to a high degree of transitivity in such visualizations, on the one hand, and limited capacity and duration of working memory, on the other hand. Less knowledgeable learners, therefore, may benefit more from a set of equivalent static diagrams. However, animations could be superior to static diagrams for more knowledgeable learners who have already acquired a sufficient knowledge base for dealing with issues of transitivity and limited working memory capacity. The chapter also briefly describes a specific empirical study that was designed to investigate the relation between levels of learner expertise and instructional effectiveness of dynamic and static visualizations (Kalyuga, 2007). The rapid diagnostic method discussed in Chapter IV, was used in this study for measuring levels of learner prior knowledge.

ADVANTAGES AND WEAKNESSES OF INSTRUCTIONAL ANIMATIONS

Instructional animations and video have been around for long time as an important part of educational technologies. There are some significant theory-based arguments in favor of greater effectiveness of animated rather than static images, and corresponding principles have been suggested for designing and using animation in instruction (e.g., Mayer & Anderson, 1992; Mayer & Moreno, 2002; Reed, 2005; Rieber, 1990; Weiss, Knowlton, & Morrison, 2002). Some empirical evidence was also obtained to support instructional effectiveness of animations. For example, Rieber, Smith, Al-Ghafry, Strickland, Chu, and Spahi, (1996) found that animated graphical feedback improved learner performance, reduced solution time and learner frustration in a computer-based simulation on the laws of motion in comparison with simple textual feedback. In the area of learning electronic troubleshooting skills, Park and Gittelman (1992) demonstrated that animated visual feedback was more effective than static visual feedback.

On the one side, since animations belong to visual representations in general, cognitively-based principles for designing and using visual representations apply to animations as well (Rieber, 1990). On the other side, animations represent dynamic visualizations that are capable of representing movements and trajectories.

The need to represent these characteristics of objects and processes (changes over time, according to Rieber and Kini, 1991) is the most important reason for using animation in instruction. Because of this difference between animations and static visuals, specific additional principles and rules for the effective use of animations in instruction are required.

Several different functions of instructional animations have been described (Large, 1996; Rieber, 1990; Rieber & Kini, 1991; Weiss, Knowlton, & Morrison, 2002). Cosmetic or decorative function is not related to instructional goals and may inhibit learning by distracting students from essential learning tasks. Most animations carrying this function are superficial and not very good as instructional tools (Large, 1996). Although important for learning in general, the motivation function, similarly to the decorative one, may not be relevant to instructional goals (for example, by strengthening wrong responses when used with feedback). Attention capturing function, including signaling significant elements of information, may be essential for directing learner attention, but may also not be of much benefit when overused. Presentation function (e.g., providing examples, procedures) could be relevant when used for presenting dynamic or abstract content that is difficult to appropriately depict in traditional form. Clarification function may also help in comprehending difficult or abstract material.

An important feature of animations, as well as static images, is their fidelity level that characterizes the degree of realism. Physical fidelity relates to the resemblance to the real world, while functional fidelity relates to behaving like the corresponding real world object. High fidelity levels (especially physical fidelity with many non-essential details that may distract learner attention) may not always be instructionally effective (Park, 1994; Romiszowsky, 1993). Schnotz and Grzondziel (1996) found that schematic low-fidelity illustrations were retained better than analogical high-fidelity illustrations.

Schnotz and Rasch (2005) compared static and animated versions of instruction on time zone differences and circumnavigation problems. The animated diagram was more beneficial for understanding time differences, however, the static diagram group performed better on circumnavigation questions. Both these topics involved movements that could be better illustrated by animated graphics. The suggested explanation was based on levels of learner involvement in essential cognitive processing associated with germane cognitive load. The animated diagram could have made the circumnavigation aspects easier to understand and resulted in less cognitive processing, leading to relatively more wrong answers. On the other hand, static images might have effectively increased germane cognitive load that enhanced learning outcomes.

For concepts and situations that are difficult to describe and/or illustrate verbally (e.g., abstract concepts and processes, changes over time, trajectories of movements, and motion processes), animations could be effective instructional tools (Casey, 1996; Chee, 1995; Park, 1994; Rieber, 1991). Also, when illustrating invisible movements, for example, on molecular or atomic levels, animations could help learners to build corresponding mental images and models (Flemming, Hart, & Savage, 2000; Williams & Abraham, 1995). Another important application area for instructional animations is simulating a context where learned procedures could be utilized, e.g., in teaching troubleshooting skills (Park & Gittleman, 1992). Thus, animations could be effectively used for relatively complex concepts and procedures that involve simultaneous influences of several factors, changes over time, or invisible levels of processes (especially when costly equipment is involved or high fidelity is required). Learning already simple concepts and procedures is unlikely to be made much more easier when animations are used.

In the study of Cohen and Hegarty (2007), learners were required to perform a spatial inference task of imaging and drawing a cross section of a complex fictitious 3-D object. Two user-controlled animations were provided which gave different perspectives of the object. The results demonstrated that learners who were provided with auxiliary animations of imaging and drawing a cross section of the 3-D object were more successful in making spatial inferences. A high level of correlation was found between use of animation and test task success. Learners with high spatial ability (high expertise) used the external representations more often than learners with low spatial ability (low expertise). Betrancourt (2005) also noted that more experienced learners generally benefited more from interactive animations.

Jamet, Gavota, and Quaireau (2007) investigated the effects of attention guiding means such as color change and step-by-step presentation of diagram elements synchronized with a spoken explanation. The diagrams of the cerebral lobes and the spoken explanations were provided to the learners. The study compared four different presentation formats: (1) a static presentation of the diagram; (2) a sequential presentation of the same diagram; (3) a static presentation in which an element of the diagram was highlighted; and (4) a sequential presentation of the diagram with the relevant element highlighted.

The names corresponding to the cerebral lobes were written on the screen at all times and the spoken explanations were the same for all experimental conditions. The display condition (static or step-by-step animated) and salience (highlighted elements) were the two independent factors in this study. For the static condition, all the areas were presented in gray at the beginning of the spoken explanation of the diagram. For the animated condition, areas were displayed sequentially in gray, following the spoken presentation and remained visible. For the salient groups, the areas were colored in red when mentioned and then turned gray. For the non-salient groups, the areas were always displayed in gray. Jamet et al. (2007) found that salience improved learning for both sequential and static presentations.

Sequential instruction was superior to static presentation for retention and diagram completion tasks. Thus, sequential presentations and salience had additive effects in terms of guiding attention.

Even though animated visualizations could be appropriate for presenting dynamic information, there was no very convincing evidence obtained indicating higher learning effects of animations as compared to static diagrams (Park & Hopkins, 1993). Tversky, Morrison, and Bétrancourt (2002) noted that in order to effectively convey information about complex systems, graphics should conform to the congruence principle. According to this principle, the content and format of the graphics should correspond to the content and format of the concepts to be conveyed. For example, animated graphics should be effective to represent change over time.

However, when conveying complex systems that change over time, animations as sequences of discrete steps could be too complex or fast to be accurately perceived. Lowe (2003) suggested that perceptually salient features of animations may distract learner attention from relevant elements of information. Tversky et al. (2002) associated possible ineffectiveness of animations with their transitory nature that makes it difficult for learners to perceive the depicted changes simultaneously.

Hegarty, Kriz, and Cate (2003) examined the effects of static diagrams and computer animations on learner mental models of a mechanical system. Students viewed static diagrams, predicted motion from static diagrams, viewed computer animations, and viewed static and animated diagrams accompanied by verbal commentaries. No evidence was obtained that animated diagrams led to superior understanding compared to static diagrams. Comprehension of diagrams was enhanced by asking students to predict the behavior of the machine from static diagrams and by providing them with a verbal description of the dynamic processes. Predicting motion from static diagrams presumably engaged students' spatial visualization and mental animation processes that were more important for learning and comprehension than presentation formats .

Koroghlanian and Klein (2004) demonstrated that participants who studied animation as opposed to static diagrams spent more time on studying the information, with no corresponding gains in learning. Lowe (1999, 2003) noted that learners need to extract relevant information form animation and integrate it into their available knowledge structures in order to build comprehensive mental models. Perceptually salient but irrelevant features of animations may distract learners from more subtle but relevant features.

Mayer, Hegarty, Mayer, and Campbell (2005) conducted a series of experiments that involved students studying an animation with narration or paper-based static diagrams with text that used the same words and graphics. On subsequent retention and transfer tests, the static diagram groups performed significantly better than the computer groups on 4 out of 8 comparisons, with no significant differences on the remaining 4 comparisons. Static illustrations may have reduced extraneous processing load and promoted germane cognitive load as compared to narrated animations.

Mayer et al. (2005) suggested that animations could obtain some features of static diagrams when learners have control over the pace and sequence of animations (e.g., by using slider bars and pause buttons); animations are segmented into meaningful sections with transition between them initiated by a learner (e.g., by using a "continue" button); learners are engaged in active processing by predicting, generating explanations, or answering questions during learning. Segmenting animations into smaller sections, allowing learner control, cuing or signaling key information could enhance instructional effectiveness of animations (De Koning, Tabbers, Rikers, & Paas, 2007; Hasler, Kersten, & Sweller, 2007; Lusk & Atkinson, 2007; Moreno, 2007).

Thus, static pictures have some clear advantages over animated visualizations. They may allow better learner control of the presentation pace and the possibility to revisit previous discrete stages of the depicted processes (however, not all intermediate steps could be explicitly shown in static representations). In addition, research indicates that people usually construct mental representations of procedures with discrete steps rather than in a continuous linear manner (Zacks & Tversky, 2003).

At the same time, animations allow visualizing objects from multiple perspectives and with different scales (Hegarty, 2004; Schnotz, 2002; Schwan & Riempp, 2004). They allow focusing learner attention on most essential elements by using flashing or movements (which is especially valuable feature for novice learners) (Park & Hopkins, 1993; Rieber, 1990; Wetzel, Radtke, & Stern, 1994). The most important feature of instructional animations is their ability to present information dynamically, with changes in time (Ainsworth, & VanLabeke, 2004; Tversky, Morrison, & Betrancourt, 2002; Weiss, Knowlton, & Morrison, 2002).

COGNITIVE LOAD IN DYNAMIC VISUALIZATIONS

As mentioned above, some reviews and studies concluded that animations are no more (and sometimes less) effective than the equivalent static graphics (e.g., Chan-Lin, 1998; Hegarty, Kriz & Cate, 2003; Koroghlanian & Klein, 2004; Lai, 1998; Park, 1998; Reed, 1985; Rieber, 1989; Rieber & Hannafin, 1988; Schnotz, Böckler, & Grzondziel, 1999; Spotts & Dwyer, 1996; Tversky, Morrison, & Betrancourt, 2002; Wright, Milroy, & Lickorish, 1999). The transient nature of animations and limited duration and capacity of working memory could be the major reason for these failures of animated instructions to demonstrate clear advantages (Chandler, 2004; Lowe, 1999). The cases when animations were more effective could be attributed to more detailed and/or additional information presented in the dynamic visualizations as compared to static versions of experimental materials. The important task in cognitive load theory is identifying conditions under which animations may actually enhance learning.

When learning from animations, many new elements of information may need to be processed in very limited time. New elements of information can be hold in working memory for no more than few seconds (unless rehearsed). In order to be able to construct an integrated mental representation of novel material in working memory, a learner needs to hold information from earlier frames of the animation while attending to the following frames. If a later frame in the animation needs to be processed before the information from previous frames has been incorporated into an organized knowledge structure and comprehended, the new information may interfere with the earlier information (retroactive inhibition, Baddeley, 1997; Lowe, 1999, 2003). Alternatively, some essential components of the preceding frames could be lost before the related elements of the following frames appear.

Thus, from a cognitive load point of view, the transient dynamic nature of animations with limited time for studying each frame in a sequence of frames that follow each other could create difficulties for learning. Cognitive demands of processing new information while holding previous information in active state in working memory could overburden working memory resulting in a potential cognitive overload. In contrast, static graphics do not create such transitivity problems, because elements of still pictures can be revisited any required number of times. For example, Schnotz (2001) compared dynamic and static versions of text illustrations and showed that overall comprehension of the material was better in the static condition. The animation failed to assist learner in establishing connections between text and illustrations (even though details of the text were remembered better in the dynamic condition).

Wright, Milroy, and Lickorish (1999) studied the effect of animated and static illustrations of text on different learning outcomes. By clicking on a hypertext link, learners could directly access either static or dynamic illustrations embedded in text. Both versions were equalized in relation to content: static version demonstrated entire sequence of events on the screen, while dynamic version showed the same content sequentially. A control group studied text-only instruction. When the animations were shown simultaneously with onscreen text, the learning results were significantly worse than when animations were provided before the text or when static illustrations were used, presumably because animations distracted learner attention interfering with processing the text.

Hasler, Kersten, and Sweller (2007) demonstrated that learner-paced instructional animations were more effective than system-paced animations. Continuous system-controlled animations could increase extraneous cognitive load due to the transitory nature of such animations. De Koning, et al. (2007) found that learners who received cues in animated instructions (highlighted key areas that reduced unnecessary search) performed better on comprehension and transfer questions than learners who studied the same animation without cues. Thus, even relatively small adjustments and modifications (allowing learner control over pacing or highlighting key areas in animated visualizations) may improve learner understanding of the animated material.

Arguel and Jamet (2007) suggested that complementing video animations with associated static pictures displayed permanently under the video frame might limit the transient nature of animations and enhance learning. Each picture in such permanent displays could represent a snapshot from the video depicting the critical steps of the procedure. In an experimental study, these researchers used animations accompanied by oral explanations depicting first aid techniques (short film scenes played by actors) without learner pace control. Results indicated that video animations alone were more effective than pictures alone resulting in better understanding of intermediate steps. However, video animations with static pictures were even better than videoanimations alone.

In the second study, Arguel and Jamet (2007) investigated the influence of appearance of the pictures (static pictures vs. pictures synchronized with the video) and number of pictures (low vs. high segmentation frequency) on the effectiveness of the method. The results of the experiment demonstrated that the synchronized appearance of pictures was more effective than the static appearance of the pictures. Synchronized pictures could possibly reduce cognitive load caused by temporal split-attention between audio and visual modalities and could also better guide learner attention. In regards to the second factor, low frequency segmentation was unexpectedly better than high frequency segmentation, especially for static appearance of the pictures. This result could possibly be caused by a redundancy effect, since some additional pictures were irrelevant to learning the main steps of the procedure and required additional cognitive resources to integrate these unnecessary pictures with the video thus increasing extraneous cognitive load.

ANIMATED PEDAGOGICAL AGENTS

It has been known for some time that observing skillful performance of complex cognitive (as well as physical) tasks can enhance learning outcomes (van Merriënboer, 1997). While observing an expert performance (modeling), learners can construct an appropriate mental representation that would later guide their cognitive activities (i.e., provide appropriate executive function). Such learning is also beneficial because it shows both what should be done and why certain steps need to be done. Cognitive modeling may result in constructing more generalized schemas that could be applied in a wider range of situations (van Gog, Paas, & van Merriënboer, 2004).

However, cognitive modeling can place a heavy cognitive load on novice learners when the observed task performance requires examination from several perspectives. In this case, the necessary support could be provided by an animated pedagogical agent, an onscreen character (which is not necessarily human-like) that provides guidance and necessary feedback. Pedagogical agents use various forms of communication, e.g., verbal explanations, gazing, gesturing, etc. (Atkinson, 2002; Clarebout, Elen, Johnson, & Shaw, 2002; Craig, Gholson, & Driscoll, 2002).

Moreno, Mayer, Spires, and Hiller (2001) demonstrated that pedagogical agents could effectively motivate learners. The provided explanation was based on social agency theory. According to this theory, multimedia instruction could be regarded as a social event of information delivery, and learners tend to work harder in socially-related situations. Therefore, if social cues such as pedagogical agents are incorporated into the multimedia instructional environment, the learners will be more engaged in making sense of the social conversation (Moreno et al., 2001).

From the point of view of adaptive learning, it is important that animated pedagogical agents could also be tailored to specific learner characteristics by varying the level of provided instructional guidance For example, agents can perform difficult parts of the task or provide necessary hints and feedback (Clarebout et al., 2002, Clark & Choi, 2005).

Lusk and Atkinson (2007) found that incorporating an agent into the animation to direct learner attention using motion, gesture, or gaze (as a form of cueing or signaling) may improve learning outcomes. They also demonstrated that incorporating worked examples into the animations are more effective if they are introduced step-by-step in a learner-controlled way rather than entirely at once. An agent may reduce extraneous cognitive load as the learner is spared of unnecessary searches that may consume additional cognitive resources. The segmented worked examples may also reduce extraneous cognitive load by keeping the amount of information that is processed concurrently in working memory to a minimum.

Similar to animations in general, studies of instructional effectiveness of animated pedagogical agents produced mixed results ranging from clear benefits to no differences compared with traditional environments. For example, Dehn and van Mulken (2000) concluded that the effect could depend on the specific task domain. Craig, Grasser, Sullies, and Gholson (2004) considered the preferences of learners as a factor influencing instructional effectiveness of animated pedagogical agents. For example, by ignoring an agent that does not motivate but annoys learners may impose an extraneous cognitive load. Cognitive load theory may provide important guidelines for the design of effective animated pedagogical agents.

MANAGING COGNITIVE LOAD IN DYNAMIC VISUALIZATIONS

Most methods for managing cognitive load in multimedia learning described in Chapter II and previous chapters of this part of the book could also be applied to multimedia instructional materials involving dynamic visualizations. In order to decrease intrinsic cognitive load in dynamic visualizations, isolated components of a complex interactive material could be presented before the learner is exposed to the dynamic interaction of these elements (isolated-interacting elements effect or pre-training effect: Mayer, Mathias, & Wetzell, 2002; Pollock, Chandler, & Sweller, 2002). For example, in studies of Mayer and Chandler (2001) with animated instructions on lightning developing, and in studies of Mayer, Mathias, and Wetzell (2002) with animated instructions on how brakes and pumps work, students learned better when they received first a short pre-training session about the names and behavior of the isolated components. This pre-training session was then followed by narrated animations about the causal relation between the components or the way these components interacted.

The traditional methods for reducing extraneous cognitive load could also be successfully applied in dynamic instructional visualizations. According to the contiguity (or split-attention) effect, verbal explanations accompanying dynamic visual representations should be presented concurrently in time or space to avoid learner split-attention between these sources of information. For example, animations could be accompanied by embedded onscreen notes (Moreno & Mayer, 1999) or concurrent narrated explanations (Mayer & Sims, 1994). Mayer, Moreno, Boire, and Vagge (1999) demonstrated that the temporal contiguity problems disappeared when the narration was broken up in small parts that lasted only short periods of time (e.g., few seconds each). Such frequent alternations between the narration and animation may allow the learners to make appropriate connections between the verbal and pictorial information without overloading working memory.

In accordance with multimedia redundancy effect, redundant (even though relevant) information should be eliminated to avoid wasting limited cognitive resources on unnecessary processes. For example, Mayer, DeLeeuw et al. (2007) demonstrated that using additional material about a mechanical system had a negative impact on learning from both animated and static instructions. In this case, additional material was redundant and increased extraneous cognitive load.

According to the signaling or cueing effect (Mayer & Moreno, 2002; 2003), providing cues to the learner on what to pay attention to or how to select and organize the material may enhance learning. For example, placing arrows or using flashing or highlights to attract learner attention to a particular component of animation would serve as a cue. In complex animations that involve intensive search, visual cues could help learners connect the corresponding verbal and pictorial elements of information, reduce cognitive resources for co-referencing these sources of information, and improve learning outcomes (Jeung, Chandler, & Sweller, 1997; Mautone & Mayer, 2001).

In order to reduce extraneous cognitive load in dynamic visualizations, appropriate learner-controlled pacing of the presentation (including pausing or going backward) may assist in adapting it to learner cognitive characteristics. For example, Mayer and Chandler (2001) and Mayer, Dow, and Mayer (2003) reported a positive effect of learner-controlled pacing (although instruction time or segmentation of material were not controlled in these studies). In a video-based instruction about nautical knotting, Schwan and Riempp (2004) demonstrated that instruction that allowed learner-controlled pacing (accelerating, decelerating, stopping or repeating the video) resulted in better understanding of the procedure that instruction without learner-controlled pacing. The learner-paced instruction also resulted in reduced practice time required for reproducing the learned knots.

On the other hand, Moreno and Valdez (2005) and Tabbers, Martens and van Merriënboer (2004) did not find any advantages of learner-controlled pacing, at least over system-controlled pacing. It is possible that this technique may also cause an extraneous load for novice learners that would eliminate potential benefits of this facility. Therefore, studies in learner-controlled pacing technique produced generally mixed results, and cognitive load conditions of its effectiveness need further research.

In order to reduce extraneous load, the animated instruction may also be divided into bite-size fragments that are learned sequentially (segmentation effect). The points at which the material is segmented are important. Such breakpoints should correspond to essential and informative steps in the animated process or procedure (Zacks & Tversky, 2001; Schwan & Garsoffky, 2004). With non-optimal segmenting, learners may need to use additional cognitive resources to compensate for the breaches in the coherence of the presentation, thus reducing resources available for building a coherent mental representation. Learning effects of the segmented instructional animation could also be enhanced by appropriately using learner-controlled pacing (Mayer & Chandler, 2001). The segmenting technique in animated and video-based environments was also investigated by Moreno (2007). In both these learning environments, there were positive effects of segmenting that allowed reducing cognitive load.

Another method for reducing extraneous cognitive load in dynamic visualizations suggested by Paas, Van Gerven, and Wouters (2007) is using key static frames following a continuous animation presentation. In their study, learners were required to either study the key frames or also construct or reconstruct key frames interactively. The interactive approach was found to be more effective than the non-interactive approach. Even though the interactive animation could potentially lead to increased extraneous cognitive load, in this study it was presumably compensated by an increased level of germane cognitive load that enhanced learning outcomes.

One of the effective techniques for increasing germane cognitive load in dynamic visualizations is prompting learners to predict the next step in animated processes before the explanation continues (Hegarty et al., 2003; Renkl, 1997). Mayer, Sobko, and Mautone (2003) used a pre-animation question that learners had to answer after studying the instruction. Moreno et al. (2001) engaged learners in the design task before they listened to the provided instruction. Another effective method used imagining procedures after viewing dynamic visualizations and before actually performing these procedures (Cooper, Tindall-Ford, Chandler, & Sweller, 2001). Prompting learners to imagine procedures can enhance learning for more advanced learners (see Chapter III for more details of this study).

PRIOR KNOWLEDGE EFFECTS FOR DYNAMIC VISUAL REPRESENTATIONS

Expertise reversal effect has been demonstrated in a number of studies with dynamic visual representations. Ollerenshaw, Aidman, and Kidd (1997) demonstrated that low prior knowledge students benefited more from the text with a computer-based animated simulation of the pump's operation (with labeled parts and operating stages) than from text-only or text with diagrams labeling parts only. When the same formats were used with high-knowledge students, the beneficial effect of the comprehensive multimedia animated format was substantially reduced compared to more concise diagram showing parts. Although the effectiveness of animated instruction depended on learner prior knowledge, the effect was not actually reversed in this study.

Schnotz and Rasch (2005) compared effects of animated and static pictures about time phenomena related to the Earth rotation on learners with different levels of learning prerequisites (a combination of pre-test scores of prior knowledge in the domain and intelligence measures). Two different forms of animated pictures were investigated: a picture that displayed visual simulations of changes over time (simulation picture of circumnavigating the Earth) and a more interactive picture that allowed students to manipulate the display by defining specific day and time for specific cities (manipulation picture).

The results of the experiment that compared animated with static pictures indicated that high learning prerequisite learners spent more time on studying animated than static pictures (effect size .58), whereas low learning prerequisite students spent more time studying static than animated pictures (the same effect size of .58). For circumnavigation posttest questions that required mental simulations, students with low learning prerequisites performed significantly better after learning with static pictures than animated pictures (effect size 1.07), while high learning prerequisite students performed equally in both conditions (effect size 0.0). These students were able to perform mental simulations by themselves and external support was redundant.

The results of a follow-up study that compared manipulation and simulation pictures indicated that for time-difference posttest questions, students with high learning prerequisites performed significantly better after learning from manipulation pictures than from simulation pictures (effect size 1.22), while lower learning prerequisite students performed better after learning from simulation pictures than from manipulation pictures (effect size 0.38).

According to cognitive load theory, due to high transitivity, continuous animations could be too cognitively demanding for novice learners who may benefit more from studying a set of static diagrams. For more knowledgeable learners, available knowledge structures may provide sufficient executive guidance that may help them in handling the animated instructions. On the other hand, details displayed in static graphics may need to be integrated and reconciled with knowledge base of these learners imposing additional working memory demands. Similar pattern could be expected from interactive manipulation representations in comparison with more traditional passive animated pictures: manipulation pictures could impose extraneous load on novice learners however be optimal for more experienced learners.

As the level of learner expertise in a domain increases, more domain-specific knowledge structures are acquired in long-term memory. As discussed in Chapter I, these structures allow chunking of many elements of information into familiar units that are treated as single elements in working memory. As a result, more working memory resources become available for constructing and running dynamic mental representations. Static graphics may be less beneficial for more experienced learners than for novices because their available dynamic knowledge structures would need to be integrated and reconciled with redundant for them details displayed in graphics. Additional cognitive resources may be required for such processes, increasing working memory demands and reducing relative learning effects.

Thus, static instructions could be more effective than animations for novices, and become relatively ineffective with increased levels of learner expertise in a domain (Ayres, Kalyuga, Marcus, & Sweller, 2005). This hypothesis is in accordance with the expertise reversal effect and the general role of prior knowledge as an important factor contributing to individual differences in the effect of instruction based on text and visual displays (Schnotz, 2002).

STUDY OF THE EXPERTISE REVERSAL FOR ANIMATED AND STATIC DIAGRAMS

An experimental study was designed and conducted to investigate the relationship between instructional effectiveness of animated and static diagrams and levels of learner task-specific expertise in the task domain of transforming graphs of simple linear and quadratic functions (see Kalyuga, 2007 for more details of this study). The tasks involved transforming graphs of the basic lines $y = x$ and $y = x^2$ into graphs of more complex lines, for example, $y = - 3x + 2$ and $y = 2(x - 1)^2 - 3$ correspondingly (Figure 17). The tasks required applying several of the following operations: flipping a graph because of the minus sign in front of x or x^2 (the negative slope in the case of linear function); squeezing (expanding) a graph toward (from) the y-axis according to the value of a coefficient in front of x or x^2 (more or less than 1); and horizontal/vertical shifting. For evaluating levels of learner proficiency in this task domain, the rapid verification diagnostic technique was applied.

The rapid verification test (see Chapter IV for the description of the rapid diagnostic approach) that was used for evaluating levels of learner prior experience in the domain included four tasks. Two tasks asked students to transform a provided graph of the basic line $y = x$ into graphs of more complex lines, $y = - 2x + 3$ and $y = \frac{1}{3}x - 2$. The following two tasks asked students to transform a provided graph of the basic line $y = x^2$ into graphs of more complex quadratic functions, $y = - \frac{1}{3}x^2$ and $y = 2(x - 2)^2$. The tasks required application of two or three of the previously listed operations. Each task statement was presented for 10 seconds (sufficient for comprehending task statements) and was followed by four suggested solution steps for rapid verification. Some verification subtasks indicated results of the application of only one operation, while other subtasks indicated results of the application of several operations. A score 1 was automatically allocated for each correctly verified step. Null scores were allocated for incorrect responses and "Don't know" entries.

Participants (university undergraduate students) represented variety of subject areas, from education to mechanical engineering. Most of participants did not deal regularly with the task domain used in the study, and all participants had not previously encountered tasks formulated using the current format. Based on results of the initial rapid verification test, students were subdivided into groups of relative "experts" and "novices". Students in each of these two groups were allocated to different treatments (animated vs. static instructions). The rapid verification test was used again to measure levels of learner performance after the instructional session (the tasks in the post-instruction test were relatively more difficult and included quadratic functions that required 3 or 4 transformation steps).The relative knowledge gains (based on standardized z-scores) were calculated, compared, and analyzed for an expertise reversal effect.

Figure 17. Snapshot of the statement for a graph transformation task

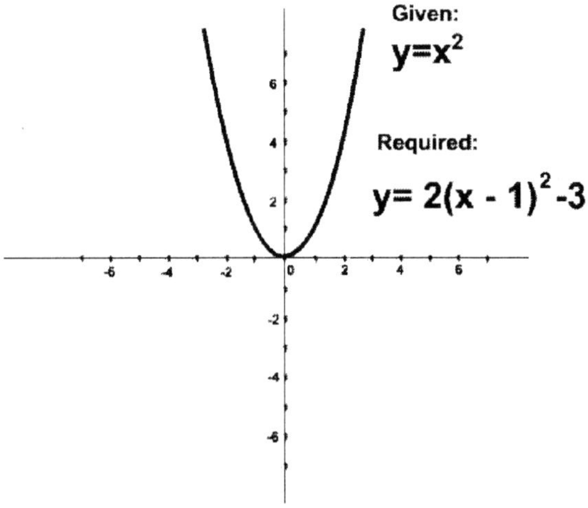

Participants in the animated instruction groups were presented two sequential animated instructional segments, each around one minute long, that showed worked examples on how to transform a given graph of the line $y = x^2$ into a graph of more complex line, e.g., $y = 2(x - 1)^2 - 3$. For each transformation step, the components of the functional expressions (signs, coefficients) that determined the corresponding step were highlighted in red color. The directions of movements were indicated by highlighted arrows. The distances for shifting transformations (in numbers of linear units) were indicated next to the corresponding arrows (see Figure 18 for a snapshot of a frame showing the process of downward shifting for the above task).

The static instruction included two consecutive screens, containing correspondingly four or five sequentially numbered frames from both animated segments depicting major stages of the transformation procedures for the corresponding tasks. Both tasks in this condition were identical to the tasks used in the animated instruction condition. Instruction times were also equalized in both conditions.

Both conditions used only pictorial explanations and contained no on-screen or narrated text to exclude possible interactions with other cognitive load effects associated with simultaneous processing of verbal and pictorial information in static and animated instructions, such as split-attention (spatial and/or temporal contiguity), redundancy, or modality effects (Mayer, 2005; Sweller, van Merriënboer, & Paas, 1998; see also overviews in Chapters II and V). Highlighted indicators of procedural steps (arrows) were embedded into the diagrams in close proximity to the corresponding diagrammatic elements to limit any unnecessary search processes that would require additional cognitive resources.

Figure 18. Snapshot of a frame from the animated instruction on graph transformations

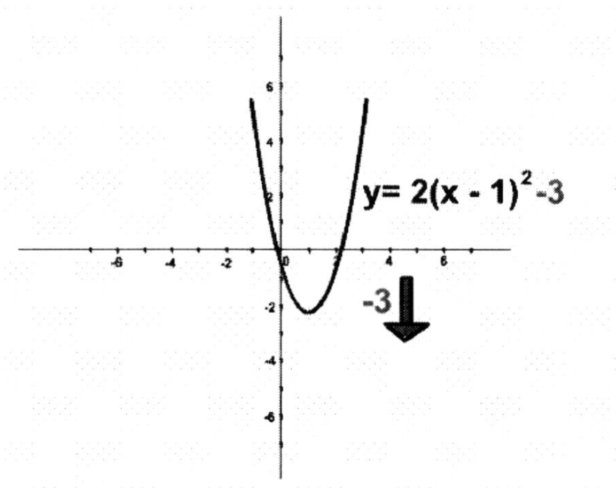

The results of the experiment indicated a significant interaction for the knowledge gains, suggesting that the most effective format of instruction depended on the level of learners' task-specific expertise. Simple effect tests indicated that novice learners benefited significantly more from static than from animated instructions (a large size effect). On the other hand, more knowledgeable learners benefited more from animated rather than from static instructions (a medium size effect). Thus, the study demonstrated an expertise reversal effect. While novice learners gained significantly more knowledge after studying static instructions, for more knowledgeable learners, there was an indication of more benefits from studying animated instructional explanations than from studying static ones.

FUTURE TRENDS IN RESEARCH ON DYNAMIC VISUALIZATIONS

The generality of the expertise reversal effect in relation to dynamic and static visual representations needs to be established, especially in poorly structured and more complex task domains. More comprehensive studies should be conducted comparing animated and static instructional procedures with different levels of interactivity and learner control over the pace of instruction.

Future studies need to verify the cognitive load explanation of the positive effect of using static visualizations depicting major stages of a procedure during animated visualizations. Traditional subjective ratings of mental effort could provide rough evidence about differences in cognitive load. Eye-tracking techniques could also reveal differences in allocating attentional resources and actual cognitive processing involved in learning from different visualization formats. Using visual cues within animated videos instead of adjacent pictures for indicating crucial steps of procedures could also provide additional insights into the nature of the effect (Arguel & Jamet, 2007).

The learner spatial ability may also influence the efficiency of animations. For example, high spatial ability learners profit more from animations with concurrent narration than low spatial ability learners (Mayer & Sims, 1994). Low spatial ability learners need to allocate additional cognitive resources to construct mental pictorial representations, thus leaving less resources for making connections between the pictorial and verbal representations.

Some neurological evidence provides an insight into the brain processes occurring while observing animated visual representations. For example, Iacoboni, Woods, Brass, Bekkering, Mazziotta, and Rizzolatti (1999) provided evidence of similarities in brain activities that occur when observing someone carrying out certain actions and when carrying out the actions oneself. Meltzoff and Prinz (2002) reported that observing actions made by others activates the cortical circuits responsible for the planning and execution of the same actions. Using fMRI scans, Tettamanti, Saccuman, Gallese, Danna, Scifo, Fazio, Rizzolatti, Cappa, and Perani (2005) demonstrated that when a person listened to another person explaining an action, the neurons in the listener's brain responsible for those exact muscle movements were activated. These mirror neurons could be responsible for human abilities to engage in imitative learning (Blandin, Lhuisset & Proteau, 1999).

This neurological evidence suggests the possibility of existence of a separate "movement" processor in our cognitive system that could possibly evolve for imitating movements of other people. Learning from animations showing human movements may trigger the use of such "movement" processor that does not occur when learning from static graphics or animations depicting processes in mechanical objects (Ayres, Kalyuga, Marcus, & Sweller, 2005; Marcus & Wong, 2007)

Observing human movements may involve biologically primary knowledge (see Chapter I) that operates in a very resource-efficient manner. Such knowledge does not require effortful conscious processing in working memory and thus leaves more resources for the acquisition of relevant secondary knowledge. We may be able to learn from animations more readily when dealing with human movements (primary knowledge) than with mechanical object movements and processes (secondary knowledge). Thus, instructional animations may be superior to equivalent static graphics when dealing with knowledge that involves human movement.

Marcus and Wong (2007) compared animations with static graphics using folding tasks with 9-year old children. The results indicated that animated instructions were better than static graphics for the task that involved human movement. In the second experiment, a task was added that was not movement-based (recognizing the next or last fold at different points of the folding procesure after the folding task was completed). The results again indicated that for motor-based folding task, animation was better than static graphics (replicating the results of the previous study). However, static graphics produced better results for the non movement-based task. This line of research represents an important direction of future studies of conditions under which instructional animations are effective and efficient learning tools.

MULTIMEDIA INSTRUCTIONAL DESIGN IMPLICATIONS

The following techniques can be used with dynamic multimedia visualizations for managing cognitive load:

- presenting isolated components of a complex visual material (or pre-training learners in such elements) before exposing learners to the dynamic interactions of these elements in order to decrease intrinsic cognitive load;
- using appropriate learner-controlled pacing of the presentation (including pausing, accelerating, decelerating, stopping, repeating the animation or going backward);
- dividing (segmenting) the animated instruction into bite-size fragments that are learned sequentially, with breakpoints corresponding to essential steps in the procedure;
- using interactively constructed key static frames following a continuous animation;
- avoiding presentation of redundant information with animated instructions;
- presenting verbal explanations of dynamic visualizations concurrently in time or space with corresponding visual components;
- breaking up the narration into small short-lasting parts with fast alternations between narration and animation;
- providing cues (e.g., arrows, highlights) to the learner on how to select and organize the material;
- prompting learners to predict the next step in dynamic animated processes before the explanation continues (in order to increase germane cognitive load);
- prompting relatively advanced learners to imagine procedures after viewing dynamic visualizations and before actually performing these procedures;
- providing novice learners with static visualizations of critical stages or steps instead of animated procedures or processes.

Adaptive instructional procedures that allow learners to progress from static to animated diagrams as levels of their task-specific expertise increase could create optimal learning environments based on different forms of visualizations. Rapid online tests of task-specific expertise with sufficient precision for diagnosing different levels of learner prior knowledge could be important components of such environments. The rapid diagnostic approach could be used for the dynamic selection of appropriate formats of instructional visual representations that are optimal for learners with different levels of expertise.

SUMMARY OF CHAPTER VIII

Animations can be effectively used to dynamically represent processes that are not directly observable. Animated pedagogical agents can motivate learners to invest more cognitive resources and provide instructional support. Advantages of static illustrations with textual explanations are better learner control over the sequence and pacing of learning and presenting only essential elements of information. System-controlled animations with narrated explanations are expected to be efficient in creating mental representations of dynamic processes and better motivate learners.

Existing research literature does not provide compelling and clear empirical evidence about educational advantages of animations over static graphics. A number of studies have shown that dynamic visualizations are generally no more effective than static visualizations. A number of traditional cognitive load management techniques could be successfully applied to enhancing learning outcomes in instructional animations.

From a cognitive load perspective, working memory could be easily overloaded by fast changes in complex animations. Animations may create a cognitive overload if they distract the learner attention away from essential information or if learners are required to search for the relevant information. Transitory nature of animations can also place great cognitive demands because current onscreen information is rapidly displaced by the content of the following frames as the animation progresses. The need to process current information while keeping active the previous content may impose an additional extraneous cognitive load.

On the other hand, static images may allow better management of cognitive load by controlling the pace and order of presentations, especially if learners are engaged in more active processing of these images. They may also reduce unnecessary processing by focusing learner attention on the main components and procedural steps.

The available studies of interactions between levels of learner task-specific expertise and effectiveness of animated and static instructional presentations show that less knowledgeable learners generally perform better after studying static diagrams. Learners with higher levels of prior knowledge show better results after studying animated instructions (an expertise reversal effect). Adaptive instructional procedures that allow learners to gradually progress from static to animated visualizations as levels of their task-specific expertise increase could provide optimal learning environments. The rapid diagnostic approach could be used for the dynamic selection of appropriate formats of visual representations in such environments.

REFERENCES

Ayres, P., Kalyuga, S., Marcus, N., & Sweller, J. (2005). The conditions under which instructional animation may be effective. Paper presented at the International workshop *Extending Cognitive Load Theory and Instructional Design to the Development of Expert Performance,* August 29 - 30, 2005. Heerlen, the Netherlands: Open University of the Netherlands.

Ainsworth, S., & VanLabeke, N. (2004). Multiple forms of dynamic representations. *Learning and Instruction, 14*, 241–256.

Arguel, A., & Jamet, E. (2007). Combining video and statics in learning procedural content. Paper presented at the International Cognitive Load Theory Conference, 24-26 March, Sydney, Australia.

Atkinson, R. K. (2002). Optimizing learning from examples using animated pedagogical agents. *Journal of Educational Psychology, 94*, 416–427.

Baddeley, A. (1997). *Human memory: Theory and practice*. East Sussex, UK: Psychology Press.

Betrancourt, M. (2005). The Animation and Interactivity Principles in Multimedia Learning. The Cambridge handbook of multimedia learning., Cambridge University Press: 287-296.

Blandin, Y., Lhuisset, L., & Proteau, L. (1999). Cognitive processes underlying observational learning of motor skills. *Quarterly Journal of Experimental Psychology, 52A*, 957–979.

Casey, C. (1996). Incorporating cognitive apprenticeship in multi-media. *Educational Technology Research and Development, 44*, 74-84.

Chandler, P. (2004). The crucial role of cognitive processes in the design of dynamic visualizations. *Learning and Instruction, 14*, 353-357.

ChanLin, Lih-Juan (1998). Animation to teach students of different knowledge levels. *Journal of Educational Psychology, 62*, 233-246.

Chee, Y. C. (1995). Cognitive apprenticeship and its applications to the teaching of Smalltalk in a multimedia interactive learning environment. *Instructional Science, 23*, 133-161.

Clarebout, G., Elen, J., Johnson, W. L., & Shaw, E. (2002). Animated pedagogical agents: An opportunity to be grasped? *Journal of Educational Multimedia and Hypermedia, 11*, 267–286.

Clark, R. E., & Choi, S. (2005). Five design principles for experiments on the effects of animated pedagogical agents. *Journal of Educational Computing Research, 32*, 209–225.

Clark, J. M., & Paivio, A. (1991). Dual coding theory and education. *Educational Psychology Review, 3*, 149–210.

Cohen, C. A. & M. Hegarty (2007). Individual differences in use of external visualizations to perform an internal visualization task. *Applied Cognitive Psychology, 21*, 701 - 711.

Cooper, G., Tindall-Ford, S., Chandler, P., & Sweller, J. (2001). Learning by imagining. *Journal of Experimental Psychology: Applied, 7*, 68–82.

Craig, S. D., Gholson, B., & Driscoll, D. M. (2002). Animated pedagogical agents in multimedia educational environments: Effect of agent properties, picture features, and redundancy. *Journal of Educational Psychology, 94*, 428–434.

Craig, S. D., Graesser, A. C., Sullins, J., & Gholson, B. (2004). Affect and learning: An exploratory look into the role of affect in learning with AutoTutor. *Journal of Educational Media, 29*, 241–250.

De Koning, B. B., Tabbers, H. K., Rikers, R. M. J. P., & Paas, F. (2007). Attention cueing as a means to enhance learning from an animation. *Applied Cognitive Psychology, 21*, 731 - 746.

Dehn, D. M., & van Mulken, S. (2000). The impact of animated interface agents: A review of empirical research. *International Journal of Human-Computer Studies, 52*, 1–22.

Flemming, S. A., Hart, G. R., & Savage, P. B. (2000). Molecular orbital animations for organic chemistry. *Journal of Chemical Education, 77*, 790-793.

Hasler, B. S., Kersten, B., & Sweller, J. (2007). Learner control, cognitive load and instructional animation. *Applied Cognitive Psychology, 21,* 713 - 729.

Hegarty, M. (2004). Dynamic visualizations and learning: Getting to the difficult questions. *Learning and Instruction, 14,* 343–352.

Hegarty, M., Kriz, S., & Cate, C. (2003). The roles of mental animations and external animations in understanding mechanical systems. *Cognition and Instruction, 21,* 325–360.

Holladay, C. L., & Quinones, M. A. (2003). Practice variability and transfer of training: The role of self-efficacy generality. *Journal of Applied Psychology, 88,* 1094–1103.

Iacoboni, M., Woods, R., Brass, M., Bekkering, H., Mazziotta, J., & Rizzolatti, G. (1999). Cortical mechanisms of human imitation. *Science, 286,* 2526-2528.

Jamet, E., Gavota, M., Quaireau, C. (2007). Attention guiding in multimedia learning. *Learning and Instruction, 18,* 135-145.

Jeung, H., Chandler, P., & Sweller, J. (1997). The role of visual indicators in dual sensory mode instruction. *Educational Psychology, 17,* 329–343.

Kalyuga, S. (2007). Relative effectiveness of animated and static diagrams: An effect of learner prior knowledge. *Computers in Human Behaviour, 24,* 852-861.

Koroghlanian, C., & Klein, J. D. (2004). The effect of audio and animation in multimedia instruction. *Journal of Educational Multimedia and Hypermedia, 13,* 23–46.

Lai, Shu-Ling (1998). The effects of visual display on analogies using computer-based learning. *International Journal of Instructional Media, 25,* 151-157.

Large, A. (1996). Computer animation in an instructional environment. *Library and Information Science Research, 18,* 3-23.

Lowe, R. K. (1999). Extracting information from an animation during complex visual learning. *European Journal of Psychology of Education, 14,* 225–244.

Lowe, R. K. (2003). Animation and learning: Selective processing of information in dynamic graphics. *Learning and Instruction, 13,* 157–176.

Lusk, M. M. & Atkinson, R. K. (2007). Animated pedagogical agents: Does their degree of embodiment impact learning from static or animated worked examples? *Applied Cognitive Psychology, 21,* 747 - 764.

Marcus, N., & Wong, A. (2007). Instructional animations that foster motor skills. Paper presented at the International Cognitive Load Theory Conference, 24-26 March, Sydney, Australia.

Mautone, P. D., & Mayer, R. E. (2001). Signaling as a cognitive guide in multimedia learning. *Journal of Educational Psychology, 93*, 377–389.

Mayer, R. (2001). *Multimedia learning.* New York: Cambridge University Press.

Mayer, R. E. (Ed.). (2005). *Cambridge Handbook of Multimedia Learning.* New York: Cambridge University Press.

Mayer, R., & Anderson, R. (1992). The instructive animation: Helping students build connections between words and pictures in multimedia learning. *Journal of Educational Psychology, 84*, 444-452.

Mayer, R. E., & Chandler, P. (2001). When learning is just a click away: Does simple user interaction foster deeper understanding of multimedia messages? *Journal of Educational Psychology, 93*, 390–397.

Mayer, R. E., DeLeeuw, K. E., & Ayres, P. (2007). Creating retroactive and proactive interference in multimedia learning. *Applied Cognitive Psychology, 21,* 795 - 809.

Mayer, R. E., Dow, G. T., & Mayer, S. (2003). Multimedia learning in an interactive self-explaining environment: What works in the design of agent-based microworlds. *Journal of Educational Psychology, 95*, 806–812.

Mayer, R. E., Hegarty, M., Mayer, S. & Campbell, J. (2005). When static media promote active learning: Annotated illustrations versus narrated animations in multimedia instruction. *Journal of Experimental Psychology: Applied 11,* 256-265.

Mayer, R. E., Mathias, A., & Wetzell, K. (2002). Fostering understanding of multimedia messages through pre-training: Evidence for a two-stage theory of mental model construction. *Journal of Experimental Psychology: Applied, 8*, 147–154.

Mayer, R. E., & Moreno, R., (2002). Animation as an aid to multimedia learning. *Educational Psychology Review, 14*, 87–99.

Mayer, R. E., & Moreno, R. (2003). Nine ways to reduce cognitive load in multimedia learning. *Educational Psychologist, 38*, 43–53.

Mayer, R. E., & Moreno, R., Boire, M., & Vagge, S. (1999). Maximizing constructivist learning from multimedia communications by minimizing cognitive load. *Journal of Educational Psychology, 91*, 638–643.

Mayer, R. E., & Sims, V. K. (1994). For whom is a picture worth a thousand words? extensions of a dual-coding theory of multimedia learning. *Journal of Educational Psychology, 86*, 389–401.

Mayer, R. E., Sobko, K., & Mautone, P. D. (2003). Social cues in multimedia learning: Role of speaker's voice. *Journal of Educational Psychology, 95*, 419–425.

Meltzoff, A. N., & Prinz, W. (2002). *The imitative mind: Development, evolution and brain bases*. Cambridge, UK: Cambridge University Press.

Moreno, R. (2007). Optimizing learning from animations by minimizing cognitive load: Cognitive and affective consequences of signaling and segmentation methods. *Applied Cognitive Psychology, 21,* 765 - 781.

Moreno, R., & Mayer, R. E. (1999). Cognitive principles of multimedia learning: The role of modality and contiguity. *Journal of Educational Psychology, 91*, 358–368.

Moreno, R., Mayer, R. E., Spires, E., & Hiller, A. (2001). The case for social agency in computer-based teaching: Do learners learn more deeply when they interact with animated pedagogical agents? *Cognition and Instruction, 19*, 177–213.

Moreno, R., & Valdez, A. (2005). Cognitive load and learning effects of having students organize pictures and words in multimedia environments: The role of student interactivity and feedback. *Educational Technology, Research and Development, 53*, 35–45.

Ollerenshaw, A., Aidman, E., & Kidd, G. (1997). Is an illustration always worth ten thousand words? Effects of prior knowledge, learning style, and multimedia illustrations on text comprehension. *International Journal of Instructional Media, 24*, 227-238.

Paas, F., Van Gerven, P. W. M., & Wouters, P. (2007). Instructional efficiency of animation: Effects of interactivity through mental reconstruction of static key frames. *Applied Cognitive Psychology, 21,* 783 - 793.

Park, O. (1994). Dynamic visual displays in media-based instruction. *Educational Technology*, 21-25.

Park, O. (1998). Visual Displays and contextual presentations in computer-based instruction. *Educational Technology Research and Development, 46*, 37-50.

Park, O., & Gittelman, S. S. (1992). Selective use of animation and feedback in computer-based instruction. *Educational Technology Research and Development, 40*, 27-38.

Park, O-C., & Hopkins, R. (1993). Instructional conditions for using dynamic visual displays. *Instructional Science, 21*, 427–449.

Pollock, E., Chandler, P., & Sweller, J. (2002). Assimilating complex information. *Learning and Instruction, 12*, 61–86.

Reed, S. K. (1985). Effects of computer graphics on improving estimates to algebra word problems. *Journal of Educational Psychology, 77*, 285-298.

Reed, S. K. (2005). From research to practice and back: The animation tutor project. *Educational Psychology Review, 17*, 55-82.

Renkl, A. (1997). Learning from worked-out examples: A study on individual differences. *Cognitive Science, 21*, 1–29.

Rieber, L. P. (1989). The effects of computer animated elaboration strategies and practice on factual and application learning in an elementary science lesson. *Journal of Educational Computing Research, 5*, 431-444.

Rieber, L. P. (1990). Animation in computer-based instruction. *Educational Technology, Research and Development, 38*, 77–86.

Rieber, L. P. (1991). Effects of visual grouping strategies of computer-animated presentations on selective attention in science. *Educational Technology Research and Development, 39*(4), 5–15.

Rieber, L. P., & Hannafin, M. J. (1988). Effects of textual and animated orienting activities and practice on learning from computer-based instruction. *Computers in the Schools, 5*, 77-89.

Rieber, L. P., & Kini, A. S. (1991). Theoretical foundations of instructional applications of computer-generated animated visuals. *American Journal of Psychology, 18*, 83–88.

Rieber, L. P., Smith, M., Al-Ghafry, S., Strickland, W., Chu, G., & Spahi, F. (1996). The role of meaning in interpreting graphical and textual feedback during a computer-based simulation. *Computers and Education, 27(1)*, 45-58.

Romiszowsky, A. J. (1993). Psychomotor principles. In M. Fleming, & W. H. Levie (Eds.), *Instructional message design: principles from the behavioral and cognitive sciences* (pp. 127-189). Englewood Cliffs, NJ: Educational Technology Publications.

Sadoski, M., & Paivio, A. (2001). *Imagery and text: A dual coding theory of reading and writing.* Mahwah, NJ: Lawrence Erlbaum.

Schnotz, W. (2001). Sign systems, technologies, and the acquisition of knowledge. In J.-F. Rouet, J. Levonen & A. Biardeau (Eds.), *Multimedia Learning - Cognitive and Instructional Issues* (pp. 9-29). Amsterdam: Elsevier.

Schnotz, W. (2002). Towards an integrated view of learning from text and visual displays. *Educational Psychology Review*, 14, 101–120.

Schnotz, W., Böckler, J., & Grzondziel, H. (1999). Individual and co-operative learning with interactive animated pictures. *European Journal of Psychology of Education, 14*, 245-265.

Schnotz, W., & Grzondziel, H. (1996). *Knowledge acquisition with static and animated pictures in computer-based learning.* Paper presented at the annual meeting of the American Educational Research Association, New York City. (ERIC No. ED 401 878)

Schnotz, W., & Rasch, T. (2005). Enabling, Facilitating, and Inhibiting Effects of Animations in Multimedia Learning: Why Reduction of Cognitive Load Can Have Negative Results on Learning. *Educational Technology Research and Development, 53*(3), 47–58.

Schwan, S., & Garsoffky, B. (2004). The cognitive representation of filmic event summaries. *Applied Cognitive Psychology, 18*, 37–55.

Schwan, S., & Riempp, R. (2004). The cognitive benefits of interactive videos: Learning to tie nautical knots. *Learning and Instruction, 14*, 293–305.

Spotts, J., & Dwyer, F. (1996). The effect of computer-generated animation on student achievement of different types of educational objectives. *International Journal of Instructional Media, 23*, 365-375.

Sweller, J., van Merriënboer, J. J. G., & Paas, F. (1998). Cognitive architecture and instructional design. *Educational Psychology Review, 10*, 251–296.

Tabbers, H., Martens, R., & van Merriënboer, J. J. G. (2004). Multimedia instructions and cognitive load theory: Effects of modality and cueing. *British Journal of Educational Psychology, 74*, 71–81.

Tettamanti, M. Saccuman, M. C., Gallese, V., Danna, M., Scifo, P. Fazio, F., Rizzolatti, G. Cappa, S., & Perani, D. (2005). Listening to action-related sentences activates fronto-parietal motor circuits. *Journal of Cognitive Neuroscience, 17*, 273-281.

Tversky, B., Morrison, J. B., & Betrancourt, M. (2002). Animation: Does it facilitate learning? *International Journal of Human-Computer Studies, 57*, 247–262.

Van Gog, T., Paas, F., & van Merriënboer, J. J. G. (2004). Process-oriented worked examples: Improving transfer performance through enhanced understanding. *Instructional Science*, *32*, 83–98.

Van Merriënboer, J. J. G. (1997). *Training complex cognitive skills*. Englewood Cliffs, NJ:Educational Technology Publications.

Weiss, R. E., Knowlton, D. S., & Morrison, G. R. (2002). Principles for using animation in computer-based instruction: Theoretical heuristics for effective design. *Computers in Human Behavior*, *18*, 465–477.

Wetzel, D. C., Radtke, P. H., & Stern, H. W. (1994). *Instructional effectiveness of video media*. Hillsdale/Mahwah, NJ: Lawrence Erlbaum.

Williams, V. M., & Abraham, M. R. (1995). The effects of computer animation on the particulate mental models of college chemistry students. *The Journal of Research in Science Teaching*, *32*, 521-534.

Wright, P., Milroy, R., & Lickorish, A. (1999). Static and animated graphics in learning from interactive texts. *European Journal of Psychology of Education*, *14*, 203-244.

Zacks, J. M., & Tversky, B. (2001). Event structure in perception and conception. *Psychological Bulletin*, *127*, 3–21.

Chapter IX
Optimizing Cognitive Load in Instructional Simulations and Games

INTRODUCTION

Instructional simulation and games are usually used as substitutes for actual equipment, processes, real-life problems, and social situations. They allow observing outcomes of different learner actions and steps without involving actual hardware and people. They also provide environments for practicing important skills in an efficient (in terms of cost and time) way. From a cognitive load perspective, using actual equipment or human actors may not necessarily lead to the acquisition of expected knowledge and skills. High cognitive load involved in operating the equipment itself, performing required procedures, interacting with other people, especially when allowed time is constrained, may inhibit learning. In such high load situations, limited cognitive resources would be left for actual learning. Instructional simulations and games allow modeling such processes without time limitations and other cognitive constrains. Instructional simulations may also allow representing abstract knowledge structures and processes that are difficult to observe in real conditions. They may enhance the development of abstract thinking and problem-solving skills by offering environments for exploring and testing hypotheses.

Many available instructional simulations and games represent mostly exploratory learning environments with limited guidance for learners. From a cognitive load perspective, any random exploratory or search procedures may impose excessive levels of working memory load thus interfering with meaningful learning (see Chapter II for more details about basic principles of cognitive load theory). Therefore, optimizing levels of instructional guidance represents the most important means of managing cognitive load and enhancing learning outcomes in such environments.

This chapter starts with examining the role of simulations as instructional technology tools and describes means of enhancing instructional effectiveness of simulations and games. Then the chapter discusses how to evaluate cognitive load in simulations using concurrent verbal reports. Some issues of cognitive load associated with instructional applications of mobile technologies are considered at the end.

SIMULATIONS AS TOOLS OF INSTRUCTIONAL TECHNOLOGY

Practical use of software products and physical equipment often does not lead to understanding of theoretical principles they try to convey because high cognitive demands of familiarization with equipment and procedures, taking measurements, interpreting data, etc. Limited (if any) cognitive resources may remain available for generalizations required for understanding the theory. In such high-load situations, learners may adopt a "recipe approach" by following step-by-step directions without clearly understanding reasons behind these steps (McFarlane & Sakellariou, 2002). Instructional simulations may help to partially avert these problems because they may eliminate the need for handling apparatus and represent simultaneously observable and theoretically predicted behaviors of the system under investigation (Hennesy, Deaney, & Ruthven, 2006).

Interactive visualizations of abstract knowledge structures by manipulating familiar objects are important benefits of simulations that enhance the development of abstract thinking and problem-solving skills (Boyle, 2004). Simulations may provide a framework for visualization of complex problems that could be encountered in real settings outside the simulation, offer environments for exploring hypotheses and receiving immediate feedback (Baggott & Nichol, 1998; Monaghan & Clement (1999). In science education, computer simulations allow many naturally occurring invisible processes, especially at molecular or atomic levels, to be made transparent and accessible to learner experimentations by manipulating (compressing or extending) natural time intervals. Such interactive manipulations of experimental situations may enhance learner abilities to apply scientific knowledge to complex real-life situations. A number of studies reported successful use of instructional simulations in educational settings, especially for teaching science classes.

For example, Lewis, Stern, and Linn (1993) conducted a longitudinal study of integrating simulations in thermodynamics curriculum for middle-school students. The modified curriculum resulted in reportedly enhanced understanding of relevant concepts and ability to explain naturally occurring phenomena. The simulations facilitated scientific knowledge construction by allowing learners to see the similarities between their simulated real-time experiments and observed real world events. On a more cautious note, Linn and Songer (1991) observed that offering students multiple models of scientific phenomena (e.g., a heat flow in everyday thermodynamics) may result in learners selecting the least explanatory and easiest model with minimal cognitive demands (which fully corresponds to the "cognitive economy principle" stated in Chapter I). Clement, Brown, and Zietsman (1989) noted that it is important for the level of model abstraction to correspond to levels of learner prior domain-specific knowledge.

Tennyson and Breuer (2002) noted that the use of simulations is associated more with learning a task as a complete whole rater than successive parts. Simulations are task-oriented and aimed at acquisition of task-relevant knowledge base. Complex dynamic simulations require learners to actually use their acquired knowledge base by constructing solutions of domain-specific tasks with focus on developing cognitive problem-solving abilities in the domain. A simulation-based system described by Tennyson and Breuer (2002) consists of two main components. One is a curriculum (macro-) component that maintains a student model (cognitive, affective, and memory components for each student) and an external knowledge base. The second component is an instructional (micro-) component that adapts the instructional strategies according to current learning progress. Complex situations modeled by the system consist of two parts. The first part establishes the problem situation with a meaningful content that requires using students' own knowledge base. The second part is the computer-based management system that presents the initial conditions of the situation, assesses the student's proposed solution, and establishes "the next iteration of the conditions based on the cumulative efforts of the student" (p. 663).

Taylor and Chi (2006) compared differences in learning effects from reading a text and using a computer simulation in the domain of project management for undergraduate university students with limited knowledge of the topic. In order to minimize interferences between the factors of instructional content and media representations, the simulation was based on the same textual material as the text used in the experiment. The text was modified to eliminate irrelevant sections and rewritten to make both conditions as equivalent in relation to their comprehensibility as possible. Only answers that could be inferred from both instructional formats were included in the assessments. The results of the post-training assessment of more abstract, deep structural and de-contextualized knowledge of project management indicated that participants in both conditions improved equally based on the pretest to posttest knowledge gains. In contrast, a contextualized case-based assessment demonstrated significantly improved learning outcomes for the simulation group only.

Thus, the analysis of results indicated that the simulation enhanced acquisition of implicit domain knowledge. The researchers claim that computer-based simulations as a delivery media have some unique features that are absent in textual paper-based information delivery means and, therefore, allow substantial increases in efficiency of learning. Among such features of simulations are dynamic interactions between learners and the environment, as well as learners' participation in a virtual environment with highly contextualized knowledge. These features allow students to learn the specific context in which the acquired domain-specific knowledge structures will be applied (Taylor & Chi, 2006).

ENHANCING INSTRUCTIONAL EFFECTIVENESS OF EDUCATIONAL GAMES

Moreno and Duran (2004) investigated benefits of instructional guidance in discovery multimedia game-based learning environments in elementary school mathematics. Addition and subtraction problems used two representations of the arithmetic procedures: a traditional symbolic representation of the number sentence and a visual representation. The visual representation used a number line and an animated bunny moving along the line according to the number operations performed. It faced the left or right sides of the screen if the corresponding numbers have the minus or plus signs correspondingly. If learners answered a problem correctly, they could see an animated sequence demonstrating major steps in solving the problem. In the guided group, the learners could also hear explanations for each step of the animation.

It was assumed that combining symbolic numerical and visual representations could help learners, especially less knowledgeable novice learners, to build connections between formal procedures and their informal intuitive conceptual knowledge (moving along a path). The results also demonstrated that the verbal guidance was an important means of enhancing learning in game-based multimedia environments using multiple representations. Another result was that students' lower computer proficiency could undermine the potential benefits of learning in such environments (see also Clarke, Ayres, and Sweller, 2005 for the importance of prior familiarity with computer spreadsheet software for learning mathematics with this software). The results supported growing evidence that guided discovery learning is more instructionally effective than pure discovery learning.

Discovery-based educational games may have positive learning effects only when students have sufficient cognitive resources to process multiple representations and parameters in working memory. High computer experienced learners (especially those who were provided with verbal guidance) outperformed low experience learners in the study of Moreno and Duran (2004). Practical implications of these results are the importance of bringing students to a higher prior level of computer proficiency and the importance of reflecting on problem solution before attempting an answer. Discovery learning may not be an effective means in learning higher-order rules when learners need to combine entirely new set of rules with previously learned prior knowledge structures (Moreno, 2004, Gagne, 1965).

Mayer, Mautone, and Prothero (2002) demonstrated that students learned better from a geology game when they received explicit guidance about how to visualize geological structures. Moreno (2004) found that students benefited more from explanatory rather than merely corrective feedback in a multimedia game about environmental problems. Learning new mathematical procedures could also be overwhelming for novice learners when no guidance is provided.

The instructional effectiveness of educational games could be low (especially for learners with low levels of prior knowledge) if no sufficient instructional support is provided and students are involved in purely discovery learning. Leutner (1993) investigated learning effects of two forms of instructional guidance, system-initiated adaptive advice and learner-requested non-adaptive pre-tutorial background information. These forms of guidance were provided to learners in an exploratory computer-based simulation game environment for geography high-school classes. The games were built around the economics situations of small farms.

As expected, students without any support learned how to play the game but acquired hardly any domain-specific knowledge. On the other hand, with adaptive advice, students were able to acquire a substantial degree of domain knowledge (as evidenced by the immediate post-test), but limited functional knowledge of how to play the game. In regards to background information, the results indicated that, if permanently available, it increased the acquisition of domain knowledge as evidenced by the delayed memory retention test. Leutner (1993) concluded that if acquisition of domain specific concepts, facts, rules, and principles of the domain is the goal of learning, then appropriate explicit instructional support should be made available during system exploration.

OPTIMIZING LEARNER GUIDANCE AND SUPPORT IN SIMULATIONS

Cognitive load theory predicts a general inefficiency of purely exploratory simulations for novice learners. According to this theory, exploratory learning environments may impose excessive levels of cognitive load for such learners. A study was designed to compare highly interactive exploratory simulations that required learners to generate and test hypotheses with a less interactive, direct instruction version of the same content. It was based on a worked-out simulation as a series of static frames demonstrating step-by-step procedures of actual hypothesis testing. In this instructional format, the learner interactions with the learning environment were limited to selecting sequential procedural steps to study (Kalyuga & Plass, 2007; Plass, Homer, Milne, Jordan, & Kalyuga, 2006).

The exploratory simulation was similar to that described in Chapter VI (see Figure 14). In this simulation, learners read a brief introductory paragraph and then manipulated the sliders, numbers, and graphs on their own until they felt they had an adequate understanding of the system. "Worked-out simulations" represented an alternative to exploratory simulations. In "worked-out" versions, a step-by-step approach was used first to demonstrate learners how to approach the exploration of the system. Participants read each fragment of the explanatory text and saw a corresponding demonstration of the action.

At the beginning of the worked-out simulation the following introduction was presented to learners:

When exploring a system with many variables, a good strategy is to change only one variable to observe its effects on another variables. In this section, you will study relationships between two different variables at a time, with the remaining third variable locked.

Suppose you wish to work out how the gas pressure changes when you change the temperature. In this case the volume of the gas remains constant.

Please follow the numbered steps and read the provided explanations carefully. Click on each note to see the corresponding changes in the simulation. Please read all the explanations before moving on.

The following numbered on-screen buttons were available (with hypertext links for triggering corresponding explanations and visualizations):

1. *Select a value for the volume and lock it.*
2. *Select a value for the temperature.*
3. *Check the value for the pressure.*
4. *Increase the temperature.*
5. *What happens to the pressure?*
6. *Increase the temperature further.*

7. *What happens to the pressure?*
8. *Decrease the temperature.*
9. *What happens to the pressure?*

An example of corresponding on-screen directions for the above steps that were accompanied by highlighted screenshots is provided below:

1. *Set the volume to 5 L and lock it.*
2. *Set the temperature to 320 K.*
3. *Notice the corresponding value for the gas pressure (5.3 atm).*
4. *Increase the temperature by 100 K to 420 K.*
5. *Notice that the pressure has increased by 1.6 atm to 6.9 atm.*
6. *Increase the temperature by another 100 K to 520 K.*
7. *Notice that the pressure has increased by the same increment of 1.6 atm to 8.5 atm.*
8. *Decrease the temperature by a halved increment of 50 K from 520 K to 470 K*
9. *Notice that the pressure dropped by the halved increment 1.6/2 = 0.8 atm from 8.5 atm to 7.7 atm.*

Within a cognitive load framework, it could be expected that worked-out instructional formats could reduce cognitive overload for less experienced learners and enhance learning outcomes. Also, adding iconic representations (see Chapter VI for the description of this cognitive load reduction technique) could possibly have stronger learning effects when used with worked-out simulations.

Sixty six high-school students in 11-12 grades (age range 16-18) participated in this experiment. Students had not studied any materials related to gas laws by the time of the experiment, and, therefore, were novices to the topic. The study was conducted in the school computer lab during regular class hours. Instructional materials included four versions of simulations designed using Macromedia Flash software and delivered on a web page that was viewed using desktop PCs. All experimental data was also collected online.

Treatment 1 contained the worked-out simulation with symbolic-only representations of input parameters. Treatment 2 contained the same worked-out simulation with added iconic representations for temperature, pressure, and volume. Treatments 3 and 4 contained exploratory simulations with, correspondingly, symbolic and added iconic representations identical to those used in the previous treatment versions. The experimental procedure included an initial pre-test of learners' knowledge, an instructional session, and a post-test. Pre- and post-tests were similar to those used in the previous experiments (described in Chapter VI).

The students' novice status in the corresponding task domain was supported by relatively low pre-test scores. Means and standard deviations were 2.97 (SD = 1.54) out of the maximum possible value of 10 for short-answer (transfer) questions; and 2.17 (SD = 1.20) out of 6 for multiple-choice (retention) questions.

The independent variable was the type of treatment. The dependent variables under analysis were differences between the final and initial test z-scores (calculated separately for multiple-choice and short-answer scores) as indicators of the relative gains in learners' knowledge due to the instructional session. Because pre- and post-tests were structurally different, standardized z-scores were used as indicators of students' relative standing and changes in performance (Table 3).

Since there was a specific cognitive load theory-generated directional hypotheses about the expected pattern of means prior to running this experiment, one-tailed planned-comparisons tests of the hypotheses were applied. Two hypotheses for this experiment (dealing with novice learners) were that worked-out simulations would be more beneficial than exploratory simulations; and that simulations using added iconic representations would be more beneficial than symbolic-only representations.

The results for corresponding contrasts for testing these hypotheses were:

- overall difference between worked-out and exploratory simulations indicated significant results favoring worked-out simulations for transfer questions; there were no statistically significant differences for retention questions, although the effect size .2 indicated a possible small effect favoring the worked-out format;
- overall difference between iconic and symbolic representations indicated marginally significant results favoring iconic representations for retention questions ($p = 0.07$);

Table 3. Means and standard deviations for different versions of simulations

	symbolic worked-out (1) N=15	iconic worked-out (2) N=16	symbolic exploratory (3) N=17	iconic exploratory (4) N=18
short answers				
M	.13	.30	-.15	-.23
SD	.78	.57	1.00	1.05
multiple-choice				
M	-.22	.32	-.22	.11
SD	1.12	.92	1.23	1.39

- difference between iconic and symbolic representations for worked-out simulations indicated marginally significant results favoring iconic representations for retention questions ($p = 0.08$); there were no statistically significant differences for transfer questions, although the effect size of 0.25 indicated a possible small-to-medium effect favoring the iconic format;
- difference between iconic and symbolic representations for exploratory simulations indicated no statistically significant results, although for retention tasks, the effect size of 0.25 indicated a possible small-to-medium effect favoring the iconic format;
- difference between worked-out and exploratory simulations using symbolic representations indicated no statistically significant results, although for transfer tasks, the effect size of 0.31 indicated a possible small-to-medium effect favoring the worked-out format;
- difference between worked-out and exploratory simulations using iconic representations indicated significant results favoring worked-out simulations for transfer tasks; for retention tasks, the effect size of 0.17 indicated a possible small effect favoring the worked-out format.

Overall conclusion from this study was that for less knowledgeable learners, using guided worked-out simulations and simulations with added iconic representations represented preferable instructional options, especially when these two features were combined together (Kalyuga & Plass, 2007; Plass, et al., 2006).

EVALUATING COGNITIVE LOAD IN ONLINE SIMULATIONS

Cognitive load associated with different formats of instructional simulations was evaluated with a small group of university students in a pilot study using concurrent verbal reports (Kalyuga & Plass, 2008; see Chapter V for the general description of the method). The four versions of the simulation were used in this study: worked-out simulation with symbolic-only representations (A); worked-out simulation with added iconic representations (B); exploratory simulations with symbolic-only representations (C); exploratory simulations with added iconic representations (D). There was only one difference between these simulations and those used in the comparative study described in the previous section: in both worked-out versions, brief animated video clips were used instead of still images with highlights.

Eight undergraduate university students with some prior knowledge in basic high school level or college freshman level chemistry were interviewed (they were paid for their participation in the study). Four instructional treatments were rotated between respondents in a way that each participant worked consecutively with three different versions in around one-hour session. The following specific participants' remarks were identified as indicators of extraneous cognitive load for different versions of the simulation:

A (symbolic worked-out):
SPATIAL SPLIT-ATTENTION:
I'm paying too much attention to little arrow.
Watching them all at the same time could be difficult.
Confusing, not sure what to do. Hard to isolate things.
I didn't pay attention to see the actual change on the graph.
A lot of things to look at once (slider and graph). I'd replay.
A lot of things.
I look at the numbers, but try to look at the graph too.
It'd be easier if there was one graph (picture) instead of two, so I'd focus on it.
A lot is going on at once, numbers are changing!

TEMPORAL SPLIT-ATTENTION:
I must go back to see previous pressure results
Clicking – everything that was before disappears
I'm struggling to figure out things.
I forgot what I did at the previous one.
I'd write down things.
If graph was on a sheet, it couldn't be ignored.
While I'm reading, this is being done. I've missed this. I keep rewinding. Rewind is a good thing.
Need to refer back to previous step to see the change.
Separate chart would make things seen better
Lost track what you are doing.
Diagram shows past trials, container shows this moment.

REDUNDANCY:
Repetitions, I've already realized the relationship from first two.
It's frustratingly slow.
A little dull.

EXCESSIVE INFORMATION:
Everything's moving at the same time.
There are three variables on the screen and a container. Even though one is locked, you expect to see only two.

B (iconic worked-out):
SPATIAL SPLIT-ATTENTION:
I didn't look at the graph much, graphics is not useful.
Moving around a lot, don't see anything else.

TEMPORAL SPLIT-ATTENTION:
Lost track what you are doing. A lot of things.

REDUNDANCY:
Slow, boring, dragging; watching things but nothing to do about it. May be previous one [version A] *could be better.*

EXCESSIVE INFORMATION:
I checked the solution but did not remembered. Looking at text, not seeing visuals (so fast!)

C (symbolic exploratory):
TEMPORAL SPLIT-ATTENTION:
It would be easier [to make predictions where the next dot on the graph is going to be] *if my old graphs stay on top of the screen.*
It's difficult to keep track of previous simulation.
I'm manipulating and seeing, but I keep storing it. It's difficult to look back.

REDUNDANCY:
Graph: I see how it's moving (rather than slowly dot-by-dot).

EXCESSIVE INFORMATION:
I am confused with temperature vs pressure or pressure vs temperature. Good to have both graphs together.
It is difficult to figure out what's happening.
It's difficult because of storing everything in my mind.
I have to remember that I'm moving Temperature or Pressure.

SEARCH:
I'm just picking numbers.

D (iconic exploratory):
SPATIAL SPLIT-ATTENTION:
This is really hard. Paying attention to gas particles, how they react to my changing aspects of the experiment; now try to pay attention to the graph.
I don't like icons: they take away from actual experiment.

TEMPORAL SPLIT-ATTENTION:
I think I missed something, I go back to see relationship between Pressure and Temperature.
Lost track what you are doing.

REDUNDANCY:
Extra stuff; flames get in the way (no need to show six flames to show temperature rising).

EXCESSIVE INFORMATION:
Too much going on the screen; extra things, like a flashy show.
A lot of things.

Based on the total numbers of extraneous cognitive load-relevant remarks for each condition, version A was the most cognitively demanding (25 remarks), and version B was the least demanding (5 remarks). Versions C (9) and D (7) were in-between, with D less loading than C. The evaluation results indicated that animated video clips in the symbolic worked out-simulation generated most cognitive load due to split attention (animations running at the same time as users read the textual explanations). Adding dynamic iconic images helped to alleviate this overload by providing an alternative, less cognitively stressful means to comprehend the dependencies between gas characteristics. There was also a positive cognitive load-reducing effect of adding iconic representations to exploratory conditions, however, the effect was weaker (the absence of simultaneously running animations eliminated a source of split attention).

COGNITIVE LOAD ISSUES IN USING MOBILE DEVICES

Mobile and ubiquitous devices become increasingly popular educational technology tools. Bay & Ziefle (2007) noted that mobile devices with small screens but complex functionality characteristics can impose high levels of cognitive load on users and cause difficulties in finding required functions. They investigated forms of instruction that may reduce such difficulties more effectively than a commonly used active exploration approach.

For example, an important factor that influences cognitive load in mobile devices is orientation in the menu of the device. When using complex menu structures, learners need to build a mental representation of the spatial structure of the menu that guides them in their search and navigation. It is especially important for small screen devices where the overall structure of the menu is not transparent and the search process is not visually supported (most of the menu functions are hidden most of the time). A correct representation of the overall structure of the menu (survey knowledge) is important, as well as the correct path to take (route knowledge) and the knowledge of salient features of the menu branch to follow (landmark knowledge) (Ziefle et al., 2006).

The development of the spatial knowledge should be supported by appropriate instructions. For example, maps of menu structures for the survey knowledge could be used if learners have sufficient level of spatial abilities (e.g., older children). For younger children with less spatial abilities, understanding and integrating the survey knowledge could be difficult. A sequential aid in the form of a step-by-step instruction of the different actions could be more useful, although still cognitively demanding (e.g., because of the need to memorize single steps to be executed). An explorative trial-and-error interaction is characteristic of children (Bay & Ziefle, 2005). However, building up a mental representation requires an initial structure as a frame of reference that may not be available in the case of younger children.

Bay & Ziefle (2007) compared three forms of instruction: 1) step-by-step instruction that provided landmark and route knowledge; 2) map of the menu structure in a graphical tree with the names and locations of the functions that provided survey as well as landmark knowledge (the functions' names); and 3) an exploratory condition in which landmark, survey, and route knowledge may be acquired. For older children (11-12 years old), the results indicated a superiority of the two instructional formats that provided survey knowledge (diagrams of the menu structure and the exploration). For younger children (9-10 years old) with lower levels of spatial abilities that were required for constructing mental representations, the landmark information in the step-by-step instructions could be more helpful. However, such instructions may impose a heavy cognitive load considering that single steps need to be held in working memory before being executed.

Bay & Ziefle (2007) concluded that constructing spatial mental representations in the form of survey knowledge of the menu structure is important, especially for children. This process should be supported by appropriate instructions. A diagrammatic instruction that provides survey knowledge by presenting the menu structure and the location of the functions appropriate for the task could reduce time almost four times.

Empirical studies provided convincing evidence of a possible heavy cognitive load when using mobile phones. Children without much experience in using mobile devices may have major difficulties carrying out simple and basic phone operations (e.g., changing a setting of the phone). For example, when exploring four phone tasks, 13-14 year old children performed 130 detouring steps and returned 17 times to the previous higher levels in menu hierarchy (only 36 steps in total were necessary to solve the four tasks) (Ziefle et al., 2006).

For younger children (9-10 years old), a simplified diagram of the menu structure with less detail can reduce cognitive overload (Bay & Ziefle, 2007). It was shown with adult participants that a diagram of the menu tree without the names of the functions to be selected could be more efficient than a menu tree with the function labels (a possible redundancy effect). Also, orientation aids could be placed onto the displays of mobile phones instead of separate manuals (Ziefle & Bay, 2006).

From a more general perspective, mobile learning is learning across contexts rather than just learning with portable devices. Instead of replicating traditional instructional approaches and methods in mobile devices, such learning needs to reflect the complexity of the relationship between learner and technology, explore new learning activities supported by mobile technology, and to investigate possible innovations in a broader social context (Sharples, 2006). Mobile learning may create rich environments for implementing non-traditional pedagogical approaches, such as collaborative and contextual learning environments, gaming and simulation-based learning. However, if not kept under control, excessive cognitive load may eliminate all advantages of this new educational technology tool.

FUTURE TRENDS IN INSTRUCTIONAL SIMULATIONS AND GAMES

Any learning process, especially in predominantly exploratory-based environments such as instructional simulations and games, involves learning events that trigger associated affective responses. A significant share of such events is related to cognitive load conditions. An important research direction in this area is establishing relations between cognitive load and emotional states that are important for learning, as well as their links with self-regulation and meta-cognitive processes in knowledge construction and elaboration. Affect-sensitive models of learning in multimedia environments need to be developed and used in optimizing cognitive load conditions.

From this point of view, rapidly developing research field of affective computing is an important source of relevant knowledge on the intersection of emotion and computer science. This field is aimed at studying the role of emotion and other affective phenomena in relation to human-computer interaction, graphics, vision, speech, synthetic characters, educational simulations, games, and related areas. Some particularly important research areas for future improvements in adaptive multimedia learning environments could be:

- recognizing affective body language (e.g., face/body/gesture affect recognition, modeling, and animation; motion capture for affect recognition);
- affective speech and language processing (e.g., affective speech analysis, recognition and synthesis; affective text processing);
- design of affective interactions (multimodal dialogue systems' interfaces; affective tutoring systems);
- affective agents in dynamical systems (e.g., models of emotion and personality in agent architectures).

The advanced game design is currently focused on generating human-like intelligent characters using various adaptive learning techniques based on rich forms of human-machine interaction. It is assumed that intelligent behaviors would enhance the player/learner satisfaction and knowledge gains from the game. However, there is generally little evidence and analyses of whether such designs in fact enhance learning. Another important research area is the design of optimized adaptive game-based learning environments based on learner cognitive models in order to provide the appropriate resources adapted to learner needs and personal cognitive characteristics. It is important to develop adaptive methodologies for enriching learner gaming experiences.

Finally, the issues of instructional effectiveness of collaborative learning (including simulation and gaming) environments remain an important area of research. In the framework of computer supported collaborative work research, Mason & Cooper (2007) investigated instructional effects of pair computing as a form of cooperative gaming. In this from of collaboration, two learners use one personal computer sharing one keyboard, one mouse, and one monitor. The important question is under what conditions is the paired computing most beneficial? Based on the cognitive load theoretical framework, Mason & Cooper (2007) suggested that the paired computing approach is more effective when dealing with problems that are characterized by higher intrinsic cognitive load ("difficult" problems) rather than those with lower intrinsic cognitive load ("easy" problems). Puzzles like Tower of Hanoi with well established levels of difficulty (e.g., Kotovsky, Hayes and Simon, 1985) were used in the experimental study. Based on the quality and quantity of learners' verbal and physical interactions captured by videotape and other recorded data, studies with Grade 6-8 students demonstrated that there were significantly more personal interactions as task difficulty increased. Results also indicated that there was a clear advantage to the paired approach in casse of moderately difficult problems.

MULTIMEDIA INSTRUCTIONAL DESIGN IMPLICATIONS

Previously described techniques (Chapters II, III, VI-VIII) for managing cognitive load in multimedia learning environments could be used in specific instructional simulations and games (e.g., split-attention, contiguity, redundancy, cueing, modality and other cognitive load effects). Expertise reversal effect requires considering levels of learner prior knowledge in a specific task domain before applying these techniques.

The following general implications of the expertise reversal effect for the design of instructional simulations and games could be outlined:

- formats of simulations need to be tailored to levels of learner prior knowledge in a specific domain;
- for novice learners, fully or partially worked-out simulations and simulations with added iconic representations need to be used;
- when designing simulations in the absence of information about levels of task-specific expertise of intended learners, elements of worked-out simulations and iconic representations should be incorporated in order to provide optional instructional support (e.g. hints on exploratory strategies);
- developing adaptive procedures for simulation-based learning environments could be the best way to cognitively optimize such environments.

SUMMARY OF CHAPTER IX

The optimal use of instructional simulations and games needs to be consistent with human learning processes. Since most of these educational technology tools are designed as exploratory learning environments with relatively limited guidance provided to learners, they may impose excessive levels of working memory load thus interfering with meaningful learning. Optimizing levels of instructional guidance in such environments represent an important means of managing cognitive load and enhancing learning outcomes. The selection of an appropriate format of interactive dynamic visual representations in such environments should take into account levels of learner prior knowledge in a specific task domain in order to successfully manage cognitive load.

Concurrent verbal reporting methods (with audio and screen capture of learner online behavior) could be used to evaluate and compare levels of extraneous cognitive load in simulations and educational gaming environments. Based on such evaluation procedures, the technology could be improved to better match the nature of human cognition. For example, similar to other learning environments, split attention situations need to be checked and eliminated by integrating graphics and text or using auditory modality for presenting verbal information; redundant representations should be eliminated to reduce unnecessary distractions of cognitive resources; and cueing techniques could be used for appropriately directing learner attention.

REFERENCES

Bay, S., & Ziefle, M. (2005). Children using cellular phones. The effects of shortcomings in user interface design. *Human Factors, 47*, 158-168.

Bay, S., & Ziefle, M. (2007). Landmarks or surveys? The impact of different instructions on children's performance in hierarchical menu structures. *Computers in Human Behavior.*

Boyle, T. (2004). Designing multimedia e-learning for science education. In R. Holliman & E. Scanlon (Eds.), *Mediating science learning through information and communication technology* (pp. 103-119). London: Routledge Falmer.

Baggott, L., & Nichol, J. (1998). Multimedia simulation. A threat to or enhancement of practical work in science education? In J. Wellington (Ed.), *Practical work in school science* (pp. 252-270). London: Routledge.

Clarke, T., Ayres, P., & Sweller, J. (2005). The impact of sequencing and prior knowledge on learning mathematics through spreadsheet applications. *Educational Technology Research and Development, 53(3).* 15-24.

Clement, J., Brown, D. E., & Zietsman, A. (1989). Not all preconceptions are misconceptions: Finding "anchoring conceptions" for grounding instruction on students' intuitions. *International Journal of Science Education, 11*, 554-565.

Gagne, R. M. (1965). *The conditions of learning.* New York: Holt.

Hennesy, S., Deaney, R., & Ruthven, K. (2006). Situated expertise in integrating use of multimedia simulation into secondary science teaching. *International Journal of Science Education, 28*, 701-732.

Kalyuga, S., & Plass, J. (2007). Managing cognitive load in instructional simulations. In M. B. Nunes & M. McPherson (Eds.), Proceedings of the IADIS International Conference E-Learning 2007, July 6-8, 2007, Lisbon, Portugal (Volume 1, pp. 27-34). International Association for Development of the Information Society (IADIS) Press. ISBN: 978-972-8924-34-8

Kalyuga, S., & Plass, J. (2008). Evaluating and managing cognitive load in games. In R. Ferdig (Ed.), *Handbook of Research on Effective Electronic Gaming*. Hershey, PA: IGI Global (in press).

Kotovsky, K., Hayes, J. R., & Simon, H. A. (1985). Why are some problems hard? Evidence from Tower of Hanoi. *Cognitive Psychology, 17,* 248-294.

Leutner, D. (1993). Guided discovery learning with computer-based simulation games: Effects of adaptive and non-adaptive instructional support. *Learning and Instruction, 3*, 113-132.

Lewis, E. L., Stern, J. L., & Linn, M. C. (1993). The effect of computer simulations on introductory thermodynamics understanding. *Educational Technology, January*, 45-58.

Linn, M. C., & Songer, N. B. (1991). Teaching thermodynamics to middle school students: What are appropriate cognitive demands? *Journal of Research in Science Teaching, 28*, 885-918.

Mason, R., & Cooper, G. (2007). When are two heads better than one? A study on the effects of task difficulty on pair computing. Paper presented at the International Cognitive Load Theory Conference, 24-26 March, Sydney, Australia.

Mayer, R., Mautone, P. D., & Prothero, W. (2002). Pictorial aids for learning by doing in a multimedia geology simulation game. *Journal of Educational Psychology, 94*, 171-185.

McFarlane, A., & Sakellariou, S. (2002). The role of ICT in science education. *Cambridge Journal of Education, 32*, 219-232.

Monaghan, J. M., & Clement, J. (1999). Use of a computer simulation to develop mental simulations for understanding relative motion concepts. *International journal of Science Education, 21*, 921-944.

Moreno, R. (2004). Decreasing cognitive load for novice students: Effects of explanatory versus corrective feedback on discovery-based multimedia. *Instructional Science, 32*, 99-113.

Moreno, R., & Duran, R. (2004). Do multiple representations need explanations? The role of verbal guidance and individual differences in multimedia mathematics learning. *Journal of Educational Psychology, 96*, 492-503.

Plass, J., Homer, B., Milne, C., Jordan, T., & Kalyuga, S. (2006). Molecules and Minds: Optimizing Cognitive Load in Simulations for Science Education. Paper presented at *the 2006 Research Conference of the Institute of Educational Sciences (IES), US Department of Education,* 15 – 16 June, 2006, Washington, DC.

Sharples, M. (Ed.) (2006) *Big Issues in Mobile Learning: Report of a workshop by the Kaleidoscope Network of Excellence Mobile Learning Initiative*. Available at http://telearn.noe-kaleidoscope.org/warehouse/Sharples-2006.pdf

Taylor, R. S., & Chi, M. T. H. (2006). Simulation versus text: Acquisition of implicit and explicit information. *Journal of Educational Computing Research, 35(3)*, 289-313.

Tennyson, R. D., & Breuer, K. (2002). Improving problem solving and creativity through use of complex-dynamic simulations. *Computers in Human Behavior, 18*, 650-668.

Ziefle, M., & Bay, S. (2006). How to overcome disorientation in mobile phones. Menus: A comparison of two different types of navigation aids. *Human Computer Interaction, 21*, 393-432.

Ziefle, M., Bay, S., & Schwade, A. (2006). On key's meaning and modes: The impact of different navigation key solutions on children's efficiency using a mobile phone. *Behaviour and Information Technology, 25*, 413-431.

SUMMARY OF SECTION II

This part of the book reviewed empirical findings related to managing cognitive load in verbal and pictorial representations, interactive multimedia, dynamic visual representations, and instructional simulations and games. Empirically established interactions between levels of learner expertise and different formats of multimedia presentations (expertise reversal effect) were described.

The expertise reversal effect has been consistently replicated with a large range of instructional materials and participants either as a full reversal (with significant differences for both novices and experts) or, more often, as a partial reversal (with a non-significant effect for either novices or experts, but with a significant interaction). The estimates of effect size differences for novices and experts ranged from 0.45 to 2.99, with the overall mid-range value of 1.72. This number could be interpreted in a simplified way as indicating that if there were effects of a similar magnitude on both sides (for novices and experts), the effect size for each side would be around 0.86, a large-size effect by accepted standards. If the effect is of relatively lower magnitude on one side (the case in most studies), then it would be accordingly stronger on the other side.

In cognitive load theory, the expertise reversal effect is associated with imbalances between learner organized knowledge base and provided instructional guidance. Two major types of such imbalances are described. One could be caused by an insufficient learner knowledge base that is not complemented by appropriate instructional guidance, especially at the initial stages of novice learning. Another type of imbalance could be caused by overlaps between available knowledge of more advanced learners and provided instructional guidance. The need for higher knowledge learners to integrate and cross-reference redundant instructional guidance with available knowledge structures that relate to the same situations may consume additional cognitive resources. A minimal instructional guidance would allow these learners to take advantage of their knowledge base in the most efficient way.

The expertise reversal effect is a logical extension of the aptitude-treatment interaction studies. Although the need to consider levels of learner prior knowledge was recognized early within that approach, few research studies and instructional design recommendations demonstrated explicitly how to use the aptitude-treatment interaction approach in practice. Aptitudes and instructional treatments were investigated without taking into account associated cognitive processes. Applied psychometric rather than cognitive diagnostic measurement instruments were not suitable for real-time use in adaptive instructional systems.

Cognitive load theoretical framework creates conditions for effectively handling these shortcomings. However, a limited number of studies in optimal instructional methods that could be used for balancing executive guidance at different levels of learner expertise is a major limitation of the research in this area. Identifying broader range of instructional methods and procedures that are optimal for learners with different levels of expertise remains an essential direction for future research. Extending findings from mostly well-defined technical domains to relatively poorly defined tasks and domains represents another important research direction.

General guidelines for managing cognitive load in multimedia learning could be briefly summarised in three separate directions. *Managing intrinsic cognitive load* could be achieved by, for example, appropriately sequencing learning tasks from simple to complex or by presenting isolated elements first followed by the presentation of all interactions between them. *Decreasing extraneous cognitive load* could be accomplished by presenting verbal explanations that accompany pictorial material contiguously in time or space, preferably as narrations, adapting the pacing of presentations to learner cognitive characteristics, properly segmenting presentations, presenting cues to prevent unnecessary visual search, etc. Finally, *increasing germane cognitive load* could be done, for example, by presenting problems that vary in relevant features, prompting learners to predict the next step in a process or imagine procedures and concepts.

Online or computer-based multimedia environments allow plenty of opportunities for implementing cognitively-based design principles and techniques for managing cognitive load. For example, dynamic onscreen presentations could display only relations and links corresponding to selected elements of the text or diagrams when needed by individual learners. Also, on-screen diagrams could be combined with auditory explanations instead of conventional visual-only formats. For more experienced learners, however, elimination of redundant audio and visual sources of information could be beneficial for learning by turning off the auditory mode.

According to the expertise reversal effect, in order to balance the executive function and optimize cognitive load, direct guidance should be provided to low-prior knowledge learners at the appropriate time; unnecessary redundant support should be timely removed as a learners becomes more experienced with the task domain; the rates of information presentations could be regulated to ensure that the learner cognitive capacity is not exceeded. Information presentation formats should also be dynamically tailored to changing levels of learner task-specific expertise.

Eventually, adaptive applications that allow dynamic tailoring of instructional multimedia presentations to changing cognitive characteristics of individual learners have the best potential for optimizing cognitive load and working in harmony with human cognitive architecture. The recent studies in rapid diagnostic assessment methods may offer appropriate real-time tools for the dynamic optimization of instruction. Such assessment methods may provide adequate fine-grained measures of levels of task-specific expertise with a sufficient diagnostic power for learner-tailored instructional procedures. These issues and specific examples will be considered in the following part of the book.

Section III
Towards Cognitively Efficient Adaptive Multimedia

Chapter X
Tailoring Multimedia Environments to Learner Cognitive Characteristics

INTRODUCTION

Personalized adaptive multimedia environments provide individual learners or learner groups with experience that is specifically tailored to them. To achieve effective personalization, a variety of information about the learner is required. Tailoring multimedia environments to individual learner cognitive characteristics is becoming a major means for achieving a true learner-centered experience for learners through their interaction with multiple content sources, presentation formats, and delivery means. Personalized multimedia environments are capable of realizing advanced learning and instruction strategies based on a continuous process of adaptation between the learners and instructional systems. This adaptation process could be accomplished through personalized interaction and adaptive presentation of content, learner feedback, adaptive navigation and search, and different adaptation methodologies.

As was mentioned in earlier chapters of this book, a major instructional implication of the expertise reversal effect is the need to tailor dynamically instructional techniques and procedures, levels of instructional guidance to current levels of learner task-specific expertise. In online multimedia instructional systems, the levels of learner task-specific expertise change as students develop more experience in a specific task domain. Therefore, the tailoring process needs to be dynamic, i.e. consider learner levels of expertise in real time as they gradually change during the learning sessions.

This Chapter describes general approaches to the design of adaptive learning environments from the perspective of tailoring learning procedures and techniques to individual cognitive characteristics of learners. Studies in aptitude-treatment interactions offered a possible approach to adaptive instruction. Intelligent tutoring systems and adaptive web-based hypermedia systems use learner models to tailor learning tasks and instructional content to individual learner characteristics. This approach accommodates learner characteristics (e.g., knowledge, interests, goals) into explicit learner models that guide adaptive procedures. On the other hand, advisement and adaptive guidance approaches realize a greater learner control over instruction and provide individualized prescriptive information in the form of recommended material and tasks based on learner past performance.

APTITUDE-TREATMENT INTERACTIONS AND ADAPTIVE INSTRUCTION

Tobias (1989) reviewed the state of research on aptitude-treatment interactions as the basis for adaptive instruction. He noted that the adaptation of instruction to student characteristics had been a much sought after idea with a long history of studies. However, it was very difficult to develop evidence-based theoretical approaches for such adaptations that could provide guidelines to practitioners. The idea of adaptive instruction was clearly articulated within the ATI approach. Cronbach (1967) and Glaser (1977) suggested that aptitude-treatment interactions and measures of aptitudes can be used for adapting instructional treatments to learner characteristics in order to reach learning goals more efficiently.

Cronbach (1967) distinguished several ways of adapting instruction to individual differences. Adaptation within a predetermined program assumes fixed sets of educational goals and instructional treatments. Possible modifications to meet individual needs in this environments include altering duration of schooling by sequential selection (e.g., dropping students out along the way) or training students to criterion on any skill or topic, which also results in altering the duration of instruction. The rate of learning is the key concept in this approach.

The second approach, the adaptation by matching goals to the individual, assumes differentiated or optional goals and fixed instructional treatments within an optional goal. Possible modifications to meet individual needs include providing a curriculum that prepares each student for her or his determined prospective adult role. The third approach, adaptation by erasing individual differences, assumes educational goals fixed within a course or program and alternative instructional treatments provided to students. Possible modifications to meet individual needs include providing remedial adjuncts to fixed main instructional procedures and teaching different students by different methods.

Finally, the fourth approach is the adaptation by altering instructional method. "It may become possible to use level of prior achievement adaptively; that is, students with high prior familiarity in a given area may be assigned to an instructional treatment, with minimal instructional support, or to a forward-ranching sequence. On the other hand, students with low prior achievement may require maximal instructional support each step of the way. Such adaptation to individual differences would be a notable step towards individualizing the method of instruction rather than merely the instructional rate" (Tobias, 1976). This approach is closely related to the contemporary methods for the design of adaptive instruction, including those proposed later in this chapter.

Cronbach & Snow (1969) mentioned different ways in which to deal with learner individual differences "from procrustean methods that involve little adaptation, through intuitive and little tested rules for adaptation, up to, in principle, tested rules derived from theory" (p. 175). The first two approaches adjust instruction through an initial selection or/and varying rate of completion. Each unit creates a basis for building the next level. A theory-based approach requires understanding of factors that cause an individual to learn better from one instructional method than from another.

Cronbach's (1967) adaptive model was elaborated by Tennyson (1975) as a pre-task adaptation model. According to this model, instructional treatments are determined from aptitude measurements taken before the actual learning situation, and then certain types of students are assigned to specific instructional treatments depending on these measurements. Federico (1999) referred to this model as a macro-treatment adaptation approach typical to all ATI research. In contrast, an alternative micro-treatment adaptation approach is based on within-task measures taken while students are in the instructional situation. These two approaches should supposedly be used together. Macro-treatments could be selected first based on initial pre-task measures. Then, instructional procedures could be further refined and optimized using micro-treatments based on continuous monitoring of learning behavior (Federico, 1980, 1999).

In the traditional ATI approach (Cronbach & Snow, 1969, 1977), variations in aptitudes were examined and instructional treatment selected without considering differences in cognitive processes among the learners. Adaptive cognitive-based systems should be designed based on relevant learner cognitive attributes and processes (knowledge and rules that students bring to learning) rather than on irrelevant psychometric measures of abilities and aptitudes (Federico, 1999). The latter measures are in fact results of students' use of these cognitive attributes and processes. Learners' cognitive processes change as they acquire more proficiency, and these changes represent the essence of individual differences. Adapting instruction to these changes is most important for optimizing learning processes (Boutwell & Barton, 1974).

Federico (1980) noted that traditional psychometric measures of abilities and aptitudes were developed primarily for predictive and selective purposes, and not for measuring processes that actually occur during learning and performance. Such psychometric characteristics cannot be used for establishing instructional treatments that facilitate the cognitive processes of knowledge acquisition. Traditional ATIs were studied by using pre-task measures of aptitudes (abilities) and then prescribing instructional treatments based on learners' characteristics (a macro-treatment approach). In contrast, micro-treatment approach (Federico, 1999) uses within-task measures while the learner is in the instructional situation, This measurement is conducted on a more refined scale and with varying amount of prompting, feedback, examples, etc. When these two approaches are used conjointly, they may complement each other by selecting macro-treatments based on entry pre-task measures, and then refining instruction using micro-treatments for optimizing prescribed instructional treatments using continuous monitoring of learner behavior (Federico, 1980, 1999).

Merrill (1975) noted that main assumptions of ATI research were:

1) relative stability of aptitudes (characteristics of the individual) for a period of at least few months;
2) relative stability of treatments retaining similar patterns from occurrence to occurrence;
3) instructor- or system-based decision on what treatment is best for the student (the environment is adapted to the learner).

He suggested a set of alternative assumptions (Merrill, 1975, p.221):

1) Multidimensional dynamic aptitudes that change from moment to moment determine the treatment that is most appropriate for a given individual at a given moment in time.
2) The tactic that is of maximum value to a specific learner at one moment is likely not to be appropriate a moment later (dynamic, continually changed experience). The optimal next tactic for a given student at a given moment is determined by his position in multidimensional, dynamic state (aptitude space). The search for the interactions of stable aptitudes and fixed treatments could be valuable for psychology, but not for instructional science.
3) Individuals should be enabled to adapt the environment to themselves by making decisions on what tactics they want next rather than having this decision

made for them. An adapting-to-the-student procedure may make the student system-dependent and unable to cope with real life situations.

The ideas of the dynamic adaptation (using variable instructional treatments depending on changing learner cognitive characteristics) and the learner-controlled adaptation appeared to be productive directions for subsequent research and development efforts.

ADAPTIVE APPROACHES IN COMPLEX LEARNING ENVIRONMENTS

Expertise reversal effect is a special case of aptitude-treatment interactions with learner prior knowledge as an aptitude of interest. An adaptation methodology based on the expertise reversal effect essentially realizes a combined macro-micro adaptation approach (mentioned in the previous section) suggested by Federico (1999). According to the expertise reversal effect, appropriate information needs to be presented at the right time, and unnecessary redundant information should be timely removed as learners gain more expertise. Optimizing executive function in cognitive processes during learning assumes using only necessary instructional guidance and continuously removing redundant components as the level of learner task-specific expertise gradually increases.

Detailed direct instructional support should be provided to novice learners as a substitute for missing knowledge structures in performing the executive role for high-level cognitive processes. At intermediate levels of expertise, a mix of direct external support for constructing new knowledge and problem solving practice for exercising and strengthening previously acquired knowledge could be optimal instructional procedures. At higher levels of expertise, problem-solving or exploratory tasks that require using available in long-term memory knowledge structures could be cognitively optimal instructional methods. Changes in domain-specific knowledge base need to be evaluated in real time and specific instructional techniques and procedures tailored accordingly.

Some instructional design principles developed within a cognitive load theoretical framework effectively implemented this general approach to tailoring levels of instructional guidance to levels of learner expertise. For example, the principle of scaffolding suggests using worked examples, completion assignments, and conventional problems combined in a completion strategy (van Merrienboer, 1990; van Merrienboer & Paas, 1989; van Merrienboer, Kirschner & Kester, 2003). Faded worked-out examples (Renkl, 1997; Renkl & Atkinson, 2003; Renkl, Atkinson, Maier, & Staley, 2003) gradually reduce the number of worked-out steps with increased levels of learner expertise replacing them with corresponding problem solving steps. As levels of learner task-specific expertise increase, less guided exploratory, problem-solving, or game-base environments could effectively assist in learning advanced knowledge and skills in specific task domains.

The described adaptive approach is mostly system-controlled. With this approach, computer program or instructor selects dynamically an instructional method that is most appropriate at the current level of learner expertise. As mentioned previously, Merrill (1975) noted that traditional aptitude-treatment interaction research generally was based on the assumptions of relative stability of aptitudes and treatments and system- or instructor-controlled decisions on what treatment was best for the learner. He suggested that since student attributes are dynamic rather than static and continuously change from moment to moment, learners should be enabled to adapt the environment to themselves. They could actively and continuously select treatments most appropriate to their cognitive states. This learner-controlled approach to individualization of instruction represents an alternative way of dynamic tailoring of instruction to learner cognitive characteristics.

Despite expected advantages (e.g., positive attitudes, sense of control), research findings in regards of the effects of learner control do not support benefits of unrestricted learner control over instructional treatments, especially for low-achieving students. The results of relevant studies have been inconclusive in respect to the benefits of learner control, and more often negative rather than positive in terms of learning outcomes (Chung & Reigeluth, 1992; Kay, 2001; Lin & Hsieh, 2001; Niemec, Sikorski, & Walberg, 1996; Steinberg, 1977; 1989; Williams, 1996). The effectiveness of the learner-controlled approach depends on student ability to select appropriate learning strategies and most of all, on levels of learner prior knowledge. The recommendation of cognitive load theory is that students could have control over the content and instructional sequences when they have sufficient prior knowledge in the task domain. Low-knowledge learners, on the other hand, should be provided with appropriate levels o f assistance.

One form of such assistance is providing advisement to learners for making their own decisions (Tennyson, 1980, 1981; Tennyson & Rothen, 1979). Such advisement strategy combines a degree of learner control with the system-controlled evidence-based task selection. An advanced form of this approach is an adaptive guidance strategy that provides learners with diagnostic information on the current level of knowledge, advise on what to study or practice to achieve mastery, how to sequences learning tasks for gradual transition from basic to more complex strategies, and how to allocate cognitive resources (Bell & Kozlowski, 2002). As learners acquire basic lower-level knowledge, adaptive guidance tailors subsequent more advanced learning tasks.

Complex learning environments may impose high levels of cognitive demands on the learner (Azevedo, 2005). A possible way to offer additional support to learners is to integrate help facilities and hypertext glossaries into instructional computer-based presentations. Metacognitive support could be embedded into learning environments by using prompts or instructions on specific metacognitive activities integrated into the learning context (e.g. prompting students to give reasons for their actions). However, the integration of prompts into learning environments may increase cognitive load by demanding additional cognitive resources for processing this information, at least some part of which could not be directly relevant to the learning task. Nevertheless, Hsieh & O'Neil (2002) demonstrated that giving learners adapted knowledge of response feedback (customized information about their improvement from previous access to the feedback in addition to verification information on whether student answers were correct or incorrect) was significantly more beneficial than just knowledge of response feedback (verification information on whether student answers were correct or incorrect).

Intelligent tutoring systems represent an example of learning and assessment environments based on complex problem solving embedded in a content domain using technology. In such systems, instruction occurs as a function of learner responses to complex tasks (Baker & O'Neil, 2002). A model of learner knowledge is the basis for selecting and sequencing learning tasks in such systems (Anderson, Corbett, Koedinger, & Pelletier, 1995; Matin & vanLehn, 1995). Computer-based performance assessment for complex tasks substantially extends the range of skills assessed, as well as increases the precision of measurement (Baker & Mayer, 1999; O'Neil, 1999). Rowe, Cooke, Hall, and Halgren (1996) noted that intelligent tutoring should incorporate individualized instruction using detailed assessment of learner knowledge and appropriately directing instructional interventions.

Using an expert concept-mapping method, Stoyanov and Kirshner (2004) identified the following conceptual continuums as a framework for defining the concept of adaptation in learning environments: pre-assessment versus monitoring adaptation; system-centered versus learner-centered adaptation; single versus multiple adaptations; and preferential versus developmental adaptation. Based on the pre-assessment of different personal constructs (e.g., through tests or check-lists for knowledge, questionnaires for learning styles and locus of control), the learner may receive advice on what and how to study. Such a pre-specified adaptation approach may coexist with dynamic adaptation based on continuous tracking of learner activities. However, these two adaptation approaches are rarely combined in instructional theory and practice, even though both of them belong to system-centered forms of adaptation. In the learner-centered adaptation, learners are provided with possibilities to select available options themselves.

Most of existing adaptive systems match instruction to a single construct (e.g., level of prior knowledge or learning styles). Currently, the most commonly used approach to the design of adaptive computer-based environments is based on asking learners what they want using questionnaires and interviews (adaptation to user preferences). The developmental adaptation as an alternative to the preferential mode may help learners to develop their weak characteristics, and thus be more effective for achieving specific learning objectives (Stoyanov & Kirshner, 2004).

LEARNER MODELING IN ADAPTIVE ONLINE ENVIRONMENTS

The currently available approaches to adaptive multimedia are best articulated and implemented in the area of adaptive hypermedia systems. Hypermedia learning environments add navigation support to traditional linear multimedia environments. This capability of hypermedia systems provides appropriate levels of learner interactivity and learner control. It is usually implemented as an organized network of hyperlinks that allow learners nonlinear access to graphics, sound, animation, and other multimedia elements.

Adaptive hypermedia learning environments accommodate learner characteristics (knowledge, interests, goals, etc.) into an explicit learner or user model and then use this model to adapt interactions with each learner (user) to her or his characteristics and needs. For example, adaptive content selection and presentation could be provided, or a set of most relevant links to proceed could be suggested (see Brusilovsky, 2001; Brusilovsky, Kobsa, & Nejdl, 2007; Brusilovsky & Millan, 2007; De Bra & Calvi, 1998; Federico, 1999; Kobsa, 2001 for comprehensive overviews of the adaptive hypermedia field). Selecting the most relevant modes of presentations for an individual learner from text, narration, animation, video, etc. is an important part of adaptive presentation techniques based on the user modeling technology.

Hypermedia enhances learner control and flexibility by allowing learner themselves to adapt instruction to their needs. However, keeping track of activated links and navigational paths may substantially increase cognitive load and inhibit the acquisition of new knowledge (Locatis, Letourneau, & Banvard, 1989). It is especially relevant for novice learners who do not have sufficient knowledge and metacognitive skills for selecting optimal links in hypermedia learning environments.

Adapting navigational paths to levels of learner knowledge was suggested as a means of resolving this issue (Federico, 1999). In order to benefit from hypermedia learning environments, students should have appropriate levels of domain-specific knowledge and metacognitive skills. Alternatively, they need sufficient levels of guidance or advice in navigating through the learning environments in order to establish an appropriate balance between program and learner control. The suggested forms of advice include completing or repeating examples, lesson sequences and navigation paths (Large, 1996). Federico (1999) indicated that hypermedia learning environments allow learners to take individual navigational paths through the subject matter information space thus increasing the level of learner control. When appropriately tracked, this information can be used by intelligent tutors to implement adaptive instruction.

User or learner models (in learning systems) represent the key component of an adaptive hypermedia system. These models are multidimensional constructs that may include many different user characteristics in addition to subject matter knowledge. These characteristics may include levels of computer literacy, experience in using specific software applications, learning styles, background, preferences, goals, interests, etc. User or learner models are usually constructed by using traditional testing and survey methods, or recording the history of user interactions with the system (e.g., browsing behavior or navigation trace). These methods allow determining users' knowledge and experience, background, interests, preferences, learning styles and other characteristics.

User or learner models are regularly updated as learners work their way through the environment. Such models are utilized by the system to individualize components of the content and user activities (the domain model) according to a specified adaptive methodology (the adaptation model). For example, adaptive navigation support may tailor the links accessible to a particular learner using such techniques as direct guidance, adaptive link sorting, adaptive link hiding, removal, or disabling (Brusilovsky, Eklund, & Schwarz, 1998; Brusilovsky, 2007).

Levels of learner domain expertise are usually represented by the knowledge component of traditional learner models. As a major factor that directly influences learning processes, domain-specific knowledge is commonly included in most learner models. However, the way it is modeled and the levels of granularity of the models may vary considerably. In most cases, they are rather coarse-grained representations that use a few numeric or categorical values for a few concepts. For example, available knowledge could be described by high, intermediate, low levels, or no knowledge; or just "yes" or "no" categories. Even systems that allow many gradations (e.g., percentage values from 0 to 100) use only a few discrete levels in the actual adaptation process (De Bra & Calvi, 1998).

Initial information about learner knowledge is usually obtained from tests at the beginning of the first session or is set as default values. Thereafter, the system updates the level of knowledge in the user model based on direct assessment tests or history of student actions (e.g., number of reattempts during task solutions, number of requests for help, etc.). The adaptation model then uses the updated knowledge levels to adapt multimedia presentations to individual users.

The accuracy of information in learner models is an essential factor that influences quality of adaptive environments. An important direction of improvement of learner models for adaptive hypermedia and multimedia learning environments is constructing richer and more diagnostically informative models that better capture the nature and levels of learner proficiency. Using traditional (mostly multiple-choice) tests and tracing sequences of user mouse clicks provide rather limited sources of diagnostic information. Analyses of student solutions to presented problems usually deal with final answers to those problems without considering details of how those answers were actually obtained.

The data available from tracing user interactions with the system are usually imprecise, incomplete, and uncertain. Applying modern artificial intelligence approaches and methods (e.g., machine learning, Bayesian inference networks, neural networks, etc.) allows significant increases in the precision of adaptive technologies. For example, intelligent solution analyses could diagnose missing or defective components of knowledge and skill, and provide learners with more accurate feedback and support. On the other hand, quality of adaptive environments could also be improved by implementing new rapid real-time cognitive diagnostic techniques to replace traditional assessment methods used in constructing learner models. Possible implementations of this approach will be described in the following chapters.

LEARNER CONTROL AND ADAPTIVE GUIDANCE AS MEANS OF INDIVIDUALIZING INSTRUCTIONAL PROCEDURES

As mentioned previously, the learner-controlled approach to the individualization of instruction was suggested as an alternative to the aptitude-treatment interaction-based approach (Merrill, 1975). The measurements of aptitudes are not necessary in this approach. Learner control is also considered as a possible approach to dynamic tailoring of instruction to learner characteristics. Its effectiveness depends on the student ability to decide on the best learning strategy.

The Merrill's (1975) major suggestion is that student performance is affected by dynamic rather than static attributes making them more suitable for adapting instruction to individual differences. In his learner control approach to dynamically adaptive instruction, learners actively and continuously select treatments most appropriate to their cognitive states. These treatments are optimal to learners' unique configuration of aptitudes at a given moment in time. The questions that need to be answered in this approach are: How many parameters can a learner control in a given learning situation before the number of controls produces a disruptive effect on learning? Are there learner characteristics that enable one student to benefit from one type of learner control while another student might benefit from a different type of learner control? (Merrill, 1975).

Generally, the issue of learner control in technology-based learning environments has occupied educational research for quite a long time (Niemec, Sikorski, & Walberg, 1996; Steinberg, 1989; 1977). Most of this research has indicated that high levels of control in such environments do not necessarily benefit learners. It is often believed that allowing more control may increase learner motivation (Kinzie, 1990). However, the expected motivational advantages followed by higher learning outcomes in student-controlled instructional systems were not demonstrated with any degree of consistency. Learners were not able to select good learning strategies on their own and clearly needed assistance in effective use of provided control facilities. Thus, the instructional efficiency and effectiveness of this approach still remains to be established (even 30 years after similar conclusion by Steinberg, 1977).

Chung & Reigeluth (1992) also noted that research findings regarding the instructional effects of learner control have been inconclusive, and more often negative rather than positive. They assumed that one of the reasons was that many students lacked knowledge necessary for making appropriate decisions. In regards to learner prior knowledge, Chung & Reigeluth (1992) provided certain prescriptions that generally are in line with recommendations based on cognitive load considerations.

For example, when students have significant prior knowledge in a domain, they could be allowed the content control (to avoid irrelevant, redundant, and uninterested materials) and sequence control. These students are better able to construct knowledge that is meaningful to them, or to use their prior knowledge to determine an appropriate instructional sequence. In hypermedia learning systems, low-ability and low-knowledge learners are advised to be provided with more guidance to develop their metacognitive skills. They could be provided default paths or guided tours through the knowledge base. Audit trails (histories of previously visited nodes and links) are also recommended to help students encode the structure of the knowledge base. Pace control should be provided when students could benefit from additional time to integrate new information with their available previously acquired schemas.

Dynamic learner control involves establishing a set of possible strategies and developing instructional systems that enable the deliberate and differential manipulation of these strategies by the student. An argument in favor of dynamically adaptable instructional systems in which learners actively and continuously select instructional treatments is that they will produce system independent learners in contrast to traditional approach that may produce system dependent learners (Federico, 1980).

As mentioned above, a relatively well investigated form of providing guidance to learners in selecting appropriate learning means is an advisement strategy approach (Tennyson, 1980, 1981; Tennyson & Rothen, 1979). An advanced extension of the advisement strategy approach is the concept of adaptive guidance as an instructional strategy that provides learners with information necessary for making effective decisions about learning improvement (Bell & Kozlowski, 2002).

Adaptive guidance strategy complements traditional feedback strategies (Kluger & DeNisi, 1996) with additional diagnostic and interpretative processes and information that enhance learner self-regulation and decision making in regards to allocating their cognitive resources. By monitoring and assessing learner progress, adaptive guidance provides individual recommendations on future learning activities. As learners acquire basic lower-level knowledge and skills, adaptive guidance tailors subsequent learning tasks and activities to focus attention on relatively more advanced knowledge and skills (Bell & Kozlowski, 2002).

Santiago and Okey (1992), Tennyson (1980), Tennyson and Buttrey (1980) demonstrated that providing guidance and advisement to learners as they proceed through the instructional program may combine advantages of both learner control (positive attitudes toward learning, sense of control, etc.) and program control (evidence-based learning decisions). Using the provided information, learners can make effective decisions themselves.

Bell and Kozlowski (2002) noted that both advisement and adaptive guidance provide learner control over instruction and provide individualized prescriptive information in the form of recommended learning materials and tasks based on past performance. On the other hand, adaptive guidance is an elaboration and extension of advisement. Advisement usually provides unidimensional recommendations that emphasize repetition, for example, how much to study and practice (e.g., recommending to study more examples if performance on sample items is poor). Adaptive guidance provides multidimensional suggestions emphasizing content to study and activities to practice in order to achieve mastery (what to study or practice). This form of guidance provides specific evaluative information on the current level and state of knowledge that would allow learners to better allocate their cognitive resources. Adaptive guidance also sequences learning tasks so that basic aspects are learned earlier with gradual transition to more complex strategic aspects of the task domain.

In an experimental study, Bell and Kozlowski (2002) compared learner control condition with adaptive guidance condition in a radar simulation learning environment. In the learner control condition, learners received descriptive feedback on their performance, but not any guidance information. In both conditions, learners were given control over content and order of studying and practicing the material.

Students in the learner control group were provided with a randomized list of learning topics at the beginning to choose from. Learners in the adaptive guidance condition were given a topic list that was ordered in a sequence with gradually increasing level of difficulty. Guidance was based on three levels of performance (cut-off scores at 50th and 85th percentiles) discriminating among low, medium, and high performance. Based on the standards and learner prior performance, adaptive guidance procedure provided evaluative information on current progress. It suggested individualized recommended actions (skills and strategies to practice) the learner could choose from to improve shortcomings.

Providing students with adaptive guidance in addition to learner control improved learning outcomes, especially in complex learning environments. It was found that adaptive guidance could have significant impact not only on the acquisition of basic knowledge and performance capabilities for novice learners, but also on the acquisition of strategic knowledge and skills and transfer capabilities for more advances learners. Individuals who received adaptive guidance demonstrated higher levels of basic and strategic knowledge and performance, and were better able to transfer their skills to more complex situations. Adaptive guidance had a positive effect on learner self-efficacy, especially for novice learners.

Thus, complex learning environments "should include information that helps trainees to make effective use of the control they are given over their own learning. Without such information, the benefits offered by Web-based training, simulations, multimedia applications, and other similar training mediums may not be fully realized" (Bell & Kozlowski, 2002, p. 299). In this study, guidance was adapted only to three major levels of performance. More refined differences in performance among learners should be used in further studies. The degree of adaptability to individual learner progress also needs to be enhanced.

Leutner (1993) compared instructional effects of providing adaptive advice with providing permanent access to explicit non-adaptive background information in a computer simulated game learning environment. The results of three experiments indicated that adaptive advice significantly enhanced learning of domain-specific knowledge. At the same time, there was no improvement in the functional game-specific knowledge of how to play the game. When the exploration time was reduced by working on a tutorial unit first, the differences in learning domain-specific knowledge with or without adaptive advice disappeared (both for seventh-graders and university students). The study also established that while adaptive advice increased immediate post-test performance, permanently available background information increased the level of acquisition and long-term (delayed) retention of domain-specific knowledge. Thus, a continuously available instructional support is important even when adaptive advice is provided to learners.

FUTURE TRENDS

In order to have adaptive capabilities based on learner modeling, the comprehensive adaptive multimedia systems need to be able to conduct the learner profiling and profile elicitation, recognition of learning patterns, content personalization, personalized information retrieval, and include agents for adaptive intelligent navigation. Comprehensive knowledge representation techniques describe the context and the structure of the learning material and play an important role in improving the adaptability of learning environments. The prospective developments include techniques for matching different representations of content with the learner knowledge in order to support personalized and adaptive learning; adaptive information retrieval, curriculum sequencing, and problem solving support.

Designs of efficient adaptive educational hypermedia environments require rich learner models and appropriate models of learning processes that would connect adaptive hypermedia and multimedia systems with cognitive characteristics of learners. Efficient adaptive multimedia also requires effective systems for retrieving text, images, audio, video and mixed-media components. In order to support learners in the search processes, the retrieval tools should be adapted to the learner needs and interests and provide adapted information about search results. Such adaptive multimedia systems require appropriate multimedia data modeling and indexing, metadata for multimedia retrieval, and methods for adaptive data visualization. For example, personalizing explorations of rich (especially poorly structured) contents may enhance learner experiences with digitized materials and virtual representations that interconnect dispersed objects. Personalized adaptive tools would simplify finding relevant content among many sources of available information that are located in different places by effectively reducing the information space only to the relevant content.

Most currently available common web-based educational environments based on learning management systems (e.g., WebCT, Blackboard) have no adaptive features. Some of such features can be integrated into the available systems to improve the efficiency of these learning environments. For example, adaptive curriculum sequencing, adaptive presentation and navigation support (including intelligent agents), adaptive collaboration support, and adaptive testing will be implemented in online educational systems. Advanced e-learning systems require comprehensive modeling of learning processes and automatic learner model acquisition, online monitoring for learner attentiveness, motivation, cognitive load, and interactions between learners.

Computer-supported collaborative learning environments may enhance acquisition of the skills that are essential in the context of collaborative work, guided cooperative knowledge construction, decision making, and conflict resolution. Such environments may also support acquisition of metacognitive and self-regulation skills (e.g., evaluating one's own learning goals, limitations of cognitive capabilities, levels of cognitive load, emotional states, and reflecting on the quality of collaborative learning). Online collaborative tools may support communication and collaboration skills using prompts, templates, explicit representational forms for shared mental models, and other scaffolding devices embedded into online learning environments.

Efficient collaborative e-learning is assumed to lead to a deeper level of learning, critical thinking, and provide opportunities for developing social and communication skills. Until recently, designing adaptive instructional systems have been mainly focused on individual learning. Adaptation and personalization at a group level could be directed to both the individual learners within a group and to the whole collaborating group. Implementing this level of adaptation requires deeper understanding of learning processes at a group level and means of support for such learning processes in adaptive environments. An important research issue is modeling the whole group of learners, including characteristics that represent learners as members of a group, such as individual differences, interaction, collaboration, and communication behavior, and reflect the group dynamic and learning processes. Other important research directions are developing effective means for collecting and analyzing this information, assessment and feedback techniques to guide the adaptation process, effective approaches to the formation of a group that is adapted to learner individual differences.

Small computerized devices that are networked with each other are rapidly moving into our daily life and education. "Smart" environments are emerging that react in an adaptive way to activities of learners in order to provide the content and other services they request or are presumed to need. Such environments require non-intrusive methods for recognizing and modeling cognitive characteristics and emotional states of learners; methods for profiling such information and tracing long-term patterns in interaction histories; and methods for making decisions on how to adapt the environment to specific situations. Adaptive personalized services in such new environments require appropriate forms of real-time learner modeling within a network of systems that share their models for group or individual adaptation. When the content is assembled dynamically from several sources, it should be coordinated in order to be appropriately adapted to the learner. Sharing and integrating learner models would improve the quality of adaptation.

Current interfaces of mobile devices are still very limited in their adaptation capabilities. For example, they do not use the information about the learner behavior, personal preferences and goals to adapt to the current situation and available resources. For example most mobile instructional systems do not consider functional requirements of older age learners or people with disabilities. These categories of learners may have specific cognitive and perceptual characteristics. Such characteristics need to be taken into account when developing learner models and considering adaptive characteristics of mobile instructional systems.

Social dynamic computing applications engage learners in creating and sharing content as well as in virtual worlds populated with other learners. Collaborative learning technologies support social interaction and knowledge sharing in multi-user environments ranging from small groups to online communities and forums. The difficulties for learning in such environments could be caused, in part, by potential cognitive overload. Therefore, adaptation to learner cognitive characteristics is important for facilitating effective knowledge acquisition for members of online groups and communities.

MULTIMEDIA INSTRUCTIONAL DESIGN IMPLICATIONS

In general, the level of cognitive load in complex multimedia learning environments is determined by the degree of balancing of the learner executive function in cognitive processes. In order to appropriately balance this function and thus optimize cognitive load, appropriate levels of guidance should be provided to learners at the appropriate time, while unnecessary support removed as learners progress to more advanced levels of proficiency in a specific task domain. Adaptive multimedia learning environments that dynamically tailor levels of instructional support to changing individual cognitive characteristics and levels of learner expertise in a domain have the best potential for optimizing cognitive load. Such environments could be built using learner modeling with specific diagnostic instruments for evaluating components of these models.

Existing adaptive multimedia environments are mostly based on external characteristics of learner behavior rather than on real cognitive characteristics. Learner levels of prior knowledge or expertise should be made the primary factors in adaptive instructional systems, complemented with relevant secondary factors (e.g., navigational patterns, learning styles, and preferences). Individualized adaptive instruction should be based on detailed diagnostic assessment of learner knowledge structures that could appropriately direct instructional interventions. Different variable levels of learner control and adaptive guidance approach should be implemented in these environments as means of enhancing their adaptive capabilities.

Students that have significant prior knowledge in a domain may be allowed control of the instructional content. These students could be able to use their prior knowledge to determine an appropriate instructional sequence. Low-ability and low-knowledge learners need to be provided with more guidance and default paths through the knowledge base. Pace control should be provided when students could benefit from additional time to integrate new information with their available knowledge base.

Complex learning environments should assist learners in making effective use of the control they are provided. Adaptive guidance could be used to monitor and assess learner progress and provide learners with diagnostic information and individual recommendations on future learning activities. As learners acquire basic lower-level knowledge and skills, adaptive guidance should tailor subsequent learning tasks and activities to focus attention on more advanced knowledge and skills. A continuously available instructional support is important even when adaptive advice is provided to learners.

SUMMARY OF CHAPTER X

The idea of adaptive instruction was clearly articulated within the aptitude-treatment interaction approach. It later lead to the ideas of dynamic adaptation (using variable instructional treatments depending on learner changing cognitive characteristics) and learner-controlled adaptation. These two approaches generated significant subsequent research and development efforts.

Nevertheless, the research in adaptive instruction is in its early stages. As a consequence, practical outcomes from the research on adaptive instruction still remain limited. Most of existing adaptive online environments are based on monitoring learner external characteristics rather than on deep cognitive characteristics, such as prior knowledge or levels of expertise. For example, most existing multimedia tutoring systems are based on monitoring students' navigational routes (e.g., using log files) and solution moves, and feeding them back to learners to guide their interactions with the system, both with high and low levels of learner control.

Research in effectiveness of learner control has indicated that high levels of control in complex learning environments do not necessarily benefit learners. Expected motivational advantages followed by higher learning outcomes in student-controlled instructional systems did not show up. Learners may not be able to select appropriate learning strategies on their own and require assistance in effective use of provided control facilities.

Providing guidance and advisement to learners as they proceed through the instructional program may combine advantages of both learner control and system control. Using this information, learners can make effective decisions themselves. Advisement and adaptive guidance approaches are based on providing individualized prescriptive information in the form of recommended learning materials and tasks based on past performance.

Adaptive guidance provides specific evaluative information on the current level and state of knowledge that would allow learners to better allocate their cognitive resources and appropriately sequence learning tasks. It was demonstrated that adaptive guidance in complex learning environments improved learning outcomes. It had significant impact on the acquisition of basic knowledge and skills for novice learners, as well as strategic knowledge and transfer capabilities for more advances learners.

The recent studies in rapid diagnostic assessment methods may offer appropriate real-time tools for the dynamic optimization of instruction. Such techniques may provide adequate fine-grained measures of levels of expertise with sufficient diagnostic power for learner-tailored instructional procedures. Some specific examples will be considered in the following chapters.

REFERENCES

Anderson, J. R. (1983). *The architecture of cognition.* Cambridge, MA: Harvard University Press.

Anderson, J. R. (1993). *Rules of the mind.* Hillsdale, NJ: Erlbaum.

Anderson, J. R., Boyle, C. F., & Reiser, B. J. (1985). Intelligent tutoring systems. *Science, 228*, 456-462.

Anderson, J. R., & Corbett, A. T. (1993). Tutoring of cognitive skill. In J. R. Anderson (Ed.), *Rules of the mind.* Hillsdale, NJ: Erlbaum.

Anderson, J. R., Corbett, A. T., Fincham, J. M., Hoffman, D., & Pelletier, R. (1992). General principles for an intelligent tutoring architecture. In V. Shute & W. Regian (Eds.), *Cognitive approaches to automated instruction* (pp. 81-106). Hillsdale, NJ: Erlbaum.

Anderson, J. R., Corbett, A. T., Koedinger, K. R., & Pelletier, R. (1995). Cognitive tutors: Lessons Learned. *The Journal of the Learning Sciences, 4*, 167-207.

Anderson, J. R., Farrell, R., & Sauers, R. (1984). Learning to program in LISP. *Cognitive Science, 8*, 87-129.

Azevedo, R. (2005). Using hypermedia as a metacognitive tool for enhancing student learning? The role of self-regulated learning. *Educational Psychologist, 40*, 199-209.

Baker, E. L., & Mayer, R. E. (1999). Computer-based assessment of problem solving. *Computers in Human Behavior, 15*, 269-282.

Baker, E. L., & O'Neil, H. F., Jr. (2002). Measuring problem solving in computer environments: current and future states. *Computers in Human Behavior, 18*, 609-622.

Bell, B. S. & Kozlowski, S. W. J. (2002). Adaptive guidance: Enhancing self-regulation, knowledge, and performance in technology-based training. *Personnel Psychology, 55*, 267-306.

Boutwell, R., & Barton, G. (1974). Toward an adaptive learner-controlled model of instruction: a place for the new cognitive aptitudes. *Educational Technology, 14*, 13-18.

Brusilovsky, P. (2001). Adaptive hypermedia. *User Modeling and User-Adapted Interaction, 11*, 87-110.

Brusilovsky, P. (2007). Adaptive Navigation Support. In P. Brusilovsky, A. Kobsa, & W. Nejdl (Eds.), *The Adaptive Web: Methods and Strategies of Web Personalization* (pp. 263 - 290). Springer Lecture Notes in Computer Science, Vol. 4321/2007. Berlin - Heidelberg: Springer.

Brusilovsky, P., Eklund, J., & Schwarz, E. (1998). Web-based education for all: A tool for developing adaptive courseware. *Computer Networks and ISDN Systems, 30*, 291-300.

Brusilovsky, P., Kobsa, A., & Nejdl, W. (Eds.) (2007). *The Adaptive Web: Methods and Strategies of Web Personalization*. Springer Lecture Notes in Computer Science, Vol. 4321/2007. Berlin - Heidelberg: Springer.

Brusilovsky, P., & Millan, E. (2007). User Models for Adaptive Hypermedia and Adaptive Educational Systems. In P. Brusilovsky, A. Kobsa, & W. Nejdl (Eds.), *The Adaptive Web: Methods and Strategies of Web Personalization* (pp. 3- 53). Springer Lecture Notes in Computer Science, Vol. 4321/2007. Berlin - Heidelberg: Springer.

Camp, G., Paas, F., Rikers, R., & van Merriënboer, J. J. G. (2001). Dynamic problem selection in air traffic control training: A comparison between performance, mental effort, and mental efficiency. *Computers in Human Behavior, 17*, 575-595.

Chung, J., & Reigeluth, C. M. (1992). Instructional prescriptions for learner control. *Educational Technology, 32*, 14-20.

Corbalan, G., Kester, L., & van Merriënboer, J. J. G. (2006). Towards a personalized task selection model with shared instructional control. *Instructional Science, 34*, 399-422.

Cronbach, L. (1967). How can instruction be adapted to individual differences. In R. Gagne, *Learning and individual differences* (pp. 23-39). Columbus, OH: Merrill.

Cronbach, L. & Snow, R. (1969). *Individual differences in learning ability as a function of instructional variables* (Final Report). Stanford, CA: School of Education, Stanford University.

Cronbach, L. & Snow, R. (1977). *Aptitudes and instructional methods: a handbook for research on interactions.* New York: Irvington.

De Bra, P., & Calvi, L. (1998). AHA! An open Adaptive Hypermedia Architecture. *The New Review of Hypermedia nad Multimedia, 4*, 115-139.

de Croock, M. B. M., Paas, F., Schlanbusch, H., & van Merriënboer, J. J. G. (2002). $ADAPT^{IT}$: tools for training design and evaluation. *Educational Technology, Research and Development, 50*, 47-58.

Federico, P-A. (1980). Adaptive instruction: trends and issues, In R. Snow, P-A Federico & W. Montague, *Aptitude, learning, and instruction: Vol. 1, Cognitive process analyses of aptitude* (pp. 1- 26). Hillsdale, NJ: Erlbaum.

Federico, P-A. (1999). Hypermedia environments and adaptive instruction. *Computers in Human Behavior, 15*, 653-692.

Gay, G. (1986). Interaction of learner control and prior understanding in computer-assissted video instruction. *Journal of Educational Psychology, 78*, 225-227.

Gabrys, G., Weiner, A., & Lesgold, A. (1993). Learning by problem solving in a coached apprenticeship system. In M. Rabinowitz (Ed.), *Cognitive science foundations of instruction* (pp. 119-147). Hillsdale, NJ: Erlbaum.

Gentner, D., & Stevens, A. L. (Eds.) (1983). *Mental models.* Hillsdale, NJ: Erlbaum.

Glaser, R. (1977). Adaptive instruction: individual diversity and learning. New York: Holt, Rinechart, and Winston.

Glaser, R. (1990). The reemergence of learning theory within instructional research. *American Psychologist, 45*, 29 - 39.

Greeno, J. G., & Simon, H. (1988). Problem solving and reasoning. In R. C. Atkinson, R. Herrnstein, G. Lindzey, & R. D. Luce (Eds.), *Stevens' handbook of experimental psychology.* New York: Wiley.

Hsieh, I-L. G., & O'Neil, H. F., Jr. (2002). Types of feedback in a computer-based collaborative problem-solving group task. *Computers in Human Behavior, 15*, 255-268.

Kay, J. (2001). Learner control. *User Modeling and User-Adapted Interaction, 11*, 111-127.

Kester, L., Kirschner, P.A., & van Merriënboer, J.J.G. (2004). Timing of information presentation in learning statistics. *Instructional Science, 32*, 233-252.

Kester, L., Kirschner, P. A., van Merrienboer, J. J. G., & Baumer, A. (2001). Just-in-time information presentation and the acquisition of complex cognitive skills. *Computers in Human Behavior, 17*, 373-391.

Kieras, D. E., & Bovair, S. (1984). The role of a mental model in learning to operate a device. *Cognitive Science, 8*, 255-273.

Kinzie, M. B. (1990). Requirements and benefits of effective interactive instruction: Learner control, self-regulation, and continuing motivation. *Educational Technology Research and Development, 38*, 5-21.

Kluger, A. N., & De Nisi, A. (1996). The effects of feedback interventions on performance: A historical review, a meta-analysis, and a preliminary feedback intervention theory. *Psychological Bulletin, 119*, 254-284.

Kobsa, A. (2001). Generic user modelling systems. *User Modeling and User-Adapted Interaction, 11*, 49-63.

Kogan, N. (1971). Educational implications of cognitive styles. In G. S. Lesser (Ed.), *Psychology and educational practice*. Glenview, Ill: Scott, Foresman.

Large, A. (1996). Hypertext instructional programs and learner control: a research review. *Education for Information, 4*, 95-106.

Lesgold, A., & Lajoie, S. (1991). Complex problem solving in electronics. In R. J. Steinberg, & P. A. Frensch (Eds.), *Complex problem solving: Principles and mechanisms*. Hillsdale, NJ: Erlbaum.

Leutner, D. (1993). Guided discovery learning with computer-based simulation games: effects of adaptive and non-adaptive instructional support. *Learning and Instruction, 3*, 113-132.

Lin, B., & Hsieh, C. (2001). Web-based teaching and learner control: A research review. *Computer & Education, 37*, 377-386.

Locatis, C., Letourneau, G., & Banvard, R. (1989). Hypermedia and instruction. *Educational Technology Research and Development, 37*, 65-77.

Martin, J., & van Lehn, K. (1995). A Bayesian approach to cognitive assessment. In P. D. Nichols, S. F. Chipman, & R. L. Brennan (Eds.), *Cognitively diagnostic assessment* (pp.141-165). Hillsdale, NJ: Erlbaum.

Mayer, R. E. (1989). Models for understanding. *Review of Educational Research, 59*, 43-64.

Mayer, R., & Anderson, R. (1991). Animations need narrations: An experimental test of a dual-coding hypothesis. *Journal of Educational Psychology, 83*, 484-490.

Mayer, R., & Anderson, R. (1992). The instructive animation: Helping students build connections between words and pictures in multimedia learning. *Journal of Educational Psychology, 84*, 444-452.

Mayer, R. E., & Sims, V. K. (1994). For whom is a picture worth a thousand words? Extensions of a dual-coding theory of multimedia learning. *Journal of Educational Psychology, 86*, 389-401.

McArthur, D., & Stasz, C. (1988). Skill-oriented task sequencing in an intelligent tutor for basic algebra. *Instructional Science, 17*, 281-307.

Merrill, M. D. (1975). Learner control: Beyond aptitude-treatment interactions. AV Communication Review,

Merrill, M. D. (1984). What is learner control? In R.K.Bass and C.D.Dills (Eds.), Instructional development: The state of the art II. Dubuque, IA: Kendall/Hunt.

Messick, S. (Ed.). (1976). *Individuality in learning.* San Francisco: Jossey-Bass.

Niemec, P., Sikorski, C., & Walberg, H. (1996). Learner-control effects: A review of reviews and a meta-analysis. *Journal of Educational Computing Research, 15*, 157-174.

O'Neil. H. F., Jr. (1999). Perspectives on computer-based performance assessment of problem solving. *Computers in Human Behavior, 18*, 699-715.

Reigeluth, C. M. (Ed.). (1983). *Instructional design theories and models: An overview of their current studies*. Hillsdale, NJ: Erlbaum.

Renkl, A. (1997). Learning from worked-out examples: A study on individual differences. *Cognitive Science, 21*, 1-29.

Renkl, A., & Atkinson, R. K. (2003). Structuring the transition from example study to problem solving in cognitive skills acquisition: A cognitive load perspective. *Educational Psychologist, 38,* 15-22.

Renkl, A., Atkinson, R. K., Maier, U. H., & Staley, R. (2002). From example study to problem solving: Smooth transitions help learning. *Journal of Experimental Education, 70,* 293-315.

Rowe, A., Cooke, N., Hall, E., & Halgren, T. (1996). Toward an on-line knowledge assessment methodology: building on the relationship between knowing and doing. *Journal of Experimental Psychology: Applied*, 2, 31-47.

Salden, R. J. C. M., Paas, F., & van Merriënboer, J. J. G. (2006). Personalized adaptive task selection in air traffic control: Effects on training efficiency and transfer. *Learning and Instruction, 16,* 350-362

Santiago, R. S., Okey, J. R. (1992). The effects of advisement and locus of control on achievement in learner-controlled instruction. *Journal of Computer-Based Instruction, 19,* 47-53.

Spector, M. J., Christensen, D. L., Sioutine, A. V., & McCormack, D. (2001). Models and simulations for learning in complex domains: using causal loop diagrams for assessment and evaluation. *Computers in Human Behavior, 17,* 517-545.

Spiro, R. J., & Jehng, J. (1990). Cognitive flexibility and hypertext: Theory and technology for the nonlinear and multidimensional traversal of complex subject matter. In D. Nix & R. Spiro (Eds.), Cognition, education, and multimedia: Exploring ideas in high technology. Hillsdale, NJ: Lawrence Erlbaum Associates.

Steinberg, E. R. (1977). Review of student control in computer-assited instruction. *Journal of Computer-Based Instruction, 3,* 84-90.

Steinberg, E. R. (1989). Cognition and learner control: A literature review, 1977-1988. *Journal of Computer-Bsed Instruction, 16,* 117-121.

Stoyanov, S., & Kirshner, P. (2004). Expert concept mapping method for defining the characteristics of adaptive e-learning: ALFANET project case. *Educational Technology, Research and Development, 52,* 41-56.

Tennyson, R. (1975). Adaptive instructional models for concept acquisition. Educational Technology, 15, 7-15.

Tennyson, R. D. (1980). Instructional control strategies and content structure as design variables in concept acquisition using computer-based instruction. *Journal of Educational Psychology, 72,* 525-532.

Tennyson, R. D. (1981). Use of adaptive information for advisement in learning concepts and rules using computer assisted instruction. *American Educational Research Journal, 18,* 425-438.

Tennyson, R. D., & Buttrey, T. (1980). Advisement and management strategies as design variables in computer-assissted instruction. *Educational Communication and Technology Journal, 28,* 169-176.

Tennyson, R. D., & Rothen, W. (1979). Management of computer-based instruction: Design of an adaptive control strategy. *Journal of Computer-Based Instruction, 5*, 126-134.

Tobias, S. (1976). Achievement treatment interactions. *Review of Educational Research, 46*, 61-74.

Tobias , S. (1989). Another look at research on the adaptation of instruction to student characteristics. *Educational Psychologist, 24*, 213-227.

Van Merriënboer, J. J. G. (1990). Strategies for programming instruction in high school: Program completion vs. program generation. *Journal of Educational Computing Research, 6*, 265-287.

van Merriënboer, J. J. G. (1997). *Training complex cognitive skills: A four-component instructional design model for technical training.* Englewood Cliffs, NJ: Educational Technology Publications.

van Merriënboer, J. J. G., Clark, R. E., & de Croock, M. B. M. (2002). Blueprints for complex learning: The 4C/ID* model. *Educational Technology Research and Development, 50*, 39-64.

van Merriënboer, J. J. G., & Dijkstra, S. (1997). The four-component instructional design model for training complex cognitive skills. In R. D. Tennyson & F. Schott (Eds.), *Instructional design: Theory and research* (Vol. 1). Hillsdale, NJ: Lawrence Erlbaum.

van Merriënboer, J. J. G., Jelsma, O., & Paas, F. G. W. C. (1992). Training for reflective expertise: A four-component instructional design model for training complex cognitive skills. *Educational Technology, Research & Development, 40(2)*, 23-43.

Van Merrienboer, J.J.G., Kirschner, P.A., & Kester, L. (2003). Taking the load off a learner's mind: Instructional design principles for complex learning. *Educational Psychologist, 38*, 5-13.

Van Merrienboer, J. J. G., & Luursema, J. J. (1996). Implementing instructional models in computer-based learning environments: a case study in problem selection. In T. Liao (Ed.), *Advanced educational technology: research issues and future potential* (pp. 184-206). Berlin: Springer-Verlag.

Van Merrienboer, J. J. G., & Paas, F. G. W. C. (1989). Automation and schema acquisition in learning elementary computer programming: Implications for the design of practice. *Computers in Human Behavior, 6*, 273-289.

White, B. Y., & Frederiksen, J. R. (1986). *Progressions of quantitative models as a foundation for intelligent learning environments* (Tech. Rep. No. 6277). Cambridge, MA: Bolt, Beranek, & Newman.

Williams. M. D. (1996). Learner-control and instructional technologies. In D.H. Jonassen (Ed.), *Handbook of research for educational communicarions and technology* (pp. 957-983). New York: MacMillan.

Chapter XI
Adapting Levels of Instructional Support to Optimize Learning Complex Cognitive Skills

INTRODUCTION

This chapter describes some specific adaptive procedures for tailoring levels of instructional guidance to individual levels of learner task-specific expertise to optimize cognitive resources available to learning. Recent studies in expertise reversal effect that were reviewed in previous chapters indicate that instructional design principles that benefit low-knowledge users may disadvantage more experienced ones. This reversal in the relative effectiveness of different instructional methods is due to the increase in cognitive load that is required for integration of presented supporting information with learners' available knowledge structures. The major implication of these findings for multimedia design is the need to tailor levels of instructional support to individual levels of learner task-specific expertise.

The procedures for adapting levels of instructional guidance suggested in this chapter have been developed in conjunction with empirically established interactions between levels of learner expertise and optimal instructional techniques and procedures. The chapter starts with the description of the processes and approaches to learning complex cognitive skills. The appropriate design models for learning complex skills are reviewed and different ways of varying levels of learner control in such models are described. The relations between levels of learner task-specific expertise and optimal levels of instructional guidance are then discussed. Also, empirical studies of the expertise reversal for instructional guidance and sequencing of learning tasks are reviewed. The completion tasks and faded worked examples are specific instructional methods used in the described studies for managing levels of instructional guidance in adaptive learning environments. Real-time monitoring of levels of learner task-specific expertise using rapid cognitive diagnostic methods was used in some of these studies.

LEARNING COMPLEX COGNITIVE SKILLS

A cognitive-based approach to designing learning environments that aim at achieving students' expert performance in specific task domains distinguishes between the actual expert performance sequence and the sequence of learning tasks. Different instructional procedures could be implemented for learning separate parts of task performance. For example, some skills could be developed first to a high degree of fluency to free limited working memory resources for the following changes in long-term memory knowledge structures. In other cases, general structures of conceptual knowledge could be acquired at the beginning and then elaborated and followed by practice with complex procedures. In this case, a big picture is learned first, followed by more specific knowledge. Moving from a central idea to its elaboration and back results in the acquisition of specific knowledge as part of whole rather than isolated information (Glaser, 1990).

General conceptual models that highlight the major parts, states, and actions in the system as well as the causal relations among them perform an executive guiding role in cognitive processes involved in learning. Such models help learners to build specific mental representations of the system by directing attention toward important information, organizing this information and integrating it with existing knowledge.

However, such externally provided conceptual models should be used cautiously when dealing with more advanced students who already possess well-organized schematic knowledge in the domain. The simplified conceptual models may conflict with these students' more sophisticated knowledge structures and thus inhibit their learning (Mayer, 1989). This phenomenon is directly related to the expertise reversal effect. A cognitive conflict between instruction-based conceptual models and learners' internal knowledge structures may increase processing demands on limited working memory, thus causing the effect. To eliminate such conflicts, instructional design should take into account expert-novice differences and knowledge of processes of cognitive transition from novice to expert states.

Glaser (1990) distinguished two major approaches to using the results of cognitive research in human knowledge structures in instructional design. The first approach originated in artificial intelligence area and expert systems and was aimed at learner direct exposure to the characteristics of well- developed expertise. For example, in coached-practice learning environments, learners observe the expert's decision process, reasons behind it, the overall goal structure of the expert performance, and compare their own performance with expert performance.

The process of comparing and reflecting on long or complicated solution paths may place significant demands on working memory. In order to reduce such demands, a replay of the learner's and an expert's performance could be made available to the learner together with summaries of the information that has been encountered during previous steps. This technique may reduce the cognitive load associated with remembering the details of learner own performance while observing the expert's actions (Gabrys, Weiner, & Lesgold, 1993).

The second and more learner-centered approach originated in cognitive science itself. It is based on developing cognitive models of students' knowledge and then creating environments where learners progress from simple to more sophisticated domain-specific conceptual models. Such progression usually takes place while learning to solve specifically designed tasks with gradually increasing levels of complexity (White & Frederiksen, 1986).

For example, intelligent tutoring systems based on the model-tracing methodology (Anderson, 1993) simulate student cognition in real time and maintain current models of student knowledge state. They provide example-based learning environments in which students induce rules from examples of correct expert-based performances. The learner actual performance is traced and compared to the ideal solution structure using a production rules model, and the student is kept on the correct solution path. The tutor evaluates the probability of acquisition of targeted rules based on correctness of their applications and selects appropriate problems for further exercises. Successful tutoring programs based on the model-tracing methodology have been effectively used in the fields of programming, geometry proofs, solving algebraic equations (Anderson, Boyle, & Reiser, 1985; Anderson & Corbett, 1993; Anderson, Corbett, Fincham, Hoffman, & Pelletier, 1992; Anderson, Corbett, Koedinger, & Pelletier, 1995; Anderson, Farrell, & Sauers, 1984).

According to the theory of skill acquisition (Anderson, 1983), learning the concepts, rules, and principles of how things work (declarative knowledge) should precede the instruction in specific procedures. In complex domains, it is impossible to describe all possible future task situations in advance. In such domains, knowledge of specific procedures may not be sufficient for successful performance. Therefore, the instruction should combine knowledge of system principles with procedures of how to use this knowledge in a specific context.

Thus, in complex systems, a deeper understanding of their components and operation is required (Lesgold & Lajoie, 1991). Providing students with conceptual models of a complex system before learning how to use that system produced better recall, faster learning, and fewer errors in the operation of the system (Kieras & Bovair, 1984). Accordingly, complex learning environments need to include basic conceptual explanations of how things work, practice in carrying out basic procedures, and variation in experiences for tuning procedural knowledge (Gentner & Stevens, 1983; Greeno & Simon, 1988).

DESIGN MODELS FOR COMPLEX LEARNING

Salden, Paas, and van Merriënboer (2006b) noted that specific instructional methods for complex cognitive skills have evolved in three major ways: 1) a shift from non-adaptive to adaptive methods (adjusting task sequences dynamically during training); 2) a shift from part-task based to whole-task based training methods; and 3) a shift from group-based to personalized methods that take individual cognitive demands into account. Cognitive research studies reviewed in previous chapters suggest that in order to provide consistency between instruction and human cognitive processes, instruction should be adapted to levels of learner prior task-specific expertise.

To evaluate the adequacy of available knowledge of individual learners and design appropriately tailored instructional procedures, cognitive task analysis should be used to determine underlying knowledge structures and cognitive skills required for the task. A general-to-specific approach was proposed which requires identifying the main idea of a task followed by determining the specific aspects of this idea (Reigeluth, 1983). Broader concepts are consequently differentiated into ones that are more specific. Knowledge engineering methods that have been developed in the field of artificial intelligence could also be used to extract expert knowledge structures and use them in the design of instructional materials.

High-level cognitive skills are required for solving complex realistic problems, especially in relatively poorly defined task domains such as management, commerce, law, etc. In order to enhance acquisition of such skills, instruction needs to be focused on whole learning tasks rather than on learning simple separate fragmented components of complex tasks. Whole learning tasks are capable of combining routine components of performance that involve rule-based and mostly automated subtasks with non-routine components of problem solving. Such non-routine components require high degrees of intentional conscious reasoning and transfer. Because of many components that need to be processed simultaneously rather than sequentially, complex whole learning tasks may impose a heavy cognitive load. Therefore, appropriate scaffolding of complex task performance that is dynamically adjusted to learning situations and cognitive characteristics of learners is an essential condition of successful learning (van Merriënboer & Kirshner, 2006).

In the framework of a competency-based approach, van Merriënboer (1997) developed the four-component instructional design model (4C/ID). This model provides methods for analysis of complex cognitive skills, knowledge structures required for performing these skills, and development of appropriate sequences of whole task practice situations that would support acquisition of these skills. A whole task-based approach is an essential feature of the model. The model also takes into account the limited processing capacity of working memory by gradually increasing the level of complexity in the sequences of whole tasks (van Merriënboer, Kirschner, & Kester, 2003). Thus, the level of cognitive load imposed by these sequences is kept under control. A set of software tools that assist designers in applying the 4C/ID methodology has been also developed (de Croock, Paas, Schlanbusch, & van Merriënboer, 2002).

According to the 4C/ID methodology, cognitively complex learning environments include four interconnected components: 1) *learning tasks* organized in a sequence of simple-to-complex task classes with gradually diminishing levels of support within each class (process of scaffolding); 2) *supportive information* for more general aspects of the learning tasks that change over different specific problem situations; 3) *just-in-time (algorithmic) information* for invariant aspects of the learning tasks; and 4) *part-task practice* that provide additional repetitive practice for constituent skills that need to be performed at a very high level of automaticity (van Merriënboer, Clark, & de Croock, 2002). The model makes a clear distinction between non-recurrent and recurrent skills. Non-recurrent skills require acquisition of complex organized knowledge structures (schemas) that guide subsequent conscious problem-solving processes. Recurrent skills require acquisition of automated task-specific rules and procedures.

To specify these four components when designing complex learning environments, it is necessary to perform the following sequence of steps (Kester, Kirschner, & van Merriënboer, 2004; van Merriënboer & Dijkstra, 1997; van Merriënboer, Jelsma, & Paas, 1992):

- deconstructing complex skills and building an intertwined skills hierarchy;
- sequencing task classes around authentic whole-task problem situations;
- conducting cognitive analysis of mental models and cognitive strategies to determine knowledge structures guiding non-recurrent aspects of competent performance;
- conducting cognitive analysis of rules and procedures, and prerequisite knowledge supporting recurrent skills;

- selecting appropriate timing of supportive and procedural information presentation.

In the first component of this design model, learning tasks represent concrete, authentic whole task experiences. Within the same task class, learning tasks start with high built-in learner support that disappears at the end of the task class. In the second component, information that supports the performance of non-recurrent aspects of the complex skills (including mental models, strategic approaches to problem solving, and cognitive feedback) should be presented before students learn corresponding classes (clusters) of tasks. This information should always be available to the learners. Such sequencing would promote construction and elaboration of relevant schematic knowledge structures.

The third component of the model consists of information displays, demonstrations, and corrective feedback and requires just-in-time presentation of information. This component is a prerequisite to the learning and performance of recurrent aspects of learning tasks. Learners should receive the information necessary for accomplishing a specific task precisely at the time this information is required during the task performance. Prerequisite just-in-time information necessary for performance of recurrent or routine aspects of the skill (fact, concepts, rules, etc.) should be presented during practice of these tasks to promote formation of automated procedures and rules. The fourth component provides part-task practice for constituent skills that need to be performed at a very high level of automaticity. It is usually organized in practice sessions intermixed with learning tasks (van Merriënboer, Clark, & de Croock, 2002).

Just-in-time presentations of prerequisite information could be considered as a means of avoiding temporal split-attention effect (Mayer & Anderson, 1991; 1992; Mayer & Sims, 1994). By eliminating temporal split attention, just-in-time information presentation reduces extraneous cognitive load and releases cognitive resources for learning non-recurrent components of complex cognitive skills. Whole-task practice includes a sequence of simple-to-complex learning tasks (or classes of tasks) that promote schema construction for non-recurrent aspects, and schema automation for recurrent aspects of complex skills. As a result, learners will construct schemas for controlled effortful performance of unfamiliar task aspects and automated schemas for effortless performance of familiar task aspects (Kester, Kirschner, van Merrienboer, & Baumer, 2001).

In an exploratory study using a computer-based simulation of a water-alcohol distillery plant, Kester, Kirschner, van Merrienboer, & Baumer (2001) demonstrated that learners who showed behavior that was consistent with this theoretical model (i.e., who requested supportive information before practicing task classes and prerequisite information during practice of learning tasks) achieved higher transfer task performance than other learners.

According to Van Merriënboer (2007), a traditional self-directed learning cycle (scaffolding - assessment – planning) involves system-supported task performance, followed by learner- or system-initiated assessment of task performance, and learner- or system- conducted selection of the following learning task. Salden, Paas, van der Pal, & van Merriënboer (2006) demonstrated that selecting the next learning task and the level of scaffolding based on self-assessment of performance and mental effort produced similar learning results on transfer tasks to those obtained when the selection was based on the assessment by the system. Both these approaches were superior to no-assessment approach (using a fixed sequence of learning tasks).

VARYING LEVELS OF LEARNER CONTROL IN COMPLEX ENVIRONMENTS

In regards to selecting appropriately supported learning tasks, it is possible to outline several approaches that are based on different levels of learner control and different levels and types of adaptation. Levels of learner control could include, for example, full system control or shared control where the learner selects from a system pre-selected set of tasks. Different types of adaptation may include adaptation to performance indicators only, adaptation to mental effort indicators only, or adaptation to combined performance and mental effort indicators. Therefore, the approaches to selecting learning tasks could range from a system-controlled selection from only a limited number of system-adapted learning tasks to the learner-controlled selection from many non-adapted tasks.

Corbalan, Kester, & van Merriënboer (2007) demonstrated that, based on the efficiency of learning outcomes, adaptive task selection approaches consistently outperformed non-adapted selection. However, there was an interaction between adaptive vs. non-adaptive task selection approaches and shared control vs. system control of task selection. The shared control approach was more efficient than the system control approach for adaptive task selection, while system control was relatively more efficient than shared control for non-adaptive task selection.

The currently available approaches to scaffolding complex task performance use different fading guidance strategies and the completion strategy (a gradual transition from fully worked-out solution procedures to completion assignments and, finally, to conventional unsupported problem solving practice). Most recent studies have been directed on distinguishing and appropriately sequencing two major types of worked examples: process-oriented and product-oriented examples (van Gog, Paas, & van Merriënboer, 2006; 2008). While product-oriented worked examples focus mostly on demonstrating procedural steps required for achieving specific results (or products), process-oriented worked examples focus on expert reasoning behind these steps and the corresponding cause-effect relationships.

Van Merriënboer (2007) suggested a double-loop learning sequence for complex tasks as an extension of a traditional self-directed learning cycle (scaffolding - assessment – planning). The double-loop sequence includes an outer layer for reflection and monitoring tools: reflection-in-action (tools for monitoring task performance), reflection-on-action (reflective tools for evaluating performance), and "preflection" (tools for planning learning trajectory). The selection of appropriate levels and forms of scaffolding is important for each component of this sequence.

Scaffolding reflection-in-action may range from "reflection prompts" to fully independent study. Van den Boom, Paas, & van Merriënboer (2007) demonstrated that eliciting reflection on own task performance in an introductory psychology course using reflection prompts was more effective that instruction without prompts, however only when such prompts were followed by tutor feedback. Appropriate scaffolding reflection-on-action involves tools that help learners to reflect on assessments of task performance and may range from given evaluations to self-evaluations. Finally, scaffolding preflection may range from detailed advice to learners on selecting learning tasks to no advice on process of task selection.

Thus, for self-directed learning of complex tasks, providing the instructional support may involve several important processes: scaffolding of performance, assessment, and task selection (the "inner loop"), as well as scaffolding of reflection-in-action, reflection-on-action, and preflection (the "outer loop") (Van Merriënboer, 2007). Following this structure may provide a systematic approach to the design of instructional support for managing cognitive load in complex learning environments.

Corbalan, Kester, & Van Merriënboer (2006) suggested a personalized task selection approach, the shared instructional control model that combines two approaches: a system-controlled task selection based on learner levels of expertise and a learner-controlled task selection. According to the proposed combined model, the system selects a subset of tasks from the full available task pool based on the current level of learner expertise, and then the learner makes the final decision. As the learner proceeds through the training session, the system continuously assesses performance and invested mental effort and selects an optimal subset of tasks for the following learning step. This subset is presented to the learner who makes the final selection.

This model was compared to a fully system-controlled procedure in a preliminary experimental study using a simulation-based learning environment in the domain of dietetics. The results of this study demonstrated that the shared control was more effective and more efficient than fully system-controlled condition. There were small effect sizes on both mentioned indicators. Shared control condition resulted in higher learner post-test performance scores with effect size 0.25. In addition, higher performance was achieved with lower invested mental effort, effect size 0.37. Measures of motivation using interest/enjoyment subjective rating scale indicated marginally significant differences favoring the shared instructional control condition, thus supporting the suggestion that learner control may enhance learner motivation (Corbalan et al., 2006).

Another possible approach mentioned by Corbalan et al. (2006) and briefly described in the previous chapter, was originally raised by Bell & Kozlowski (2002). According to this advisory model, students in learner controlled condition receive some form of advice, for example, on how to assess their own performance and select new learning tasks accordingly. This approach may enhance student abilities to regulate their own learning. Shared instructional control could also be combined with advisory models.

It should be noted that optimal levels of learner control depend on levels of learner task-specific expertise. Novices in a specific task domain may not have enough knowledge to make effective use of allowed control. As the levels of learner expertise increase, system control could be decreased while learner control increased (Niemec, Sikorski, & Walberg, 1996; Gay, 1986).

Shared responsibility models may vary the level of student control as learners develop higher levels of expertise and self-regulation skills that are sufficient for selecting learning tasks independently. Advisory models could also provide learners with variable degrees of additional support in the task selection process. Based on their adaptive guidance approach, Bell and Kozlowski (2002) demonstrated that providing students with adaptive guidance in addition to learner control in a complex learning environment was beneficial for learners (see Chapter X for more details of this study).

Learner control over the task selection process may have certain advantages over system-controlled task selection. It could be implemented with different degrees of control over various elements of instruction ranging from full control to minimum control. The availability of choice may facilitate the perceived learner control and positively influence performance and learning involvement. For example, Hasler, Kersten, & Sweller (2007) observed that even when available choices are not actually used by learners, solely the availability of control may improve learning outcomes. On the other side, there is little empirical support for the positive effects of actual learner control on learning. In some learner-controlled instructional environments, learners may have simply overlooked essential instructional material and did not use the available control capabilities (Merrill, 2002). Even more importantly, learner-controlled instruction may have caused cognitive overload (Gerjets & Scheiter, 2007).

Corbalán, Kester, & van Merriënboer (2007) further suggested that shared instructional control model combined with variability over surface features of the tasks may enhance the perception of control and decrease the chance of making poor instructional choices. Using the task domain of genetics (inheritance laws of Mendel) Corbalan et al. (2007) investigated variability conditions (low / high) under which shared control would be most beneficial for learning. The results indicated a significant interaction effect. The shared control yielded higher transfer performance and higher task involvement in the condition of high variability over surface features. On the other side, system control resulted in higher transfer performance and higher task involvement in the condition of low variability. There were no main effects of levels of variability neither on transfer or mental effort. In this study, the task involvement was calculated according to the scale suggested by Paas, Tuovinen, van Merriënboer, & Darabi, 2005 that was based on performance scores and mental effort ratings (see Chapter V for more details).

Thus, the variability over surface features of the learning tasks may not enhance the learning effects by itself, but only in combination with shared control. It could also be detrimental with system control. Shared control could be optimized by ensuring high variability over surface features in the sequence of learning tasks. Providing selection only from very similar tasks may lead to a diminished level of perceived control and be detrimental for transfer performance and learner involvement (Corbalán et al., 2007).

LEARNER EXPERTISE AND LEVELS OF INSTRUCTIONAL GUIDANCE

Procedures for the selection of learning tasks need to tailor provided instructional guidance to levels of learner expertise. Differential learning effects of different methods of learning task selection in computer-based training for air traffic control were investigated by Camp, Paas, Rikers, & van Merrienboer (2001). In one method, learning tasks were provided to learners in a fixed predetermined sequence, from simple to more complex tasks. In other three methods, learning tasks were selected dynamically using three different learner characteristics: reported mental effort, performance scores, and mental efficiency indicator that combined these two variables (see Chapter V for more details about this indicator). Based on post-test transfer performance results, dynamic task selection generated better results than non-dynamic task selection, and led to more efficient training. However, no significant advantages of efficiency-based task selection over remaining two dynamic selection methods were demonstrated.

Camp et al. (2001) suggested that dynamic task selection based on performance indicators could result in a different type of learning than selection based on mental effort or mental efficiency. Schema automation process usually demands significantly less effort than the initial schema acquisition process. Therefore, performance indicators could be best suitable for use in dynamic task selection when training recurrent aspects of a skill, while mental effort and mental efficiency could be more suitable for training non-recurrent aspects of a skill.

With a dynamic selection of learning tasks, there is no pre-determined sequence of tasks that a learner needs to complete. The tasks are selected on-the-fly using certain current (online) measures of learner characteristics that change during learning as it progresses. Performance is a most commonly used variable for dynamic task selection processes (McArtur & Stasz, 1988; van Merriemboer & Luursema, 1996). Measures of cognitive load had never been used directly prior to Camp et al. (2001) study. As learner acquires more schematic knowledge structures in the task domain and automates more procedural rules, cognitive load involved in performing tasks will decrease.

In the air traffic control training program used by Camp et al. (2001), the difficulty of learning tasks was determined by the number of possible conflicts in the task (e.g., two planes are approaching each other at the same flight level; or an aircraft is given a command that could cause the aircraft to conflict with another aircraft, etc.). The total task difficulty was calculated using different weights for conflict situations of different complexity. When a student finished a problem, depending on the experimental condition he or she was in, the difficulty of the next problem presented to the student was determined using measures of mental effort, performance, or mental efficiency. The following task was then selected from a database of tasks with different complexities.

A simple algorithm for selecting the level of difficulty of the next task was developed. The overall relative learner performance was represented by a number between 1 and 5. In the performance condition, if a participant scored 1, problem difficulty was decreased by 2 units. If the score was 2, problem difficulty decreased by one unit. Score 3 left the level of problem difficulty on the same level, score 4 increased it by one unit, and score 5 increased the difficulty by 2 units.

In the mental effort condition, task difficulty depended on the mental effort a learner indicated after completing the previous task on a five-point subjective rating scale (with 1 corresponding to very low effort and 5 to very high effort). If a learner scored 1, task difficulty was increased by two units, while score 2 increased it by one unit. Score 3 left the difficulty level unchanged, score 4 decreased it by one unit, and score 5 decreased the task difficulty level by two units.

Finally, in the mental efficiency condition, the efficiency was calculated as a difference between performance and mental effort scores. If the efficiency score was more than zero (indicating that mental effort score was lower than the performance score and the problem was relatively easy), problem difficulty was increased. If it was less than zero (indicating that mental effort score was higher than the performance score and the problem was relatively hard), problem difficulty was decreased. A specific difficulty level of the next task was selected using a simple algorithm based on the above relation between mental efficiency and changes in problem difficulty.

For example, if the mental effort score is 1 (the lowest level) and the performance score is 5 (the highest level), task difficulty is increased significantly by four units (the maximum possible increment). However, if the performance is not at the highest level (while the effort is at the lowest level 1), the increment will accordingly decrease (to three units for a performance score 4, two units for a score 3, one unit for a score 2, and 0 for a score 1). If a student indicates a higher level of mental effort by a score 2, the increments in the next task difficulties levels will be lower by one unit in comparison with the previous scale: increase by three units for a performance score 5, two units for 4, one unit for 3, same level for a performance score 2 and decrease by one unit for a performance score 1.

With higher levels of mental effort, the increments in the next task levels of difficulty will accordingly be shifted downwards. For example, for the highest level of mental effort rating of 5, the next task difficulty level remains the same (increment zero) if the performance score is highest (5), decrease by one unit for a performance score 4, decrease by two units for a score 3, decrease by three units for a score 2, and decrease by the maximum possible four units for a score 1 (the lowest performance score).

EXPERTISE REVERSAL FOR INSTRUCTIONAL GUIDANCE AND SEQUENCING OF LEARNING TASKS

An adequate sequencing of learning tasks (or classes of tasks) according to levels of their difficulty is an essential part of the adaptation procedure. In most situations, it amounts to selecting appropriate levels of instructional guidance or support provided in specific learning tasks. The learning tasks that provide optimal levels of instructional guidance for novice learners may not be optimal for more experienced learners. These learners may have already acquired sufficient knowledge base to provide them with required levels of support internally. Using learning tasks with higher levels of instructional guidance with these learners may, in fact, inhibit learning resulting in the expertise reversal effect.

This section provides an overview of most recent studies demonstrating the reversals in instructional effectiveness and efficiency of instructional methods with different levels of instructional guidance as levels of learner expertise change. Brief descriptions of results of earlier studies by Kalyuga, Chandler, and Sweller (2001), Kalyuga, Chandler, Tuovinen and Sweller (2001), and Tuovinen and Sweller (1999) were provided in Chapter III.

Kalyuga & Sweller (2004) studied an interaction between levels of learner expertise in a specific task domain of calculating distances and projections in coordinate geometry and levels of instructional guidance. A first-step rapid diagnostic method was used in this study for evaluating levels of learner task-specific expertise (see Chapter IV for more details about the method). Participants (high school students) were divided into two groups of more and less knowledgeable learners based on a median split using scores obtained in the pretest. Results of the posttest indicated that less knowledgeable high-school students benefited significantly more from well-guided worked examples. For more knowledgeable learners, there was a clear indication of problem solving benefits (a medium to large effect size). There was a significant interaction between knowledge levels and instructional formats indicating that the most effective instructional format depended on the level of learner task-specific expertise. As the level of knowledge increased, the performance of the problem solving group improved more than performance of the worked examples group.

Reisslein, Atkinson, Seeling, & Reisslein (2006) compared effectiveness of three different sequence approaches to example-based instructional procedures in the task area of serial and parallel electrical circuit analysis for learners (university engineering students) with different levels of prior knowledge in the domain. One approach used traditional example-problem pairs with worked examples followed by isomorphic practice problems. Another approach provided practice problems first with an accompanying worked example for reference if needed (problem-example pairing). The third condition included backward faded worked examples in which increasingly more steps at the end of the solution procedure were omitted. Although no overall differences between the instructional procedures were found, the study demonstrated that novices benefited more from example–problem pairs while experts from problem–example pairs and faded example sequences.

Reisslein (2005) examined the effect of the pace of transitioning from worked examples to independent problem solving for learners with different levels of prior knowledge in the area of electrical circuit analysis (engineering college freshmen). In the immediate transitioning condition, learners started practicing problems immediately after an introduction. In the fast fading condition, worked solution steps were faded at a rate of one step with each example. In the slow fading condition, the rate was halved (one step for every second example). The results of the retention posttest indicated significant interactions between levels of learner prior knowledge and the pace of transitioning. More knowledgeable learners performed significantly better in the fast and immediate transitioning groups than in the slow transitioning group indicating that worked examples provided redundant guidance for these learners. On the other hand, learners with low level of prior knowledge benefited more from slow transitioning condition than from immediate or fast transitioning conditions, thus demonstrating the importance of detailed guidance for novice learners.

Seufert (2003) studied the effect of providing verbal semantic assistance for coherence formation (mapping a structure of the material) when learning from scientific text and pictures. Two kinds of support were investigated: a specific direct support and non-directive support (e.g., questions to students providing non-specific hints). The post-test results indicated that for learners with a relatively lower level of prior knowledge in the task domain, both directive and non-directive help conditions were significantly better than no-help conditions, with more benefits from the direct help condition. On the other hand, for learners with a higher level of prior knowledge, there were no differences between conditions (in fact, a small decrease in post-test results).

Clarke, Ayres, and Sweller (2005) investigated interaction between the timing of learning spreadsheet skills when using spreadsheet applications in learning mathematics and levels of learner expertise in this area. The sequential experimental condition provided instructions on spreadsheets prior to applying this knowledge to learning mathematics. In the concurrent condition, instructions on spreadsheet use and mathematical concepts were presented in an integrated format. The results of the study indicated that students with low-level knowledge of spreadsheets learned mathematics more effectively in the sequential formats in which the relevant spreadsheet skills were acquired prior to attending the mathematical tasks. On the other hand, students who were more experienced in using spreadsheets benefited more from an integrated format in which relatively new spreadsheet skills were acquired during learning corresponding mathematical concepts. Reversed measures of cognitive load (using subjective ratings) supported the cognitive load interpretation of the effect.

If information on both spreadsheet applications and mathematics is presented concurrently for novices, their working memory could be overloaded and learning inhibited compared to a sequential presentation. In contrast, more experienced learners are already familiar with basic spreadsheet skills and providing such information may cause redundant activities and imbalanced executive guidance. These learners need to concentrate on learning the relationship between their spreadsheet knowledge and mathematics instead, which is best supported by the integrated instructional presentation. The major instructional implication of this study is that the technology should be learned prior to learning a specific subject area. Concurrent learning may only be effective for more technologically experienced learners who need to familiarize themselves with relatively new technological skills. Acquiring basic technology skills while learning a specific subject discipline is unlikely to be effective (Clarke et al., 2005).

In all of the above experiments, novice learners benefited most from well-guided low-paced instructional procedures that reduced extraneous cognitive load for these learners, especially when learning structurally complex materials. For more expert learners, studying redundant worked examples and integrating the externally provided instructional guidance with learners' available knowledge structures that provided essentially the same guidance might have imposed a greater cognitive load than problem solving. These learners were able to use their relevant knowledge base to guide constructing integrated mental representations without overloading working memory, and therefore benefited more from a minimally guided instruction.

There are situations where intrinsic complexity of the learning material (the level of intrinsic cognitive load) may exceed cognitive capacity of novice learners. In such situations, initially presenting complex material as a set of isolated elements of information that could be processed serially, rather than simultaneously, may eliminate the cognitive overload in working memory. Pollock, Chandler, and Sweller (2002) demonstrated that using an isolated elements learning task followed by the fully interacting elements instruction benefited low-knowledge learners (isolated-interacting elements effect). However, for learners with higher levels of prior knowledge in the domain, there were no differences between this method and the traditional approach that used complex materials during both stages.

In a simple learning environment with a relatively limited size of problem space (number of possible intermediate problem states), cognitive load for novice learners could be reduced by eliminating a specific problem goal (goal-free effect, see Sweller, 1999 for an overview). For example, instead of "Find the value of x" in an equation, a goal-free problem statement would asks "Find the values of as many parameters you can". On the other hand, in the case of poorly specified learning goals in complex learning environments, a learner (even a relatively experienced one) could be lost in search for relevant sub-goals, experiencing a heavy working memory load. Spiro and Jehng (1990) suggested traversing of the information space along few well-defined overlapping lines of representation, thus effectively reducing the number of relevant sub-schemas to a few overlapping contexts covering the information space.

According to cognitive flexibility theory (Spiro & Jehng, 1990), in complex and ill-structured domains, nonlinear forms of learning which allow exploring the domain by revisiting the same content material in a variety of different contexts (nonlinear multidimensional traversal) could be a cognitively efficient learning approach. Suggesting learners to explore few representational dimensions prevents irrelevant activities that might unnecessary overload working memory during random unguided exploration and provides a means of gradual reduction of instructional guidance. Providing these sub-goals for advanced students in complex environments may have similar cognitive load consequences as eliminating specific goals in simple situations for novice learners (goal-free effect). Both techniques could reduce cognitive load and facilitate learning.

MEANS FOR THE GRADUAL CHANGE OF LEVELS OF INSTRUCTIONAL SUPPORT IN ADAPTIVE LEARNING

Multiple research studies demonstrated that for novice learners, worked examples represent a very efficient form of instruction (Cooper & Sweller, 1987; Paas, 1992; Paas & van Merriënboer, 1994a; Quilici & Mayer, 1996; Rieber & Parmley, 1995; Sweller & Cooper, 1985; Trafton & Reiser, 1993). However, for more experienced learners, integrating provided detailed instructional guidance with knowledge structures available in learner long-term memory may require additional cognitive resources and impose unnecessary cognitive load. Instructional formats that provide reduced guidance or minimal support (such as problem solving practice or exploratory learning environments) could be more cognitively suitable for relatively advanced learners.

A possible way to implement a gradual transition from worked examples to problem solving practice or exploration is using completion assignments (van Merriënboer, 1990; van Merriënboer et al., 2003). A completion assignment provides a problem statement, a partially worked out solution procedure, and asks learners to complete the solution. In this way, it effectively combines worked examples with problem solving tasks.

Atkinson, Derry, Renkl, & Wortham (2000), Renkl (1997), and Renkl, Atkinson, and Maier (2000) suggested another version of this approach, a faded worked examples technique. With this instructional method, worked examples are gradually faded as levels of learner knowledge increase. Parts of worked examples are progressively replaced with problem-solving steps for learners to complete. The gradual reduction of guidance as levels of learner experience in a domain increase is more effective instructional procedure than abrupt switch from worked examples to problems (Renkl, Atkinson, Maier, and Staley, 2002; Renkl and Atkinson, 2003)

An alternative instructional method for gradually replacing worked examples when instructing relatively more knowledgeable learners could be realized as imagining procedures and concepts. For example, Cooper, Tindall-Ford, Chandler, and Sweller (2001) asked students to imagine the computer-presented instructional procedures on how to use a spreadsheet application rather than repeatedly study the instructions. The instructional procedures were designed as worked examples consisting of a set of diagrams with embedded textual explanations of sequential steps.

The imagining technique was beneficial for more knowledgeable learners. The results also indicated that the imagining technique was not useful for low-knowledge students because of heavy working memory load it generated for these learners. Worked examples provided much more effective guidance for novice learners. More experienced learners had already acquired sufficient task-relevant schematic knowledge structures and continued studying of worked examples was a redundant activity for them. Imagining practice provided additional practice for such learners and lead to higher levels of knowledge acquisition.

A gradual transition from well-guided instructional formats to unguided forms of instruction as learners acquire more experience in a specific task domain was implemented in a computer-based tutorial in solving elementary algebra equations (Kalyuga & Sweller, 2004). The tutorial was designed as a series of worked examples, completion assignments, and conventional problems. The initial allocation of learners to appropriate completion assignments or stages of the faded worked examples was based on the outcomes of the rapid first-step diagnostic pretests in the relevant class of tasks (see Chapter IV for more details about rapid diagnostic assessment methods). The learner progress through the stages was also monitored by rapid diagnostic probes and instruction was accordingly tailored to changing levels of expertise.

Novice learners initially studied a series of fully worked-out examples (Figure 19), each followed by a problem solving exercise. Depending on results of a diagnostic probe at the end of this phase, a set of additional shortened worked examples (showing major steps without detailed explanations) was provided, if necessary, before proceeding to the next stage. The second stage contained completion assignments (faded worked examples) in which the explanations of the last procedural step were omitted and learners were asked to complete the solution themselves (Figure 20). Each of the following stages was similar to the previous one, except for a lower level of instructional guidance provided to learners. In completion assignments, explanations of progressively more procedural steps were eliminated. The final stage contained only problem solving exercises without any explanations provided.

Studying worked-out examples at the initial stages of cognitive skill acquisition is capable of providing deeper task understanding and patterns of meaningful problem solving procedures for novice learners. In example-based learning, effective means of developing learner expertise could be implemented by gradually fading worked-out steps in appropriately sequenced set of learning tasks as levels of learner knowledge in the task domain gradually increase. The four-component instructional design model (4C/ID model; van Merriënboer, 1997; van Merriënboer, & Kirshner,

Figure 19. A fully worked out example used in the computer-based algebra tutor.

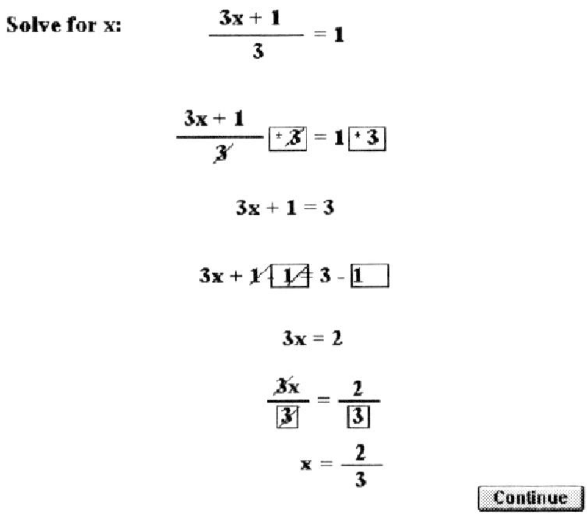

Figure 20. A faded worked example used in the computer-based algebra tutor.

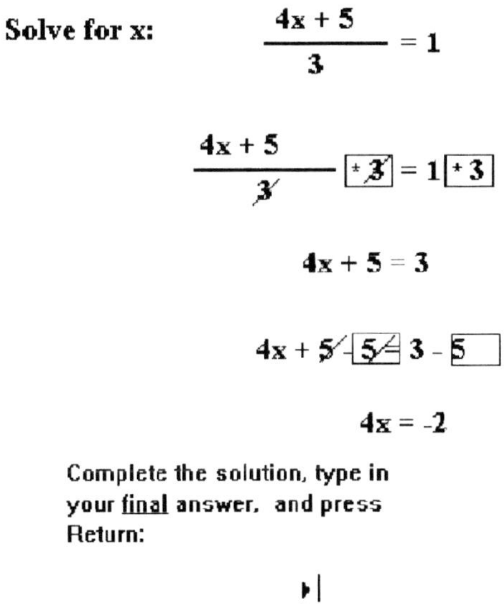

2007) provides an effective instructional design framework for implementing these methods in realistic complex adaptive learning environments.

Involving learners in quality self-explanation activities or using imagination techniques may enhance learning outcomes by increasing levels of effective (germane) cognitive load. Interactive complex learning environments may increase such cognitive load by prompting learners for self-explanations and predictions of the subsequent solution steps (Atkinson & Renkl, 2007). The self-explanation technique requires learners to explain explicitly suggested solution steps or actions based on learned principles of the domain, while the second method asks learners to predict the next procedural step before demonstrating or describing this step. These techniques could also be implemented within the 4C/ID framework by placing appropriate prompts after explaining each procedural step.

Another effective instructional approach to developing learner expertise is based on model-tracing intelligent tutoring systems. For example, cognitive tutors were developed within a theoretical framework of ACT-R (Anderson, 1983) primarily to enhance student learning of mathematics. In such intelligent tutoring systems, learning by problem solving is supported by providing explicit sub-goal structures, immediate feedback, hints, dynamic system-based evaluation of student progress in skill acquisition (using so-called "skillometers" or "skill bars") based on model and knowledge tracing, and appropriate remedial problems.

Because of the comprehensive instructional support component embedded into cognitive tutors, a reported instructional effectiveness of guided learning by problem-solving in intelligent tutoring systems could effectively be a worked example effect. Renkl, Schwonke, Wittwer, Krieg, Aleven, & Salden (2007) reported a series of experiments designed to investigate if this effect could be found in cognitive tutors with respect to different outcome measures, such as conceptual knowledge acquisition, transfer, learning time, and efficiency of learning. A "standard" problem-based tutor in circle geometry area (with self-explanation prompts and integrated format) was compared with an example-enriched tutor based on faded worked examples. The results indicated no differences in learning performance (transfer performance was very low in both conditions), however lower instruction time and higher efficiency indicators were obtained for example-enriched tutor.

In a follow-up study reported by Renkl et al. (2007), the tutor was modified in order to eliminate observed learner difficulties in working with it (e.g., the introduction to the tutor was improved, individual learning sessions with concurrent verbal reports were used). The results indicated higher post-test conceptual knowledge scores, lower instruction time, and higher efficiency indicators for example-enriched tutor.

Observations of learning processes and self-explanations showed that example group participants made many errors in the beginning of the learning phase with a quick catch-up and expressed more principle-based self-explanations. Problem group participants uttered more superficial procedure-based self-explanations. The general conclusion of Renkl et al. (2007) was that example-enriched tutor resulted in more efficient learning and conceptual knowledge acquisition. Integrating intelligent cognitive tutors with example-based learning could be an effective instructional approach to developing learner expertise.

Generally, a specific form in which instructional support is provided to learners may not be important. For example, extended feedback messages could serve the same guiding role as embedded worked examples. However, it is essential to provide the necessary guidance when learners lack sufficient task-specific knowledge base. Such external instructional guidance would serve in the executive role and prevent unproductive random search activities.

Therefore, worked-out examples embedded into interactive multimedia learning environments (such as intelligent cognitive tutors) that already provide extended feedback and hints, may not improve learning because these redundant examples could duplicate the feedback and hint messages. Interactive problem-solving environments that provide rich hints on learner request are effectively represent a form of annotated worked examples (Koedinger & Aleven, 2007). It is also possible that in some situations, embedding worked examples into such environments could even inhibit learning because additional cognitive resources would be required for coordinating different sources of duplicated guidance.

FUTURE TRENDS

The use of technology-rich multimedia learning environments in complex domains is steadily increasing. Therefore, a systematic instructional design framework is required to facilitate acquisition of complex cognitive skills as well as provide reliable diagnostic methods for evaluating these skills. Cognitive load theory could be instrumental in meeting these challenges. However, a limited number of studies in optimal instructional support methods that could be used at different levels of learner cognitive characteristics, first of all levels of task-specific expertise, is a major limitation of research in this framework.

In future studies, more refined levels of adaptability to the individual learner progress need to be investigated instead of relying on course-grained expertise levels (e.g., novice, intermediate, expert). Also, the development of learner skills in self-managing cognitive load (as an essential part of self-regulation skills) should be investigated in conjunction with adaptive guidance, shared responsibility, and advisory models for adaptive learning environments. Cognitive efficiency of different forms of external instructional guidance in specific areas should be evaluated.

Integration of intelligent cognitive tutors with example-based learning could be an effective means of optimizing cognitive load in adaptive learning. Adaptive fading of instructional support based on using rapid assessment techniques is another direction of improving example-based adaptive multimedia learning environments.

MULTIMEDIA INSTRUCTIONAL DESIGN IMPLICATIONS

In order to enhance acquisition of high-level cognitive skills required for solving complex realistic problems, especially in poorly structures task domains, instruction needs to be focused on whole learning tasks rather than on learning simple components of such complex tasks. Because of the need to process and learn many components simultaneously rather than sequentially, such complex whole learning tasks may impose heavy levels of cognitive load. Therefore, appropriate scaffolding and timely instructional support that are dynamically tailored to learning situations and cognitive characteristics of individual learners represent essential conditions of successful learning and performance of complex tasks (van Merriënboer & Kirshner, 2006).

There are several approaches to the selection of appropriately supported learning tasks that are based on different levels of learner control. The degree of learner control may range from full system control, through the shared control where the learner selects from a system pre-selected set of tasks, and to full learner control. Learner and shared instructional control could also be combined with advisory models. According to the advisory models, students receive some form of advice on how to assess their own performance and select new learning tasks accordingly. This approach has the potential to improve learner self-regulation skills and abilities of self-managing cognitive load.

Different levels and types of dynamic adaptation could also be used: adaptation to performance indicators, adaptation to mental effort indicators, and adaptation to combined performance and mental effort indicators. According to available data, while dynamic adapted task selection consistently lead to more efficient learning than non-dynamic task selection, no significant differences between different types of adaptation methods have been demonstrated.

Studying worked-out examples is an effective method of initial cognitive skill acquisition for low-knowledge or novice learners. A gradual transition from worked examples to problem solving practice or exploratory learning could be accomplished by using completion assignments or faded worked examples. As levels of learner task-specific expertise increase in example-based learning environments, gradually fading worked-out steps represents an effective means of optimizing instructional support and developing higher levels of expertise. The gradual reduction of guidance with increases in learner expertise is more effective instructional procedure than an abrupt switch from worked examples to problems.

Specific forms of instructional support may not be important as soon as the necessary guidance is provided to learners when they lack sufficient task-specific knowledge base to serve in executive role. Different forms of extended feedback, hints, etc. may serve the same function as worked examples. In this case, using additional redundant forms of support may not provide any benefits and could, in fact, inhibit learning in some circumstances.

SUMMARY OF CHAPTER XI

The procedures for adapting levels of instructional guidance to individual learners described in this chapter have been described in conjunction with the expertise reversal effect for levels of instructional support. The effect relates to empirically established interactions between levels of learner task-specific expertise and instructional methods that provide different levels of instructional support. The major instructional implication of the expertise reversal effect is the need to tailor dynamically external instructional guidance to current levels of learner expertise as they gradually change during learning.

Dynamic tailoring procedures may provide optimal and well-balanced executive function throughout the process of knowledge construction and elaboration. Such adaptive procedures could be effectively implemented within appropriate instructional design models that were developed for managing cognitive load while learning complex skills (e.g., 4C-ID model). These models allow using different levels of learner control, including shared responsibility, advisory models, and adaptive guidance. The completion tasks and faded worked examples could be effectively used for managing levels of instructional guidance in adaptive learning environments.

In general, the practical outcomes from the research on adaptive learning environments are still very limited, especially for instruction adapted to learner deep cognitive characteristics such as levels of knowledge or expertise. Cognitively supported learner-adapted instruction should be based on detailed real-time diagnosis of learner knowledge and skills. Real-time monitoring of levels of learner task-specific expertise using rapid cognitive diagnostic methods (first-step and rapid verification techniques) could be instrumental in selecting appropriate levels of instructional support at different stages of acquisition of complex cognitive skills. More research in using such methods in adaptive learning environments will be described in the following chapter.

REFERENCES

Atkinson, R. K., Derry, S. J., Renkl, A., & Wortham, D. W. (2000). Learning from examples: Instructional principles from the worked example research. *Review of Educational Research, 70,* 181-214.

Atkinson, R. K., & Renkl, A., (2007). Interactive example-based learning environments: Using interactive elements to encourage effective processing of worked examples. *Educational Psychology Review, 19,* 375-386.

Clarke, T., Ayres, P., & Sweller, J. (2005). The impact of sequencing and prior knowledge on learning mathematics through spreadsheet applications. *Educational Technology Research and Development, 53(3).* 15-24.

Cooper, G., & Sweller, J. (1987). The effects of schema acquisition and rule automation on mathematical problem-solving transfer. *Journal of Educational Psychology, 79,* 347-362.

Cooper, G., Tindall-Ford, S., Chandler, P., & Sweller, J. (2001). Learning by imagining procedures and concepts. *Journal of Experimental Psychology: Applied, 7,* 68-82.

Corbalan, G., Kester, L., & Van Merriënboer, J.J.G. (2006). Towards a personalized task selection model with shared instructional control. *Instructional Science, 34,* 399-422.

Corbalán, G., Kester, L., & van Merriënboer, J. J. G. (2007). Optimizing shared control with task variability over surface features: Effects on transfer and task involvement. Paper presented at the International Cognitive Load Theory Conference, 24-26 March, Sydney, Australia.

Gerjets, P., & Scheiter, K. (2007). Learner control in hypermedia environments. *Educational Psychology Review, 19,* 285-307.

Hasler, B. S., Kersten, B., & Sweller, J. (2007). Learner control, cognitive load and instructional animation. *Applied Cognitive Psychology, 21,* 713 - 729.

Kalyuga, S., & Sweller, J. (2004). Measuring knowledge to optimize cognitive load factors during instruction. *Journal of Educational Psychology, 96,* 558-568.

Koedinger, K., & Aleven, V. (2007). Exploring the assistance dilemma in experiments with cognitive tutors. *Educational Psychology Review, 19,* 239-264.

Merrill, D. (2002). First principles of instruction. *Educational Technology Research and Development, 50,* 43–59.

Paas, F. (1992). Training strategies for attaining transfer of problem solving skill in statistics: A cognitive load approach. *Journal of Educational Psychology, 84*, 429-434.

Paas, F., Tuovinen, J. E., van Merrienboer, J. J. G., & Darabi, A. A. (2005). A motivational perspctive on the relation between mental effort and performance. *Educational technology, Research and Development, 53*, 25-34.

Paas, F., & van Merriënboer, J. J. G. (1994a). Variability of worked examples and transfer of geometrical problem-solving skills: A cognitive-load approach. *Journal of Educational Psychology, 86*, 122-133.

Pollock, E., Chandler, P., & Sweller, J. (2002). Assimilating complex information. *Learning and Instruction, 12*, 61-86.

Quilici, J. L., & Mayer, R. E. (1996). Role of examples in how students learn to categorize statistics word problems. *Journal of Educational Psychology, 88*, 144-161.

Reisslein, J. (2005). *Learner achievement and attitudes under varying paces of transitioning to independent problem solving.* A dissertation presented in partial fulfillment of the requirements for the degree Doctor of Philosophy. Arizona State University.

Reisslein, J., Atkinson, R. K., Seeling, P., & Reisslein, M. (2006). Encountering the expertise reversal effect with a computer-based environment on electrical circuit analysis. *Learning and Instruction, 16*, 92-103.

Renkl, A. (1997). Learning from worked-out examples: A study on individual differences. *Cognitive Science, 21*, 1-29.

Renkl, A., Schwonke, R., Wittwer, J., Krieg, C., Aleven, V., & Salden, R. (2007). Worked-out examples in an Intelligent Tutoring System: Do they further improve learning? Paper presented at the International Cognitive Load Theory Conference, 24-26 March, Sydney, Australia.

Renkl, A., & Atkinson, R. K. (2003). Structuring the transition from example study to problem solving in cognitive skills acquisition: A cognitive load perspective. *Educational Psychologist, 38*, 15-22.

Renkl, A., Atkinson, R. K., & Maier, U. H. (2000). From studying examples to solving problems: Fading worked-out solution steps helps learning. In L. Gleitman & A. K. Joshi (Eds.), *Proceeding of the 22nd Annual Conference of the Cognitive Science Society* (pp. 393-398). Mahwah, NJ: Erlbaum.

Renkl, A., Atkinson, R. K., Maier, U. H., & Staley, R. (2002). From example study to problem solving: Smooth transitions help learning. *Journal of Experimental Education, 70,* 293-315.

Rieber, L. P., & Parmley, M. W. (1995). To teach or not to teach? Comparing the use of computer-based simulations in deductive versus inductive approaches to learning with adults in science, *Journal of Educational Computing Research, 13*, 359-374.

Salden, R. J. C. M., Paas, F., van der Pal, J., & van Merriënboer, J. J. G. (2006). Dynamic Task Selection in a Flight Management System Training. *The International Journal of Aviation Psychology, 16*, 157-174.

Salden, R. J. C. M., Paas, F., & van Merriënboer, J. J. G. (2006a). A comparison of approaches to learning task selection in the training of complex cognitive skills. *Computers in Human Behavior, 22*, 321-333.

Salden, R. J. C. M., Paas, F., & van Merriënboer, J. J. G. (2006b). Personalised adaptive task selection in Air Traffic Control: Effects on training efficiency and transfer. *Learning & Instruction, 16*, 350-362.

Seufert, T. (2003). Supporting coherence formation in learning from multiple representations. *Learning and Instruction, 13*, 227-237.

Spiro, R. J., & Jehng, J. (1990). Cognitive flexibility and hypertext: Theory and technology for the nonlinear and multidimensional traversal of complex subject matter. In D. Nix & R. Spiro (Eds.), Cognition, education, and multimedia: Exploring ideas in high technology. Hillsdale, NJ: Lawrence Erlbaum Associates.

Sweller, J. (1999). *Instructional Design in Technical Areas.* Melbourne: ACER.

Sweller, J., & Cooper, G. A. (1985). The use of worked examples as a substitute for problem solving in learning algebra. *Cognition and Instruction, 2*, 59-89.

Trafton, J. G., & Reiser, B. J. (1993). The contribution of studying examples and solving problems to skill acquisition. *Proceedings of the 15th Annual Conference of the Cognitive Science Society* (pp. 1017-1022). Hillsdale: Erlbaum.

Tuovinen, J., & Sweller, J. (1999). A comparison of cognitive load associated with discovery learning and worked examples. *Journal of Educational Psychology, 91,* 334-341.

Van den Boom, G., Paas, F., & Van Merriënboer, J.J.G. (2007). Effects on elicited reflections combined with tutor or peer feedback on self-regulated learning and learning outcomes. *Learning and Instruction, 17*, 532-548.

Van Gog, T., Paas, F., & Van Merriënboer, J J.G. (2006). Effects of process-oriented worked examples on troubleshooting transfer performance. *Learning and Instruction, 16,* 154-164.

Van Gog, T., Paas, F., & Van Merriënboer, J.J.G. (2008). Effects of studying sequences of process-oriented and product-oriented worked examples on troubleshooting transfer efficiency. *Learning and Instruction, 18*, 211-222.

van Merriënboer, J. J. G. (1990). Strategies for programming instruction in high school: Program completion vs. program generation. *Journal of Educational Computing Research, 6*, 265-287.

van Merriënboer, J. J. G. (1997). *Training complex cognitive skills: A four-component instructional design model for technical training.* Englewood Cliffs, NJ: Educational Technology Publications.

van Merriënboer, J. J. G. (2007). Cognitive Load Theory and self-directed learning: Systematic design of scaffolding. Paper presented at the International Cognitive Load Theory Conference, 24-26 March, Sydney, Australia.

van Merriënboer, J. J. G., & Kirshner, P. A. (2007). Ten steps to complex learning: A systematic approach to four-component instructional design. Mahwah, NJ: Lawrence Erlbaum.

van Merriënboer, J. J. G., Kirschner, P. A., & Kester, L. (2003). Taking the load off a learner's mind: Instructional design principles for complex learning. *Educational Psychologist, 38*, 5-13.

Chapter XII
Adaptive Procedures for Efficient Learning

INTRODUCTION

The rapid diagnostic approach to evaluating levels of learner task-specific expertise was introduced in Chapter IV and used in several studies that were subsequently described throughout this book. The rapid diagnostic techniques (first-step method and rapid verification technique) were instrumental in investigating some instances of the expertise reversal effect and in optimizing levels of cognitive load in faded worked example procedures (Section II and Chapter XI). This chapter describes some specific adaptive procedures based on rapid diagnostic methods for evaluating ongoing levels of learner task specific expertise. Two specific approaches to the design of adaptive instruction are considered, adaptive procedures based on rapid measures of performance and adaptive procedures based on combined measures of performance and cognitive load (efficiency measures).

The expertise reversal effect established interactions between learner levels of task-specific expertise and effectiveness of different instructional methods. The major instructional implication of this effect is the need to tailor instructional methods and procedures to dynamically changing levels of learner expertise in a specific class of tasks within a domain. The rapid diagnostic approach was successfully used for real-time evaluation of levels of learner task-specific expertise in adaptive online tutorials in the domains of linear algebra equations (Kalyuga & Sweller, 2004; 2005) and vector addition motion problems in kinematics (Kalyuga, 2006) for high school students. Both first step diagnostic method and rapid verification technique were applied in adaptive procedures.

According to the rapid assessment-based tailoring approach, these tutorials provided dynamic selection of levels of instructional guidance that were optimal for learners with different levels of expertise based on real-time online measures of these levels. The general designs of those studies were similar. In learner-adapted groups, at the beginning of training sessions, each student was provided with an appropriate level of instructional guidance according to the outcome of the initial rapid pretest. Then during the session, depending on the outcomes of the ongoing rapid tests, the student was allowed to proceed to the next learning stage or was required to repeat the same stage and then take the rapid test again.

At each subsequent stage, a lower level of guidance was provided to learners (e.g., worked-out components of solution procedures were gradually omitted and progressively replaced with problem solving steps), and a higher level of the rapid diagnostic tasks was used at the end of the stage. In control non-adapted groups, learners either studied all tasks that were included in the corresponding stages of the training session of their yoked participants, or were required to study the whole set of tasks available in the tutorial.

ADAPTIVE PROCEDURES USING RAPID MEASURES OF PERFORMANCE

Two rapid assessment methods described in Chapter IV, first-step diagnostic method and rapid verification diagnostic method, were used for measuring learner levels of task-specific expertise in different studies. For example, in an experiment using coordinate geometry tasks, the rapid assessment approach (first-step method) was used for the first time to successfully predict which students should be presented with worked examples and which should be presented with problems (Kalyuga & Sweller, 2004, Experiment 3).

Then, the rapid first-step testing method was used in a simple adaptive computer-based tutor in linear algebra equations for real-time adaptation of instructional procedures (worked examples, faded worked examples, and problem-solving practice) to ongoing levels of individual learners' knowledge (Kalyuga & Sweller, 2004, Experiment 4). The aim of the study was to demonstrate that the rapid test could be effectively used in a computer-based training environment for adapting instruction to changing levels of learners' knowledge of specific solution procedures.

The rapid test was used for initial selection of the appropriate levels of instructional materials according to levels of learner preliminary knowledge, as well as for monitoring learner progress during instruction and real-time selection of the most appropriate instructional formats. For learners with lower levels of expertise, as measured by the rapid test, additional worked examples were provided. For learners with higher levels of expertise, less worked example information and more problem solving exercises were provided. A flow-chart of the complete procedure is represented in Figure 21.

The learner-adapted procedure was compared to an equivalent procedure without real-time adaptation of instruction to levels of learner task-specific expertise. Learning was enhanced by the adaptive instruction with the effect size 0.46 for relative knowledge gains (differences between the sum of the test scores for the final rapid test and sum of the test scores for the initial rapid test). This study provided the initial evidence of the usability of the rapid test for tailoring instructional methods, although in a relatively simple and not media-rich domain. Similar rapid diagnosis-based approaches could be used in more complex environments for the initial selection of the appropriate formats of multimedia materials according to levels

Figure 21. Flowchart of the adaptive procedure using rapid first-step diagnostic assessment method. Reprinted from Kalyuga & Sweller (2004). Copyright © 2004 American Psychological Association. Used with permission.

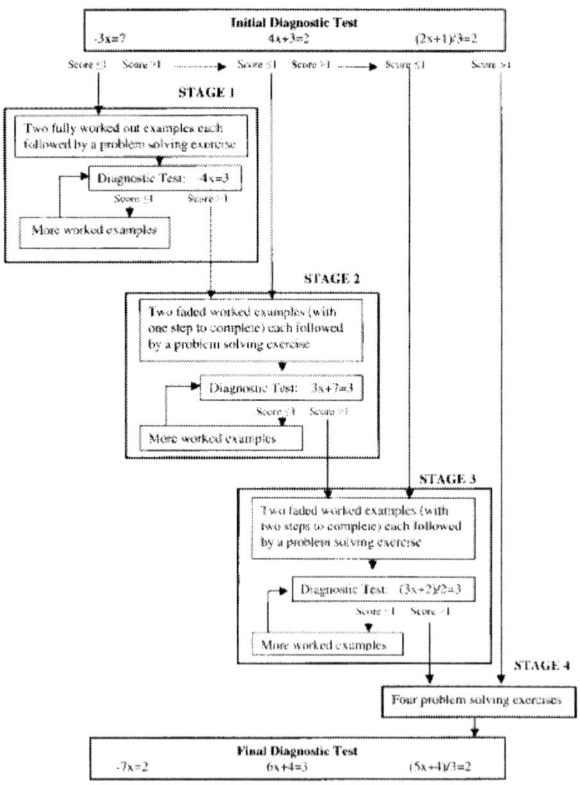

of learner preliminary domain-specific knowledge, for monitoring their progress during training, and real-time selection of the most appropriate multimedia formats to build fully learner-adapted presentations.

However, in more complex task domains, rapid diagnostic tasks may require responses that cannot always be specified precisely in advance as those in well-structures algebra equations. Therefore, recording and analyzing students' first-step responses in online multimedia environments may be technically challenging. In such situations, an alternative rapid verification diagnostic method could be more suitable for dynamic online assessment. As described in Chapter IV, with the rapid verification method, after studying a task for a limited time, learners are presented with a series of possible (both correct and incorrect) solution steps reflecting various stages of the solution procedure. They are required to rapidly verify the suggested steps, for example, by pressing corresponding keys on the computer keyboard.

The usability of the rapid verification method as a means of real-time adaptation of simple multimedia presentations (diagrams with on-screen textual explanations) to current levels of learner expertise was tested in the task domain of solving vector addition motion problems in kinematics. A sample of Grade 11 high-school students in the school's computer lab was used in the study. The learner-adapted procedure in computer-based tutor was compared to an equivalent instruction without real-time adaptation to the level of learner task-specific expertise. The training packages included an initial rapid diagnostic test, an adaptive training session for the experimental group and a non-adaptive version for the control group, and a final rapid diagnostic test.

The design of possible rapid verification tests in this task area was described in Chapter IV. As was noted in that description, in order to limit the task domain to relatively simple classes of problems, a restricted range of five angle values between vectors were used in the tasks. The diagnostic items in this restricted domain included one diagnostic task statement for each angle value, followed by a series of five possible (both correct and incorrect) solution steps for rapid verification with gradually increasing levels of graphical and numerical solution details provided to students.

For example, the first step indicated only directions of vectors; the second step also showed their numerical values; the third step indicated the direction of the resulting vector; the fourth step included the numerical expression for calculating the value of the resulting vector; and the fifth step indicated only the final answer. Each task statement was presented to students for around 15 seconds that were sufficient for reading the statement. Instead of technically restricting response times to several seconds (what could have forcefully interrupted some genuine responses), students were 'coached' in responding rapidly during pre-test exercises with a sample of tasks from a different area.

Learner prior knowledge is an important factor contributing to learning effects of instruction that is based on text and visual displays (e.g., Schnotz, 2002). Therefore, for learners with lower levels of task-specific expertise, based on the rapid diagnostic assessment, additional pictorial and textual information was provided. For learners with relatively higher levels of task-specific expertise, redundant representations were eliminated. Similar to the previously described tutorials in algebra, the adaptive training session in this domain was also based on a series of faded worked examples or completion tasks (Renkl & Atkinson, 2003; Van Merriënboer, 1990) each followed by a problem-solving practice. According to this approach, novices learn most effectively when instructed using fully worked out examples. As levels of learners' knowledge in the task domain increases, parts of worked examples should be gradually faded thus increasing a relative share of problem solving practice in instruction.

In the learner-adapted group, learners were allocated to appropriate stages of the instruction based on the performance indicators that were determined by the outcomes of the initial rapid verification test that covered the whole class of tasks. Appropriate fully and partially worked-out examples were presented, each followed by a problem solving exercise. Depending on the outcome of rapid diagnostic probes during specific stages of the instruction, each learner was allowed to proceed to the next stage of the training session or was required to repeat the same stage and then take the rapid test again. The rapid diagnostic probes measured performance only in specific types of tasks that were used at corresponding stages.

At each subsequent stage of the training session, a lower level of instructional guidance was provided to learners by eliminating increasingly more explanations of initial procedural steps in faded examples, and a higher level of the rapid probe task was used at the end of the stage. How long each learner stayed at each stage depended on her or his performance on rapid diagnostic tasks during the session. Thus, according to the number of levels of acquisition of the solution skill, there were five levels of adaptation for each of the five types of tasks corresponding to different angle values.

In contrast, in the non-learner-adapted group, all learners went through all the stages of the training session regardless of their performance on the initial rapid test. Each learner had to study all worked examples, perform all problem exercises, and undertake all rapid diagnostic tasks. However, the outcomes of these tests were not used for selecting the subsequent instructional materials. Thus this group was intentionally exposed to the maximum number of learning tasks and materials possible in the tutorial.

Even though studying less examples and solving less problems, the learner-adapted group demonstrated better knowledge gains with the effect size 0.52 (a medium size effect). Training session time was reduced by the factor 1.5 with the effect size 0.73. The higher knowledge gains for the learner-adapted format in comparison with the non-adapted format and significantly reduced training time provided evidence that the suggested rapid verification technique can be used to tailor instructional procedures in multimedia learning environments.

ADAPTIVE PROCEDURES USING MULTIPLE COGNITIVE MEASURES

As was mentioned in Chapter V, higher levels of task-specific expertise in a domain are characterized not only by rapid and effective performance due to well-organized knowledge base in long-term memory. Also, expert performance is usually relatively effortless because experts are capable to process information efficiently without exceeding available working memory capacity. Therefore, when both an expert and a novice successfully solve a task, the cognitive costs of their performance (in terms of required cognitive effort and time) could be different. On the other hand, if the same level of cognitive load is involved in solving a problem, experts are expected to achieve higher performance results. Therefore, measuring levels of cognitive load in addition to performance tests may provide better indicators of expertise. The cognitively optimal status of multimedia presentations themselves could also be verified by directly monitoring cognitive load during learner-tailored sessions.

Adaptive multimedia environments could be more efficient if rapid diagnostic tests of task-specific expertise are combined with measures of cognitive load. There are different methods, both quantitative and qualitative, that could be used to combine measures of performance and cognitive load (see Chapter V for details). Paas and van Merriënboer (1993) defined a quantitative integrated indicator of instructional efficiency as a difference between standardized z-scores of performance and standardized z-scores of subjective ratings of mental effort. Camp, Paas, Rikers, & van Merriënboer (2001) and Salden, Paas, Broers, and van Merriënboer (2004) used this indicator for the dynamic selection of learning tasks in air traffic control training (see Chapter XI for the description of their approach).

Methods for combining measures of performance and cognitive load could also be based on simple matrix-like approach (e.g., the approach described in Chapter XI) or on qualitative threshold considerations. With the latter approach, different levels of expertise could be associated with combinations of certain ranges of values of rapid performance indicators and ratings of cognitive load. For example, the top level of expertise may be defined as achieving the top performance scores combined with difficulty ratings that are not higher than a certain threshold level (e.g., "easy").

The efficiency-based approach to optimizing cognitive load was tested using a simple adaptive algebra tutor (Kalyuga & Sweller, 2005). Cognitive efficiency (E) was defined as the level of performance P (measured by the rapid first-step diagnostic method) divided by the rating of mental effort R: E = P/R. In contrast to the approach using *z*-scores for performance and mental effort ratings, this value could be calculated in real time for each individual learner. In this study, critical values of cognitive efficiency required for achieving a sufficient level of expertise were defined as Ecr = Pmax/Rmax, where Pmax is the maximum performance score for the task and Rmax is the maximum difficulty (or mental effort) rating score. If someone invests maximum mental effort in a task but does not display the maximum level of the task performance, his or her cognitive performance is not regarded as efficient (see Chapter V for more details about this method of defining instructional efficiency).

This combined measure of rapid test performance and mental effort was used for the initial selection of the appropriate assignments, as well as for monitoring learner progress during the session and real-time tailoring of instruction to changing levels of expertise. Thirty Grade 10 students who participated in the experiment were randomly assigned to 15 pairs and for each pair, one student was randomly assigned to the experimental groups and the other was assigned to the yoked control group. The experimental procedure included an initial rapid diagnostic test, an adaptive training session for the experimental group with 'yoked controls' in the control group, and a final rapid diagnostic test (see Figure 22 for a flow chart of the experimental procedure).

The initial rapid diagnostic test was designed to assess the initial level of learners' expertise in the domain. In the task statement preceding the test, students were asked for each of three equations they would see, to type a single one-line step that they would normally make first when solving the equation on paper (see Chapter IV for more details about such tests). After learners typed their first solution step, the following instruction appeared on the screen: "Indicate how difficult this task was by clicking on an appropriate answer". The participants had to select one of the nine options ("Extremely easy", "Very easy", "Moderately easy", "Slightly easy", "Neither easy nor difficult", "Slightly difficult", "Moderately difficult", "Very difficult", and "Extremely difficult"). Thus, a mental effort rating ranging from 1 (extremely easy) to 9 (extremely difficult) was collected for each task and a corresponding efficiency indicator was calculated using both measures.

Similar to the previous studies, the training session was designed as a series of worked examples, completion assignments (faded worked examples), and conventional problems. In the learner-adapted format, the allocation of learners to appropriate stages of instruction was based on the outcomes of the initial rapid diagnostic test. For example, if a learner obtained an efficiency level of 2/9 or less

Figure 22. Flow chart of the adaptive procedure for the experimental training session. Reprinted from Kalyuga & Sweller (2005). Copyright © 2005 Association for Educational Communication Technology. Used with permission.
Note: E = Efficiency.

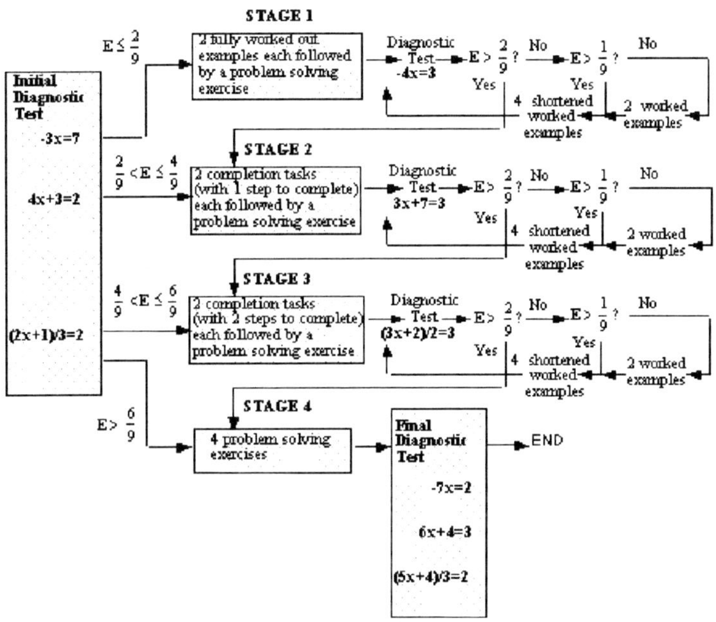

on the first task of the initial diagnostic test, he or she started training from the first stage. Two fully worked out examples were presented, each followed by a problem solving exercise. An expertise assessment procedure similar to that used in the initial diagnostic test (including both rapid task and rating of mental effort) was used for monitoring learners' progress during each stage of the training session. For example, in order to be able to get to the next stage of training from Stage 1, the efficiency indicator (based on the rapid response to the equation $-4x = 3$) had to be more than 2/9.

If a learner's efficiency measure on the first task of the initial diagnostic test was more than 2/9, but on the second task, the efficiency indicator was 4/9 or less, the learner started the training session from the second stage. This stage contained two faded worked examples, each followed by a corresponding problem exercise. At the other end of the efficiency scale, if a learner's efficiency indicators on all three tasks in the initial diagnostic test were above corresponding critical levels (indicating an expert performance level), he or she started training from the final fourth stage. This stage contained only four problem solving exercises with corresponding feedback.

Thus, in the learner-adapted format, learners who indicated the lowest level of efficiency in the initial diagnostic test went through all four stages of the training session. How long learners stayed at each stage depended on efficiency of their learning as measured by diagnostic tests and rating scales during the session. On the other hand, learners who indicated the highest efficiency level in the initial diagnostic test immediately went the last stage of the training session which included only problem solving practice.

In contrast, in the non-adapted format group, each learner started the training session from the same stage as the paired learner in the learner-adapted format group and his/her performance during the training was not monitored. The learners in both groups went through the same stages of the training session, thus equalizing experimental conditions. The only difference was that in the learner-adapted format group, the selection and sequence of training episodes was tailored to the specific current level of each learner's expertise, while in the non-adapted format group it was not (it was tailored to the level of a different learner).

Results indicated that the learner-adapted instructional format resulted in significantly higher average efficiency gains (differences between average cognitive efficiency scores for the final rapid test and average cognitive efficiency scores for the initial rapid test) than the non-adapted format with the effect size 0.69 (a medium to large effect size). The test score gains (differences between the final and initial test scores) also favored the learner-adapted group with the effect size 0.55 (a medium to large effect size). Electronic records of students' activities showed that in the learner-adapted group, the pace of learning indeed varied considerably for different learners. Together with higher efficiency and knowledge gains for the learner-adapted group, these observations demonstrated that the adaptive procedure was successful in tailoring instructional sequences to levels of task specific expertise of individual learners.

The described adaptive methodology incorporated cognitive load as an essential factor of the learning task selection procedure in a dynamic learner-tailored environment. The dynamic problem selection procedure realized in this study was in principle similar to those implemented by Camp et al. (2001) and Salden et al. (2004) in air traffic control training. However, it used a different performance assessment method based on rapid diagnostic tests, an alternative definition of instructional efficiency, and a different task selection algorithm which allowed a smoother transition between stages of training. Despite these differences, learner-adapted instructional environments proved to be more effective than non-adapted formats in all these studies.

COMPARISONS OF DIFFERENT ADAPTIVE PROCEDURES

If different adaptation methodologies could be applied for the design of learner-tailored instructional environments in the same task domain, an important research question is to find out which adaptation procedure is superior. Kalyuga (2006) compared two alternative adaptation procedures, performance-based and efficiency-based, and the control condition without real-time adaptation. The control condition included all the worked examples and problems the students in experimental groups could encounter. The first procedure used only results of rapid verification test performance for adapting levels of instructional guidance, while the second procedure combined rapid measures of performance with measures of mental load. The study involved 45 Grade 11 students and used a class of tasks in kinematics (vector addition motion problems) described previously in Chapter IV. Efficiency-based or performance-based measures of expertise were used for selecting the appropriate initial level of details in instructional explanations, as well as for monitoring learners' progress during the instruction in order to fine-tune the level of instructional guidance during the session.

The experimental procedure included an initial rapid diagnostic test (for efficiency-based condition, it was combined with the rating of mental effort), an adaptive or non-adaptive (for control group) training session, and a final rapid diagnostic test. The initial test was designed as a sequence of five tasks representing the five task classes corresponding to different values of angles between vectors (see the previous section and Chapter IV for details).

In the learner-adapted efficiency-based condition, the rapid verification method for evaluating levels of learner task-specific expertise was combined with subjective ratings of mental effort using a simple qualitative definition of efficiency. This approach is based on certain thresholds of performance and mental effort. Each diagnostic task was followed by a 9-point rating scale of mental effort. A learner's performance in a class of tasks was considered efficient if, in a rapid verification task corresponding to this class of tasks, she or he correctly verified all the suggested steps at least up to, but not including, the final numerical answer and rated task difficulty below the average value (i.e. less than 5 for the 9-point rating scale).

As in the previous studies, the training session was designed as a series of faded worked examples each followed by problem-solving practice. As levels of learner expertise increased, parts of worked examples were gradually omitted. In the learner-adapted groups, learners were allocated to appropriate stages of the instruction according to the efficiency or performance measures that had been determined during the initial rapid test. For learners with insufficient levels of expertise in a class of tasks (according to performance or efficiency criteria for corresponding groups), a fully worked-out procedure with detailed explanations of each step for this class of tasks was provided. As levels of learner performance gradually improved, explanations of increasing number of initial steps were eliminated, and graphics presented only the final results of the omitted steps. The remaining steps were explained and depicted in details. When a learner reached the top level of performance or efficiency, only final numerical answers were presented. Time allowed for studying fully worked-out and faded procedures was user-controlled. Time for solving each problem was limited to 1 minute. If the learner could not solve the problem within this time limit, a fully worked out solution of the problem was provided.

An individual's progress during the training session was monitored using single rapid verification probes at corresponding levels. As before, depending on the outcome of these rapid probes, a learner was allowed to proceed to the next stage of the training session or was required to repeat the same stage and then take the rapid probe again. In the non-adapted group, all learners went through all the stages of the training session regardless of their performance on the initial rapid test. Training sessions in all three groups ended with subjective ratings of difficulty of the instruction and the final rapid verification test. The final test was similar to the initial test with re-worded tasks and changed numerical values. Instructional efficiency measures for the training session were calculated as ratios of knowledge gain scores to ratings of mental effort for the training session.

Results indicated higher instructional efficiency indicators and lower training session difficulty together with reduced training time for learner-adapted instructional formats in comparison with the non-adapted format. Both approaches to tailoring instruction to levels of learner task-specific expertise were superior to the non-adaptive condition. However, there were no statistically significant differences between effects of these two procedures, although means and effect sizes indicated a possible superiority of the efficiency-based approach on a number of important measures (instructional efficiency, mental effort, and number of problem solving reattempts during training). Although this approach required more instruction time, the time difference was not statistically significant. This increase was partially due to additional time students required for rating levels of task difficulty during diagnostic probes.

Thus, both suggested approaches could be successfully used to adapt instructional procedures to levels of learner expertise. However, at this stage, there are no clear indications of advantages of one approach over another. The cognitive efficiency-based approach may require further fine-tuning in order to see such advantages. For example, various criteria for achieving the expert level of efficiency may need to be investigated.

The above adaptive procedures were system-controlled. As mentioned previously, decreased levels of motivation and the lack of opportunities for the development of self-regulation skills are possible disadvantages of such procedures. Therefore, the described approaches should be compared with adaptive procedures based on the learner-controlled approach to individualization of instruction. Learner-controlled selection of learning tasks offers another form of adaptive methodology by giving the students control over what learning tasks they want to study or practice next. It may provide students with the opportunity to select the appropriate tasks to practice while avoiding a possible overload of their cognitive system.

Preliminary studies indicate that when given the possibility to choose the task format, students may be capable of selecting their own learning tasks (e.g., van Merriënboer, Schuurman, de Croock, & Paas, 2002). The learners could be able to adapt the learning environment to themselves by deciding what learning tasks or instructional methods they prefer next rather than having this decision made for them by the system. However, students with lower levels of knowledge or expertise might not use the control appropriately (Niemic, Sikorski, & Walberg, 1996). Merrill (1975) also admitted that the number of variables that a learner can control should be limited, otherwise the learner control may inhibit learning.

In accordance with their previous results, Salden, Paas, & van Merriënboer (2006a; 2006b) demonstrated that tailoring air traffic control training to the individual needs of the student generally made training more efficient. However, although task selection based on efficiency approach demonstrated some training benefits, it did not lead to higher transfer performance nor was this condition more efficient. On the other side, learner-controlled (personalized preference) task selection demonstrated only minor training benefits. However, it lead to higher transfer performance and was shown to be an efficient training method. Students were capable of controlling their learning, as long as their cognitive system was not overloaded. Salden et al. (2006b) found no significant differences between specific adaptation procedures based on task selection using a system-controlled efficiency-based procedure and learner-controlled personalized preference procedure.

FUTURE TRENDS

To further investigate the applicability of the rapid diagnostic approach (both the first-step and rapid verification methods, used separately or combined with measures of cognitive load) in adaptive learning environments, it is necessary to test the described procedures in other domains, especially less structured tasks areas. Alternative measures of cognitive load may also be investigated in conjunction with rapid diagnostic techniques in adaptive learning environments. For example, it is possible to incorporate dual-task techniques that use performance on simple secondary tasks as indicators of cognitive load associated with performance on primary tasks (Brünken, Plass, & Leutner 2003) or less intrusive non-verbal formats of subjective rating scales. Various criteria of efficient expert performance for tailoring instructional methods to changing levels of learner task-specific expertise also need to be evaluated in adaptive instructional systems.

The adaptive procedures could also be modified further by combining multiple measures of cognitive load and performance. For example, a multidimensional approach combining measures of learning task effort, test task effort, and test performance indicators could be investigated (Tuovinen & Paas, 2004). The influence of user motivational characteristics on the relation between mental effort and performance could also be taken into account (Paas, Tuovinen, van Merriënboer, & Darabi, 2005).

The techniques for making branching decisions when selecting appropriate learning pathways in adaptive learning environments need further refinement. More sophisticated approaches than those based on using the results of a single test probe need to be investigated. Such approaches may reduce a possible negative influence of low reliability of a single item in assessing levels of learner expertise. Also, more comprehensive procedures are needed "to permit the learner to adjust step size to his capabilities without suffering either many errors or tedious, unneeded redundancies" (Briggs, 1968, p. 166).

Alternative adaptation procedures that combine advantages and reduce disadvantages of both system- and learner-controlled approaches need to be investigated. For example, shared-responsibility and advisory models could be incorporated into adaptive learning environemnts (Corbalan, Kester, and van Merriënboer, 2006; van Merriënboer, Sluijsmans, Corbalan, Kalyuga, Paas, & Tattersall, 2006). Providing students with adaptive guidance in addition to learner control (an adaptive guidance approach, Bell and Kozlowski, 2002) may have a great potential for enhancing learner knowledge and self-regulation skills in complex adaptive learning environments.

MULTIMEDIA INSTRUCTIONAL DESIGN IMPLICATIONS

Multimedia learning environments could be more instructionally efficient if they continuously and dynamically tailor learning tasks to changing levels of learner expertise in a specific task domain. This process involves selecting appropriate levels of instructional guidance, formats of information presentation, and levels of learner control.

Rapid diagnostic tests could be used to determine optimal instructional procedures for individuals with different levels of task-specific expertise. Appropriately constructed rapid diagnostic instruments could be used to dynamically monitor levels of learner expertise in a specific task domain. Such diagnostic techniques in combination with principles for optimizing cognitive load derived from the expertise reversal effect could provide effective adaptive procedures.

Developing appropriate rapid cognitive diagnostic techniques in specific task domains is the key task in implementing this approach to adaptive multimedia learning. For example, based on the expertise reversal effect, presenting novice learners with worked examples is superior to presenting them with problems to solve. On the other hand, more knowledgeable learners should be presented with more problems than worked examples (Kalyuga, Chandler, Tuovinen, & Sweller, 2001). However, it is not clear at what point the switch from examples to problems should occur without a suitable diagnostic instrument to measure levels of task-specific expertise in real time.

Similarly, the rapid diagnostic tests should be used to determine whether learners need to be presented with information in integrated or dual-modality format (if they are relative novices) or in non-redundant diagrammatic format (if they are relatively more expert learners). The rapid diagnostic techniques could be used to determine the point at which information should no longer be presented as textual explanations embedded into a diagram or presented as auditory narrations, but rather as a single diagram without any on-screen or auditory textual explanations. Thus, the rapid tests should direct switching instructional formats at the most appropriate time for an individual learner.

As discussed in the previous chapters, learner control approaches to individualization of instruction are considered as alternative ways of dynamic tailoring of instruction to learner cognitive characteristics. The effectiveness of learner control-based approaches obviously depends on the ability of learners to select appropriate learning strategies. Since novice learners may lack sufficient prior knowledge base, this approach may not be suitable during the early stages of learning complex cognitive skills. When students have acquired a significant prior knowledge base in a domain, they may effectively control the content and sequence of learning tasks. In this case, they would not end studying irrelevant and redundant tasks that could cause high levels of cognitive load and inhibit learning.

SUMMARY OF CHAPTER XII

Using rapid dynamic performance indicators in adaptive methodologies is a viable approach to the problem of tailoring multimedia learning environments to levels of learner task-specific expertise. The rapid diagnostic methods were used for optimizing levels of instructional guidance and cognitive load in several adaptive learning environments in algebra and kinematics (Kalyuga, 2006; Kalyuga & Sweller, 2004; 2005). All these environments used a similar adaptive procedure.

At the beginning of a session, each learner was allocated to an appropriate level of guidance according to the outcome of the initial rapid diagnostic test. Depending on the outcomes of the rapid diagnostic probes during instruction, the learner was allowed to proceed to the next stage of the session or was required to repeat the same stage and then take the rapid test again. At each subsequent stage of the tutoring session, a lower level of instructional guidance was provided to learners, and a higher level of the rapid diagnostic tasks was used at the end of the stage. Important advantages of this approach to learner-adapted learning environments are its transparency and relative simplicity.

In some of the studies, the allocation of learners to appropriate stages of instructional guidance was based on levels of task-specific expertise as measured by the rapid online first-step or rapid verification tests. In other studies, the rapid measures of task-specific expertise were combined with measures of cognitive load based on subjective ratings of task difficulty. Since expertise is associated not only with higher levels of performance but also with lower cognitive effort, combining both measures was expected to produce a better indicator of learner task-specific expertise.

Critical levels of efficiency were defined for each class of tasks as criteria for achieving proficiency in this task domain. Appropriately defined cognitive efficiency indicators were used for the initial selection of optimal levels of instructional guidance, as well as for continuous monitoring of learner progress and tailoring instruction to changing levels of task-specific expertise. With both approaches, results indicated that learner-adapted conditions resulted in significantly better knowledge gains than non-adapted conditions. However, there were no significant differences found between the two adaptation procedures when they were used in the same study and could be meaningfully compared.

Thus, dynamically adapting task selection procedures and levels of instructional guidance to levels of learner task-specific expertise using rapid diagnostic methods enhanced learning outcomes and supported previous results of Camp et al. (2001), Salden et al.(2004), and Salden et al. (2006). Despite differences in performance assessment methods, definitions of instructional efficiency, and task selection algorithms, learner-adapted conditions were superior to non-adapted formats in all these studies.

Incorporating learner control approaches into adaptive instruction represents alternative ways of dynamic tailoring of instruction to levels of learner expertise. Shared-responsibility, advisory, and adaptive guidance models could be effectively used in adaptive multimedia learning environments. For example, a shared control model demonstrated higher learning outcomes than a fully system-controlled condition (Corbalan et al., 2006). The shared control model effectively combined system- and learner-controlled environments by first selecting a subset of tasks based on learner performance and cognitive load indicators, and then presenting this subset to the learner who made the final decision.

The quality of adaptive environments depends on the accuracy of information about levels of learner knowledge and skills in specific task domains. Using traditional multiple-choice tests and tracing user interactions with the system may not produce sufficient levels of diagnostic precision. Applying modern artificial intelligence approaches and developing sophisticated fine-grained production rule-based learner models allowed a significant increase in the precision of adaptive methodologies (e.g., Anderson et al., 1992). However, implementing these methodologies requires complex computational modeling procedures. Therefore, their application has been limited to several well defined and relatively simple for modeling domains (e.g., programming and mathematics). On the other hand, the models that are used in most adaptive hypermedia and web-based environments are based on several discrete coarse-grained levels of learner expertise. An important advantage of the suggested rapid diagnosis-based approach to the design of learner-adapted environments is combining high levels of diagnostic precision with simplicity of implementation.

REFERENCES

Anderson, J. R., Corbett, A. T., Fincham, J. M., Hoffman, D., & Pelletier, R. (1992). General principles for an intelligent tutoring architecture. In V. Shute & W. Regian (Eds.), *Cognitive approaches to automated instruction* (pp. 81-106). Hillsdale, NJ: Erlbaum.

Bell, B. S. & Kozlowski, S. W. J. (2002). Adaptive guidance: Enhancing self-regulation, knowledge, and performance in technology-based training. *Personnel Psychology, 55*, 267-306.

Briggs, L. J. (1968). Learner variables and educational media. *Review of Educational Research, 38*, 160 – 176.

Brünken, R., Plass, J., & Leutner, D. (2003). Direct measurement of cognitive load in multimedia learning. *Educational Psychologist, 38,* 53-61.

Camp, G., Paas, F., Rikers, R., & van Merriënboer, J. J. G. (2001). Dynamic problem selection in air traffic control training: A comparison between performance, mental effort, and mental efficiency. *Computers in Human Behavior, 17*, 575-595.

Chung, J., & Reigeluth, C. M. (1992). Instructional prescriptions for learner control. *Educational Technology, 32*, 14-20.

Corbalan, G., Kester, L., & van Merriënboer, J. J. G. (2006). Towards a personalized task selection model with shared instructional control. *Instructional Science, 34*, 399-422.

Kalyuga, S. (2006). Assessment of Learners' Organized Knowledge Structures in Adaptive Learning Environments. *Applied Cognitive Psychology, 20*, 333-342.

Kalyuga, S., Chandler, P., Tuovinen, J., & Sweller, J. (2001). When problem solving is superior to studying worked examples. *Journal of Educational Psychology, 93*, 579-588.

Kalyuga, S., Chandler, P., & Sweller, J. (2000). Incorporating learner experience into the design of multimedia instruction. *Journal of Educational Psychology, 92*, 126-136

Kalyuga, S., & Sweller, J. (2004). Measuring knowledge to optimize cognitive load factors during instruction. *Journal of Educational Psychology, 96,* 558-568.

Kalyuga, S., & Sweller, J. (2005). Rapid dynamic assessment of expertise to improve the efficiency of adaptive e-learning. *Educational Technology, Research and Development, 53*, 83-93

Merrill, M. D. (1975). Learner control: Beyond aptitude-treatment interactions. AV Communication Review,

Niemec, P., Sikorski, C., & Walberg, H. (1996). Learner-control effects: A review of reviews and a meta-analysis. *Journal of Educational Computing Research, 15,* 157-174.

Paas, F., Tuovinen, J., Tabbers, H., & van Gerven, P. (2003). Cognitive load measurement as a means to advance cognitive load theory. *Educational Psychologist, 38,* 63-71.

Paas, F., Tuovinen, J. E., van Merrienboer, J. J. G., & Darabi, A. A. (2005). A motivational perspctive on the relation between mental effort and performance. *Educational technology, Research and Development, 53*, 25-34.

Paas, F., & van Merriënboer, J. J. G. (1993). The efficiency of instructional conditions: An approach to combine mental-effort and performance measures. *Human Factors, 35*, 737-743.

Renkl, A., & Atkinson, R. K. (2003). Structuring the transition from example study to problem solving in cognitive skills acquisition: A cognitive load perspective. *Educational Psychologist, 38,* 15-22.

Rowe, A., Cooke, N., Hall, E., & Halgren, T. (1996). Toward an on-line knowledge assessment methodology: building on the relationship between knowing and doing. *Journal of Experimental Psychology: Applied*, 2, 31-47.

Salden, R. J. C. M., Paas, F., Broers, N. J., & van Merriënboer, J. J. G. (2004). Mental effort and performance as determinants for the dynamic selection of learning tasks in air traffic control training. *Instructional Science, 32,* 153-172.

Salden, R. J. C. M., Paas, F., & van Merriënboer, J. J. G. (2006a). A comparison of approaches to learning task selection in the training of complex cognitive skills. *Computers in Human Behavior, 22*, 321-333.

Salden, R. J. C. M., Paas, F., & van Merriënboer, J. J. G. (2006b). Personalised adaptive task selection in Air Traffic Control: Effects on training efficiency and transfer. *Learning & Instruction, 16*, 350-362.

Schnotz, W. (2002). Towards an integrated view of learning from text and visual displays. *Educational Psychology Review, 14,* 101-120.

Shute, V., & Towle, B. (2003). Adaptive e-learning. *Educational Psychologist, 38*, 105-114.

Steinberg, E. R. (1977). Review of student control in computer-assited instruction. *Journal of Computer-Based Instruction, 3,* 84-90.

Steinberg, E. R. (1989). Cognition and learner control: A literature review, 1977-1988. *Journal of Computer-Bsed Instruction, 16,* 117-121.

Tennyson, R. D. (1980). Instructional control strategies and content structure as design variables in concept acquisition using computer-based instruction. *Journal of Educational Psychology, 72*, 525-532.

Tennyson, R. D. (1981). Use of adaptive information for advisement in learning concepts and rules using computer assisted instruction. *American Educational Research Journal, 18*, 425-438.

Tennyson, R. D., & Buttrey, T. (1980). Advisement and management strategies as design variables in computer-assissted instruction. *Educational Communication and Technology Journal, 28*, 169-176.

Tennyson, R. D., & Rothen, W. (1979). Management of computer-based instruction: Design of an adaptive control strategy. *Journal of Computer-Based Instruction, 5*, 126-134.

Tuovinen, J. E., & Paas, F. (2004). Exploring multidimensional approaches to the efficiency of instructional conditions. *Instructional Science, 32*, 133-152.

van Merriënboer, J. J. G. (1990). Strategies for programming instruction in high school: Program completion vs. program generation. *Journal of Educational Computing Research, 6*, 265-287.

Van Merriënboer, J. J.G., Schuurman, J. G., de Croock, M. B. M., & Paas, F. (2002). Redirecting learners' attention during training: Effects on cognitive load, transfer test performance, and training efficiency. *Learning and Instruction, 12*, 11-37.

Van Merriënboer, J. J. G., Sluijsmans, D., Corbalan, G., Kalyuga, S., Paas, F., and Tattersall, C. (2006). Performance assessment and learning task selection in environments for complex learning. In D. Clark, & J. Elen (Eds.). *Advances in Learning and Instruction* (pp. 201-220). Elsevier Science.

SUMMARY OF SECTION III

Multimedia learning environments can significantly enhance learning outcomes by integrating knowledge of cognitive processes involved in human information processing with technological capabilities. Such integration would allow using the most appropriate content and presentation formats, at the most appropriate time, and in the most cognitively efficient way for each individual user, thus providing truly learner-centered and adaptive environments (Shute & Towle, 2003).

Recent research studies in cognitive load issues in multimedia learning have demonstrated that many suggested multimedia presentation techniques that were highly effective with less knowledgeable learners could lose their effectiveness and even have negative consequences when used with more experienced learners. This expertise reversal effect represents an important phenomenon that provides an insight into the operation of our cognitive system in learning. It has been observed in many studies both within and outside of a cognitive load framework. It has also been supported by previously conducted studies in aptitude-treatment interactions. In practical terms, it provides a valuable guidance for the design of learner-adapted instructional systems.

An important implication of the expertise reversal effect is that multimedia presentation techniques and formats need to be tailored to levels of learner task-specific expertise. Dynamically (in real time) selected multimedia instructional formats and procedures should be optimized for individuals with different levels of expertise. To accomplish this goal, firstly, it is important to understand the cognitive mechanisms that influence efficiency of multimedia learning for individual learners. Secondly, it is necessary to have simple rapid diagnostic measures suitable for real-time on-line evaluation of levels of learner task-specific expertise.

Recent advances in our knowledge of human cognitive architecture, learning processes, and the nature of expertise provide a foundation for understanding changes in mechanisms of processing multimedia information that occur with development of learner expertise in a domain. Also, a rapid diagnostic approach to the assessment of levels of learner task-specific expertise has been developed and tested in several domains. Finally, prototypes of adaptive procedures using rapid diagnostic techniques were applied in adaptive computer-based training packages.

All these developments have created prerequisites for the design of comprehensive theory-based adaptive multimedia learning environments that would be dynamically tailored to changing levels of learner expertise. For example, recent studies in rapid diagnostic assessment methods may offer appropriate real-time tools for the dynamic optimization of multimedia instructional systems. These tools may provide adequate fine-grained measures of levels of expertise with sufficient diagnostic power for learner-tailored instructional procedures. Such techniques can also be used to improve the accuracy of information about levels of learner expertise required for learner modeling in adaptive multimedia and hypermedia systems. The development of adaptive multimedia learning environments in a whole range of task domains (not only for well-defined tasks in technical areas) would require rapid diagnostic instruments for measuring levels of learner expertise in poorly defined domains.

This final part of the book discussed possible adaptive methodologies that are based on real-time monitoring of learner proficiency in a domain by using rapid cognitive diagnostic methods. Such cognitively-supported adaptive learning environments are expected to be not only instrumental in achieving desired instructional effects, but achieving them efficiently, with optimal expenditures of cognitive resources and instruction time.

An important advantage of the rapid assessment-based adaptive procedures for the design of learner-tailored multimedia environments is their relative simplicity. Such procedures can be implemented with common multimedia authoring tools. They do not require the complex computational modeling and high-level programming expertise that are essential for developing sophisticated intelligent tutoring systems (e.g., systems using production rule-based learner models). These relatively simple adaptive procedures have the potential to enhance performance outcomes in multimedia learning environments, increase levels of competence for each learner and, at the same time, reduce training and diagnostic assessment time.

GENERAL CONCLUSION

Adaptive Multimedia Learning as a Means for Achieving Adaptive Expertise

In most chapters of this book, the discussed learning environments and instructional methods were aimed at acquisition of task-specific expertise as an ability to perform fluently in a specific class of tasks. For example, expertise reversal effect was investigated in relation to expertise in specific classes of tasks and used for optimizing conditions for developing task-specific expertise. Adaptive learning environments were investigated as a means of tailoring dynamically external instructional guidance to current levels of learner task-specific expertise as they gradually change during learning. However, task-specific expertise is a stage in achieving higher levels of professional expertise. The direct applicability of the expertise reversal effect to higher levels of expertise in broader professional domains (e.g., adaptive expertise) needs to be established in further studies.

In a series of studies with adaptive online tutorials reviewed in the previous chapters, the rapid diagnostic methods were successfully used for the dynamic selection of appropriate levels of instructional guidance that were optimal for learners with different levels of task-specific expertise. Adaptive learning environments based on the expertise reversal effect and rapid diagnostic methods were suitable for optimizing instructional support in developing task-specific expertise. However, they may not be the best environments for the development of self-regulation skills required for adaptive expertise. Alternative adaptive approaches, such as shared-control, advisory, and adaptive guidance models that combine system and learner control during advanced learning stages, could be better suitable for developing attributes of adaptive expertise.

In future, more comprehensive studies are needed for comparing different adaptive methodologies that are optimal for building flexible knowledge and skills. Optimal combinations of different types of control over learning processes for developing adaptive expertise in complex domains need further research. Optimized shared-control and adaptive guidance environments need to be developed and tested in complex and less structured domains leading to the acquisition of adaptive expertise.

Developing adaptive expertise requires cognitive resources for dealing with flexible, non-routine, and creative aspects of performance. Acquisition of task-specific expertise is an essential necessary condition for the release of such resources. Based on the fine-grained dynamic assessment of task-specific expertise and on the expertise reversal effect, adaptive multimedia learning environments could provide learners with individually tailored levels of instructional support. Such optimal levels of instructional guidance would allow handling new situations without a cognitive overload, thus optimizing learning pathways to higher levels of expertise.

Glossary of Terms

Adaptation level of interactivity: interactive learning environments that involve responses that are tailored to the learner previous behavior, even though they are selected from a fixed pool of options. Adaptive interactive learning environments dynamically tailor the real-time selection of learning tasks, instructional procedures and formats based on the information about learner current and past actions and online behavior.

Adaptive expertise: ability of experts to flexibly approach new situations by changing available or creating new procedures when the known approaches do not work in new situations. Developing adaptive expertise requires combining higher level general knowledge structures, practice in carrying out basic procedures in specific contexts, and variation in practice contexts for the development of flexible skills.

Adaptive guidance strategy: an advisement strategy that provides learners with diagnostic information about the current level of knowledge, advise on what to study or practice to achieve mastery, how to sequences learning tasks for gradual transition from basic to more complex strategies, and how to allocate cognitive resources. As learners acquire basic knowledge, adaptive guidance tailors subsequent more advanced learning tasks.

Adaptive hypermedia learning environments: hypermedia environments that accommodate learner characteristics into an explicit learner model and use this model to adapt interactions with each learner to her or his characteristics and needs, for example, by providing adaptive content selection, presentation formats, or suggesting a set of most relevant links to proceed.

Adaptive instructional systems: learning environments that react dynamically to learner needs and their individual characteristics (such as prior knowledge, preferences, learning goals, learning styles, and cognitive abilities), for example, by presenting suitable information, learning materials, and instructional support.

Advisement strategy: a form of instructional assistance provided to learners for making their own learning decisions that combines a degree of learner control with the system-controlled evidence-based task selection.

Animated pedagogical agents: onscreen characters (not necessarily human-like) that provide guidance and necessary feedback using various forms of communication (verbal explanations, gazing, gesturing, etc.). Pedagogical agents may also effectively motivate learners.

Aptitude-treatment interactions (ATIs): interactions that occur when different instructional treatments result in differential learning rates depending on student aptitudes. The aptitude is broadly understood as any learner characteristic that influences results of a particular educational treatment. Relevant aptitudes include knowledge, skills, learning styles, personality characteristics, etc. Learner prior knowledge is the aptitude of interest in the context of the expertise reversal effect

Assistance dilemma: balancing the executive guidance between knowledge-based and instruction-provided guidance. Within a cognitive load framework, the explanatory feedback is capable of providing external instructional guidance in place of missing internal long-term memory structures.

Automatic cognitive operations: cognitive processes that require minimal resources and do not interfere with other cognitive operations, in contrast to controlled or effortful processes that require considerable attentional capacity. Automatic operations allow to encode some elements of information directly and automatically into long-term memory without conscious effortful processing in working memory.

Cognitive architecture: a general cognitive system that underlies human performance and learning. The understanding of human cognition within a cognitive architecture requires knowledge of corresponding models of memory organization, forms of knowledge representation, mechanisms of problem solving, and the nature of human expertise.

Cognitive load: the demand for working memory resources required for achieving goals of specific cognitive activities. This is a theoretical concept reflecting resources required for information processing in specific situations by a specific person when the individual is fully committed to the task. An actual amount of resources invested in a cognitive activity depends on many factors, including levels of motivation, attitudes, and other personality characteristics.

Cognitive load theory: an instructional theory describing instructional implications of processing limitations of human cognitive architecture (capacity and duration of working memory) and evolved mechanisms for dealing with these limitations (long-term memory knowledge base and its role in cognition). Cognitive load theory distinguishes between the essential (intrinsic and germane) and wasteful (extraneous) forms of cognitive load, and suggests a variety of techniques and procedures (cognitive load effects) for managing essential and reducing extraneous load in learning.

Cognitive modelling: observing skillful expert performance of complex cognitive tasks to construct an appropriate mental representation that would later guide learner cognitive activities and enhance learning outcomes. Such learning usually shows both what and why certain steps need to be done, and results in constructing more generalized schemas that could be applied in a wider range of situations. Cognitive modeling can place a heavy cognitive load on novice learners when the observed task performance requires examination from several perspectives.

Communication level of interactivity: dynamic interactive learning environments that involve flexible, non-predetermined responses to learners live queries that may be refined in an iterative process. This level may include features of the previous levels, for example, dynamic feedback, manipulation, real-time personalized task selection and information tailoring. Examples of this level of interactivity are online prompting for and submitting self-explanations or predictions for next procedural steps.

Completion assignments: means for implementing a completion strategy as a gradual transition from worked examples to unsupported problem solving practice. A completion assignment contains a problem statement, incomplete worked out solution, and tasks to complete. It provides a partially worked out solution procedure and asks learners to complete the solution.

Concurrent verbal reports (think-aloud protocols): the method for studying cognitive processes that could also be applied for evaluating cognitive load (with audio and video tracking of participants' verbalizations and on-screen actions) by using the generated qualitative verbal data that reflects cognitive load caused by different types of sources and expressed through the participants' own language. Verbal data from think-aloud interviews is coded using rubrics based on expected verbal expressions or remarks for different types of cognitive load.

Congruence principle: design principle for complex graphic according to which the content and format of the graphic should correspond to the content and format of the concepts to be conveyed. For example, animated graphics should be effective to represent change over time.

Dual-modality (audiovisual) presentations: presenting textual information in an auditory form with pictures or diagrams in a visual modality that effectively increases working memory capacity by using combined resources of the visual and auditory channels of sensory and working memory that may exceed the processing capacity of a single channel. Dual mode presentations may be used to reduce extraneous cognitive load caused by split-attention.

Dual-task technique: measures of cognitive load that use performance on simple secondary tasks as indicators of cognitive load associated with performance on main tasks. Various simple responses are used as secondary tasks, for example, reaction times to some events, counting backwards, recalling the previous letter seen on the screen of a separate computer while encoding the new letter appearing after a tone sounded.

Dynamic adaptation: instructional adaptation approach based on continuous tracking of learner activities. Dynamic adaptation belongs to system-centered forms of adaptation that are contrasted with the learner-centered adaptation that provides learners with possibilities to select available options themselves.

Executive function in learning: cognitive function associated with the engagement and coordination of different cognitive activities and directing learner attention to appropriate information. Within the cognitive architecture based on interacting working memory and long-term memory, the executive function during complex cognitive processing is provided by available domain-specific schematic knowledge base in long-term memory.

Expertise: superior levels of professional accomplishments in a field that require many years of training and extensive deliberate practice at a challenging level of difficulty. Professional expert performance requires well-developed cognitive skills, well-organized high-level knowledge structures, and self-regulatory performance control or metacognitive strategies.

Expertise reversal effect: reversal in the relative effectiveness of information presentation formats and procedures as levels of user knowledge in a domain change. For example, extensive external support could be beneficial for novices when compared with the performance of novices who receive a low-support format, but is disadvantageous for more expert users when compared with the performance of experts who receive a low-support format.

Extraneous cognitive load: non-essential for learning cognitive load that is associated with a diversion of cognitive resources on activities irrelevant to performance and learning. It is imposed by the design of learning tasks and information presentations (e.g., separated in space and/or time related elements; an excessive step-size or rate of introducing new elements of information; insufficient instructional support that cannot compensate limited learner knowledge base; excessive externally provided guidance that overlaps with user knowledge base).

Faded worked-out examples: an instructional method that implements the principle of scaffolding by gradually fading worked-out steps in the examples (and replacing them with corresponding problem solving steps) with increased levels of learner expertise.

Faded worked examples: an instructional method for the gradual transition from worked examples to problem solving practice. Parts of worked examples are progressively replaced with problem-solving steps for learners to complete. Worked examples are gradually faded as levels of learner task-specific expertise increase, thus implementing the principle of scaffolding.

Feedback level of interactivity: interactive learning environments that provide a pre-defined feedback on specific learners' actions. The feedback could be immediate or delayed; simple, corrective or extended explanatory; with or without a learner control.

First-step diagnostic method: a method that realizes the rapid diagnostic assessment approach by presenting learners with selected tasks for a limited time and asking them to rapidly indicate their first step toward solution of each task. The first step would involve different cognitive operations for individuals with different levels of expertise in a specific task domain. For more experienced learners, their well learned higher-level solution procedures would allow these learners to rapidly generate advance steps of the solution skipping some intermediate steps.

Four-component instructional design model (4C/ID): instructional design model that provides methods for analysis of complex cognitive skills, knowledge structures required for performing these skills, and development of appropriate sequences of whole task practice situations that would support acquisition of these skills. The model includes four interconnected components: learning tasks, supportive information, just-in-time (algorithmic) information, and part-task practice.

General-to-specific task analysis: an approach to cognitive task analysis that requires identifying the main idea of a task followed by determining the specific aspects of this idea (broader concepts are consequently differentiated into more specific ones).

Germane cognitive load: learning-relevant demands on working memory traditionally associated with various auxiliary cognitive activities (e.g., explicit self-explanations during learning from worked examples or imagining procedures described in instructional materials) that are intentionally designed with the purpose of fostering learning, enhancing learning outcomes, or increasing levels of learner motivation.

Hypermedia learning environments: learning environments that add navigation support to traditional linear multimedia environments, thus providing appropriate levels of learner interactivity and learner control. They are usually implemented as an organized network of hyperlinks that allow learners nonlinear access to graphics, sound, animation, and other multimedia elements.

Iconic representations: representational formats for input parameters used in instructional simulations that contain (in addition to traditional symbolic verbal and numerical) concrete, "situated" graphics to represent the various elements of the physical environment (e.g. flames to represent temperature, weights to represent pressure, etc.). Adding iconic representations may enhance instructional effectiveness of simulations, especially for novice learners.

Imagining technique: imagining procedures and concepts rather than repeatedly studying the examples and explanations in order to increase germane cognitive load. The imagining technique is beneficial for more knowledgeable learners. It could be used to replace worked examples when instructing relatively more experienced learners

Instructional efficiency: an approach to evaluating learning outcomes that considers learning and instruction in terms of cognitive cost (cognitive resources spent, mental effort invested, or cognitive load imposed) of achieving instructional effects rather than their mere effectiveness. According to this approach, the whole point of investing considerable human and financial resources into the design and development of sophisticated interactive multimedia learning environments is to achieve returns in terms of efficiency: learning faster and without mental stress.

Intelligent tutoring systems: learning and assessment environments based on complex problem solving in which selecting and sequencing of learning tasks occur as a function of learner responses to complex tasks based on a model of learner knowledge. Intelligent tutoring incorporates individualized instruction using detailed assessment of learner knowledge and appropriately directing instructional treatments. Intelligent tutoring systems based on the model-tracing methodology simulate student cognition in real time and maintain current models of student knowledge state. The learner actual performance is traced and compared to the ideal solution structure using a production rules model, and the student is kept on the correct solution path.

Intrinsic cognitive load: cognitive load caused by levels of interactivity between elements of information that need to be processed simultaneously (relative to levels of learner expertise). It is associated with cognitive activities of establishing connections between related elements of information in working memory and integrating them with available knowledge base in accordance with specific instructional goals. These cognitive activities essentially signify comprehension of the situation and may result in modified or new knowledge structures in long-term memory.

Learner-controlled approach to individualization of instruction: an adaptive approach according to which learners are enabled to adapt the learning environment by actively and continuously selecting treatments most appropriate to their cognitive states. It is an alternative way of dynamic tailoring of instruction to learner cognitive characteristics.

Learner (student, user) models: key component of an adaptive hypermedia system that includes many different user characteristics (e.g., level of computer literacy, experience in using specific software applications, learning styles, background, preferences, goals, interests, etc) in addition to subject matter knowledge. Learner models are usually constructed by using testing and survey methods, or recording the history of user interactions with the system.

Long-term memory (LTM): a major part of our cognitive architecture, an organized knowledge base that stores massive amount of hierarchical knowledge structures.

Long-term working memory (LTWM): cognitive construct created by knowledge structures in long-term memory associated with active components of working memory. It is capable of holding virtually unlimited amount of information due to the chunking effect. For example, when reading a text, we construct and continuously update in working memory a situation model of the text using our knowledge base long-term memory. This situation model represents the current content of long-term working memory. Due to the association with a stable long-term memory knowledge base, this content is sufficiently stable, durable, and resistant to temporary interferences (e.g. interruptions in reading).

Manipulation level of interactivity: interactive learning environments that involve real-time online change or transformation of information in response to learners' actions; provide flexible, variable responses, although not tailored to the learner previous behavior. This level of interactivity may involve different degrees of learner control.

Measures of instructional efficiency: indicators of the relative efficiency of instructional conditions and the cognitive cost of learning generated by different ways of combining measures of performance with measures of cognitive load. High efficiency learning generally occurs under conditions of low cognitive load and high test performance, and low efficiency occurs under high cognitive load and low test performance.

Measures of instructional involvement: indicators of the relative levels of learner motivation in instructional conditions generated by combining measures of performance with measures of mental effort. The measure of motivation should take into account not only the invested mental effort but also the associated performance data. When learner involvement is higher, more mental effort is likely to be invested that would result in higher performance.

Micro-treatment adaptation approach: adaptation approach based on fine-grained within-task measures taken while students are in the instructional situation with varying amount of prompting, feedback, and examples. This approach is used together with macro-treatment approach (pre-task adaptation model) by selecting macro-treatments based on initial pre-task measures, and then refining and optimizing instructional procedures based on continuous monitoring of learning behavior.

Modality effect: an instructional effect according to which presenting one of the essential and related sources of information in an auditory form, thus engaging another processing channel in working memory and effectively expanding its available capacity, may reduce or eliminate split attention and facilitate learning. The amount of information that can be simultaneously processed using both auditory and visual channels might exceed the amount of information processed in a single channel. Therefore, instructional materials that present information using dual- or multiple modalities (for example, a visual diagram accompanied by an auditory text) can be more efficient than equivalent single modality formats.

Multimedia redundancy effect: an instructional effect according to which duplicating textual explanations using different modalities may inhibit learning. When auditory textual explanations of a diagram are presented concurrently with the same on-screen text, learners need to mentally relate corresponding visual and auditory components of instruction. Processing on-screen textual explanations of a diagram together with the same auditory explanations imposes an additional cognitive load. Elimination of a redundant source of information may enhance learning in this situation.

Optimization of cognitive load: the process of using essential instructional guidance and removing redundant components as the level of learner task-specific expertise gradually increases, thus reducing extraneous and enhancing essential cognitive load. Such optimization assumes not only presenting appropriate information and instructional guidance at the appropriate time, but also timely removal of unnecessary redundant information as learner levels of learner expertise increase.

Pre-task adaptation model: instructional adaptation approach according to which instructional treatments are determined from aptitude measurements taken before the actual learning situation, and then assigning certain types of students to specific instructional treatments.

Principle of scaffolding: an instructional design principle implementing the general adaptive approach to tailoring levels of instructional guidance to levels of learner expertise. The principle suggests using worked examples, completion assignments, and conventional problems combined in a completion strategy.

Process-oriented worked examples: worked examples that focus on expert reasoning behind performance steps and the corresponding cause-effect relationships.

Product-oriented worked examples: worked examples that focus mostly on demonstrating procedural steps required for achieving specific results (or products).

Rapid diagnostic approach: diagnostic assessment of expertise based on rapidly determining if and how learners use their knowledge structures while approaching a specific problem or situation. The idea of the approach is to determine the highest level of organized knowledge structures a learner applies rapidly to a task or situation. More experienced learners would immediately see the task within their higher-level knowledge structures. Novices may only be able to identify some random lower-level components. Organized knowledge base in long-term memory is the main factor determining such differences.

Rapid verification diagnostic method: an alternative method that realizes the rapid diagnostic assessment approach by presenting learners with a series of potentially possible steps at various stages of the solution procedure, and asking them to rapidly verify the correctness of these steps instead of generating the steps themselves. This method is easier to implement in online learning environments, and it is also usable for relatively poorly defined tasks when solution steps could not be specified exactly in advance.

Redundancy effect: an instructional effect according to which elimination rather than integration of redundant sources of information could produce better learning outcomes in situations when individual sources of information could be understood separately (e.g., self-explanatory diagrams or textual explanations). If a source of information is fully intelligible on its own, then any additional redundant sources of information should be removed from the instructional materials rather than integrated into it.

Retroactive inhibition: interference between new and earlier information in animations when the following frame in the animation needs to be processed before the information from previous frames has been incorporated into an organized knowledge structure and comprehended.

Segmentation effect: an instructional effect according to which concurrent presentation of the same audio and visual text by small portions (instead of one large uninterrupted chunk) may improve learning outcomes. The size of textual segments that are processed continuously without a break may influence the conditions of applicability of the multimedia redundancy effect.

Self-explanation technique: prompting learners for self-explanations and predictions. It requires explaining explicitly suggested solution steps or actions based on learned principles of the domain or predicting the next procedural step before demonstrating or describing this step. The technique could be used to increase germane cognitive load.

Shared instructional control model: an approach to personalized task selection according to which the system selects a subset of tasks from an available task pool based on the current level of learner expertise, and then the learner makes the final task selection. As the learner proceeds through the training session, the system continuously assesses performance and invested mental effort and selects an optimal subset of tasks for the following learning step. This subset is presented to the learner who makes the final selection. The model combines a system-controlled task selection based on learner levels of expertise and a learner-controlled task selection.

Signaling or cueing effect: an instructional effect according to which providing cues to the learner on what to pay attention to or how to select and organize the material (e.g., by placing arrows, using flashing or highlights to attract learner attention to a particular components of animation) may enhance learning. Visual cues could help learners connect the corresponding verbal and pictorial elements of information, reduce cognitive resources for co-referencing these sources of information, and improve learning outcomes.

Sources of cognitive load: features of external information structures and/or cognitive characteristics of individual users that determine required working memory resources.

Split-attention effect: an instructional effect according to which physically integrating different essential sources of information (e.g., textual explanations located near its matching parts on a picture) significantly improves learning performance. If neither explanations nor pictures can be understood separately, the statements in the explanatory text need to be mentally coordinated with corresponding elements in a picture. Such mental coordination processes require additional cognitive resources that are not directly related to learning. Similar problems could occur in temporal split-attention situations when corresponding words and pictures are presented successively rather than simultaneously.

Subjective ratings of cognitive load: measures of cognitive load that are based on the assumption that people are able to introspect their conscious cognitive processes. Ratings of subjective mental effort associated with learning instructional materials have been used in most of studies in cognitive load framework as they are easy to implement, do not intrude on primary task performance, are sufficiently reliable, and correlate highly with objective measures.

Task-specific expertise: ability of a person to perform fluently in a specific class of tasks. It is a "narrow" definition of expertise in contrast to expertise in a professional domain. The availability of highly organized and automated domain-specific knowledge base is a common characteristic of both task-specific and broader professional expertise. The importance of task-specific expertise is in freeing cognitive resources required for learning higher-level tasks and developing flexible and transferable skills by acquiring well automated knowledge structures and procedures.

Transient nature of animations: the need to hold in working memory elements of information from earlier frames of the animation while attending to the following frames. Cognitive demands of processing new information while holding previous information in active state in working memory could overburden working memory resulting in cognitive overload. In many situations, some essential components of the preceding frames could be lost before the related elements of the following frames appear.

Worked examples effect: an instructional effect according to which studying more worked examples (that provide all the appropriate solution steps for a problem) instead of solving equivalent conventional problems may lead to better learning outcomes (including transfer performance) achieved faster and with less wasteful cognitive load. While studying a worked example, learners attend simultaneously only to one problem state and an associated solution step. This process requires significantly less working memory capacity thus reducing extraneous cognitive load and facilitating learning.

Working memory (WM): a major part of our cognitive architecture, a functional mechanism that limits the scope of immediate changes to long-term memory. Depending on a specific model, working memory is considered either as a separate component of our cognitive system, or as an activated part of LTM. The essential attribute of working memory is its severe limitations in capacity and duration when dealing with novel information.

About the Author

Dr. Kalyuga is senior lecturer at the University of New South Wales (UNSW) in Sydney, Australia where he has worked since 1995. He received a PhD in education from UNSW in 1998. His research interests are in cognitive processes and evidence-based instructional design principles for multimedia learning environments. His specific contributions include detailed experimental studies of the role of learner prior knowledge in multimedia learning (the expertise reversal effect); the redundancy effect in multimedia learning; the development of rapid online diagnostic assessment methods; and studies of the effectiveness of different adaptive procedures for tailoring instruction to levels of learner expertise. He was awarded an Australian Research Council Postdoctoral Research Fellowship (2001-2003). He is the author of the book *Instructing and Testing Advanced Learners: A Cognitive Load Approach* (2006) and 35 research articles and chapters. During his previous work in Russia (until 1991), he published more than 30 articles and several books and textbooks. (http://education.arts.unsw.edu.au/staff/index.php)

Index

O

P

R

S

T

V

W